MW01631004

ALONG THE WAY

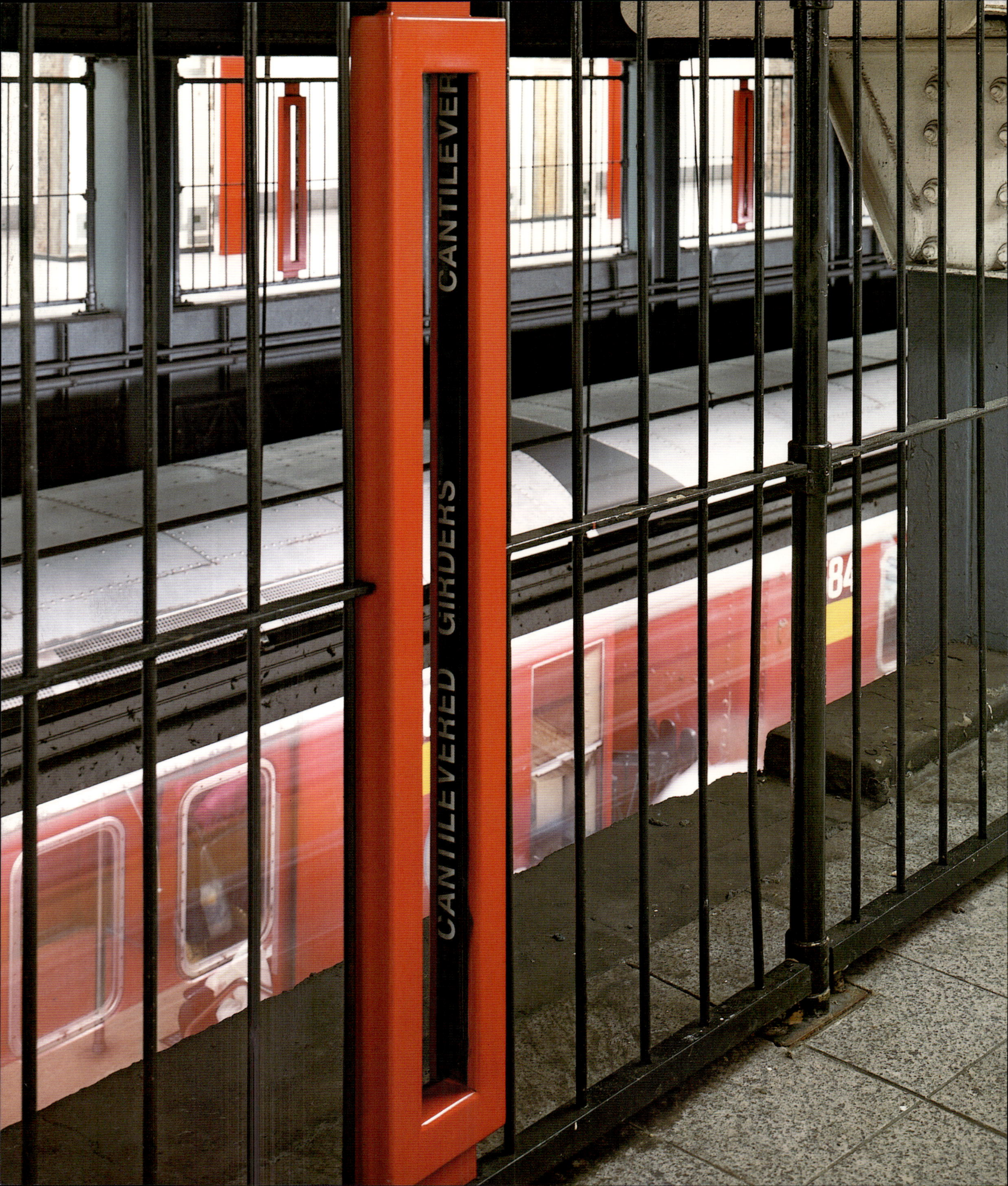
CANTILEVERED GIRDERS
CANTILEVER

ALONG THE WAY MTA ARTS FOR TRANSIT

SANDRA BLOODWORTH and **WILLIAM AYRES**

Foreword by **STANLEY TUCCI**

THE MONACELLI PRESS

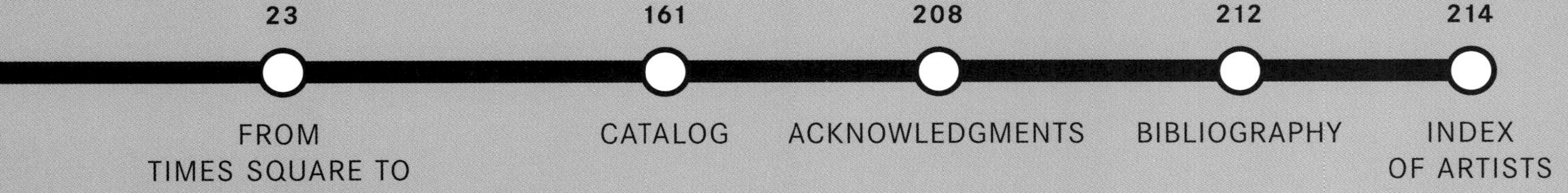

FOREWORD

I have always thought of New York City as an organism of steel and stone, forever growing and in flux, its streets and tunnels the veins through which flows the energy necessary to bring water, light, steam, heat, sound, and image to what one writer termed "the shirt-sleeved multitude." And this multitude had a real and palpable energy of its own that was as exhilarating as the city in which it lived and worked.

Nowhere is that energy more concentrated than in the warrens of the New York City subway. As a young actor, I descended into the seemingly endless burrows that connect the disparate parts of Gotham, where all New Yorkers, regardless of color, creed, wealth, or position, were instantly equalized. How thrilling it was to be a part of the scrum born of the scramble to embark on the train and experience the jolt of the first forward movement, the slow creep out of the station, the sudden swift acceleration through too dark a tunnel, and finally the screeching, teeth-piercing, sliding halt into the next station.

At the time I arrived in New York, the subway system was in a dismal state of disrepair. As one who is fascinated by art (my father taught art for forty years) as well as history, particularly urban history and particularly that of New York, I remember wandering through the streets and riding the subways into the wee hours—extended periods of unemployment breed wee-hour wandering—and searching for the architectural vestiges of what we now call lost New York. And what beautiful vestiges there were to be found, not only above the streets but also below in the subways. Such care had been taken in the design, the choice of subjects, and the craftsmanship of countless works of art, and now so much of it was in disrepair, partly obscured, neglected, ignored, or ravaged by time and by the very people it was meant to please.

I would pass my hand over dingy and fractured mosaics, sure that no one would ever be willing to repair, recreate, or create something like them again. To me, this neglect showed not only a lack of respect for those who labored so hard (mostly immigrant artisans), but also a lack of respect for our own and future generations. Here was the perfect integration of form and function, and we were carelessly letting it slip away.

In a country that has, at best, a conflicted relationship with public support for the arts, we are made to think more and more every year that art is a luxury. I was raised to believe it is a necessity. Art, in all its forms, is the expression of who, why, and where we are at any given time in history. It allows us to question, in a nonliteral, academic, or linear way, who we are, why we do what we do, and where we are going. Incorporating art into the fabric of everyday life is an obligation and a sign of a healthy democratic society.

Traveling from home to work, and back again, day after day is a necessity. It can be tedious and potentially mind-numbing. To do so in an environment that incorporates art can make the usual unusual, the ordinary—more than that—the boring, stimulating, and what is ugly . . . maybe beautiful. Art can take us out of the everyday, the mundane, and raise us up, perhaps just when we need it most.

It is this very thing to which MTA Arts for Transit has devoted the past twenty years. The program has rescued and recreated artisanal works of the past and created new works of art for the future. This visual feast, through which we are fortunate enough to move, is as ambitious as anything the WPA achieved seventy-some years ago. Arts for Transit has brought a fallow period for public art to an end and shown us respect for the past, for ourselves, and for those who will ride the same rails for generations to come.

Art touches our souls because it comes from our souls. It has been said that this program is trying to save the soul of the subway. In doing so it may be saving a piece of ours as well.

STANLEY TUCCI

PROLOGUE

For the past two decades, the MTA Arts for Transit program has admirably carried out its ambitious mission to make the New York transportation system more inviting, to bring art to the public, and to give each transit station a special character that offers an immediate identification. Arts for Transit's mandate includes administering the Music Under New York program, the transit poster program, and most important, the inclusion of art in construction of transit facilities, bus depots, and subway and commuter railroad stations.

As a former MTA board member and as a New Yorker, I am especially proud of the works of art that today are a permanent part of our subway and commuter railroad system. When I first became involved in the MTA's Capital Program in the early 1980s, the prevailing philosophy was that station improvements should be "engineered" and realized as directly and efficiently as possible without much concern for aesthetics or preserving original decorative features. During that period, I remember seeing, to my horror, a new masonry block wall being installed in the Spring Street Station over the original glass tiles, signage, and ornamentation. This and other stations were to be transformed into a "clean" but characterless environment. To its credit, the MTA responded immediately and adjusted the direction, initiating the policy that worthy design elements and materials were to be respected and preserved whenever possible. The station "modernization" program became a station "improvement" program, including art and acknowledging the preservation movement gathering strength across the city.

When the MTA began its much-needed rebuilding campaign, there were, predictably, questions about spending money on "art." But we argued that the dollars were relatively small and the potential return enormous. The art was a signal of respect by the system for the rider; the station environment was improved, vandalism reduced, and transit employees took pride in the art in their stations. In working with artists, it soon became clear that stations would also benefit from stronger design guidelines for all aspects of their renewal, including signage, lighting, materials, and organization of the fare control areas.

Arts for Transit later expanded into industrial design to encompass the whole rider experience, with well-received results. Artists were asked to design the prototypes for the attractive new grills now installed system-wide to replace the more forbidding bars that preceded them. Similarly, the office later became involved in the design of new transit cars. A charette was organized, drawing designers from around the country, to discuss what passengers wanted in the new subway cars, what colors and signage to use, in short, how the car interior might be best designed. With the launch of MetroCard, Arts for Transit led the aesthetic design of the highly successful new vending machines.

The MTA was under great pressure in the mid-1980s to rebuild a system that was in such disrepair. In some ways it was chutzpah for me to suggest that art be added to the equation. But the investment of leadership time as well as dollars was quickly rewarded. The program's success has been the result of the commitment and skill of many people, including the founding director, Wendy Feuer, and her successor, the current director Sandra Bloodworth. Both have been able to communicate the value of art to the system, while also being sensitive to the issues confronting people whose priority is making the trains run on time. They also have received critical support from MTA board leadership.

The artists have worked hard for our transportation system. They have stretched to respond to the needs of a dense and quick-paced environment. They have provided their unique perspective to solve design challenges posed by the system. And they have given us work that can hold our interest over time.

I am delighted that the program has given so many artists, architects, and designers in the city and the region an opportunity to work in this public environment where thousands of riders see their pieces daily. And I am grateful that the program has been sustained over the years by so many individuals throughout the system. As we look to the future, we are fortunate that we can build on this strength and that the city's community of artists is continually offering new work that can help sustain our transit environment.

RONAY MENSCHEL
MTA BOARD MEMBER
1979–90

PREFACE

Art has been a vitally important part of the New York transit system since the first subway line opened more than a century ago. From the beginning, its architects, planners, and designers were interested in more than simply digging tunnels, erecting stations, building cars, and moving people from one part of town to the other—they were interested in doing all these things in aesthetically pleasing ways that reflected the styles and materials of the day.

Times changed, however. During the 1960s and 1970s, the terra-cotta ornament and well-designed stations did not fare well. By the end of that period, the New York City transit system was seemingly on the brink of collapse. Commuters were afraid to enter the crumbling stations and board the subway with its graffiti-covered cars, poor lighting, and insufficient signage.

Then, beginning in 1982, the situation began to turn around. Under MTA Chairman Richard Ravitch, plans were developed to repair and maintain the transit system's infrastructure for all of the MTA transit properties, including the subway system and the commuter railroads. It was during this time that New York City passed its Percent for Art legislation, which mandated that art be a part of the design and construction of its capital building projects, at a time when billions of dollars were dedicated to repair and construction projects. Thus the MTA began to include public art as part of its projects, in conjunction with the Department of Cultural Affairs.

In 1985, under Chairman Robert R. Kiley, the MTA expanded and formalized its own art program, creating MTA Arts for Transit (AFT). In addition to commissioning permanent art, AFT has increasingly become the aesthetic eyes of the MTA, representing the agency in all aspects of aesthetic design throughout the system.

Under Chairman Peter E. Stangl, Arts for Transit continued to flourish. By 1995, ten years into the program, there were forty-eight artworks installed throughout the MTA system. The entire scheme of railings had been redesigned and Arts for Transit had played an important role with all the agencies in promoting and establishing overall design guidelines for stations and promoting the role of strong architectural design to meld with the system's established history as an engineering marvel.

By the millennium, some may have wondered if this public art program would continue. They need not have worried because the unfailing support continued under Chairman E. Virgil Conway, who actively supported the tradition of including art in the transportation environment. Public art not only survived but continued to thrive. As Arts for Transit grew significantly, it also expanded its role in industrial design, insisting that all major capital improvements should be designed in an aesthetically pleasing way, on the theory that it costs no more to build something attractive.

By the time I became chairman and Katherine Lapp took the helm as executive director, Arts for Transit was well established. It has been an honor for us to continue to support this program that has not only changed the environment of stations for our customers, but has also improved the image of the entire system.

Who could have believed that the initial efforts of the early 1980s would blossom into a system-wide collection of 162 magnificent artworks—and counting! But they did—and this has made a profound difference in the quality of life of metropolitan New York City's transit users during the millions of hours they collectively clock each day—along the way.

I take pride in having helped to make all this happen, and I am dedicated to ensuring that it continues.

PETER S. KALIKOW
CHAIRMAN
METROPOLITAN TRANSPORTATION AUTHORITY

ALONG THE WAY

As early as 1899, five years before the New York City subway opened for business, the planners behind it, with high hopes and great ambitions, made it clear that the new transit system was to be more than just a bare-bones people mover. To ensure that this would happen, William Barclay Parsons, who had been tapped as chief engineer and was responsible for the vision, plans, and specifications, made sure that this clause was written into the contract for its construction:

> The railway and its equipment as contemplated by the contract constitute a great public work. All parts of the structure where exposed to public sight shall therefore be designed, constructed, and maintained with a view to the beauty of their appearance, as well as to their efficiency.

This concept emerged from the City Beautiful movement, a planning philosophy based on the thesis that beautification and monumental grandeur would improve social conditions. Frederick S. Lamb, a well-known stained glass designer and one of the City Beautiful's chief proponents, put it succinctly, declaring that "art must appeal to the great masses of the republic to regain its educational influence," prescribing "increased use of color" and other embellishments to appeal to "the better impulses of the people." The architectural firm Heins & LaFarge, which at the time was working on the prestigious Bronx Zoo and Cathedral of St. John the Divine projects, was commissioned to carry out the design mandate.

For the "embellishments," George L. Heins and Christopher Grant LaFarge, in consultation with the engineers, decided to use ceramic materials almost exclusively, for practical reasons of durability and ease in cleaning as well as their wide range of expressive possibilities. In addition to adding color and variety to otherwise drab underground interiors, the decorative features announced stops and distinguished one station from another. Certain unifying motifs appear throughout the system, but the overall impression is of a great diversity of ornamentation. In general, the designs owed much to the

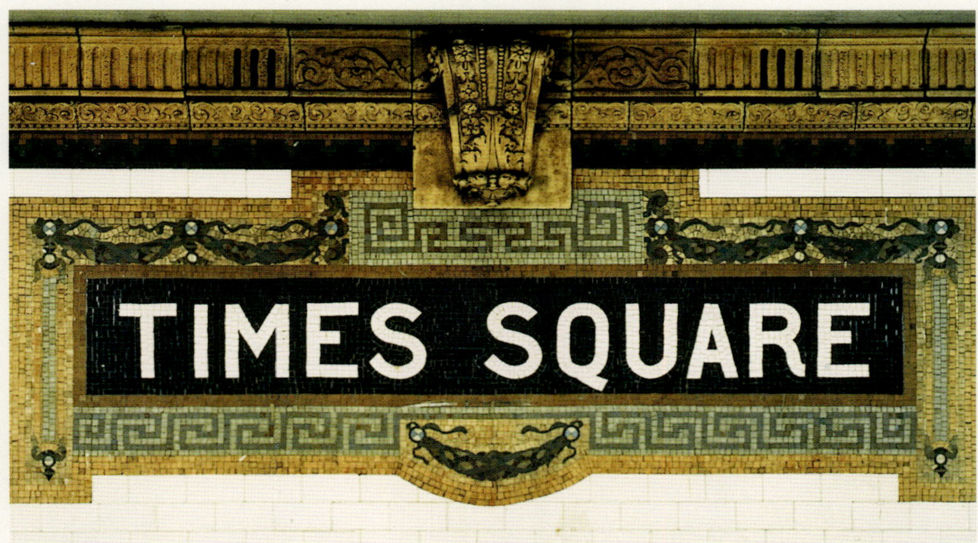

Heins & LaFarge, ceramic mosaic signage, c. 1904. Times Square–42nd Street.
PHOTOGRAPHER: DAVID LUBARSKY

classical heritage of the Beaux-Arts tradition in which Heins and LaFarge had been trained—with a few nods to the vocabulary of the Arts and Crafts movement.

Several types of ceramic were used, often in combination. These included ordinary brickwork and white "glass tiles" for major wall expanses; multiple-cast terra-cotta segments from which bands and friezes could be formed; small tile pieces, or tesserae, for mosaic work; and plaques for identifying certain stations, usually with associative symbols. These included a sailing ship for Columbus Circle, Fulton's steamboat *Clermont* for Fulton Street, a beaver for Astor Place referencing the Astor family's fur-trading fortune. These designs anticipated the contemporary mandate that public art should be site-specific and consider its location.

Among the American ceramic firms that produced the custom designs were the celebrated art pottery companies Grueby and Rookwood, as well as firms that customarily produced more ordinary work. During this period, art pottery was all the rage. Boston's Grueby Faience Company, founded in the 1880s and famous for its trademark matte green glaze, had garnered numerous awards, including medals at all the great turn-of-the-century World's Fairs. Rookwood Pottery, based in Cincinnati, was world-renowned, particularly for its hand-decorated vases and other domestic wares. Hiring firms of this caliber and prominence was intended to carry a clear message: nothing was too good for the new subway and its riders.

After the opening of the Interborough Rapid Transit system (IRT) in 1904, both press and public reacted with enthusiasm. A critic in the *Real Estate Record and Guide* proclaimed:

> The subway stations are excellent in the architectural propriety of their schemes of decorations . . . The effect of this sort of thing upon popular taste is enormous; and since the example will be imitated hereafter, New York can congratulate itself on one specimen of "Civic Art," in which a very useful structure has been decorated with the utmost propriety.

Eventually, the BRT (Brooklyn Rapid Transit, later the Brooklyn-Manhattan Transit Corporation, or BMT) and the municipally owned IND (Independent Rapid Transit) were chartered in addition to the original IRT system. With these came a change in station design and decoration, particularly on the IND, which was constructed between 1925 and 1940. On these later lines, the vocabulary of the Machine Age came into play, along with the abstracted geometric forms of Art Deco and Art Moderne. In 1940, at the end of the Depression, the City of New York bought the IRT and BMT, and,

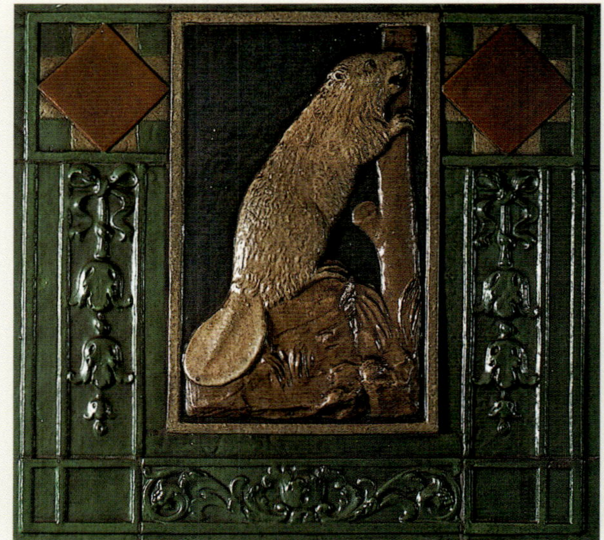

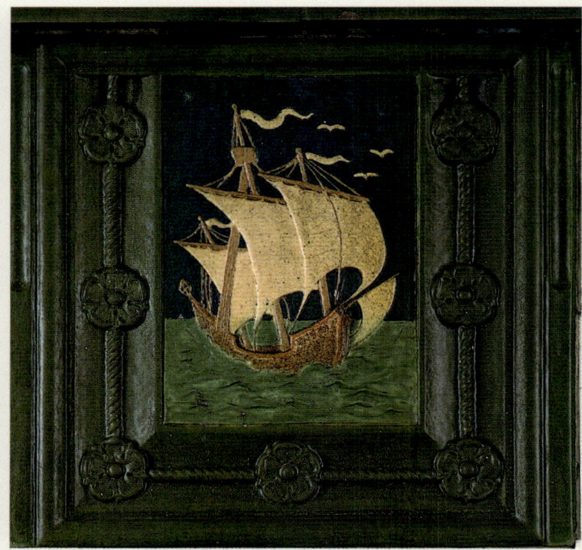

Heins & LaFarge and Grueby Faience Company, terra-cotta plaques for Astor Place (left) and Columbus Circle, c. 1904.
PHOTOGRAPHER: DAVID LUBARSKY

beginning in 1953, operated the subway under a single administration called the New York City Transit Authority. In 1968 this agency was incorporated into the Metropolitan Transportation Authority and is now known as MTA New York City Transit.

In the post–World War II era, when all attention and public money seemed to be focused on rapidly expanding automobile travel and its enormous infrastructure needs, subways came to seem old-fashioned and unfashionable. Not only did subway building come to a halt, but progressive deterioration of the lines also set in, reaching its nadir in the 1970s, when New York City was on the brink of bankruptcy. Deferred maintenance resulted in leaky, dirty, crime-ridden stations. Trains broke down with increasing frequency and were typically defaced inside and out with graffiti. As a result, subway ridership plummeted; many people were simply afraid to use the subways. Along with the city, the transit system was on the verge of collapse.

By the 1980s, the bankruptcy crisis had passed. The economy improved, and a group of government officials, civic organizations, and citizens began to focus on revitalizing the transit system. This coincided with the emergence of two nationwide phenomena: the historic preservation movement and the public art movement. As early as 1982, in conjunction with Percent for Art legislation, which allocated one percent of public building construction costs for the installation of art, there were efforts to include art in the subways as the massive rebuilding program began. An art selection panel, chaired by Henry Geldzahler, commissioner of the Department of Cultural Affairs and founding curator of the department of contemporary art at the Metropolitan Museum of Art, commissioned such notable works as Houston Conwill's *Open Secret* at 125th Street, Nancy Holt's *Astral Grating* at Fulton Street, and Milton Glaser's new work at Astor Place.

At that time, the public art movement was still in its infancy, but many issues had already been identified. Public art evolved from the nineteenth-century "statue-in-the-park" to monumental modern sculpture, often by a well-known artist, set adrift in a sterile office building plaza. James Wines of the organization SITE (Sculpture in the Environment) coined the term "Plop Art," explaining, with some justification, that these pieces seemed to have been "plopped onto the plaza" with little or no consideration for their relationship with the particular location or their function. Arts for Transit was, from the beginning, determined to change the direction of contemporary site-specific public art, to encourage something different—and better. Public art within the transportation system would look to

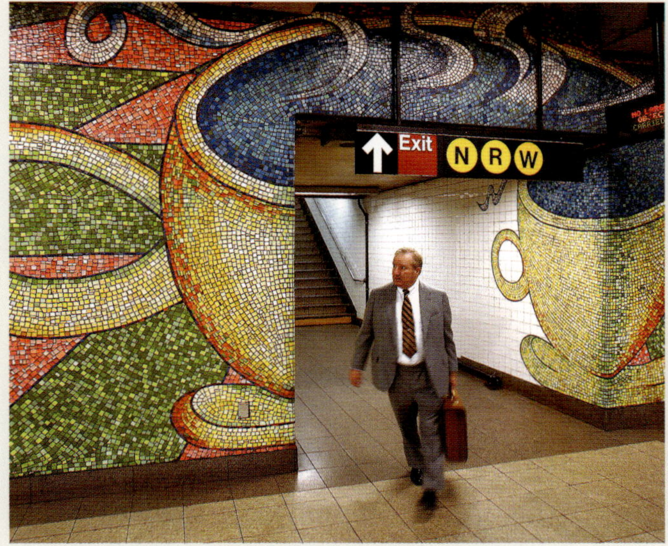

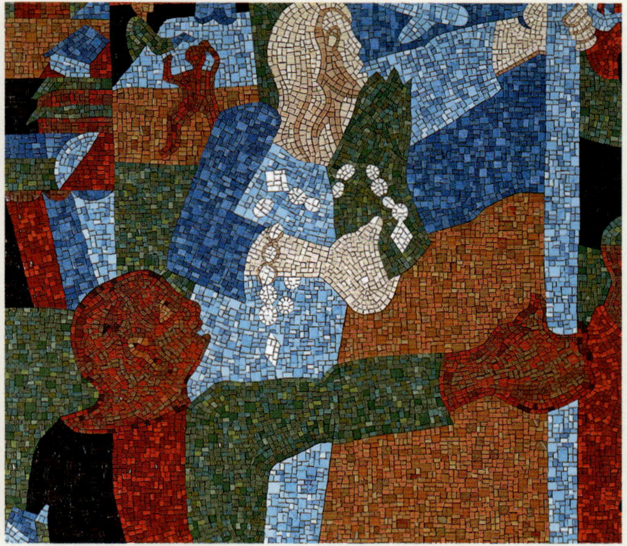

Left: Elizabeth Murray, *Blooming*, 1996, glass mosaic. Lexington Avenue–59th Street.
Right: Jacob Lawrence, *New York in Transit*, 2001, glass mosaic. Times Square–42nd Street.
PHOTOGRAPHERS: ROB WILSON (LEFT), DAVID LUBARSKY (RIGHT)

its own environment to determine its form. It seemed clear that if a system had hundreds of thousands of feet of wall space, then that wall space should be used, particularly since time had demonstrated its potential for posterity.

Public art should be just that: art created for a public place, for a public purpose, with public input. The best public art eloquently and effectively links the place where it is located to the people who come there; both the place and the people are altered, however imperceptibly, by the dialogue between art and the public. But this is not to say that public art must be narrative or didactic; indeed, some of the most effective pieces are abstract or conceptual. Setting a mood or triggering a train of thought can be just as legitimate as, and often more effective than, an artwork with an agenda.

Over the past twenty years, the Arts for Transit philosophy has been reiterated and refined. The process is ongoing, a process of learning by doing. The latest installation is never the last word. One of the early lessons was that, to be effective in a busy public environment, a work of art must be strikingly visible and call attention to itself. Clearly the subway and commuter rail stations were, and remain, a particularly difficult environment with inherent restrictions. Other obvious preliminary considerations were to identify sites within the system that would be most appropriate for art and materials that would be most appropriate in terms of visual impact and visibility.

Mosaics, terra-cotta, bronze, glass, and metals from the original installations were found to be in remarkably fine shape where there had been no major intervention from man or nature. Arts for Transit has built on this foundation, requiring that artists use the same or similar durable materials of the system and encouraging them to use the expansive walls and to incorporate their projects into the architecture.

Michael Kelly Williams's two small murals at Intervale Avenue in the Bronx were the first works to be executed in mosaic. The neighborhood knew immediately that the art had been created for them. Community efforts were directed at getting a new station built after a fire had destroyed the old one, but residents were pleased that it also included art, bringing beauty to this particular place. The success of this project led to others in the same vein, employing similar materials and using similar techniques.

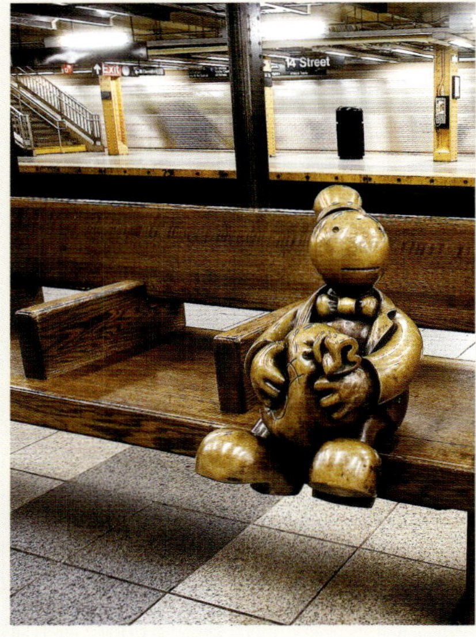

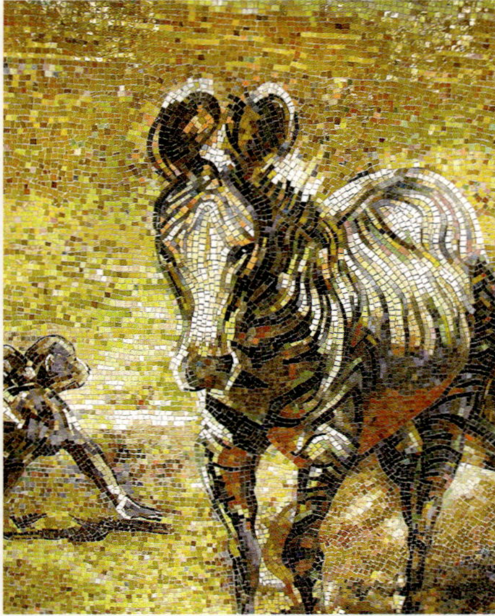

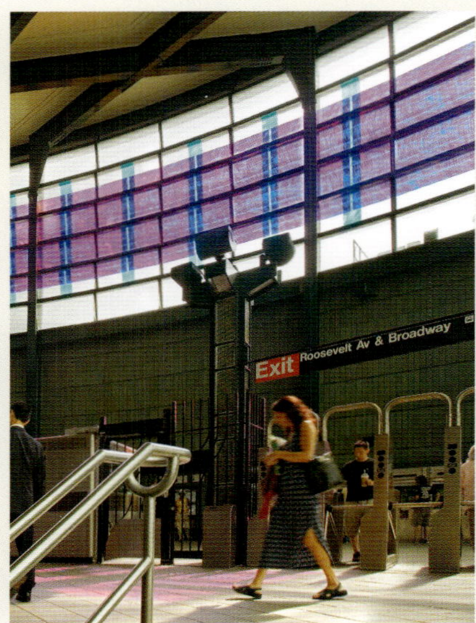

Left: Tom Otterness, *Life Underground*, 2001, bronze. 14th Street–8th Avenue.
Center: Eric Fischl, *The Garden of Circus Delights*, 2001, glass mosaic. 34th Street–Penn Station.
Right: Tom Patti, *Passage*, 2004, glass. 74th Street–Broadway–Jackson Heights–Roosevelt Avenue.
PHOTOGRAPHERS: ROB WILSON (LEFT); ROB WILSON (CENTER); DAVID SUNDBERG/ESTO (RIGHT)

Ceramic and glass mosaics brought a vibrancy to stations that was unmatched. Millions of tesserae gleaming and glittering in these previously drab places brought passageways and mezzanines to life. *Blooming*, Elizabeth Murray's room of mosaics at 59th Street and Lexington Avenue, and *Stream*, her mural in Long Island City, Jack Beal's *Onset of Winter* and *The Return of Spring*, Jacob Lawrence's *In Transit* at Times Square, and mosaic murals by Faith Ringgold, Willie Birch, and Vincent Smith on the Lenox line in Harlem have had a truly transformative effect.

In determining that mosaic would be the material of choice underground and that translation of the artwork would be done by experienced fabricators, Arts for Transit was able to open up new possibilities for artists who paint and draw and for those with no public art experience. By having Arts for Transit staff determine sites for the art in conjunction with the station architects, the art could be a dramatic part of the station, giving the renovation a new element and riders a new sense of ownership. In what might be called a holistic approach, the art became part of the larger design.

By the late 1980s, as public art grew in scope and stature nationwide, artists, architects, and particularly arts professionals, spoke of architect-and-artist collaborations with fervor. Arts for Transit developed processes to pair artists and architects who would theoretically meld into a single functional entity to create a work of art/architecture that would exceed in beauty and power what each could have achieved alone. But in reality these goals proved elusive. The genuine architect/artist collaboration is truly unusual. The very thing that drives much of the creative process–that single-willed vision–flies directly in the face of artists and architects giving and taking and coming up with a shared design concept. It quickly became clear that pairing an artist with an architect to work together cooperatively would be more successful. Projects such as Tom Otterness's *Life Underground* at 14th Street-8th Avenue with SOM, Eric Fischl's *The Garden of Circus Delights* at 34th Street-Penn Station with MTA NYCT architects, and Tom Patti's *Passage* at 74th Street Broadway-Jackson Heights-Roosevelt Avenue with FX FOWLE reflect the cooperative approach. It has become apparent that there are varying degrees of cooperation between the artist and architect. When the cooperation is a close one, as was the case with Mary Miss and Lee Harris Pomeroy Architects at 14th Street-Union Square, truly complex projects can be achieved.

MTA Arts for Transit's sphere of operation is integrated with the MTA's Capital Program. MTA typically chooses a group of stations to be renovated during each five-year period and then Arts for

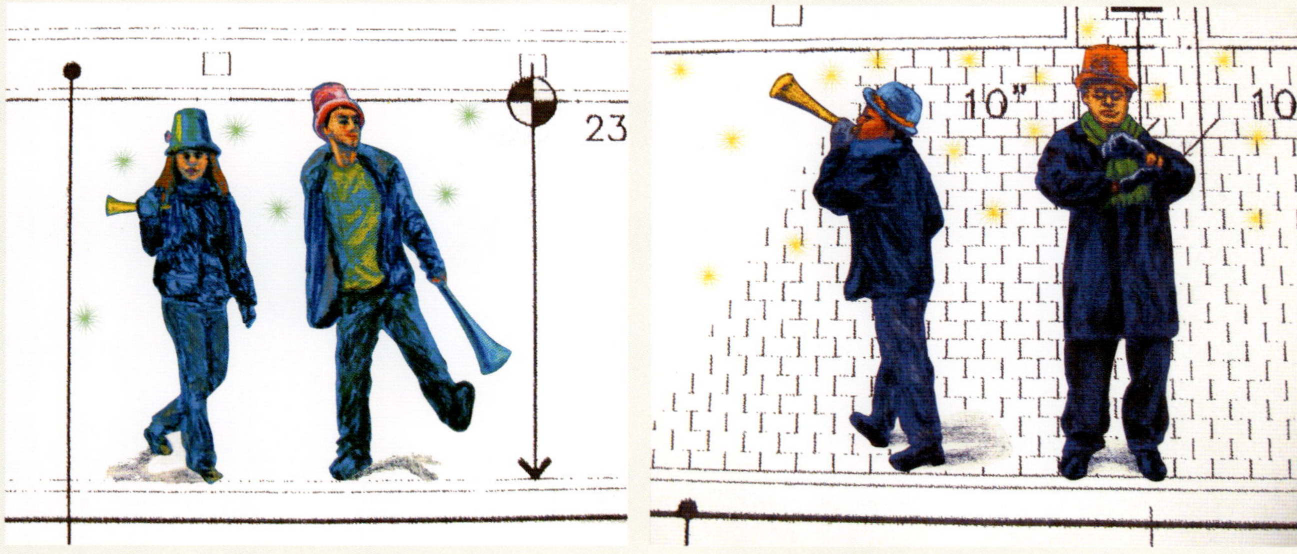

Jane Dickson, *Revelers*, maquette. Times Square–42nd Street.

Transit is allocated one percent of these funds for station renovations. Artworks are commissioned either through juried competitions or through a competitive selection process. In either case, proposals are typically submitted in both narrative and maquette form. A great deal of thought is given to the prospective work's appropriateness in terms of visual impact, durability, and suitability to the particular geographic location.

Special circumstances sometimes come into play—for instance, the opportunity to collaborate with an institution in the neighborhood, as happened with the Brooklyn Museum and the American Museum of Natural History. Other projects have a preservation aspect, as in the case of the salvaged Marine Grill murals at Fulton Street and the new Coney Island portal building where the new art, the preservation of the original BMT facade, and the architecture work together to evoke a storied past. Still other projects involve a creative dialogue with historic construction features and ornament, as in the projects of Mary Miss at 14th Street, Roberto Juarez at Grand Central Terminal, Andrew Leicester at Penn Station, and Roy Lichtenstein at Times Square.

Although the medium into which a work will be translated is theoretically the decision of the artist, in actuality only the most durable will meet the subway's inherent requirements. The medium must be hard-surfaced, relatively impervious to the elements, vandalism, and hard usage, and it must be able to retain its form and color for the foreseeable future. Thus most projects are of ceramic, glass, or bronze. In addition to the traditional media of faceted glass and ceramic tile, aluminum and granite are also being used as well as special effects of light. But even within these restrictions, there is latitude for great variety.

Currently, more than fifty new works are in progress, a program that makes MTA Arts for Transit one of the largest sources of public art commissions in the world. The challenge is to ensure that the art is of consistently high quality, fresh and vital, and appropriately site-specific. Just as the original mosaics installed in the subway in 1904 were designed with the specifics of the transit environment in mind, today's commissioned works are under a strict requirement to comply with the needs of the system's underlying substructure needs—indeed, they are dictated by the larger system's parameters. And, adding to the challenge, the system is always evolving and changing.

Arts for Transit continues to support traditional projects in traditional media. In 2005 Jane Dickson was selected to create artwork for the Times Square–42nd Street complex. Although Arts for Transit

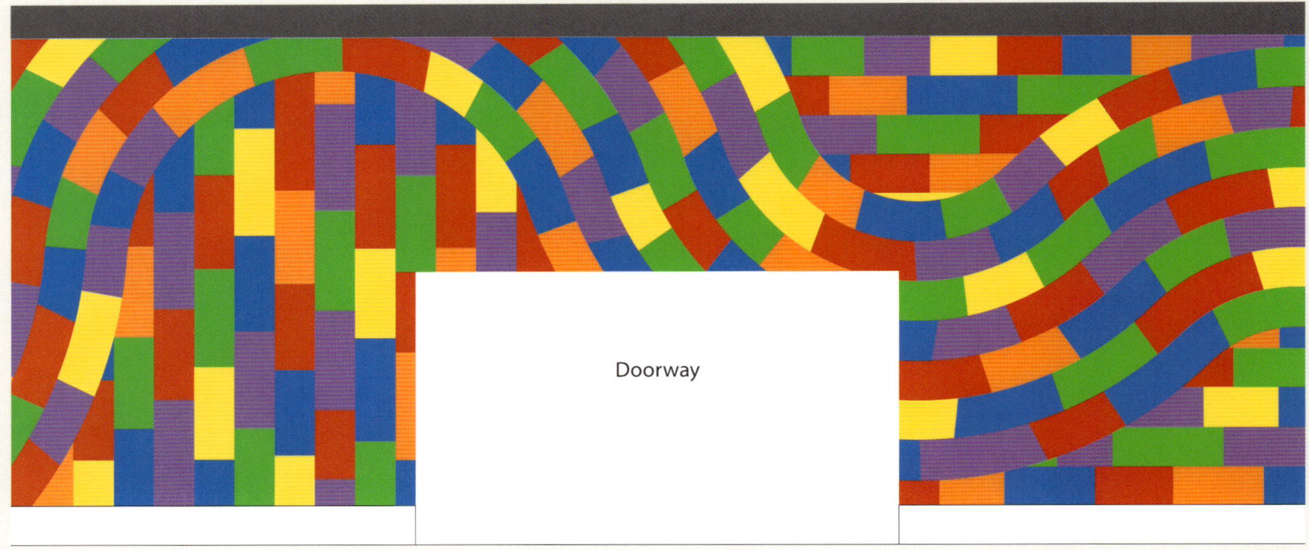

Sol LeWitt, *Whirls and Twirls (MTA)*, maquette.
59th Street–Columbus Circle.

generally believes in "one artist, one station," this enormous, central facility was an exception. The juxtaposition of many artists' visions thrives conceptually amidst the swirling energy that is 42nd Street. Now *Revelers*, a series of figures with hats and horns and all the elements of a celebration, will join the cacophony. Although the work is evocative of New Year's Eve, the artist also embraces and acknowledges a much broader spirit of celebration. Every day is a celebration for someone or something at Times Square. Dickson's revelers will appear to move along the walls of the long passageway that connects the Times Square station to the Port Authority Bus Terminal. As she explains, "Along the passageway of Times Square, everyone is hurrying by, hoping to catch the next train. I am designing these mosaics with that reality in mind. The images are meant to be enjoyed at a glance, in passing, the figures' animation enhanced by the viewer's hurrying past them. You will catch a glimpse of different figures each time you pass. Eventually some will become old friends."

For the mammoth 59th Street–Columbus Circle station, with its large mezzanine and long connecting passageways, Sol LeWitt has created a proposal for a ceramic wall drawing. "I . . . refer to the kind of art in which I am involved as conceptual art," LeWitt says. "In conceptual art the idea or concept is the most important aspect of the work. When an artist uses a conceptual form of art, it means that all of the planning and decisions are made beforehand and the execution is a perfunctory affair. The idea becomes a machine that makes the art."

LeWitt's vision for the execution of the Columbus Circle wall drawing is rigorous, the requirements challenging the parameters of ceramic; his insistence on strict control of color challenges the qualities of ceramic as a material. In order to fire a glazed ceramic piece at a temperature high enough to make it impervious to the elements, precise color control is lost. Therefore, extensive tests are under way, and the results are encouraging. Ultimately, LeWitt's ideas will be translated into durable ceramic form while maintaining his exacting standards for color, shape, and size. This truly will be a phenomenal piece, completely original in its execution.

Arts for Transit continues to seek those opportunities where architects and artists can work closely together. At the entry to subways and the terminal for the MTA Long Island Rail Road at the Atlantic Avenue Terminal in Brooklyn, Allan and Ellen Wexler have worked with di Domenico + Partners to impact the overall architectural space. The entry pavilion contains a dramatic overlook, commanding a view across Flatbush Avenue outside and the sprawling terminal area below. In addition, the expansive

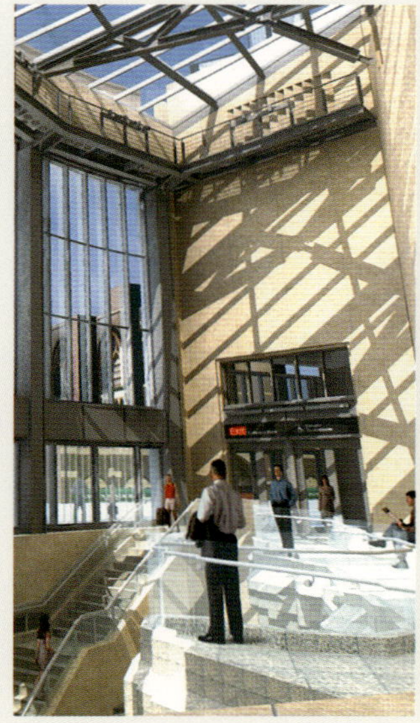

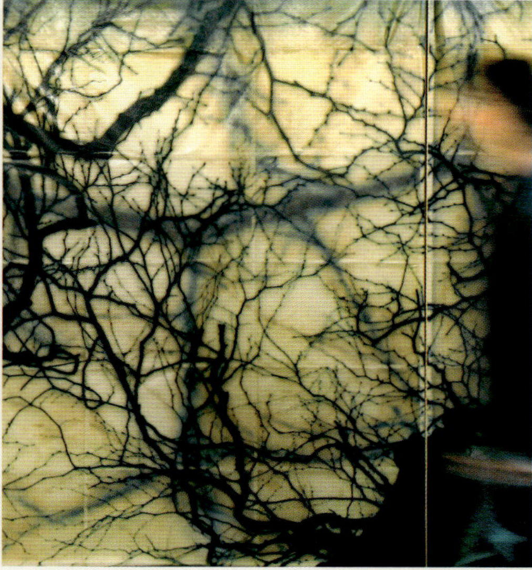

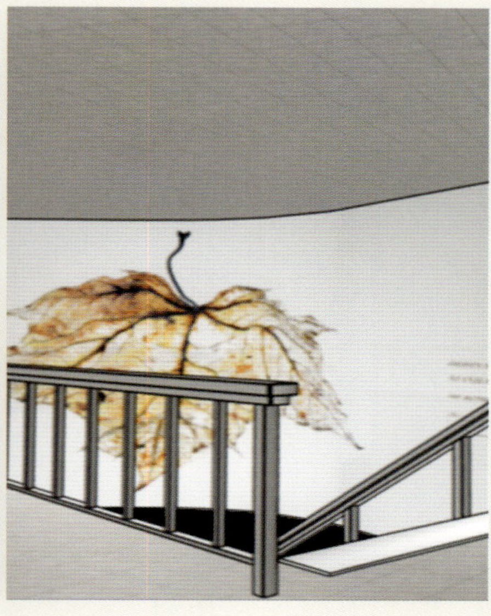

Left: Allan and Ellen Wexler, *Overlook*, rendering by di Domenico + Partners. Atlantic Avenue Terminal
Center and **Right**: Starn Studio, *Untitled*, rendering. South Ferry Terminal.

glass above provides a view upward that includes the towering form of the historic Williamsburgh Savings Bank building. The artists conceived a "rocky overlook," with allusions to stunning natural views such as those at the Grand Canyon and other national parks. The cantilevered structure will also provide harried travelers below with a sheltered place to sit and rest. Granite tiles will be used to achieve the effect, shaped into triangular segments that, when assembled, will create a monumental work that the Wexlers say "feels simultaneously man-made and natural."

The MTA has played, and will continue to play, a significant role in the rebuilding of Lower Manhattan after the catastrophic destruction of September 11, 2001. Two massive projects are under way: the building of a new South Ferry terminal and the design and construction of the Fulton Street Transit Center. Both of these greatly exceed the scope of all previous projects in their opportunities for the creation and installation of artwork in the transportation system.

The Starn twins, Doug and Mike, are internationally known photographers, constantly experimenting with the medium and creating mysterious and intriguing effects that are beautiful in their exploration of nature. Through *Untitled*, the Starns are bringing their investigation to the South Ferry Terminal. In their proposal, the artists spoke of the subway station as a point of departure: "Cut off from the surface of the streets, time bends, speeding up or slowing to a crawl; a sense of history and place is muffled." Their concept is to evoke the specificity of this site and to "re-place" the passenger with a broader context of time as well as physical location.

Riders entering the station will see a fence of photographically derived, laser-cut aluminum in the shape of trees. This recreates the feeling of walking through the park above. Passing through the turnstiles, they will face a telescopic imagining of time and place in a floor-to-ceiling reproduction of a map of the island of Manhattan. Along and above the stairwell leading down to the platform, a parallel image of a tree's discarded leaf echoes the shape of the island. Latticed branch-like structures will line the corridors. As the artists explain, "Though photography generally attempts to fix an image in time, we seek to inject time into our images, for time is a positive force: paradoxically, what endures is change. The silhouetted trees, the desiccated leaf, and the discarded topographies serve as poignant symbols for our journey because they quietly remind, while we go, from whence we came."

As if to underscore these sentiments, there are plans to showcase an archaeological artifact discovered during station excavation work. It consists of a stone wall, from the mid-eighteenth century, which will highlight the significance of the Battery in the city's history and development.

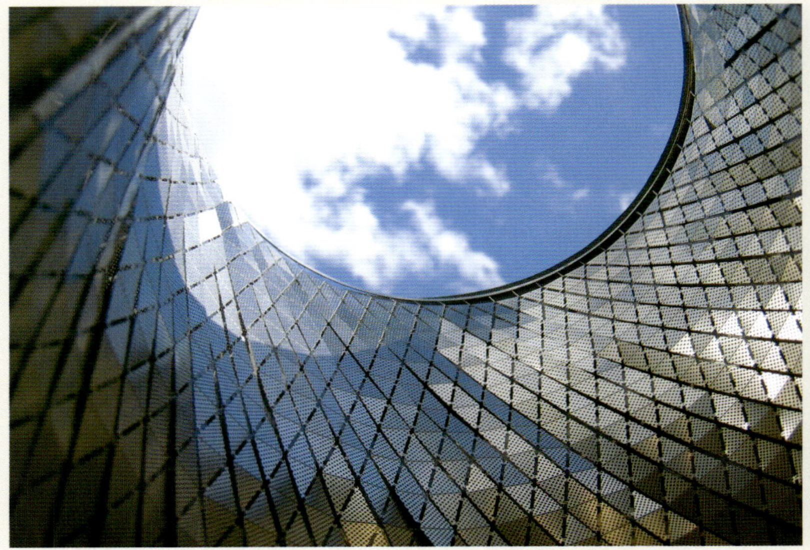

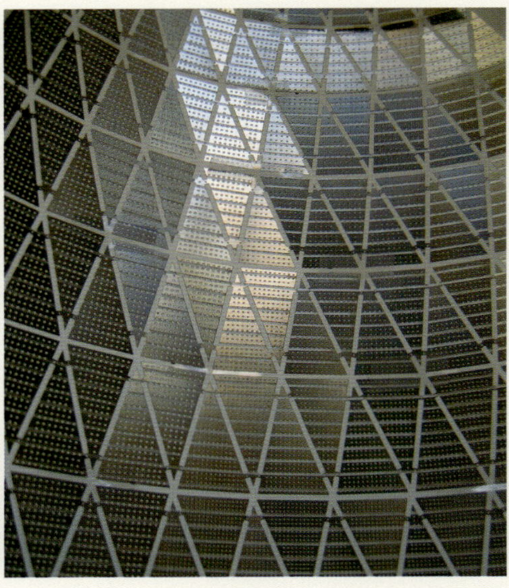

James Carpenter, *Solar Reflector Shell*, proposal. Fulton Street Transit Center.
RENDERING: JAMES CARPENTER.

The Fulton Street Transit Center project is proving to be an ideal opportunity for architect/artist collaboration. Since the main entry spaces are being built anew, art and architecture can progress together, fully integrated, as the overall design develops. The primary goal is to provide a strong visual identity and to create a welcoming space where sunlight helps to orient travelers and to assist them in finding their way through the complex. Nicholas Grimshaw & Partners and James Carpenter Design Associates are jointly developing the design.

For the Center's main space, the designers are creating a metaphor for the celestial heaven and the powerful influence of its changing continuum of light on our sense of time: day is transformed into night, months into seasons, and seasons into years. The architect and artist are currently refining both the architectural volume of the main space and developing an artwork; the result will be two, contrasting qualities of light.

The geometry of the support structure and the faceted surface of perforated aluminum panels are conceived as lightweight, reflective, and ever-changing. The result will be a beautiful, animated surface that will follow travelers as they move through the station. The configuration of the panels will alter along with lighting conditions; their surfaces will be treated in such a way that even on a cloudy day the interior of the space will feel luminous.

The aim of the Fulton Street Transit Center public art project is to create an environment and an impact that will be the best a city can provide its citizens, one that will become part of New Yorkers' memories, fulfilling the 1904 mandate and transforming it into a formula for success and beauty.

In a June 1904 article in *House and Garden* on the ornamentation of the new IRT subway, the writer commented on the importance of validation by future generations: "Whether in the end public observation will be keen enough to note the subtle differences of color and form; whether fancy's play may be compatible with the necessary conspicuousness which the stations signs must have, the future experience of riders and managers of the line can alone decide."

A century later, *New York Times* critic Roberta Smith made a similar observation about Arts for Transit's introduction of new art into the transit system and the test of time: "Liking subways, art, and democracy, I want the three to collaborate brilliantly. This doesn't always happen, but it may happen often enough. Not all the new art in our dramatically renewed subway system will stand the test of time, but every last bit of it will become part of a living museum never-to-be-finished creation that, despite its many imperfections, is more perfect than not. New York's subway system expresses an urban body electric that Whitman only glimpsed and connects each of us to the more personal one that he eloquently envisioned. It enables us to encounter in awe-inspiring physical form and complexity the energy of the past mingling with the present and evolving into the future, all in the process of getting to work on time."

In his "Crossing Brooklyn Ferry," as originally published in 1856 in *Leaves of Grass*, Walt Whitman reflected on the passage of time and wondered about the possibility of a dialogue with future generations:

> These, and all else, were to me the same as they are to you;
> I project myself a moment to tell—also I return.
>
> I loved well those cities;
> I loved well the stately and rapid river;
> The men and women I saw were all near to me;
> Others the same—others who look back on me, because I look'd forward to them;
> (The time will come, though I stop here to-day and to-night.)
>
> What is it, then, between us?
> What is the count of the scores or hundreds of years between us?
>
> Whatever it is, it avails not—distance avails not, and place avails not.

Walt Whitman spoke across time to New Yorkers of the future, and the original subway planners at the turn of the twentieth century are still in dialogue with the designers and artists of today. Now, after the turn of a different century, it is appropriate that MTA Arts for Transit staff and the many others concerned with improvements in New York's transit system wonder how their contributions will fare in the test of time. Our hope is that coming generations will appreciate and treasure their creations, not as sterile artifacts from a dark past, but as valuable, functioning parts of an ever brighter future. May the process continue to evolve and change—this *is* New York!—but may those involved never lose touch with the art and ideas of those who came before in the shared quest for the Subway Beautiful.

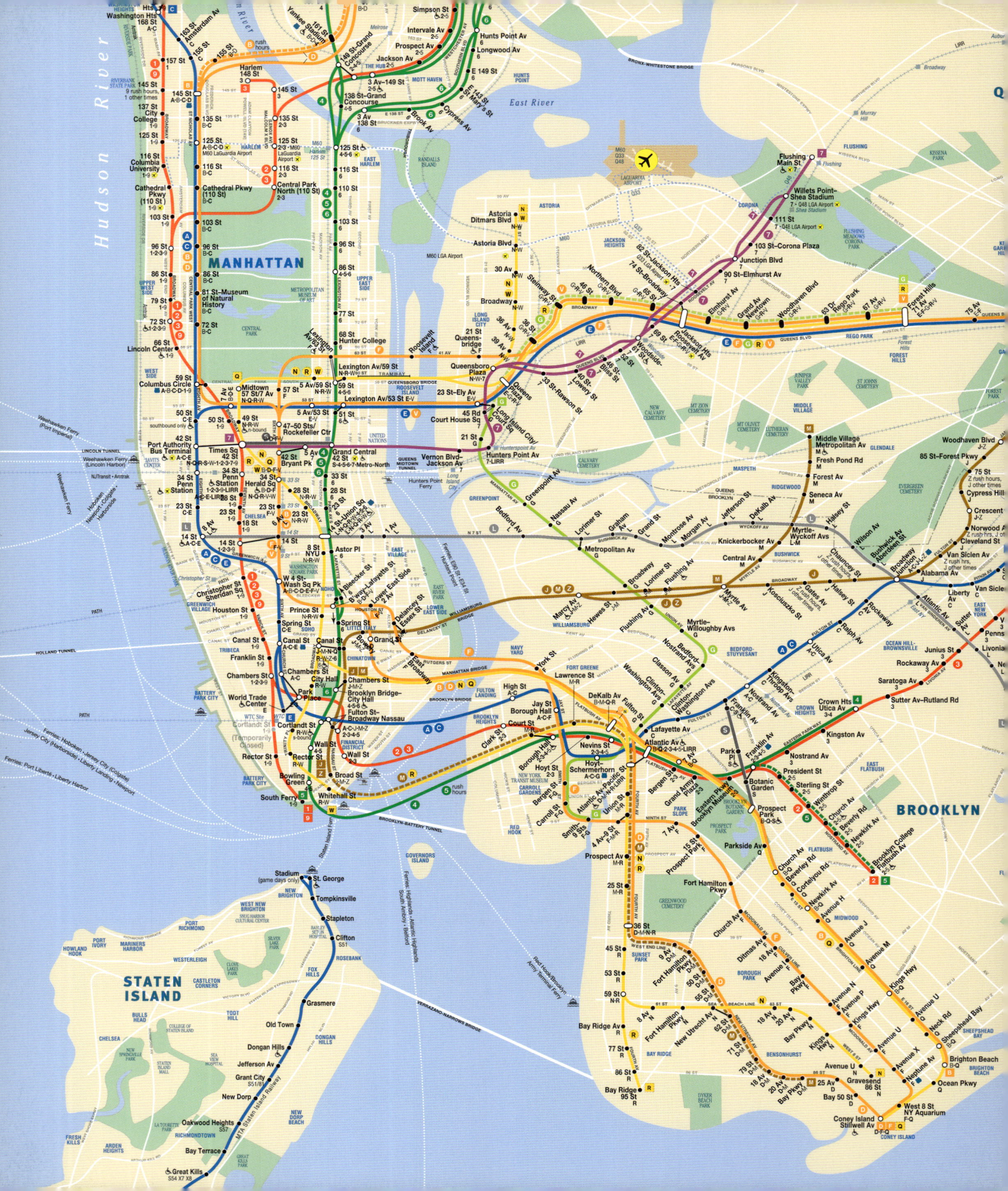

Hudson River
East River
MANHATTAN
BROOKLYN
STATEN ISLAND
Washington Hts 168 St
Harlem 148 St
145 St
137 St City College
125 St
116 St Columbia University
Cathedral Pkwy (110 St)
103 St
96 St
86 St
81 St–Museum of Natural History
79 St
72 St
66 St Lincoln Center
59 St Columbus Circle
50 St
42 St Port Authority Bus Terminal
Times Sq 42 St
34 St Penn Station
Herald Sq 34 St
23 St
18 St
14 St
Christopher St Sheridan Sq
Houston St
Canal St
Franklin St
Chambers St
World Trade Center
Cortlandt St
Rector St
Wall St
South Ferry
Bowling Green
Whitehall St
Broad St
Fulton St–Broadway Nassau
Brooklyn Bridge–City Hall
City Hall
Park Place
Spring St
Prince St
W 4 St–Wash Sq Pk
8 St NYU
Astor Pl
Bleecker St
Union Sq 14 St
Grand Central 42 St
5 Av/53 St
47-50 Sts/Rockefeller Ctr
49 St
57 St
Lexington Av/59 St
Lexington Av/53 St
51 St
33 St
28 St
125 St
116 St
110 St
103 St
96 St
86 St
77 St
68 St Hunter College
Roosevelt Island
Queensboro Plaza
Queens Plaza
Court Sq
Hunters Point Av
Vernon Blvd–Jackson Av
Astoria Ditmars Blvd
Astoria Blvd
30 Av
Broadway
36 Av
39 Av
Steinway St
46 St
Northern Blvd
65 St
74 St–Broadway
82 St–Jackson Hts
90 St–Elmhurst Av
Junction Blvd
103 St–Corona Plaza
111 St
Willets Point–Shea Stadium
Flushing Main St
Roosevelt Av Jackson Hts
Elmhurst Av
Grand Av Newtown
Woodhaven Blvd
63 Dr Rego Park
67 Av
Forest Hills 71 Av
75 Av
LaGuardia Airport
Greenpoint Av
Nassau Av
Metropolitan Av
Lorimer St
Graham Av
Grand St
Montrose Av
Morgan Av
Jefferson St
DeKalb Av
Myrtle–Wyckoff Avs
Halsey St
Wilson Av
Bushwick Av Aberdeen St
Broadway Junction
Marcy Av
Hewes St
Flushing Av
Myrtle Av
Myrtle–Willoughby Avs
Bedford–Nostrand Avs
Classon Av
Clinton–Washington Avs
Lafayette Av
Atlantic Av
Nevins St
Hoyt–Schermerhorn
Borough Hall
Court St
Jay St Borough Hall
High St
York St
DeKalb Av
Bergen St
Carroll St
Smith 9 Sts
Grand Army Plaza
Eastern Pkwy Brooklyn Museum
Franklin Av
Botanic Garden
Prospect Park
Parkside Av
Church Av
Nostrand Av
Kingston Av
Crown Hts Utica Av
Sutter Av–Rutland Rd
Saratoga Av
Rockaway Av
Junius St
President St
Sterling St
Winthrop St
Beverly Rd
Newkirk Av
Brooklyn College Flatbush Av
Fort Hamilton Pkwy
Prospect Av
25 St
36 St
45 St
53 St
59 St
Bay Ridge Av
77 St
86 St
Bay Ridge 95 St
Avenue J
Avenue M
Kings Hwy
Avenue U
Neck Rd
Sheepshead Bay
Brighton Beach
Ocean Pkwy
West 8 St NY Aquarium
Coney Island Stillwell Av
Bay 50 St
Gravesend 86 St
Bay Pkwy
Stadium
St. George
Tompkinsville
Stapleton
Clifton
Grasmere
Old Town
Dongan Hills
Jefferson Av
Grant City
New Dorp
Oakwood Heights
Bay Terrace
Great Kills
Verrazano-Narrows Bridge
Brooklyn-Battery Tunnel
Holland Tunnel
Lincoln Tunnel
Queensboro Bridge
Williamsburg Bridge
Manhattan Bridge
Brooklyn Bridge
Bronx-Whitestone Bridge

FROM TIMES SQUARE TO GREENPORT

An Arts for Transit Tour through the MTA System

ROY LICHTENSTEIN

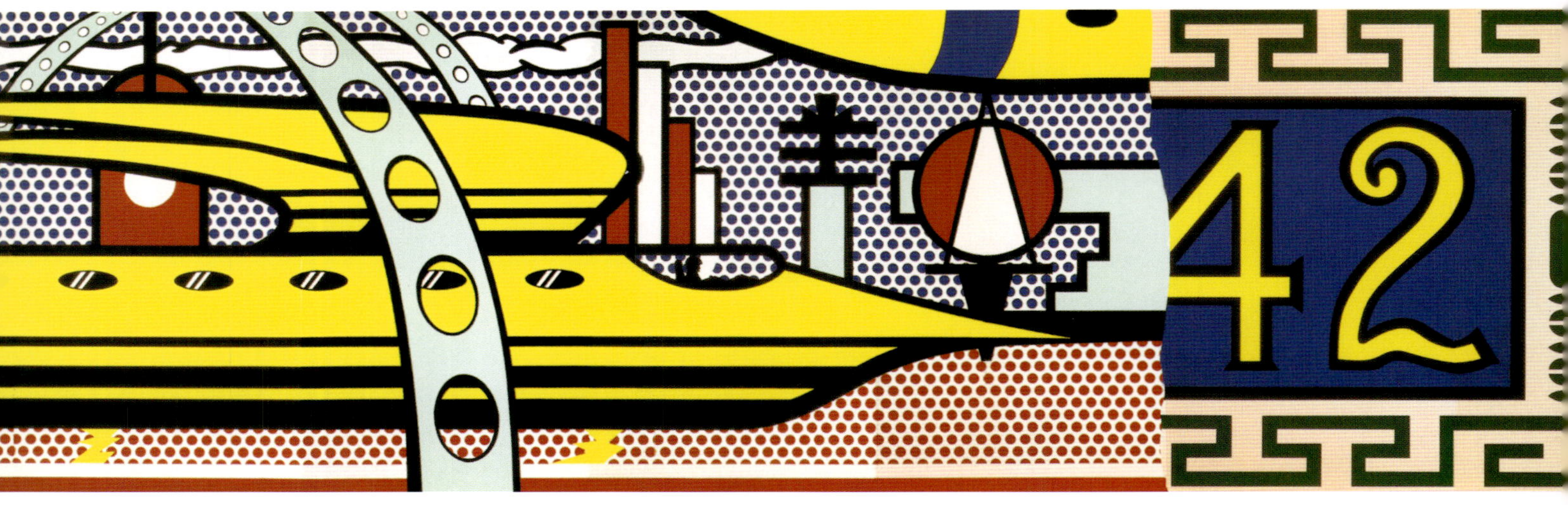

TIMES SQUARE MURAL, 2002
Times Square–42nd Street N Q R S W 1 2 3 7
(Collage 1990, fabricated 1994)
Porcelain enamel
COPYRIGHT © ESTATE OF ROY LICHTENSTEIN; PHOTOGRAPHERS: ROBERT MCKEEVER (ABOVE); ROB WILSON (OPPOSITE)

Roy Lichtenstein's *Times Square Mural* captures the spirit of the subway, its linearity and its dynamism. It tips its hat to both the past and the future, with its retro-futuristic forms. The central image is a levitating winged tubular car making its way through the tunnels of a subterranean station. And not just any station, for the specific architectural details and particularly the giant 42 sign indicate that this is Times Square, the throbbing heart of Manhattan.

Lichtenstein was a true son of the city. He was born in New York in 1923 and studied at the Parsons School of Design and the Art Students League. His work is often viewed as emblematic of mid-twentieth-century New York, particularly Manhattan, with its emphasis on surface, large scale, mass marketing, and modernist design.

Times Square Mural is in many ways a synthesis of Lichtenstein's career. It is replete with references to and variations on the artist's earlier works. For instance, the futuristic transporter can be directly linked to his painting *Emeralds* and also to the abstract ships in his *New York State Mural* images. The architectural ornament is adapted from his *Entablatures* of the 1970s. And he has taken the building and billboard forms from a combination of his *Imperfect* paintings and his *Modern* series that began with his poster for the Lincoln Center Film Festival of 1966.

For *Times Square Mural* Lichtenstein also freely appropriated and incorporated images from the works of other artists and designers. Indeed, in an interview with Bob Adelman, he declared, "All my art is in some way about other art, even if the other art is cartoons." The hooded figure at the right of the mural is from the Buck Rogers comic strips that ran from the 1920s through the 1960s, a favorite of the artist. And a more literal borrowing is the iconic 42 image from Philip Coppola's *Silver Connections* series of drawings of the architectural detail of the subway.

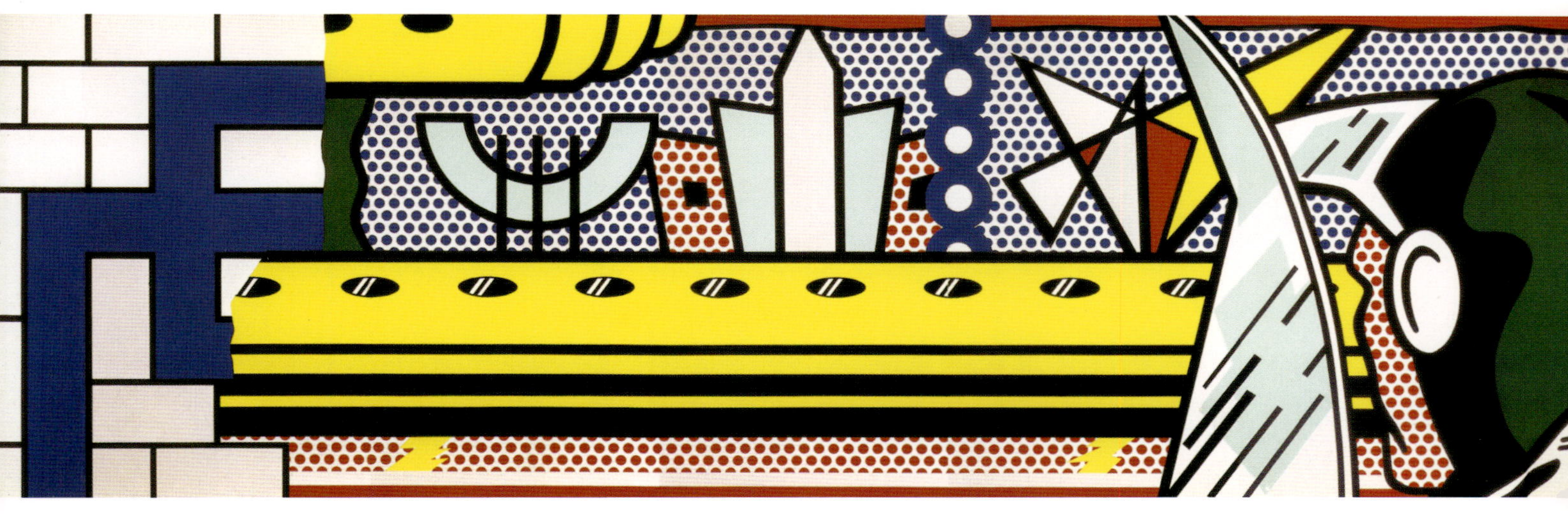

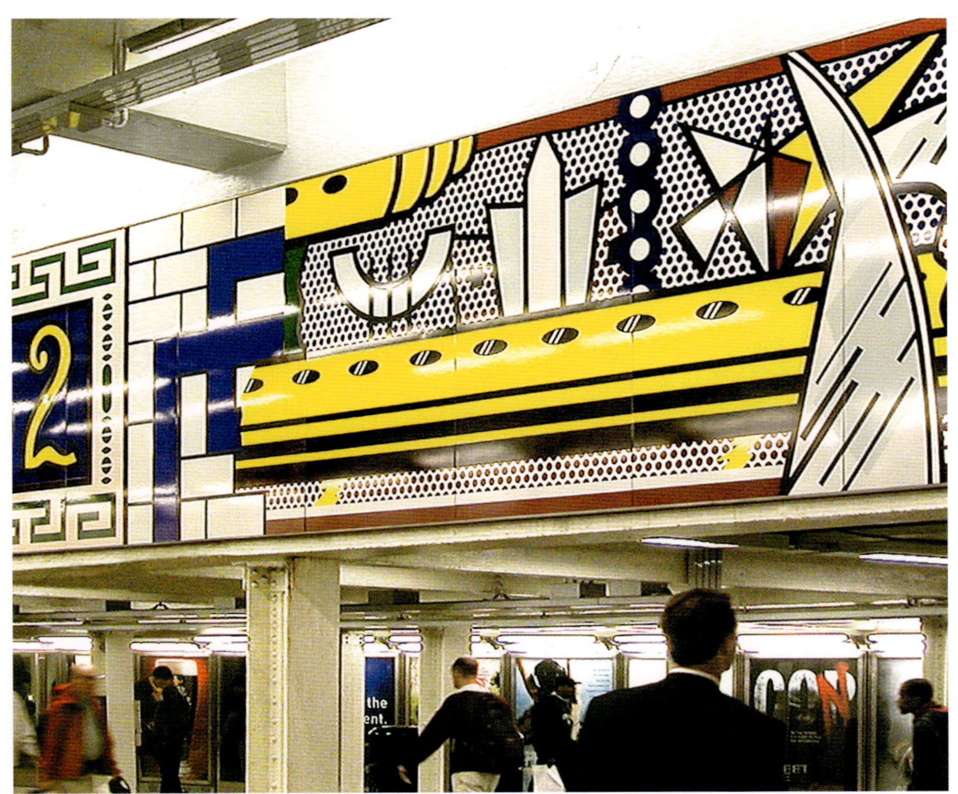

JACOB LAWRENCE

NEW YORK IN TRANSIT, 2001

Times Square–42nd Street N Q R S W 1 2 3 7

Glass mosaic

PHOTOGRAPHERS: JEFFREY STURGES (BELOW); DAVID LUBARSKY (OPPOSITE)

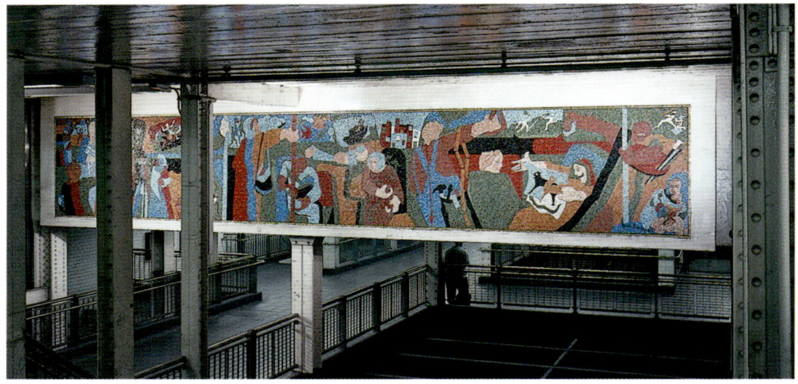

The enormous mosaic mural *New York in Transit* is the focal point of the new elliptical mezzanine in the Times Square subway complex. Taken together, its thousands of color-washed facets constitute a hymn of praise to the city of New York, its streets, neighborhoods, sports—and its subway.

Jacob Lawrence lived in New York for much of his life, and he often incorporated his observations and memories of the city into his art. The artist spent his childhood in Harlem and then studied at the Harlem Arts Workshop under Charles Alston. He also attended the American Artist School in 1937 and worked as a painter for the WPA Federal Art Project. He is best known for historical works that depict the lives of famous African American figures, particularly those involved in the civil rights movement and their precursors. Toward the end of his career, his work became more abstract and more colorful.

In these later works, Lawrence took as his subjects the city and its people. He insisted that his characteristic bold and colorful forms were also directly linked to the living conditions he experienced in his youth.

In an interview published in the book *Over the Line: The Art and Life of Jacob Lawrence* (2001), he recalled:

> Our homes were very decorative, full of pattern, like inexpensive throw rugs. It must have had some influence, all this color and everything. Because we were so poor the people used this as a means of brightening their life. I used to do bright patterns after these throw rugs; I got ideas from them, the arabesques, the movement and so on.

New York in Transit was Jacob Lawrence's last public work. Here he evokes city life as it might be seen from an elevated train, subtle and diffuse at first but upon closer inspection detailed and striking. Undertaken when the artist was gravely ill, this work is reflective and contemplative in attitude. As in Roy Lichtenstein's *Times Square Mural* in the same station, Lawrence's *New York in Transit* is in many ways a meditation on a great artist's life—a parting gift to New York City and the millions of people who live and have lived here.

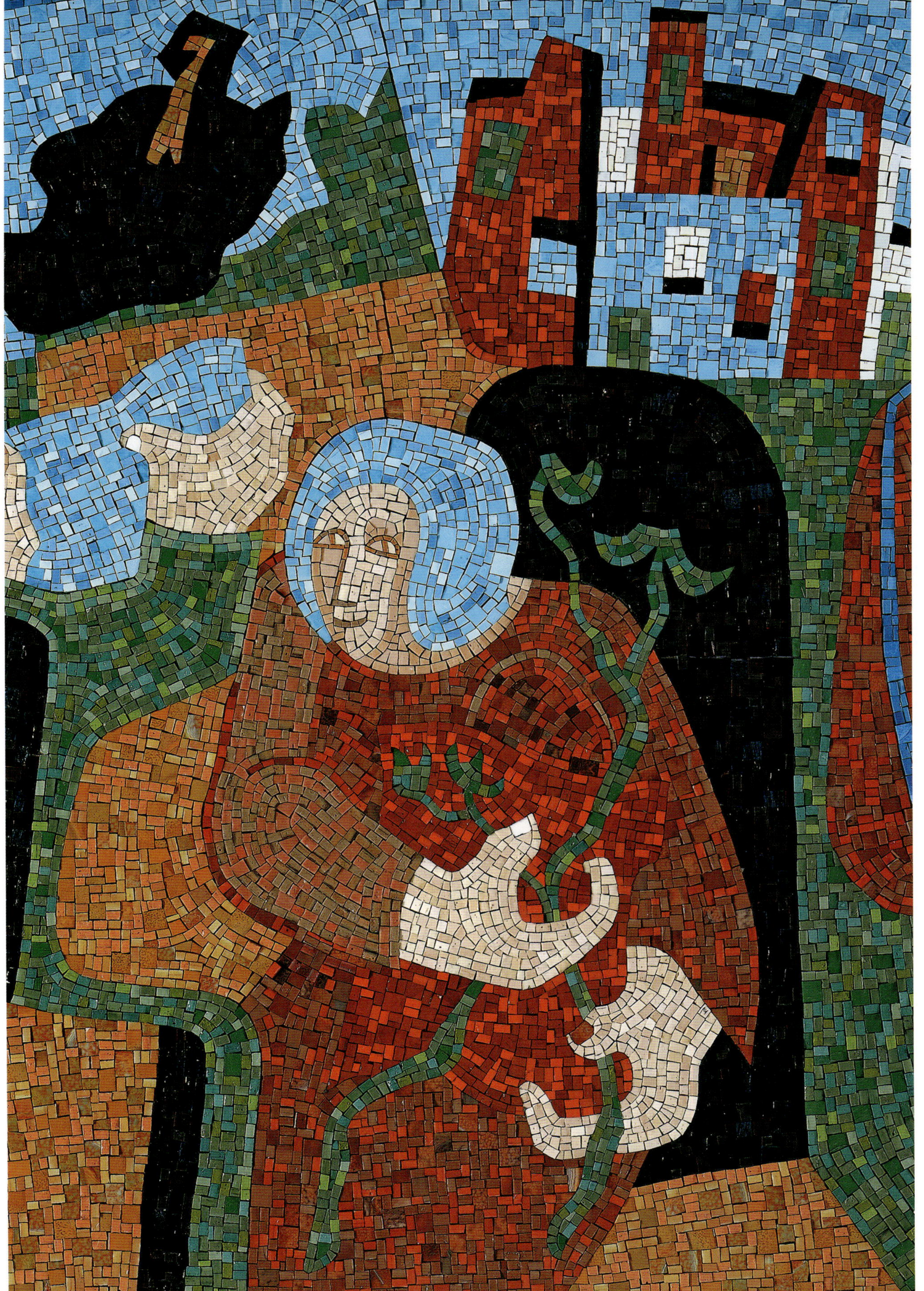

JACK BEAL

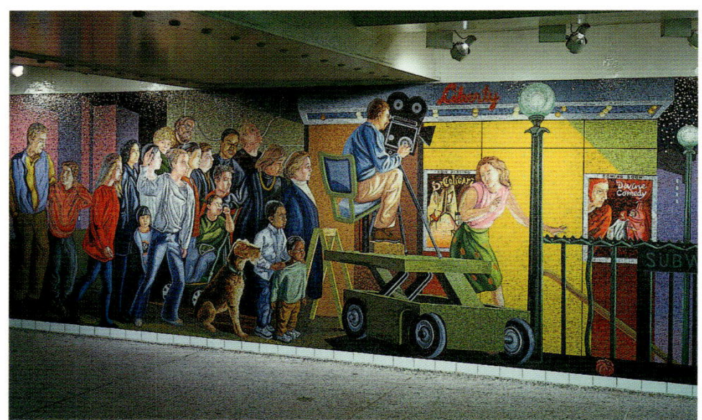

THE RETURN OF SPRING, 2001
THE ONSET OF WINTER, 2005
Times Square-42nd Street N Q R S W 1 2 3 7
Glass mosaic
PHOTOGRAPHER: JEFFREY STURGES

In these dramatic murals Jack Beal links the subway to classical myths that deal with the relationship between goings-on above ground and below.

Trained as an abstract expressionist, Jack Beal soon turned toward figuration in his works, eventually achieving great success and becoming a leading realist. He often stated, "I will never be satisfied until I obtain the believability of the seventeenth century Dutch painters." Ironically, now his interest has turned back to abstraction, he says.

The artist explains that he based this work on the Greek myth of Persephone, who was abducted by Hades and whisked away to the underworld. In *The Return of Spring* Persephone is shown running to her mother, Demeter, goddess of the Harvest. According to the terms of a pact Demeter had made with Hades, Persephone would be allowed to return to earth and her mother for the rest of eternity provided that she ate nothing before leaving the underworld. But Hades enticed her to sample a pomegranate before she left.

The Onset of Winter completes Beal's story. Having eaten the pomegranate, Persephone now is allowed to spend six months on earth, but must spend the other six down below—autumn and winter in the underworld and spring and summer with her mother —thus the origin of the seasons. A rueful Persephone is shown at the top of the stairs, knowing she must descend but not wanting to go.

As with the works of Lichtenstein and Lawrence, place and time—a particular place and a particular time, but with an implied universality—are the theme. Time passes, people and things come and go, but there is always a déjà vu quality lurking just beneath the surface.

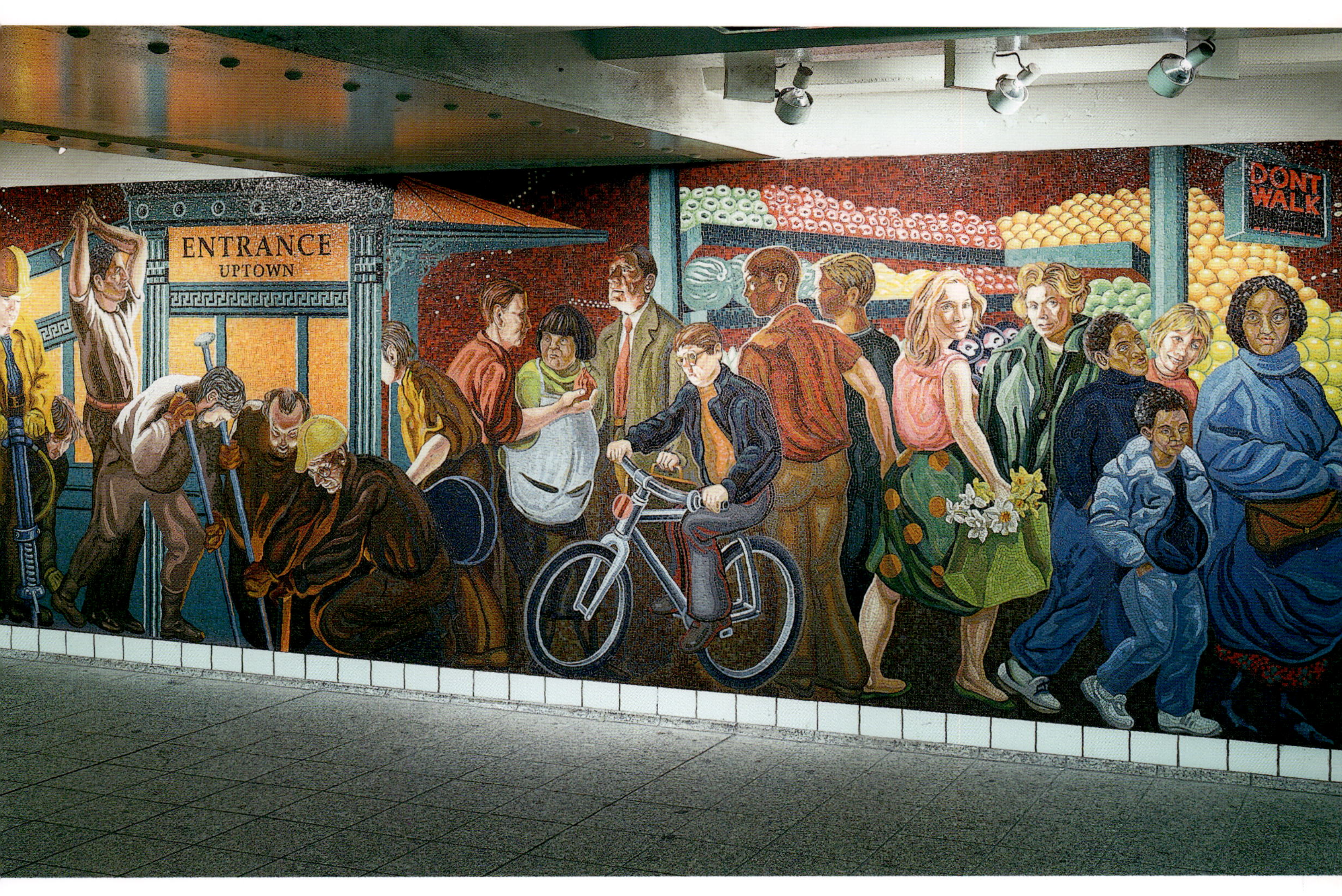
ENTRANCE
UPTOWN
DONT
WALK

TOBY BUONAGURIO

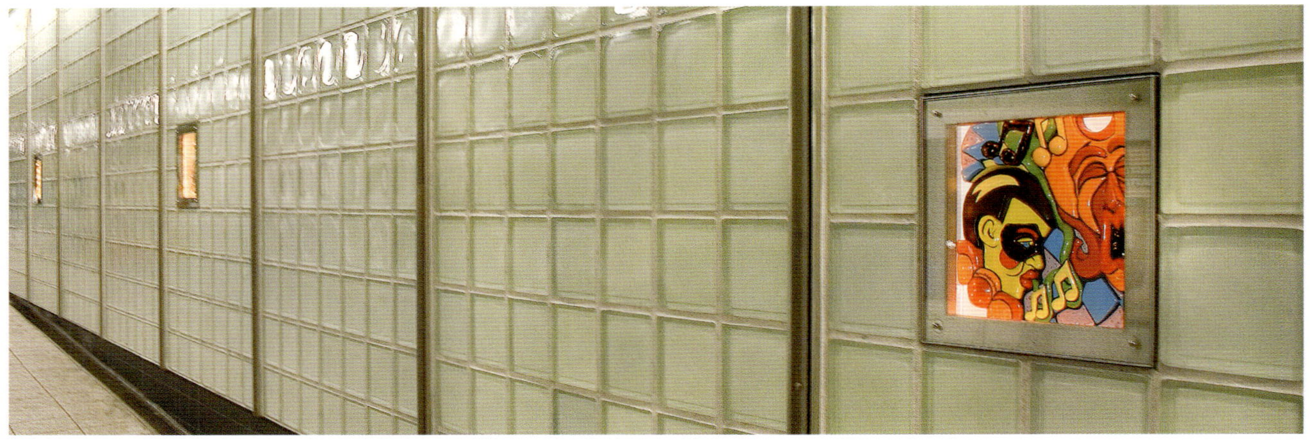

TIMES SQUARE: 35 TIMES, 2005
Times Square–42nd Street N Q R S W 1 2 3 7
Ceramic plaques inset in glass-block wall
PHOTOGRAPHER: ROB WILSON

What images does Times Square evoke? New Year's Eve? Hot dogs and pretzels? Gawking tourists snapping photographs? Ladies of uncertain virtue? Magic tricks and three-card monte? Ice-cream cones? Strange people strutting stranger clothes? The theaters? Whatever the case, it is probably represented in *Times Square: 35 Times* and its multidimensional cartoonlike artworks scattered throughout the station.

Toby Buonagurio has lived in New York all her life. She is particularly well known for her vividly colored, offbeat ceramic work, which often has tongue-in-cheek or satirical overtones. The influences of Japanese figural works, theater, and ceramics shine through in her work, including this one.

Times Square: 35 Times draws on three main elements—performing arts, fashion, and street life—that energize midtown Manhattan, and these are brought vividly to life by the artist's clever depictions of people, places, and objects that can be recognized by all. Buonagurio's panels are installed in newly designed illuminated shadowboxes that are featured in glass-block walls in various places throughout the station. Taken together, they remind passersby of Times Square's myriad wonders—both high and low.

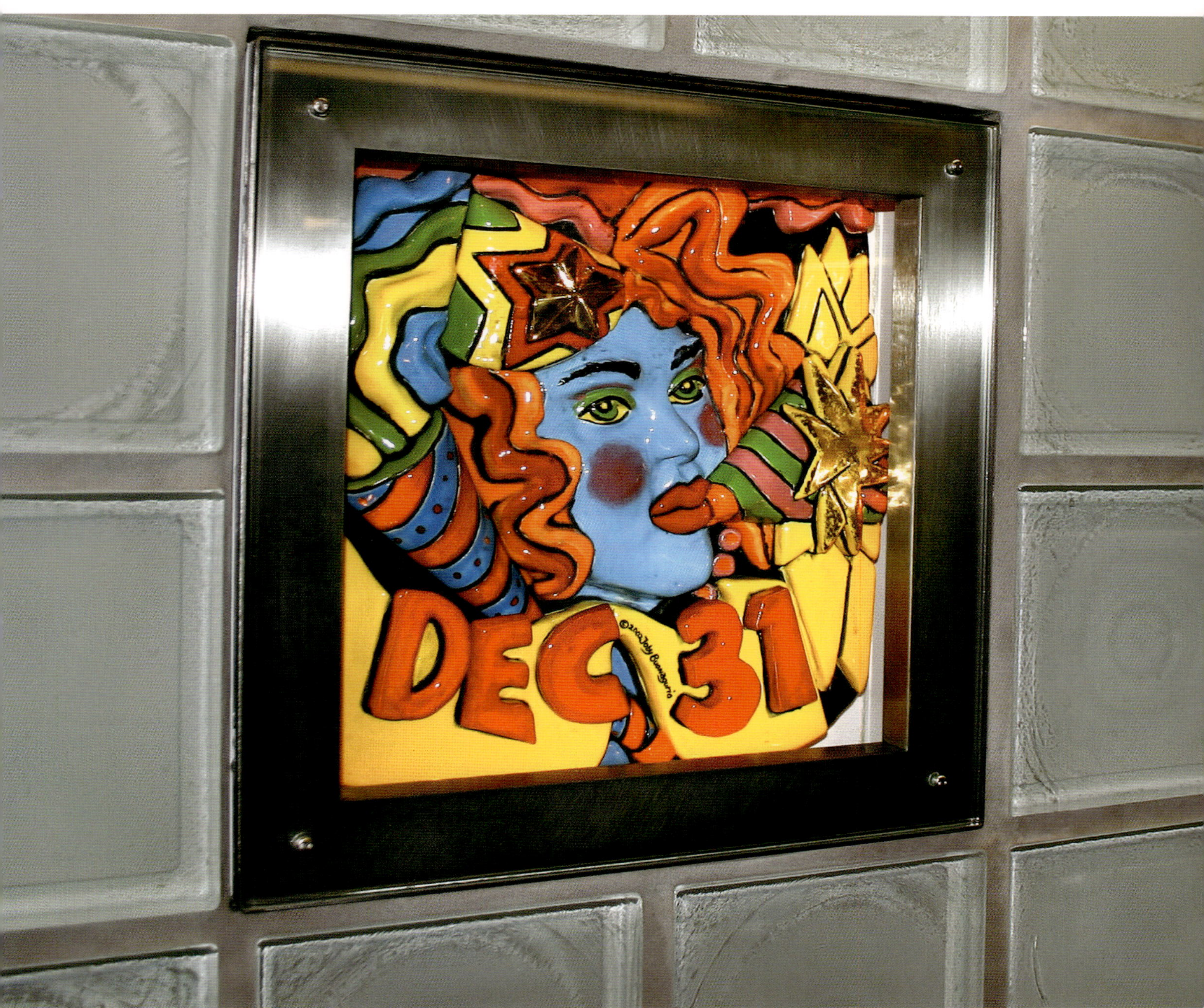
DEC 31
©2002 Joby Buonagurio

LISA DINHOFER

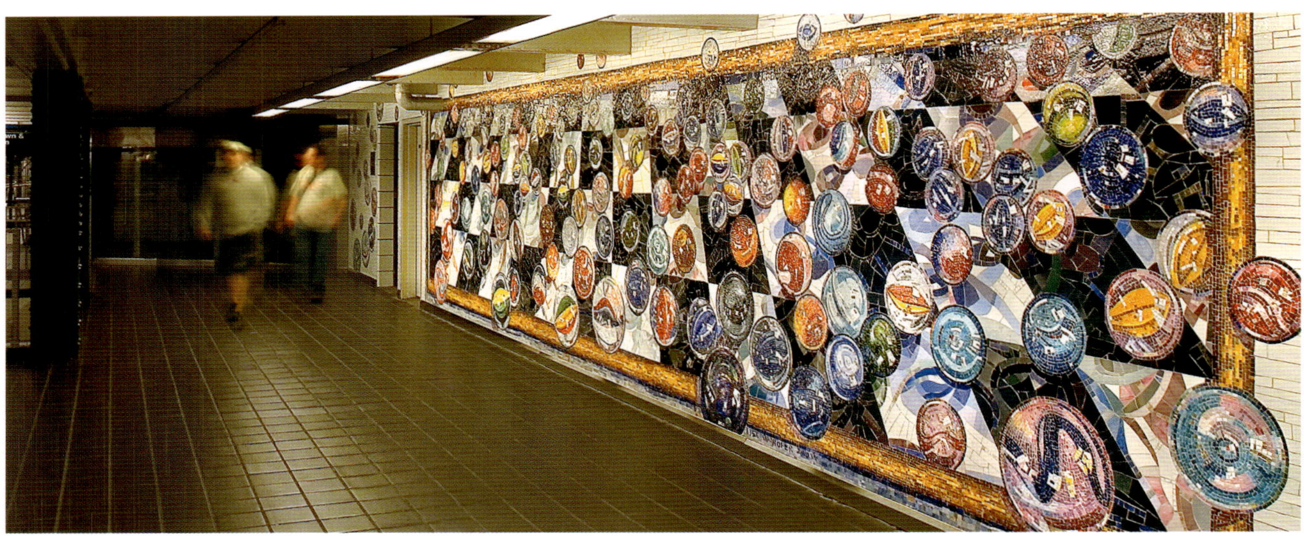

LOSING MY MARBLES, 2003
42nd Street–Port Authority Bus Terminal Ⓐ Ⓒ Ⓔ
Glass mosaic
PHOTOGRAPHER: ROB WILSON

Losing My Marbles is part of Lisa Dinhofer's ongoing fascination with marbles and other toys. "Toys are caricatures in miniature of society at large . . . they carry a collective, popular memory," she declared in her artist statement for the work.
The artwork is gigantic, taking up a large wall that subway riders encounter head-on and two flanking walls, a total of forty-four linear feet. The main wall is designed to simulate three-dimensional space, to draw the viewer into the work; the side walls help the artist to achieve a wraparound effect.

Dinhofer has described her working method and the effects she achieves:

> The goal of my work is to fascinate visually. Through color, light, orchestrated movement and playful objects the audience is drawn into an enchanted environment where people become smaller and playing marbles loom large. I am an "illusionist" painter rather than a "realist." All the objects I depict are real, they exist, but I chose to create my own special plane . . . The marbles themselves inhabit our imagination and memory. They are joyful and they are beautiful. There are smiles in this piece, there is an exuberance to this piece, and ultimately there is a true delight. And that is magic.

To stress the illusionist character of the piece, a golden trompe l'oeil frame surrounds the main image, which depicts a floor of black-and-white squares with marbles seemingly floating in space. Concave mirrors are strategically introduced to add further dimension and to literally draw viewers deeper into the work, via their distorted reflections. The marbles on the side walls seem to have burst forth from the main wall or else to be rushing to join them. In her artist statement, Dinhofer commented, "Here I can be an abstract expressionist and a realist at the same time. My space is imaginary but my objects are observed."

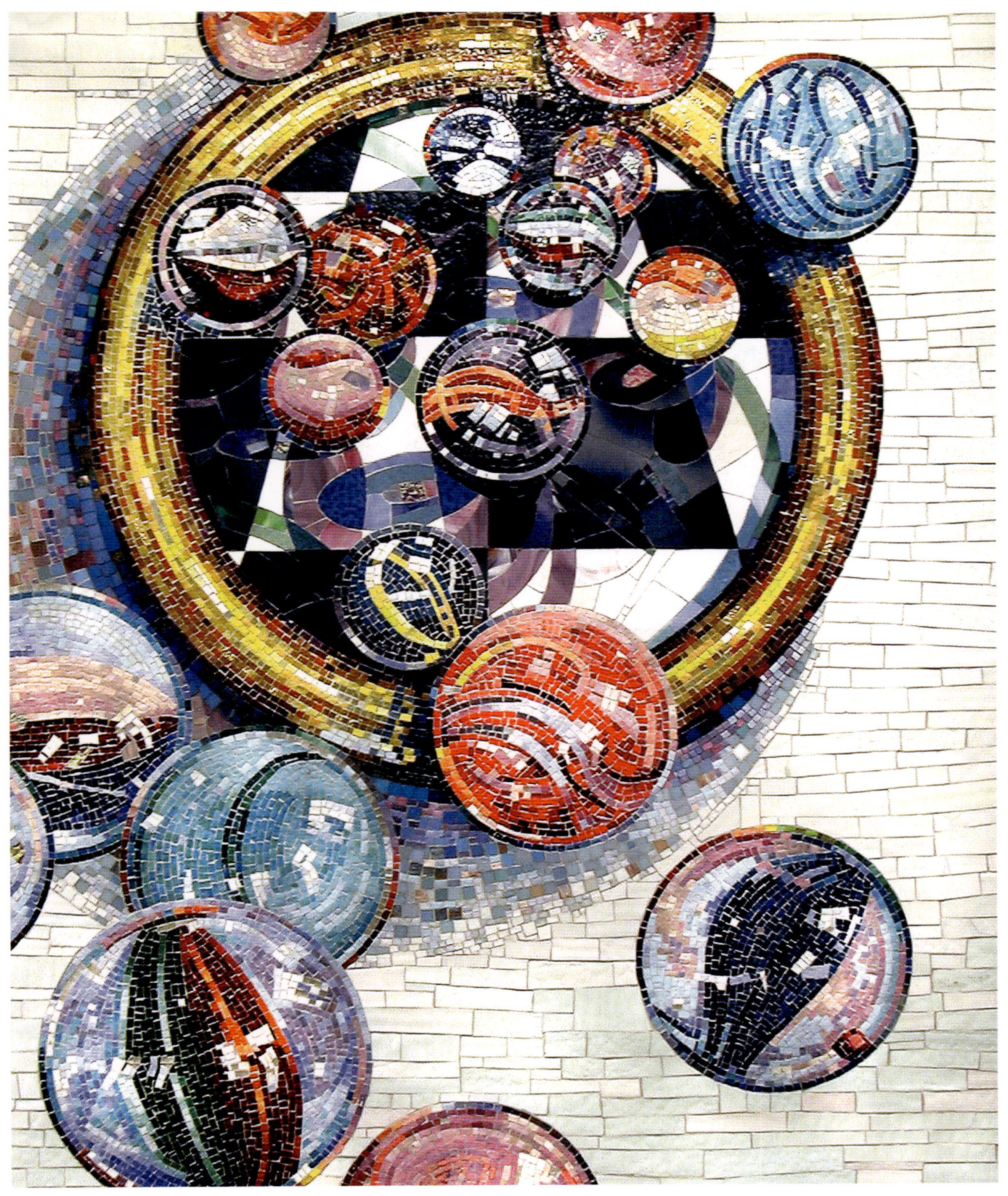

SAMM KUNCE

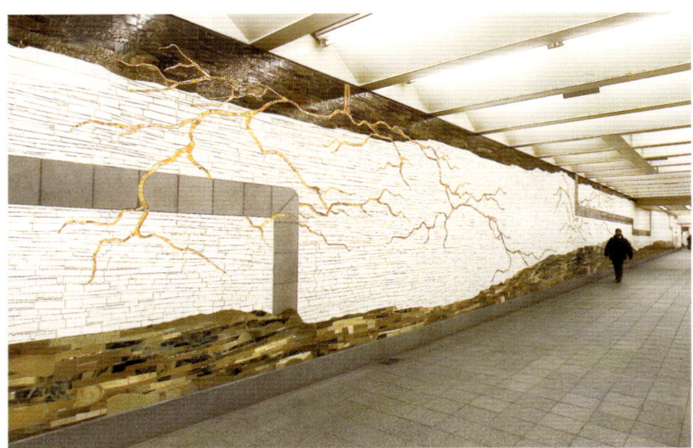

UNDER BRYANT PARK, 2002
42nd Street–Bryant Park B D F V 7
Glass mosaic and stone
PHOTOGRAPHER: ROB WILSON

Under Bryant Park is one of the largest and most provocative artworks in the Arts for Transit program. The mosaic runs under 42nd Street along the corridor connecting the east-west and north-south subway lines that intersect at the Avenue of the Americas. On both sides of the tunnel, slightly strange things start to appear on the walls. First come monochromatic rock outcroppings, followed by tree roots and more rock strata, and then animal burrows. Finally these are joined by quotations from sources as diverse as Ovid, James Joyce, and Mother Goose.

Environmental artist Samm Kunce says that *Under Bryant Park* is "based on the idea of systems–the city's water system, the system of tree routes and animal tunnels underground, and the system of language, history, and knowledge" (a nod to the New York Public Library nearby). In her words, "We travel in the subway system. Our water is delivered via a system of pipes. The plants and trees that provide grace and softness against the city's sharper edges find a way to the water that resides naturally underground by systems of roots. Literature is shared by systems of learning and lending in schools and libraries. Moles and rabbits live in systems of burrows, as most of us inhabit divided portions of larger buildings."

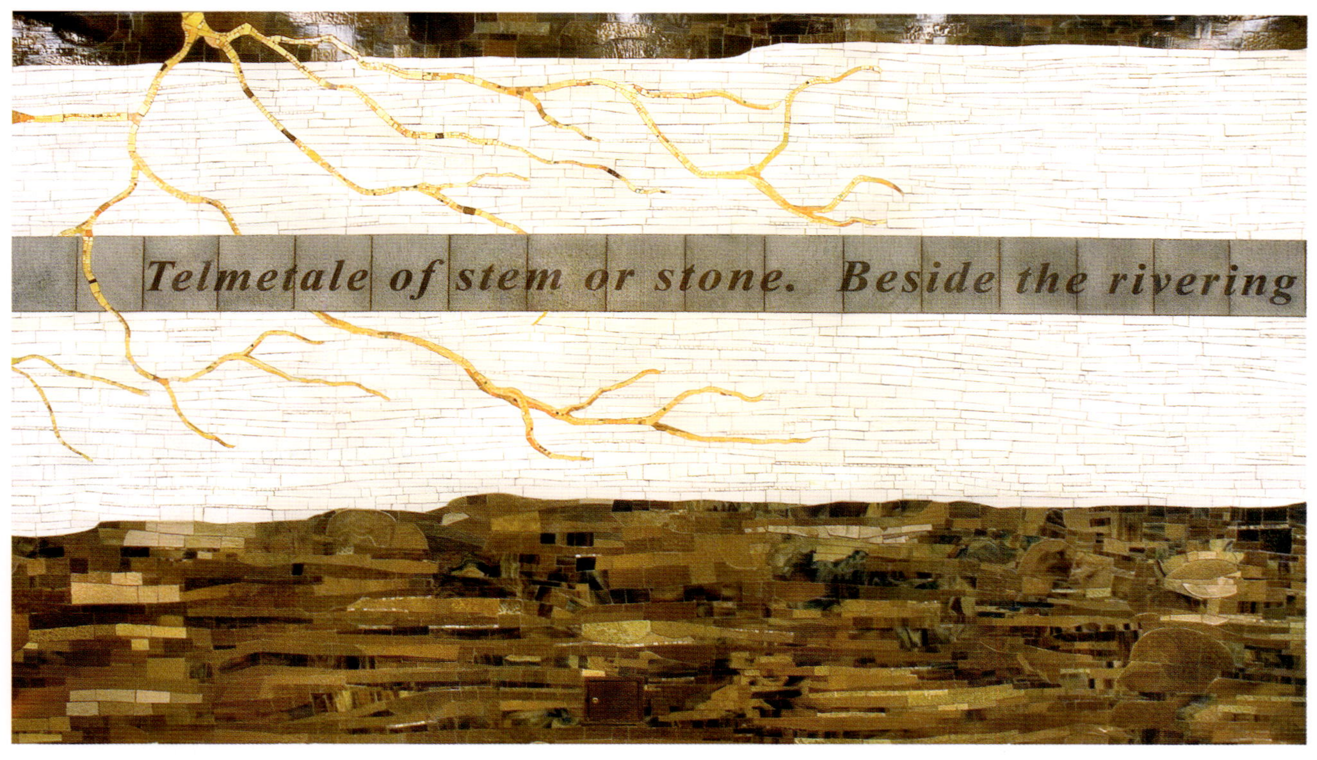
Telmetale of stem or stone. Beside the rivering

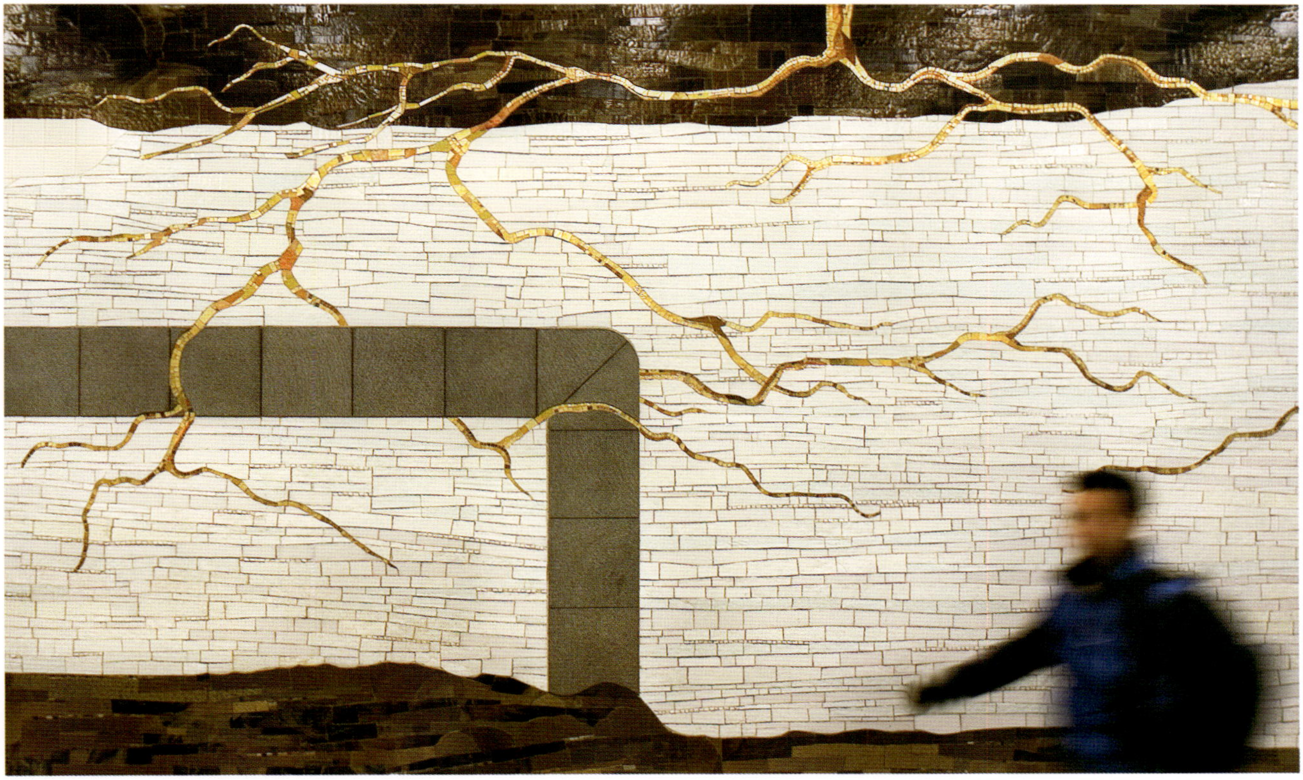

JACKIE FERRARA

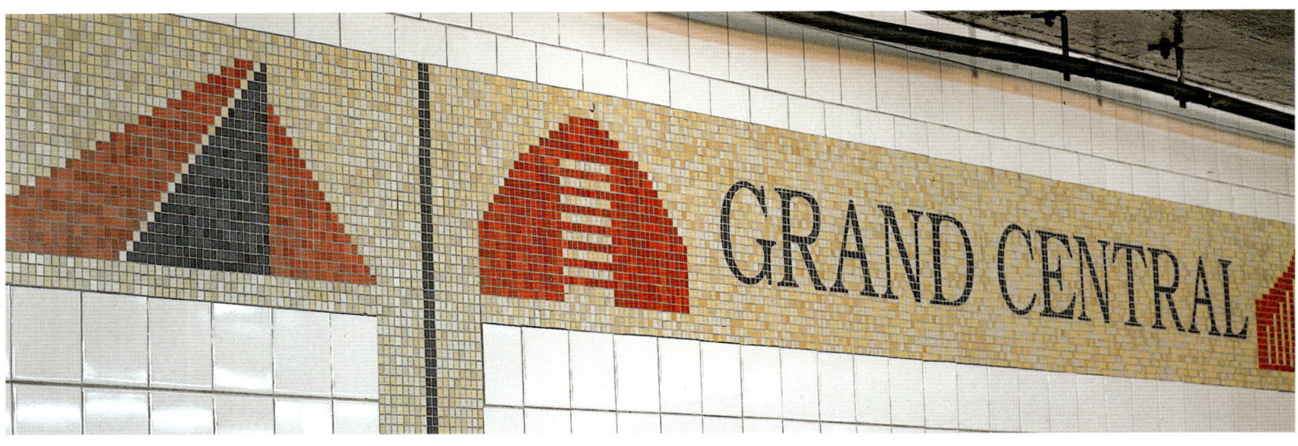

GRAND CENTRAL: ARCHES, TOWERS, PYRAMIDS, 2000
Grand Central–42nd Street S 4 5 6 7
Ceramic mosaic
PHOTOGRAPHERS: MICHAEL KAMBER (ABOVE); ROB WILSON (OPPOSITE)

The passageways and waiting areas of Grand Central's subway stations are low and labyrinthine, connecting various areas of the monumental railroad terminal with nearby buildings, the streets above, and the subway system. They have been likened to the streets of a city, and they indeed could be considered a miniature version of New York but without the skyline.

Jackie Ferrara, a minimalist architectural and landscape artist, is interested in the simple and repetitive forms of building. *Grand Central: Arches, Towers, Pyramids* harks back to one of her most celebrated works, *Stacked Pyramid*, exhibited at the Storm King Art Center in 1973.

Ferrara's building forms are structures of a curious sort—simple, schematic, almost primitive looking. Taken together, they lend a unity and meditative character to the space; as people move through the platforms and passageways, the images seem to shift and mutate. No two vistas are the same. The artist says she thinks of these as pieces of a puzzle, but not a sterile one susceptible to only one solution; rather, each viewer is invited to come up with his or her own solution by mentally putting together the various shapes in different ways.

Nothing is casual or unintentional in the artist's design. Each mosaic is placed in a predetermined position in a rigid, precisely measured grid; a narrow vertical stripe separates the images. Ferrara explains, "This sequence of stripe/image is calculated. It can be seen as images on a strip of film, or a line of faces framed in the windows of a passing train."

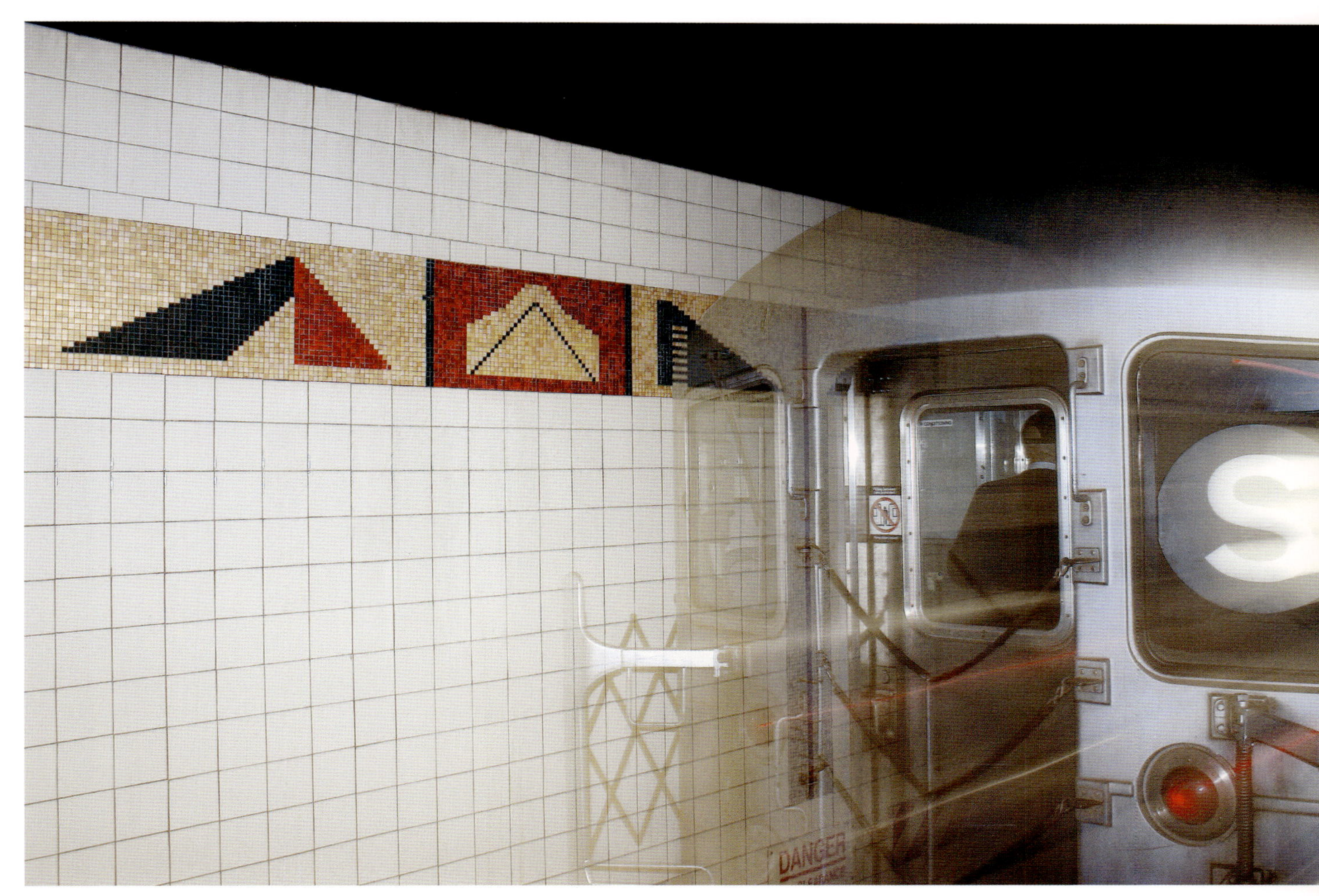
DANGER

DONALD LIPSKI in cooperation with Beyer Blinder Belle

SIRSHASANA, 1998
Grand Central Terminal Market, MTA Metro-North Railroad
Aluminum and polyester resin with crystals
PHOTOGRAPHERS: PATRICK J. CASHIN (RIGHT AND OPPOSITE); ROB WILSON (BELOW RIGHT)

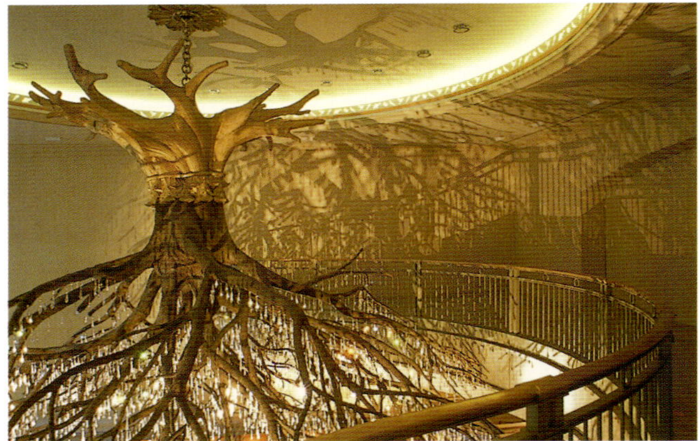

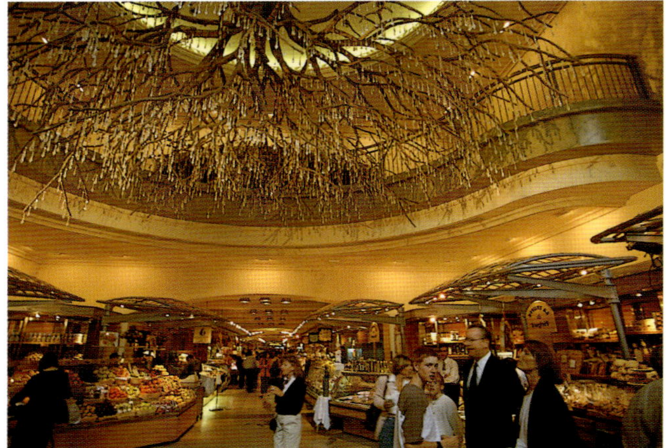

Donald Lipski based his chandelier *Sirshasana* on Greek and Hindu myths. "To the ancient Greeks the olive tree symbolized freedom and purity," he explains. "And the name *Sirshasana* refers to a yoga headstand posture—the inverted tree—that springs from the Hindu belief that humankind's highest energies flow from the infinite forces of the cosmos rather than from earth."

Since the mid-1980s, Lipski has been fascinated by the iconography of surrealism, as seen, for example in *Waxmusic and Candelabracadabra* of 1992, an assemblage of multiple white candles and empty boxes of musical instruments. *Sirshasana* partially follows in this tradition and might properly be called decorative surrealism.

Sirshasana's form has a writhing, enticing, but somewhat sinister aspect—and its unexpected components add a slightly jangling frisson. Why is the base of the tree finished in gold? And why are there precious crystals dangling on this tree and not olives? In addition to the allusion to the chandeliers in other parts of Grand Central, could this be a comment on the allure of the exotic, costly, and tempting wares for sale beneath it?

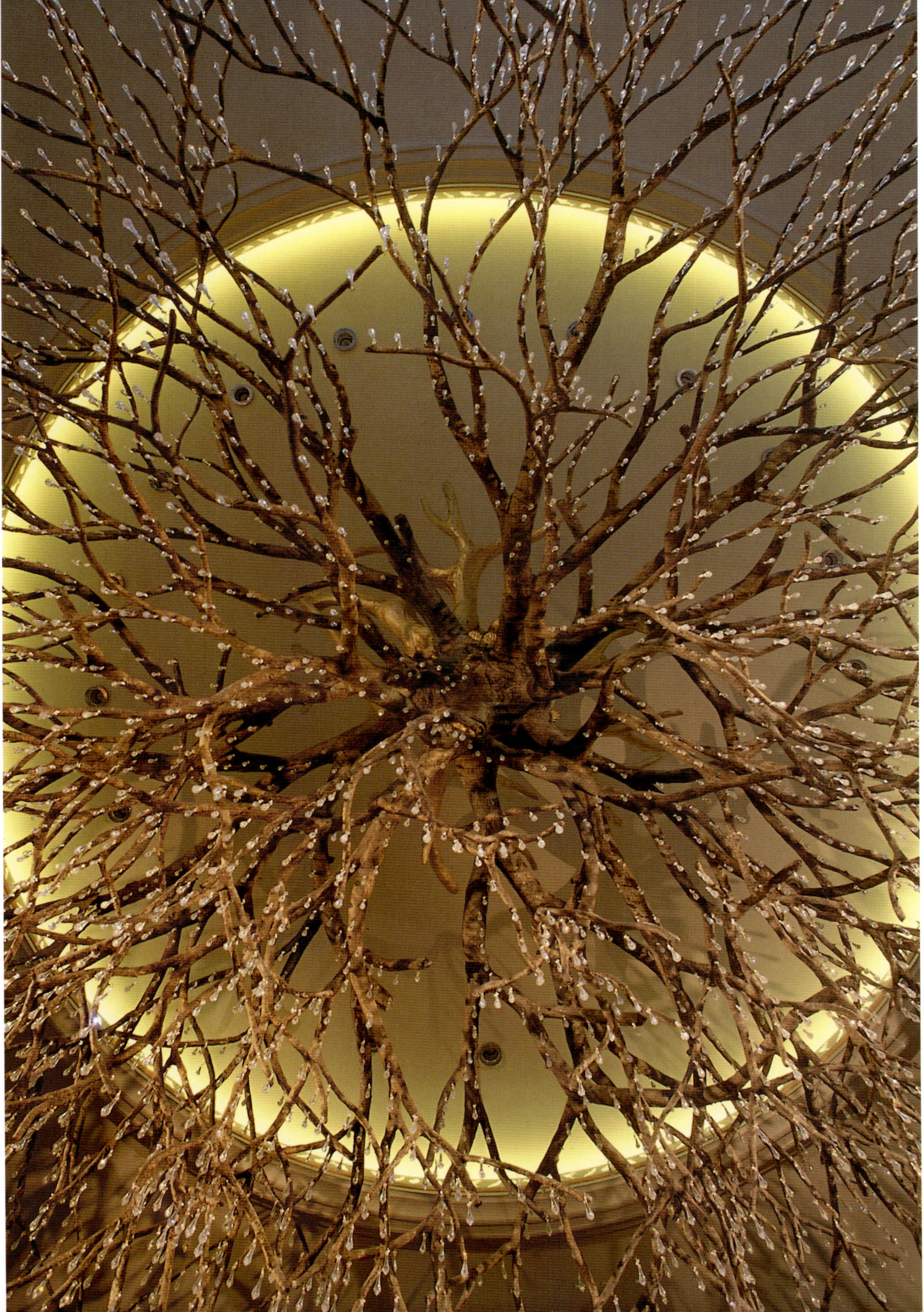

ROBERTO JUAREZ

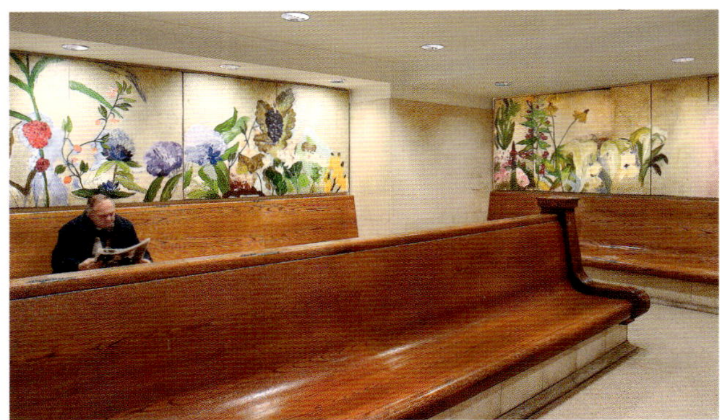

A FIELD OF WILD FLOWERS, 1998
Grand Central Terminal Waiting Room, MTA Metro-North Railroad
Mixed-media
PHOTOGRAPHER: ROB WILSON

In *A Field of Wild Flowers*, Roberto Juarez has set out to provide a place of refreshment and repose, an elongated view of a lush garden landscape, with vertical divisions as if it were being seen through the windows of a train moving slowly through it.

In the choice of medium, the work is one of the more fragile and complex in the system—a collage of multiple components, typical of the artist's work. Juarez explains the process:

> My work is composed of a variety of layers, which together depict a floating, journeying state, devoid of any fixed perspective. In addition to . . . layers of gesso, under-painting, urethane and varnish, I also utilize natural materials—rice paper and a dusting of peat moss—to give my work added texture, strength and beauty.

Juarez was particularly attracted to the site of the project because it would allow him to continue with his interest in describing "tranquility, the cyclical nature . . . and the joy found in the appreciation of common daily routines." In his vision:

> The Grand Central Waiting Room will be a calming center, a beautiful respite from the surrounding terminal's cacophony of visual noise. Since Grand Central Terminal has been called New York City's cathedral, the waiting room's benches can likewise be conceived of as pews on which passengers can contemplate while looking at this triptych field of flowers, and thereby feel more comfortable and secure while regaining composure and perspective.

A Field of Wild Flowers was intended to complement the architecture of Grand Central, incorporating interior details such as the representations of fruit, acorns, and garlands used in its decoration. But at the same time, Juarez's piece provides enough visual contrast to be read as a new, contemporary work of art.

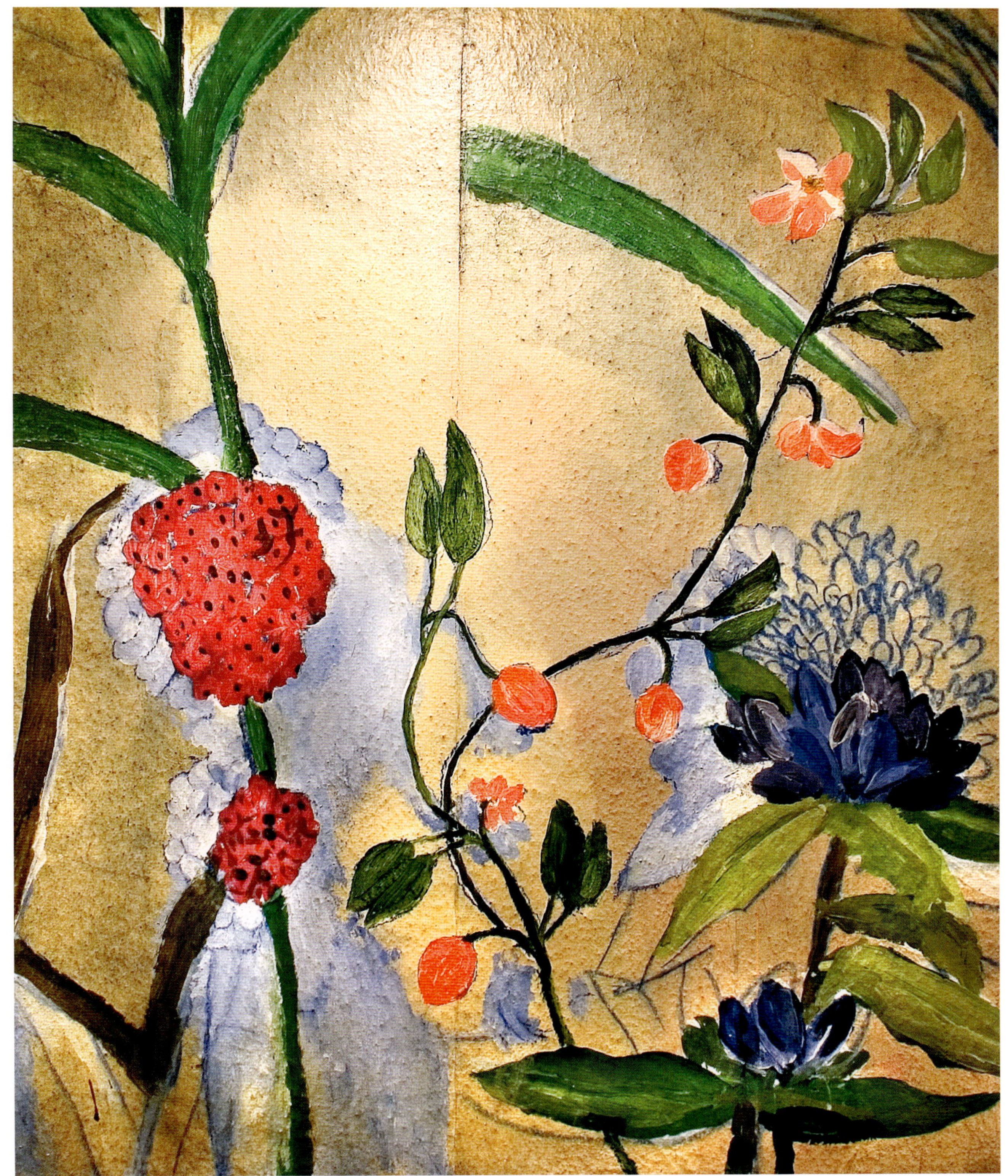

ELLEN DRISCOLL

AS ABOVE, SO BELOW, 1998
Grand Central North, MTA Metro-North Railroad
Glass, bronze, and mosaic
PHOTOGRAPHERS: MICHAEL KAMBER (BELOW AND OPPOSITE); ROB WILSON (BELOW RIGHT)

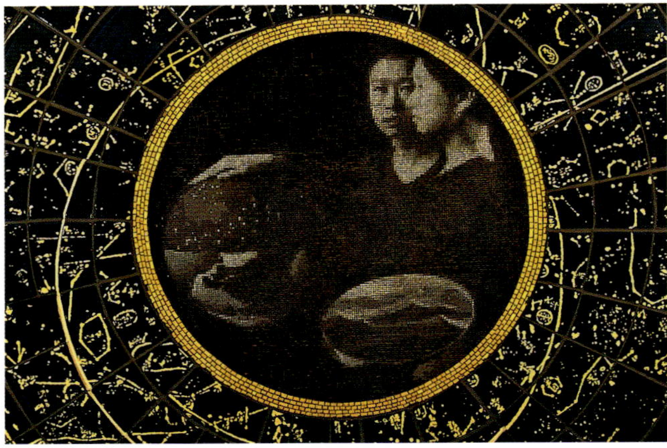

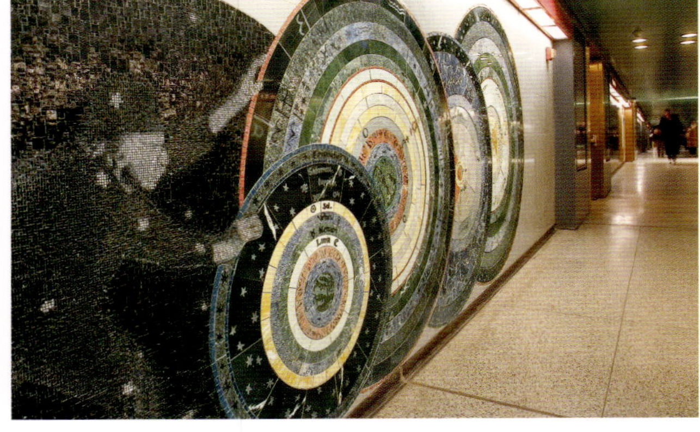

Ellen Driscoll's murals are directly related to the historic sky ceiling in Grand Central Terminal, a particularly beautiful example of our abiding fascination with the night sky. Constellations of luminous stars cover an azure ground. Pegasus, the winged horse, regarded as the source of poetic inspiration and the guardian of Zeus's thunderbolt, charges across the heavens as bustling travelers rush below.

In *As Above, So Below*, Driscoll conducts a tour of the continents, the heavens, and even the underworld, illustrated by their distinctive myths and legends–stories purporting to explain to us the movement of the stars, the creation of the planets, and the way mankind is affected, indeed ruled, by these forces.

To emphasize the connection between the myth and reality, the artist photographed everyday people and then manipulated the images digitally so that they assume the traditional poses of mythological figures. Driscoll's message to riders is that they are part of an overarching cosmos with an infinitely deep and meaningful past, extending back until the beginning of time.

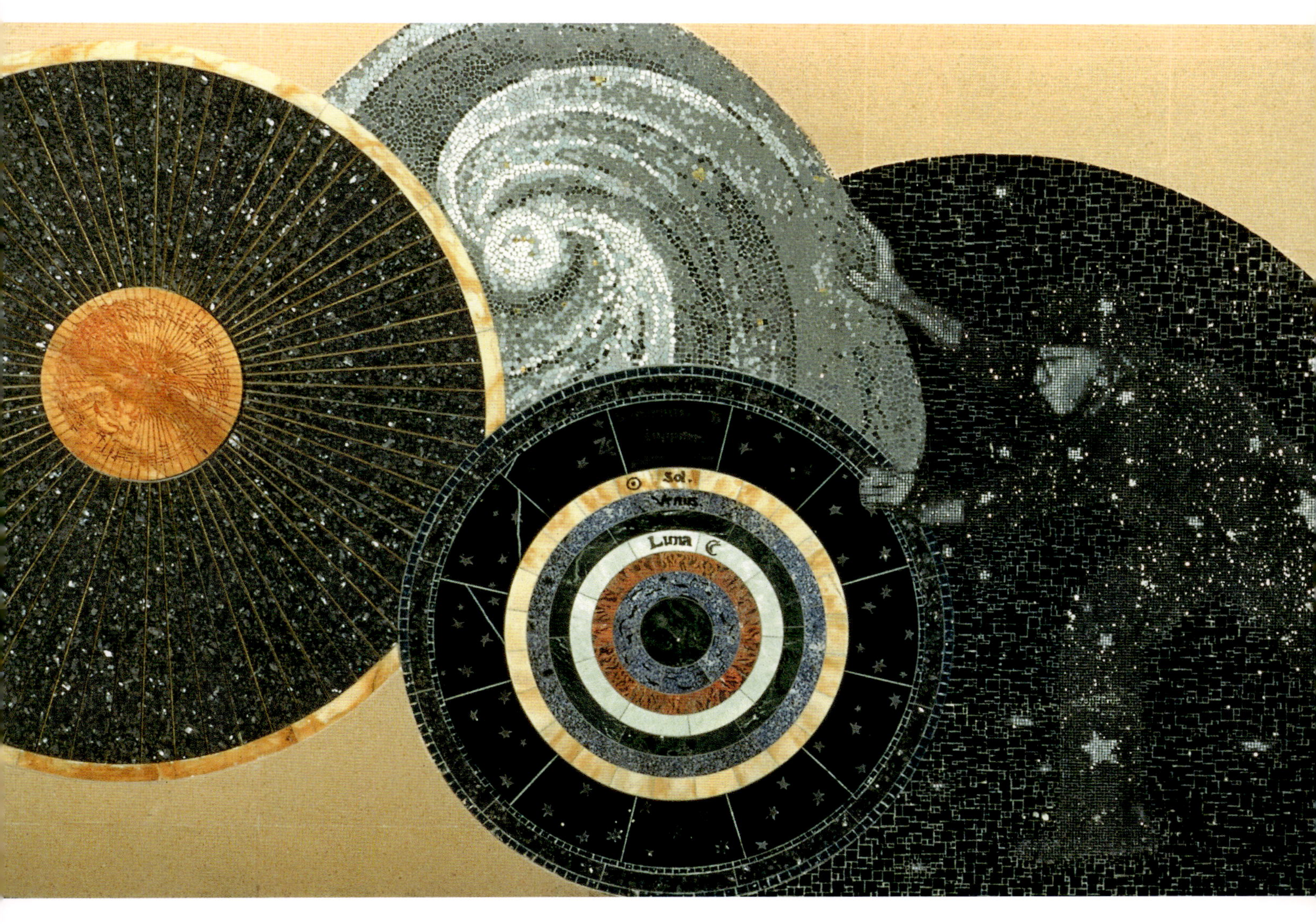
Sol.
Venus
Luna

ELIZABETH MURRAY

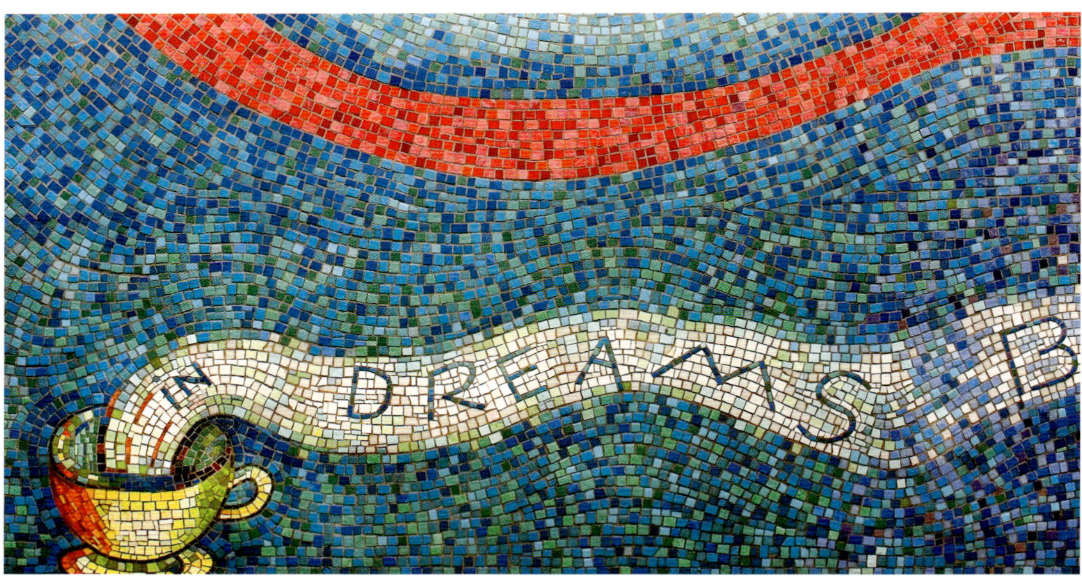

BLOOMING, 1996
Lexington Avenue–59th Street 4 5 6
Glass mosaic
PHOTOGRAPHER: ROB WILSON (ABOVE); DAVID ALLISON (OPPOSITE)

Blooming, one of the most ambitious works of art in the MTA system, transforms a drab, utilitarian space into a seemingly magical environment. The floor-to-ceiling glass-mosaic walls literally escape the confines of the space to wrap around corners, sneak down steps, and ooze through doorways. Elizabeth Murray says that she intended *Blooming* as a catalyst that "provokes the imagination and makes the passage brighter, more positive." Her concept directly echoes that of the original subway designers, who set out to create art to bring out the best in human nature.

Murray has called the subway a "dreamy underworld," a place that many riders almost sleepwalk through. If so, *Blooming* is a kind of wakeup call. All of a sudden, even the most somnambulant person is confronted with startling and vivid images—giant red women's shoes with whiplash laces, enormous pink tree trunks with writhing shoots and branches, and huge yellow mugs filled to the brim with blue coffee.

"After the blooming tree," says Murray, "I added the stepping shoes and steaming coffee cups, part of the ritual of every morning or evening subway trip." According to the artist, the images "stimulate thoughts about passage, as does the poetry." Here she is referring to William Butler Yeats's line "In dreams begin responsibility," which is incorporated into the mural, as well as Gwendolyn Brooks's "Conduct your blooming in the noise and whip of the whirlwind."

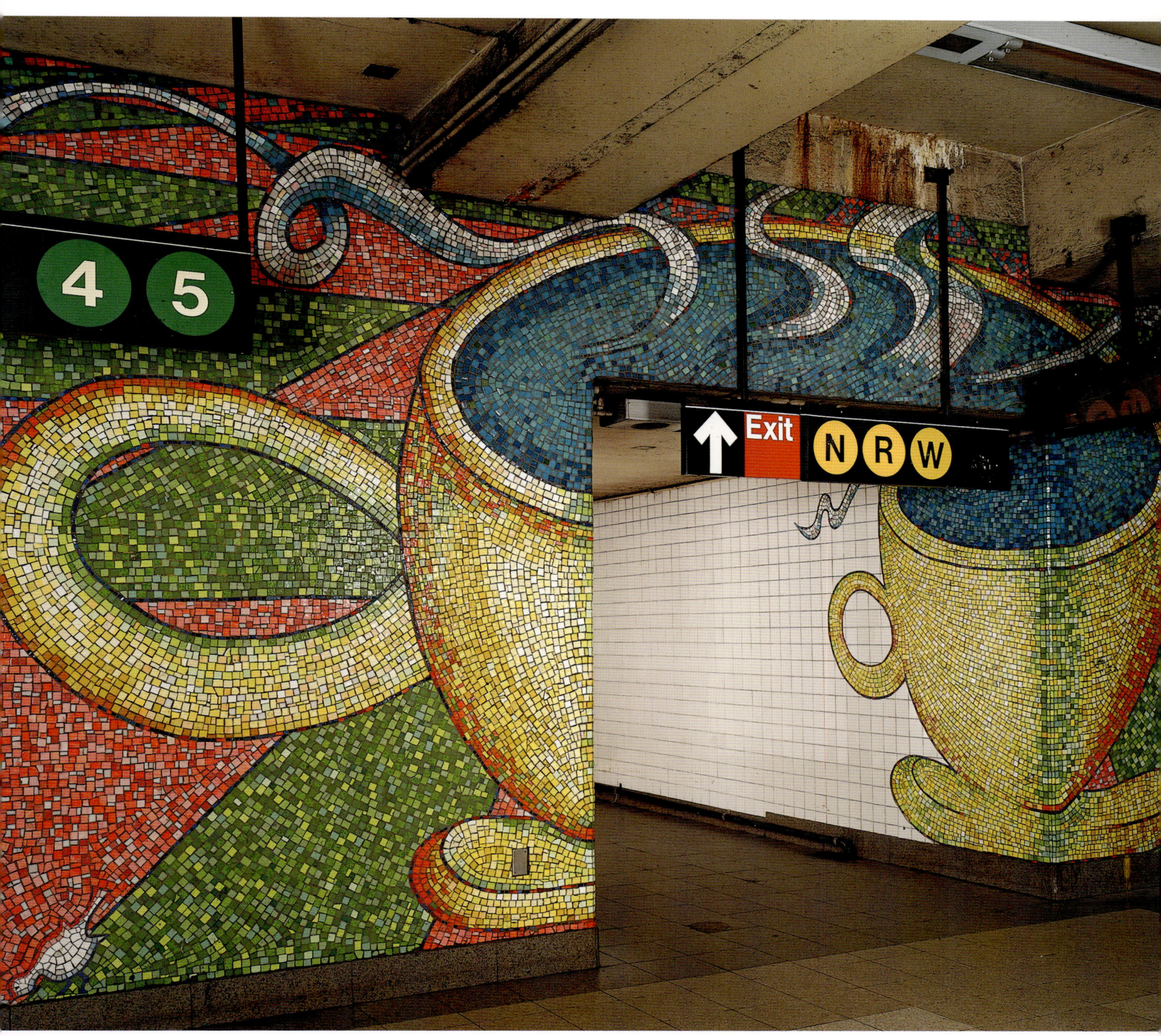
4 5
Exit
N R W

RALPH FASANELLA

SUBWAY RIDERS, 1995
Fifth Avenue–53rd Street 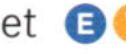
(Created by artist, 1950)
Oil on canvas
On permanent loan from The American Folk Art Museum, New York
PHOTOGRAPHER: AMERICAN FOLK ART MUSEUM, NEW YORK

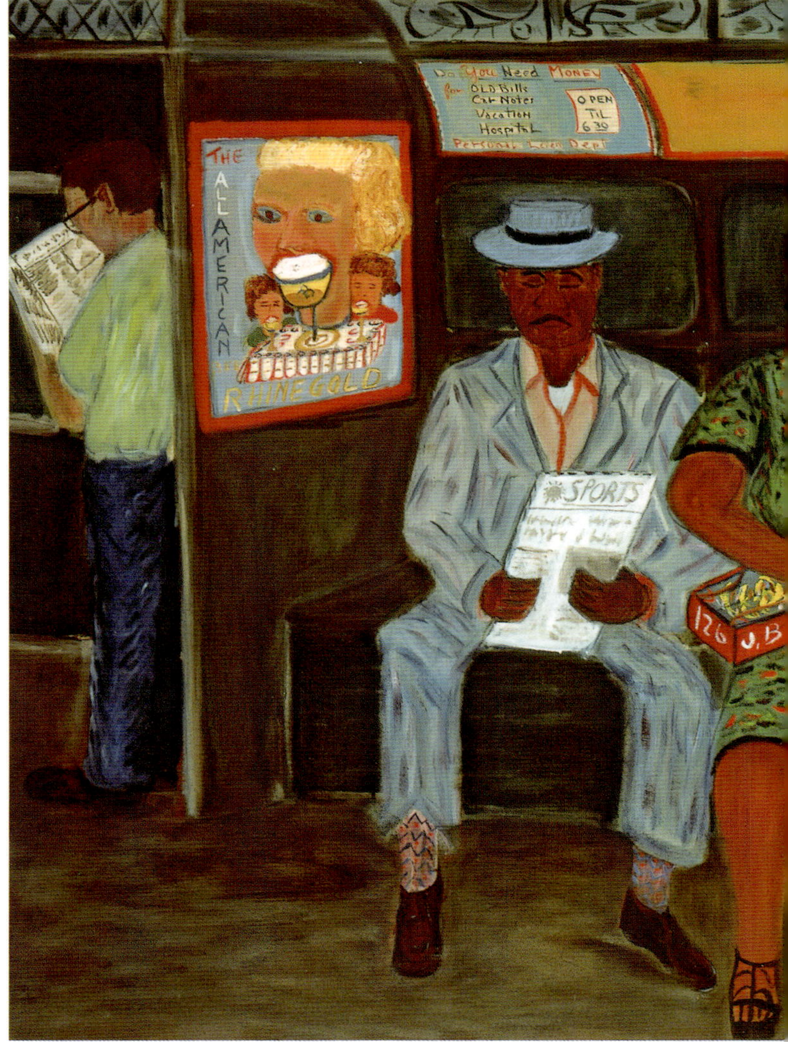

Talking about *Subway Riders* forty-five years after he completed it, Ralph Fasanella reflected:

> I'd ride the subway every day, back and forth to my machine shop job. I'd ride and ride and sketch and sketch. I love the subway. It pulls the city together, pulls people together in a magic way. Here I show the subway riders at night after a hard day's work. Everyone is separate, alone, but very much together. It's noisy with the creaks and squeals, but peaceful too, because we move to a rhythm and cadence that gets inside us; that's comforting, like the noise of the city itself. The subway makes the city work, makes the city great. And behind the scenes—unseen and unheard—the transit workers drive the trains, grease the wheels, and keep the engines running. They perform miracles. They get us through another day.

A lifelong New Yorker, Ralph Fasanella was born in the Bronx and grew up in Greenwich Village. He worked as an iceman and then as a union organizer, and on the side he produced paintings in what would become known as urban folk style. Many have somber overtones, focusing on political and labor struggles. Others have happier subjects, including sports, the city's dynamic street life—and of course subway rides.

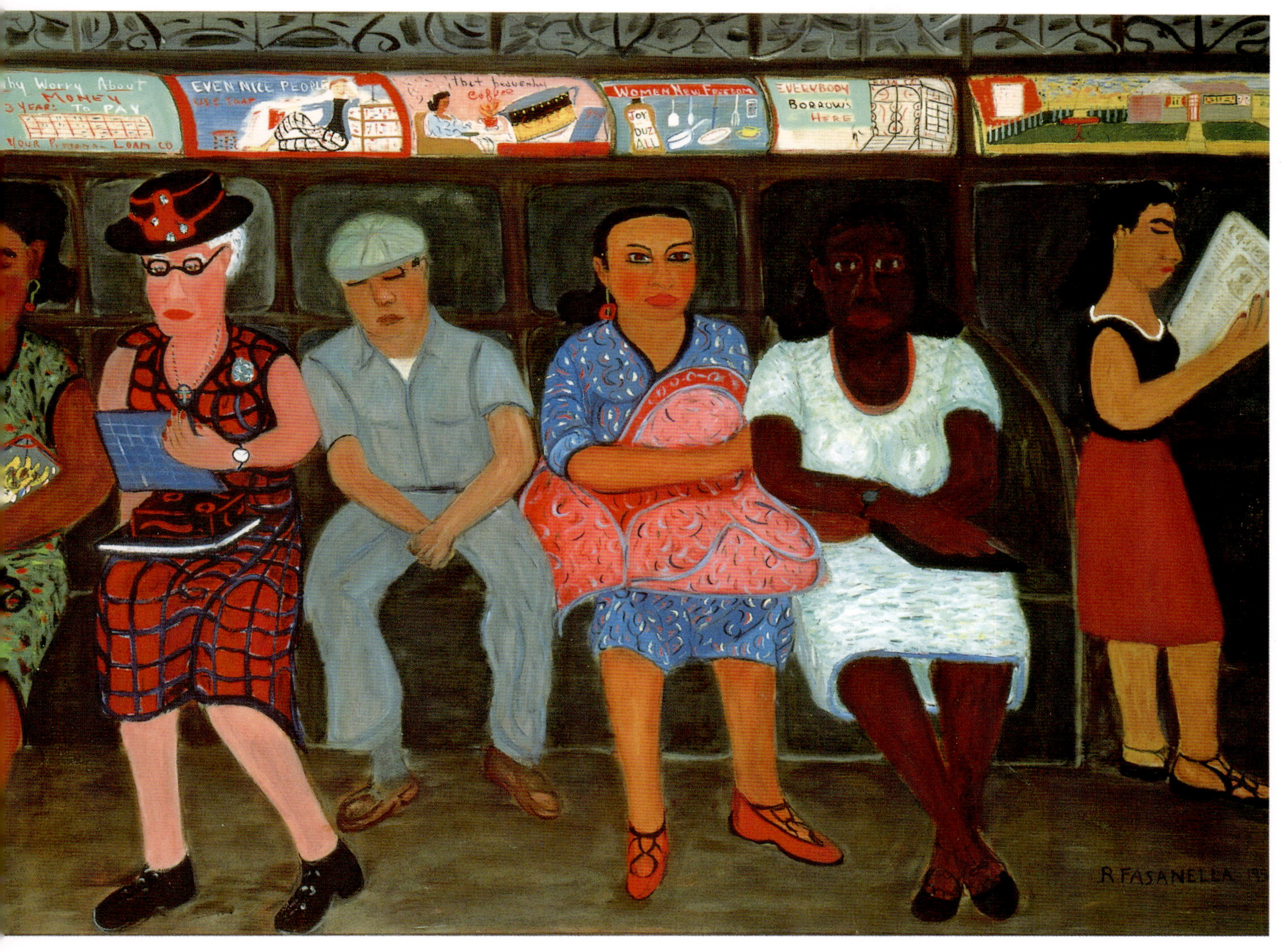
Worry About
MONEY
3 YEARS TO PAY
EVEN NICE PEOPLE
that heavenly
coffee
WOMEN NEW FREEDOM
JOY
DUZ
ALL
EVERYBODY
BORROWS
HERE
R FASANELLA

AL HELD in cooperation with Urbahn Architects

PASSING THROUGH, 2004

Lexington Avenue–53rd Street 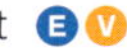

Glass mosaic

PHOTOGRAPHER: JEFFREY STURGES

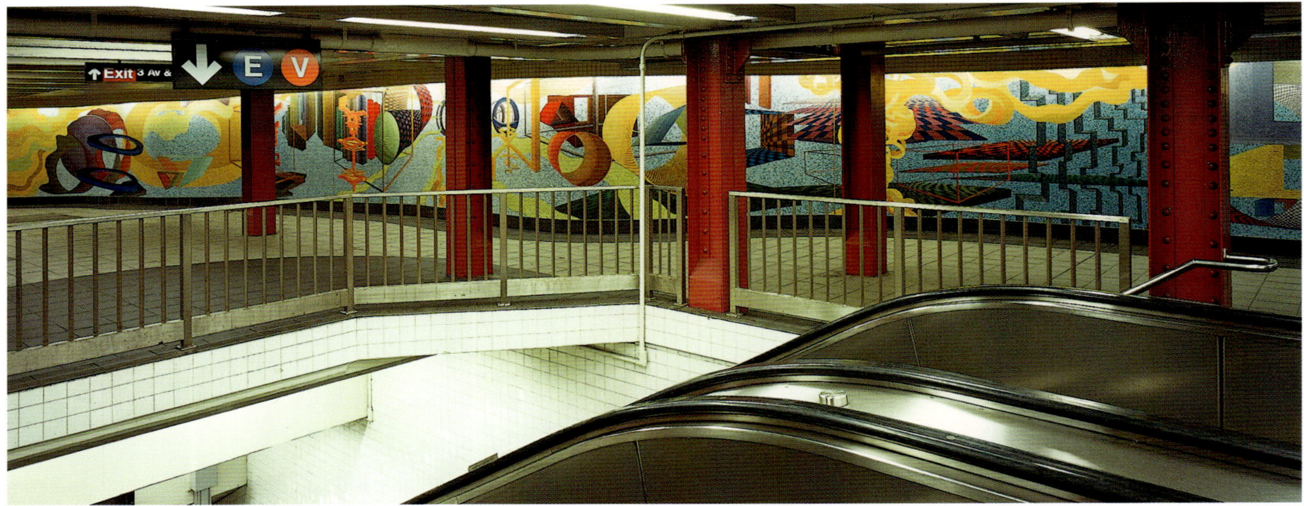

Passing Through is one of Al Held's last great public works and one of his most vital and provocative. It is enormous, wildly colorful, and transfixing. Here Held set out to depict nothing less than the universe, conceived as a geometric abstraction, with precise multi-hued shapes afloat in space, dizzily defying gravity.

In the 1960s, Held turned from abstract expressionism to tightly controlled, geometric pieces, with two-dimensional figures that seem weightlessly suspended on the canvas or even appearing to burst forth from it. The earliest works of this type were in black and white, but later Held became a master of saturated, mannerist color. At the same time, his works became larger and larger. *Passing Through* is an excellent example of his mature style.

Held was a polymath, curious about everything and how it works, especially at the level of theoretical physics. He was particularly fascinated by chaos theory, cosmic strings, black holes, and all other arcane descriptions of the cosmos and explanations of how it works. In his art, he attempted to represent these concepts in a way that suggests both their complexity and beauty—"images that we believe in but that are beyond our senses and that we can never experience directly." In *Passing Through* he asks us to leave our everyday concerns and think about these imponderables.

But there is also a more down-to-earth subject here—building and buildings—architectural forms and how they are conceived and constructed, how they evolve. Held's imagery powerfully evokes New York City's contemporary energy and complements, and sometimes mimics, the forms and styles of the Midtown skyscrapers overhead.

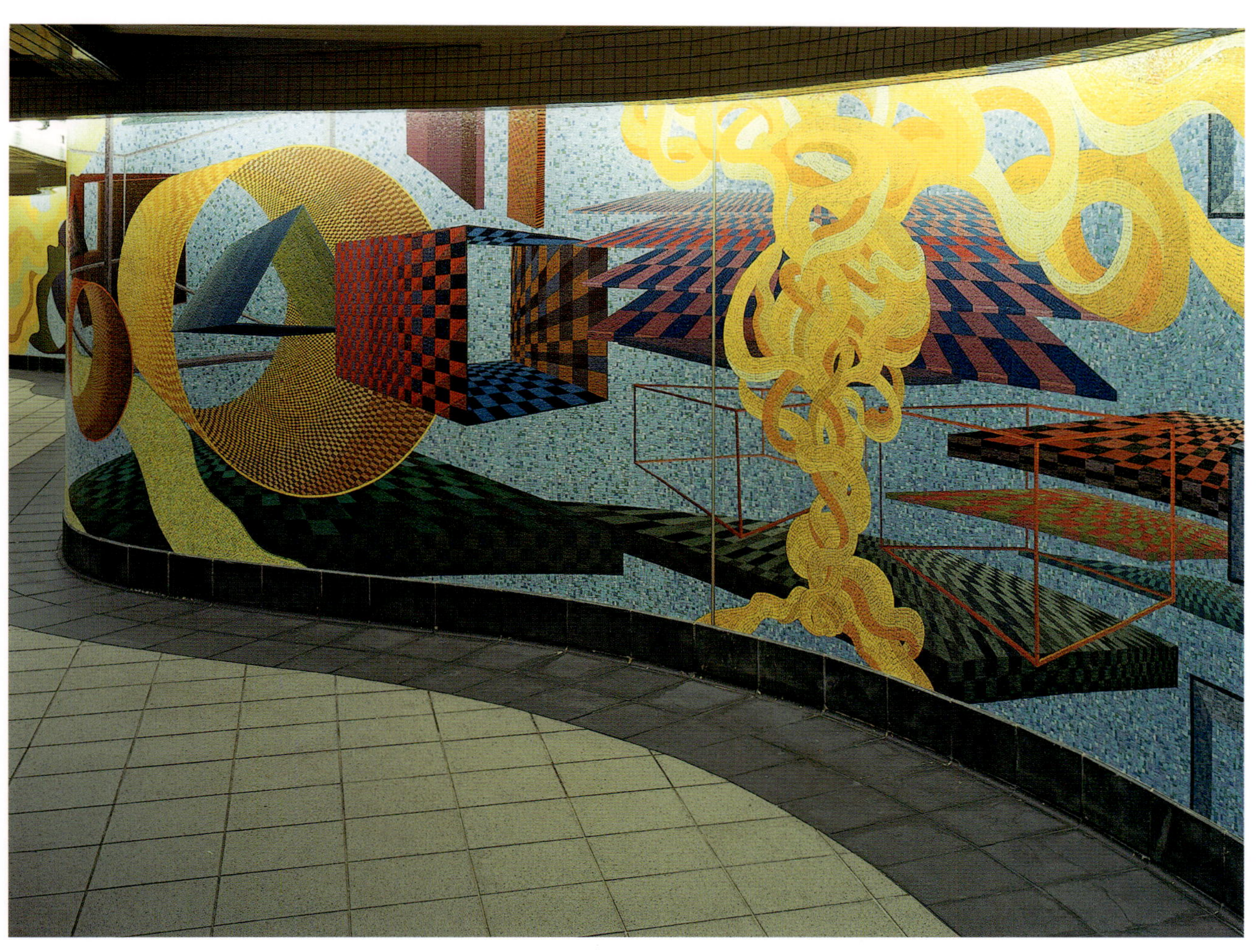

ANDREW LEICESTER

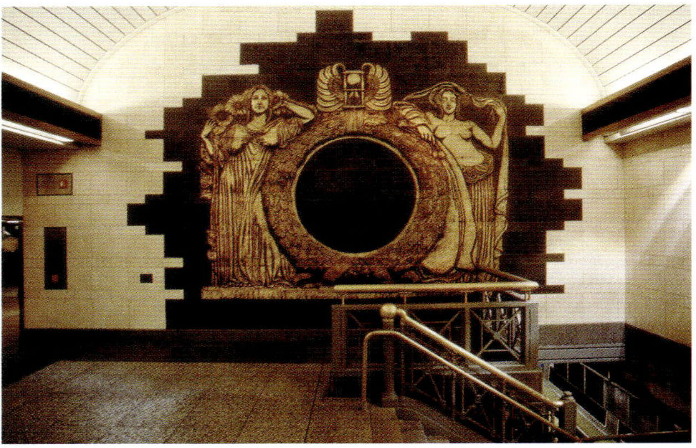

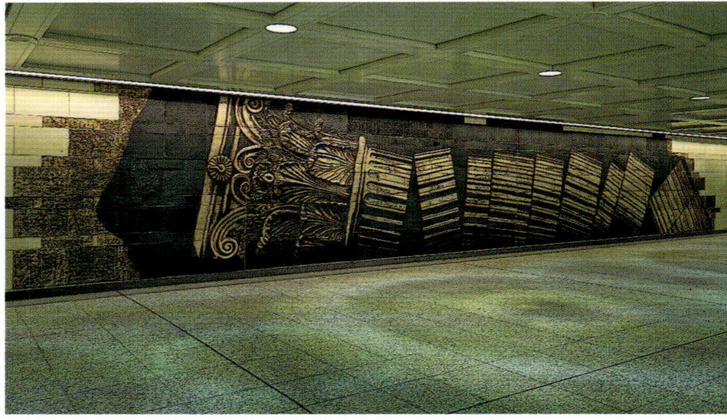

GHOST SERIES, 1994

Penn Station, MTA Long Island Rail Road

Terra-cotta and porcelain enamel on steel

PHOTOGRAPHERS: ROB WILSON (LEFT); DAVID LUBARSKY (BELOW LEFT AND OPPOSITE)

Andrew Leicester's *Ghost Series*, five towering bas-relief terra-cotta murals scattered throughout the station corridors, evoke the lost world of the original Pennsylvania Station, the majestic Beaux-Arts structure by McKim, Mead & White that was demolished in the 1960s. Leicester points out that fragments are hidden in the lower depths of the building that replaced it; these murals symbolically reveal the original architecture now ignominiously concealed behind new walls—and buried in the landfills of the New Jersey Meadowlands.

In *Ghost: Day and Night*, a 500-square-foot mural at the Seventh Avenue end of the main concourse, Leicester has reinterpreted the Adolph Weinman sculptures that presided over the original entrances, depicting two voluptuous women flanking a gigantic clock. The artist has embedded the date on which demolition began—10/28/63—into the clock's otherwise blank face. Other murals include *Mercury Man,* a reproduction of another sculptural figure with anonymous fragments from the original building, as well as a large-scale porcelain-on-steel rendering of one of the plans. Taken together, *Ghosts Series* is a thoroughly compelling and fitting memento mori.

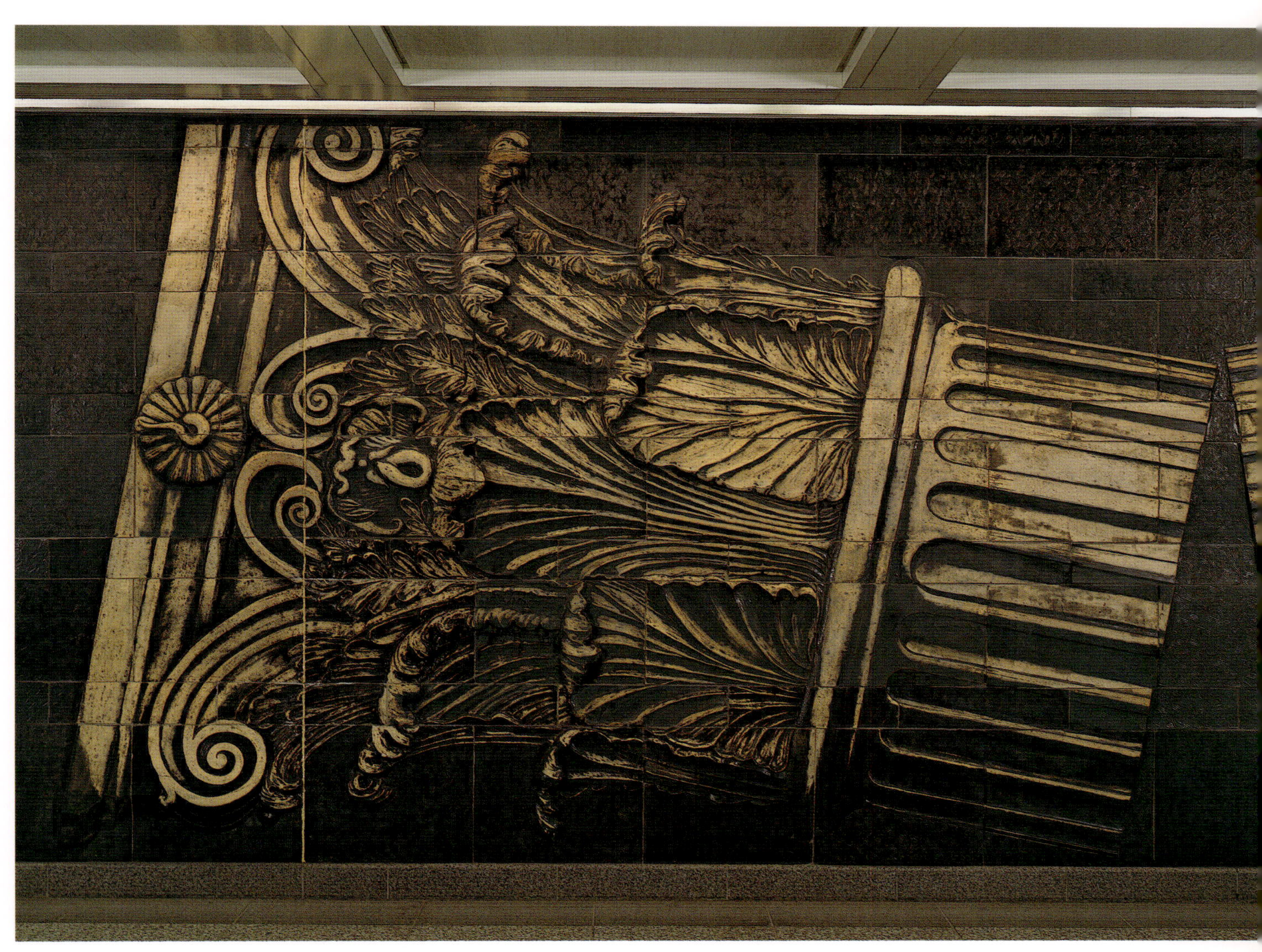

MAYA LIN

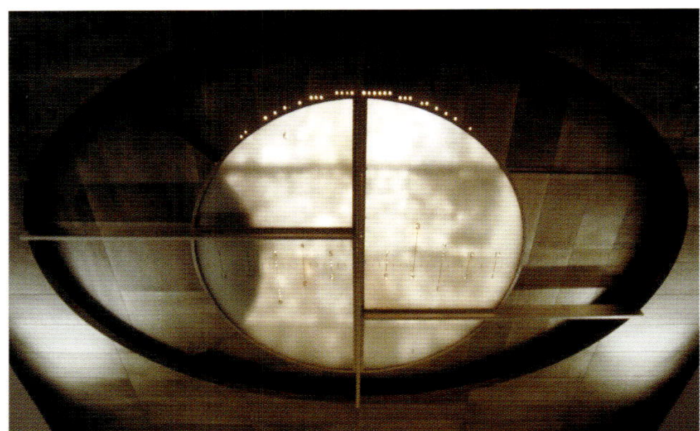

ECLIPSED TIME, 1994
Penn Station, MTA Long Island Rail Road
Frosted glass, aluminum, stainless steel, and fiber optics
PHOTOGRAPHER: ROB WILSON

In *Eclipsed Time* Maya Lin urges commuters to think differently about time. This is particularly poignant given the location of the sculpture in one of the busiest rail terminals in the country, where time is of the essence to passengers as they move through their daily commuting ritual.

This large work combines sculpture and technology, all in the service of telling time. "When people think about the clocks, they usually envision hands or digital numbers," Lin explains. "Time is measured mathematically and specifically. I wanted to reflect time more naturally and chose to use the concept of an eclipse. We all have internal natural clocks based on the monthly phases of the moon, and this timepiece refers to that cycle."

The effect of the eclipse is created by the overlapping of two disks with a halogen light source situated above and behind them. The bottom of the piece is a glass circle fixed in place, while the upper circle is aluminum and moves back and forth, casting a shadow-line crescent on the glass. At noon, the disks admit the maximum amount of light to the floor below; at midnight they are precisely synchronized one directly above the other, and only a thin glowing ring of penumbral light can be observed around them. Day and night, they silently turn, repeating their endless cycles as a tide of humanity ebbs and flows below.

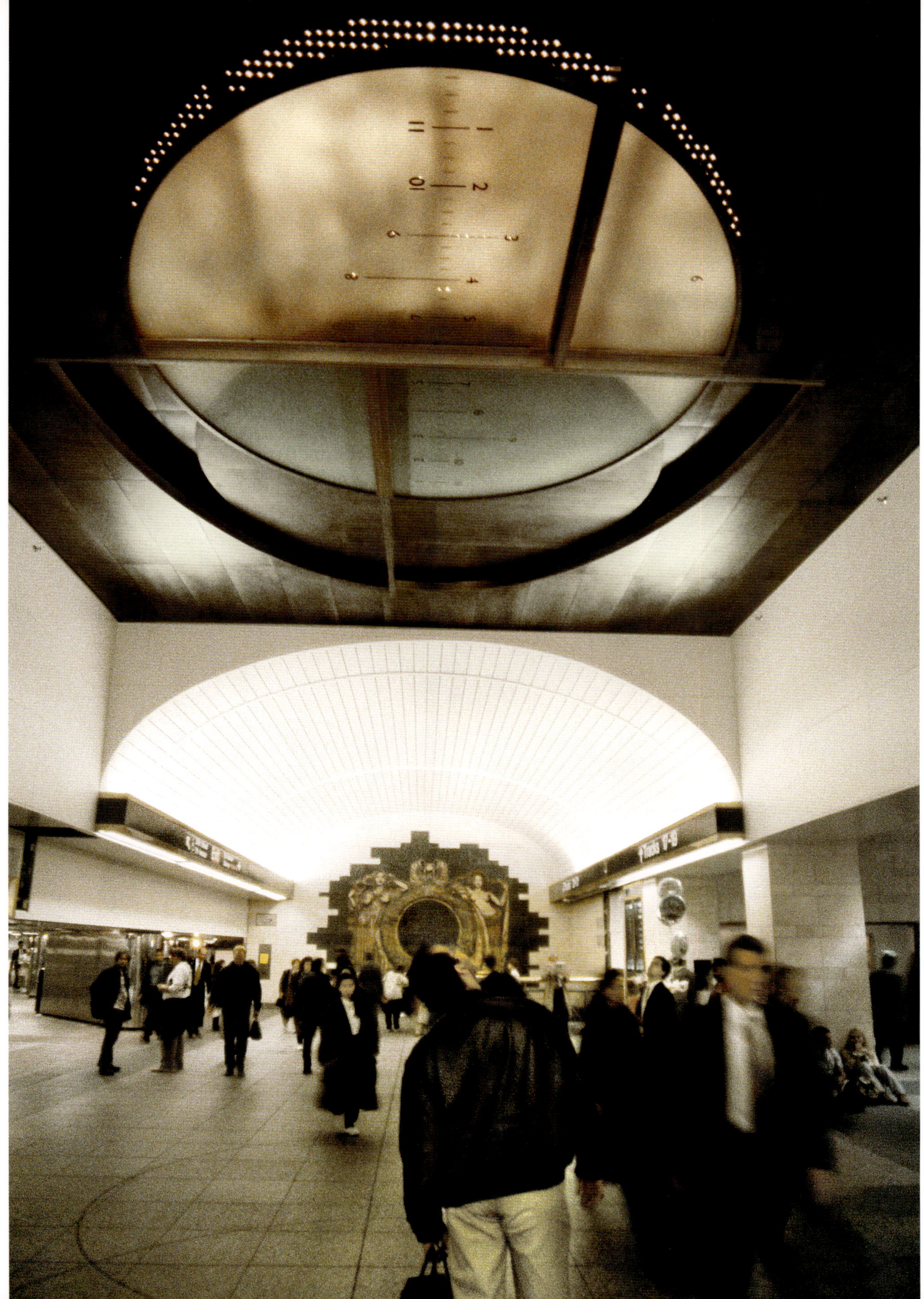

ERIC FISCHL

THE GARDEN OF CIRCUS DELIGHTS, 2001

34th Street–Penn Station Ⓐ Ⓒ Ⓔ

Glass mosaic

PHOTOGRAPHER: ROB WILSON

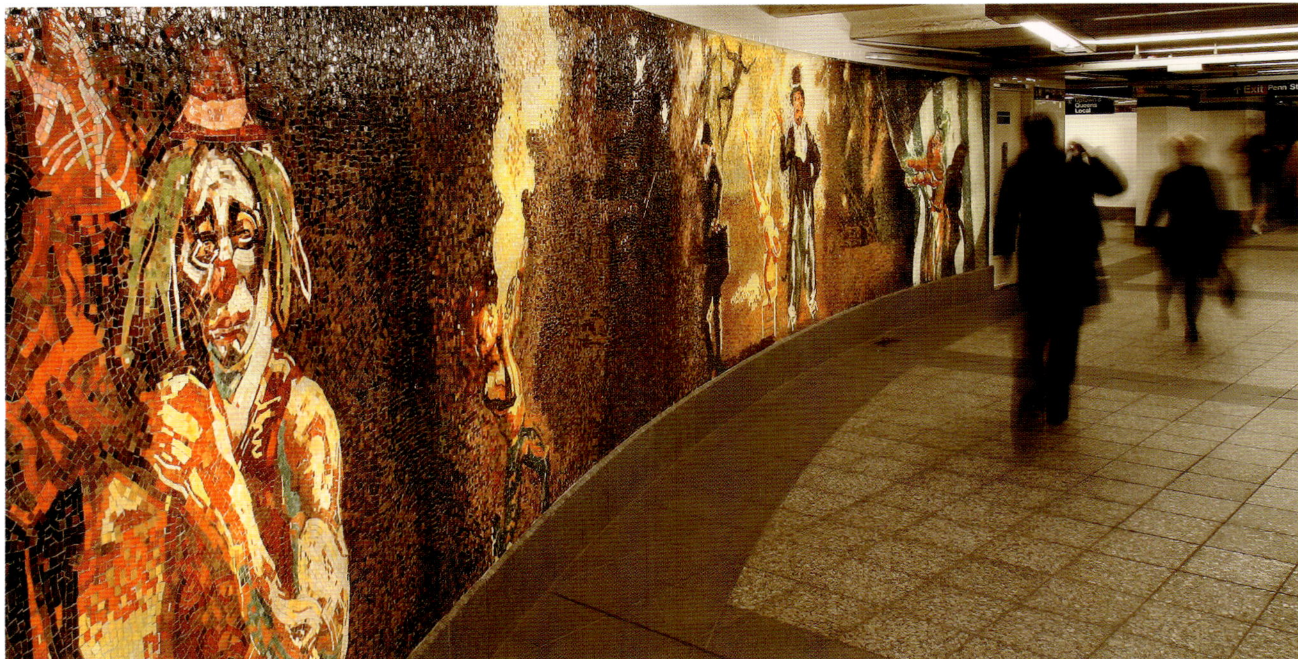

The Garden of Circus Delights both recalls and anticipates "The Greatest Show on Earth," an event held annually in Madison Square Garden, immediately above Penn Station.

Eric Fischl earned a reputation as a New Image painter for his provocative and harshly realistic figure and genre scenes. Much of his work is narrative, loaded with everyday drama, a conscious and deliberate departure from the canon of abstraction. *The Garden of Circus Delights* follows in this tradition.

Fischl created these murals to snap commuters out of their everyday routines and into "a journey of the spirit that goes from serenity and harmony though strangeness and chaos and back." The murals surround riders with a circus world of fire-breathers, acrobats, and animals; only gradually do viewers realize that there is a narrative: a commuter leaves home on an otherwise normal day and is pulled into the circus action.

"When you encounter him on the far wall," says Fischl says of the commuter, "he's surrounded by circus figures and he begins a journey with them. On the way he meets incredible and bizarre characters as the circus gets stranger and stranger. On the other side of the tent, he emerges in the white light and harmony, a commuter once again, but transported and transformed."

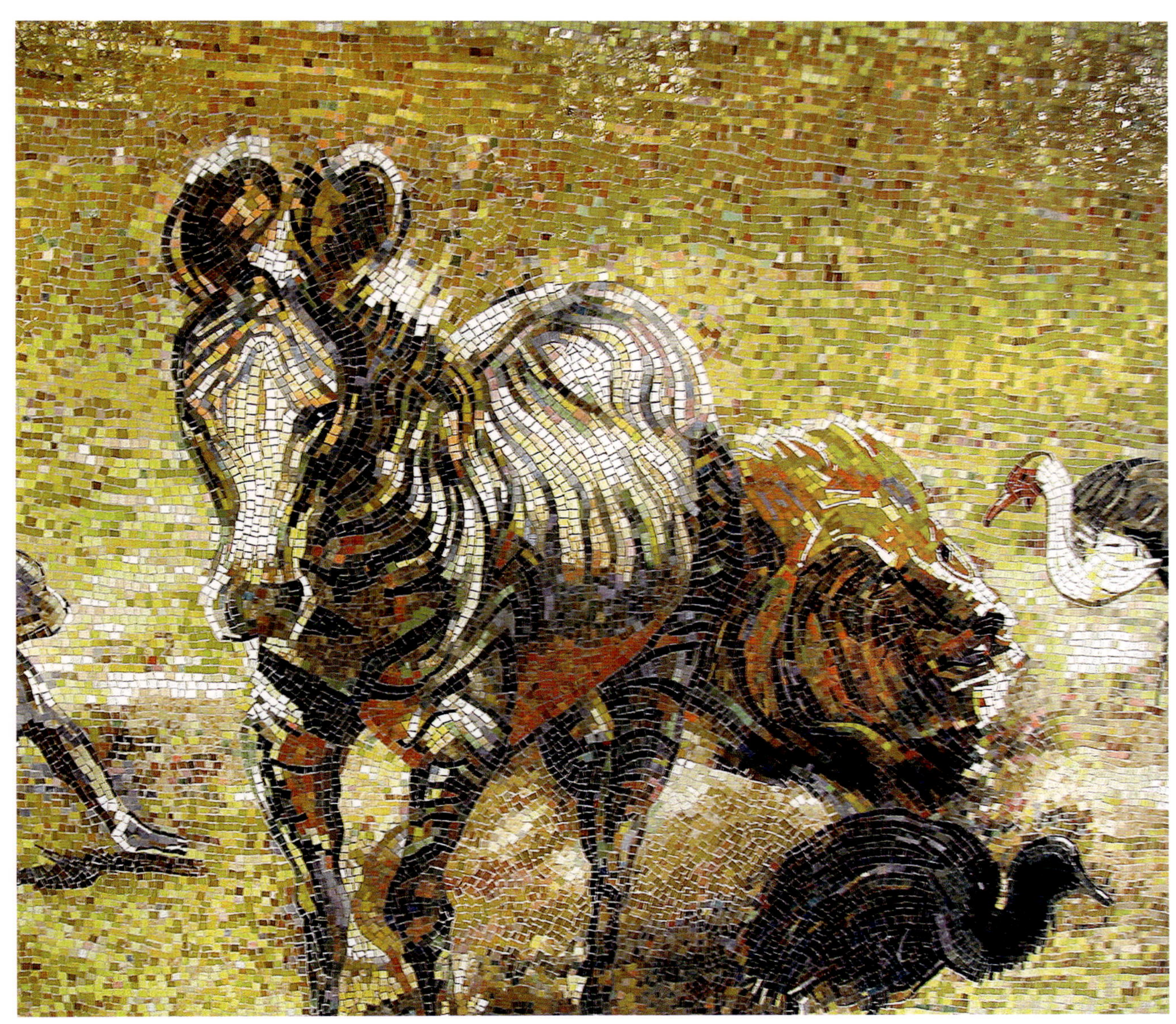

MICHELE OKA DONER

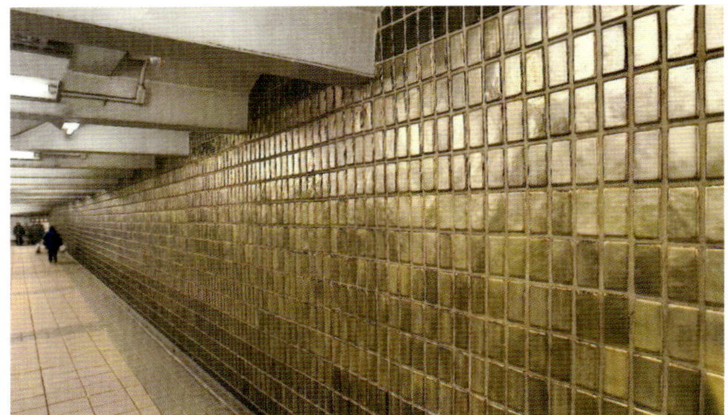

RADIANT SITE, 1991
34th Street–Herald Square 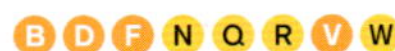
Handmade bronze-colored tiles
PHOTOGRAPHER: ROB WILSON

Radiant Site is a rectilinear floor-to-ceiling passage bathed in a pervasive golden light. The midsection of the corridor is the brightest, glazed in coppery tiles, but these darken and are less reflective toward the top and bottom of the passage, where the tiles are glazed in black. The resulting glow seems to pulse with gentle energy.

In order to ensure control over the effects of her work in *Radiant Site,* Michele Oka Doner made the 11,000 tiles by hand on a century-old foot press at the venerable Pewabic Pottery in Detroit. Their slightly irregular shapes and uneven surfaces were then hand-glazed by the artist who varied the formula in tiny increments to achieve the desired luminous effect. Irregularities are intentionally left, to stress the organic nature of the process.

The artist says that in thinking about prospective art projects she considers not only the physical and chemical properties of the materials she will use but also "their psychic and cosmic qualities." In *Radiant Site* the composition of the tiles and glazes is manipulated in such a way as to make what would be a gloomy place into one that is reflective and inviting. "I don't believe in confrontational art," she explains. "The amount of aggression in the city is already overwhelming. I think of the project as a spiritual sculpture . . . Each of the thousands of people who walk along the wall each day becomes enveloped by this mysterious power."

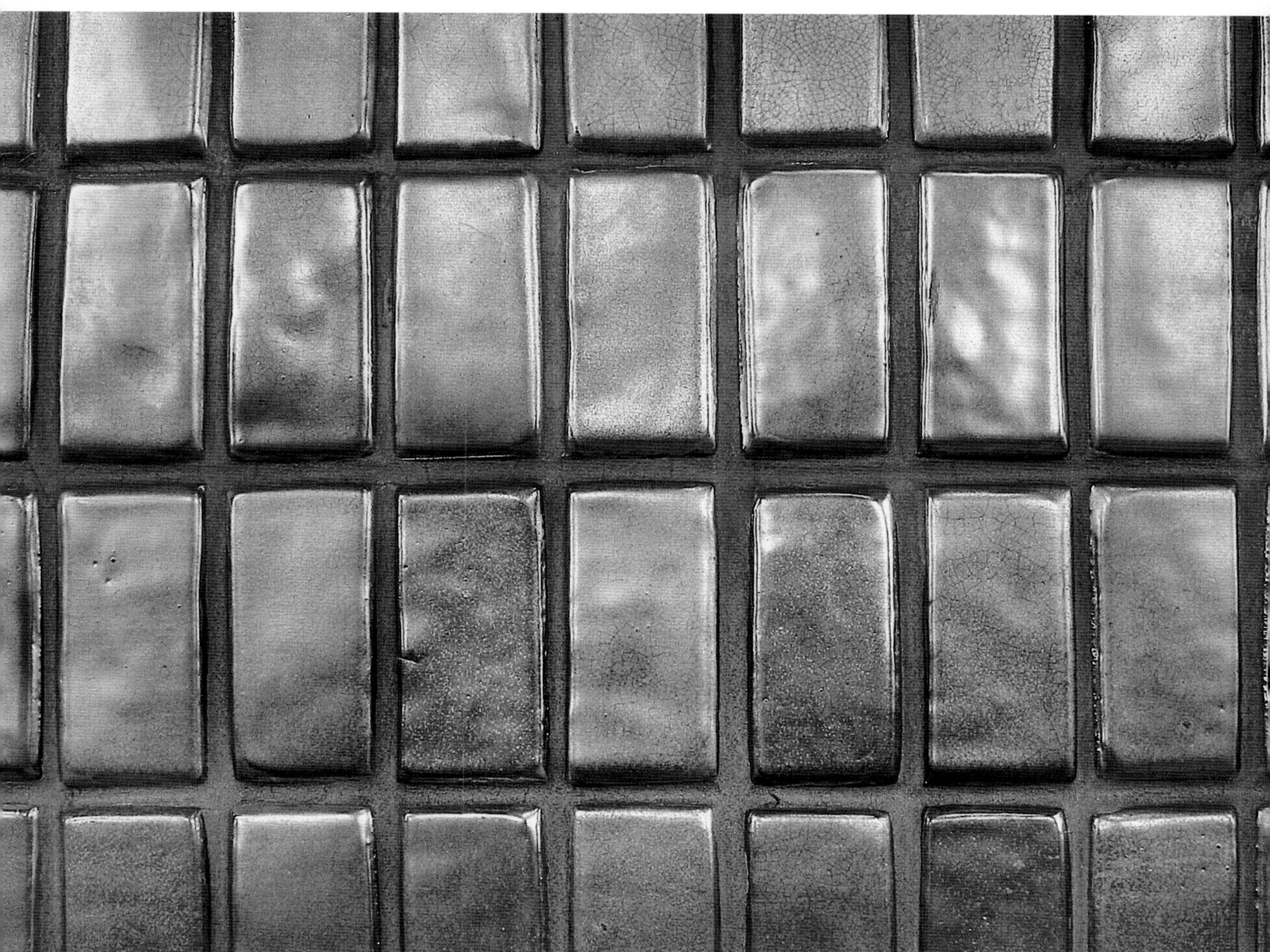

JAMES GARVEY

LARIAT SEAT LOOPS, 1997
33rd Street (6)
Hand-forged bronze
PHOTOGRAPHER: MICHAEL KAMBER

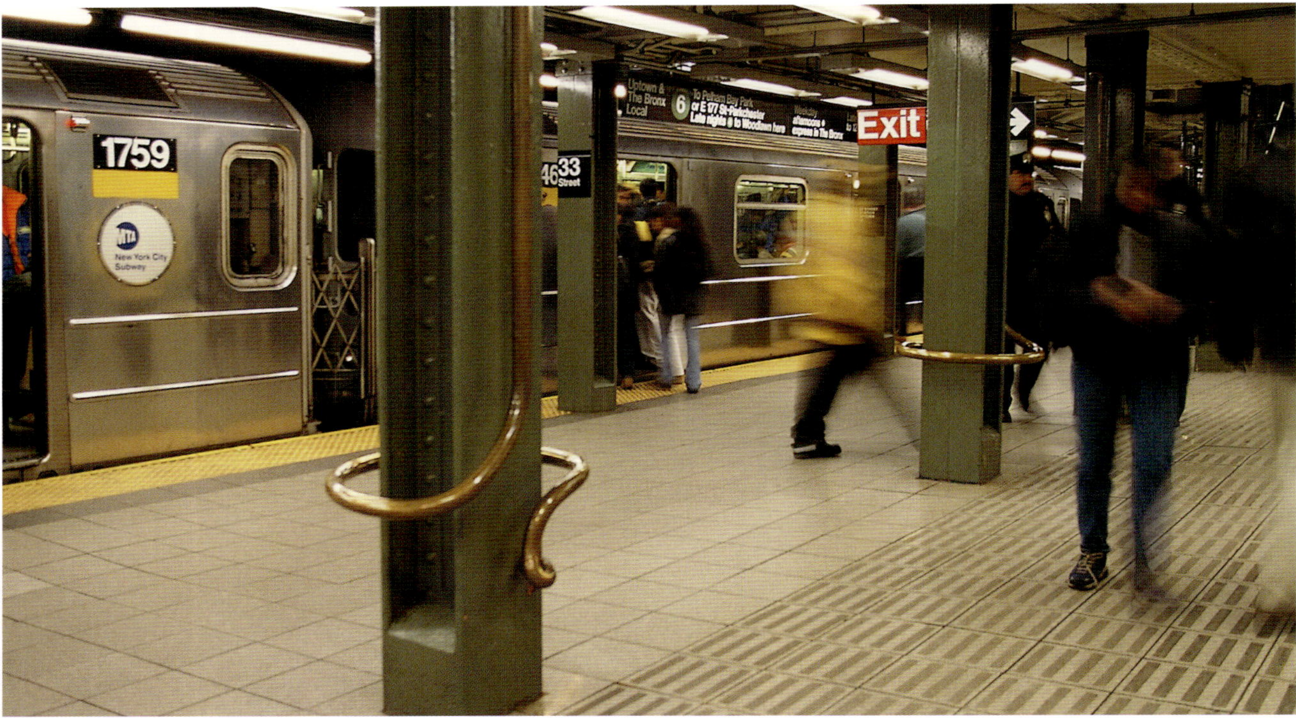

James Garvey's fourteen sinuous and sculptural *Lariat Seat Loops* wrap around columns at the 33rd Street station in a variety of configurations. In each of the loops, "the thick bronze bar encircles the structural column and resembles the lasso demonstration in a Will Rogers film clip," Garvey explains. "When a seat rest or handhold design really works, it invites you to touch, to hold on. You want to use it. My aim is to put inspiration into routine treks and refresh people caught up in mundane thoughts."

Garvey is trained as both an artist and an artisan. To him, the fact that the loops were individually crafted is critical:

I think the labor-intensive blacksmith approach is worthwhile because it has a shared appreciation in our collective unconscious; it demonstrates a traditional work ethic that is recognized by cultures throughout the world. I remain mindful of the most obvious thing about the New York City streetscape; it is a complicated place for people, and I intend to go beyond helping people cope with the conditions. Some people are thinking in conversation, and some are hearing tunes. I am visualizing objects and formations . . . resolving, refining, and approaching my world with creations.

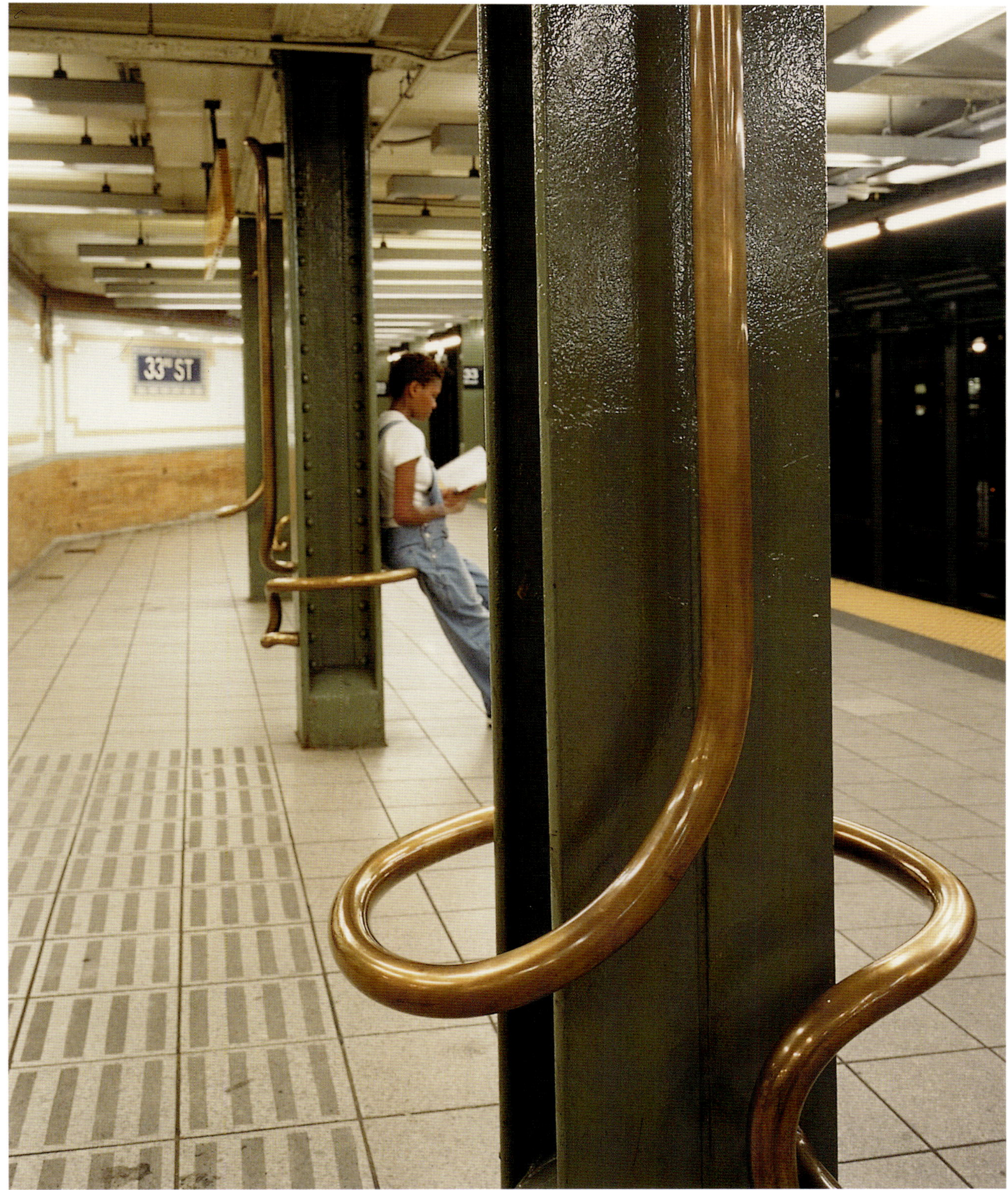
33rd ST

VALERIE JAUDON

LONG DIVISION, 1988
23rd Street 6
Painted steel
PHOTOGRAPHER: DAVID LUBARSKY

Long Division seamlessly combines the practical and the aesthetic. In its purely functional role, it is a sturdy steel fence serving as a security barrier. But it is a work of art as well, a beckoning welcome into the subway. Valerie Jaudon explains, "The idea was to make a fence that functions as a combination of wall, door, window, and column that allows you to see the entire station . . . a sort of transparent lens through which people can see where they are going and where they have been."

The work is divided into panel units. When these are placed together, their straight and arched lines form decorative patterns. The abstract stylized motifs and the way they are combined relate directly to Jaudon's paintings of that time. The hard imagery that dominated her canvases became three dimensional while maintaining the sense of hard-edged flatness on the same plane.

Jaudon's successful transformation of the 23rd Street gates inspired the MTA to commission another artist, Laura Bradley, to develop a system-wide design for new gates that would be both aesthetically pleasing and functional. Bradley's design is based on *Wave and Medallion*, her mosaics for the 96th Street Station (see page 172).

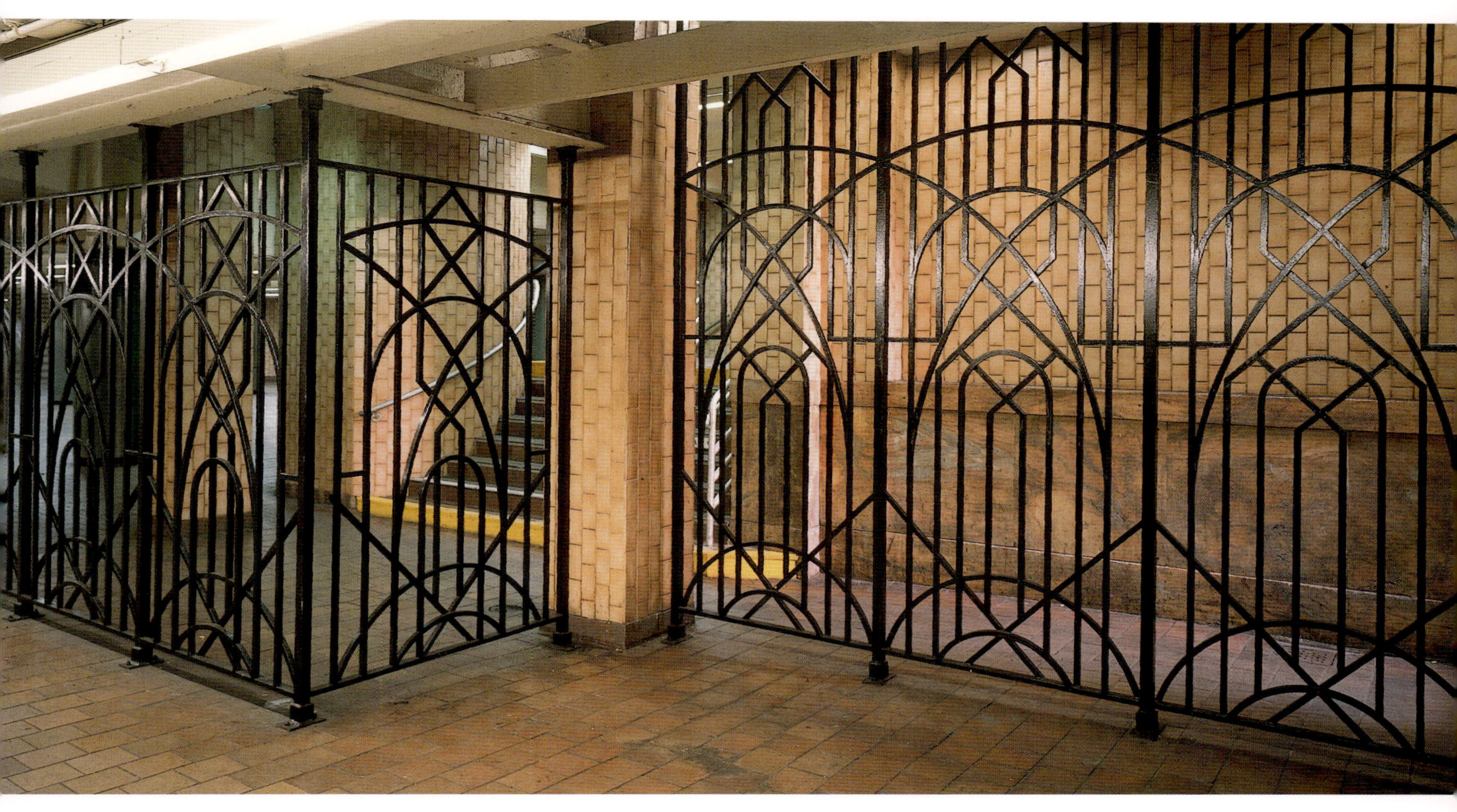

ROBERT KUSHNER

4 SEASONS SEASONED, 2004
77th Street 6
Glass mosaic
PHOTOGRAPHER: ROB WILSON

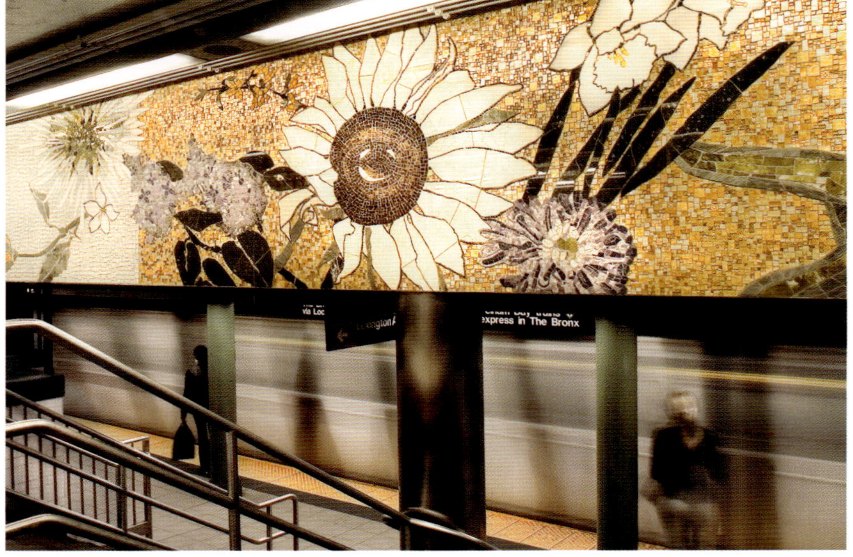

Robert Kushner has created two large flower arrangements—bouquets for any season and no season—blending diverse artistic traditions such as Dutch flower paintings and Japanese screens.

A member of the Pattern and Decoration Movement, he continues to feature vegetal motifs in his works, often along with geometric patterns and architectural shapes. His work is influenced by Chinese and Japanese art, in both subject matter and composition, and is also inspired by European and American artists such as Henri Matisse, Pierre Bonnard, Odilon Redon, and Georgia O'Keeffe.

The artist has a special affinity for the Upper East Side neighborhood where his work appears:

> My intention is for people to enter the station, pass through the turnstile, look up and take note, and then go on with their day feeling a little lighter, having glimpsed something beautiful for a passing moment. As people come and go from this stop, either to their job, home, Lenox Hill Hospital, Central Park, or the museums in the neighborhood, recreation, culture, work or healing are often on their minds. Flowers can be associated with all of these activities and become particularly apt subject matter for this station.

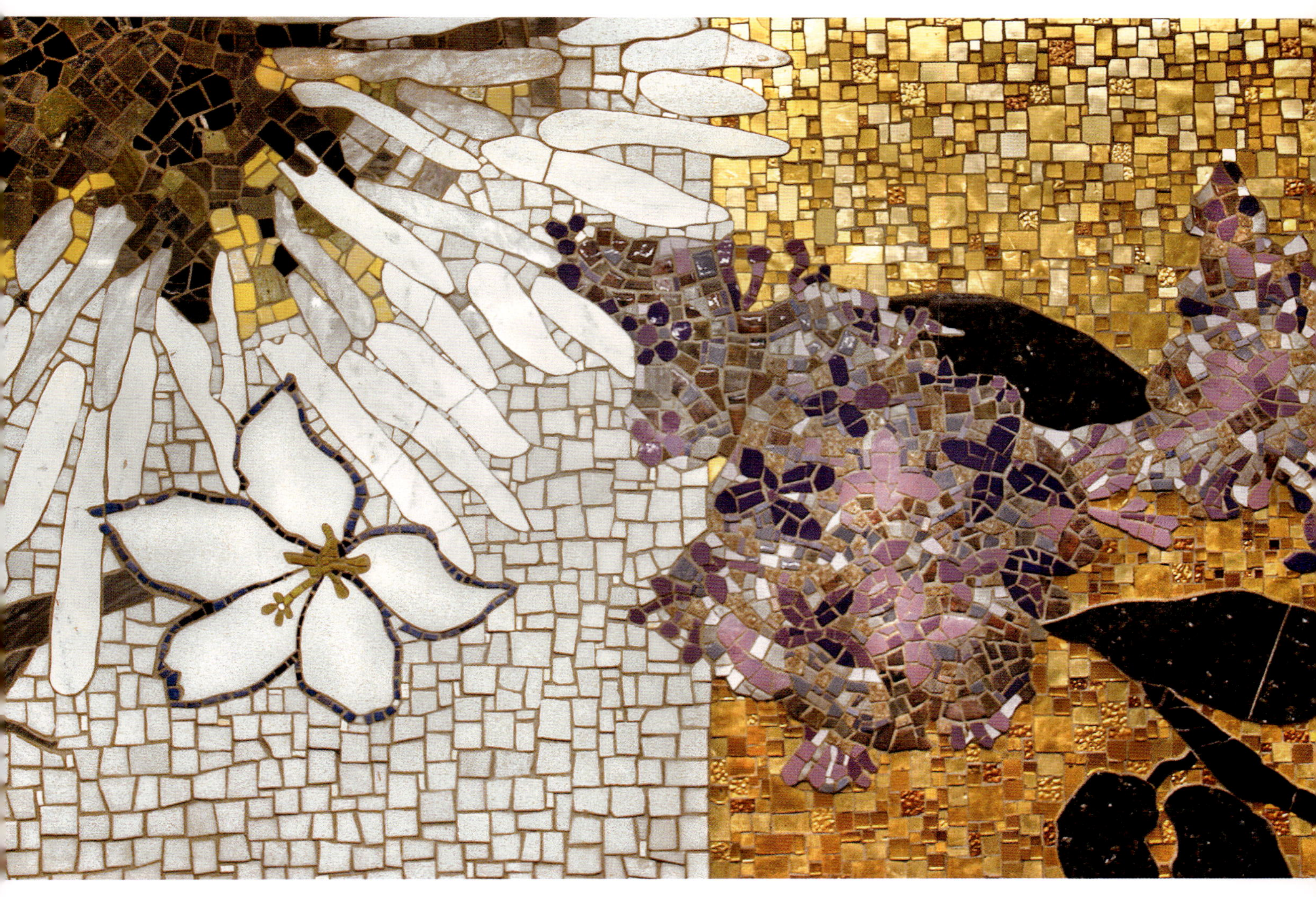

PETER SIS

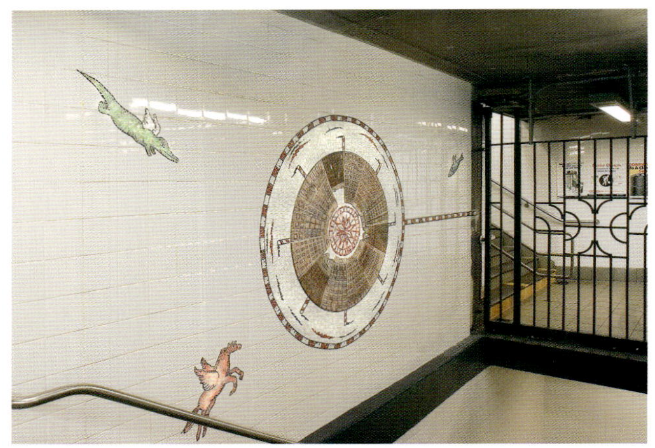

HAPPY CITY, 2004
86th Street 4 5 6
Glass mosaic and etched stone
PHOTOGRAPHER: ROB WILSON

In *Happy City,* Peter Sis depicts the evolution of an eye in stages, as a symbol of the elements of a community, the vibrant center that is New York City. The eye also observes the outside world and is part of a greater whole. The elements of the eye—pupil, eyelashes—are "drawn" with buildings from the neighborhood, incorporating such landmarks as the Metropolitan, Guggenheim, and Whitney Museums, as well as Gracie Mansion. The irises and whites of the eyes serve as a background for figurative elements that capture the diversity and vibrancy of the community.

According to the artist:

> These four murals depict the formation of the neighborhood around 86th Street. This neighborhood, depicted by an eye, is the eye of the happy city. This eye, which never sleeps, is part of a bigger organism—New York City.
>
> The [people of the city] have children and want the best for their children, so they tell them stories and fairy tales. The fairy tales are the magic animals which appear to float in throughout the four murals. In the end they form the carousel with the happy children of all nationalities enjoying the ride. That is the future of the city.

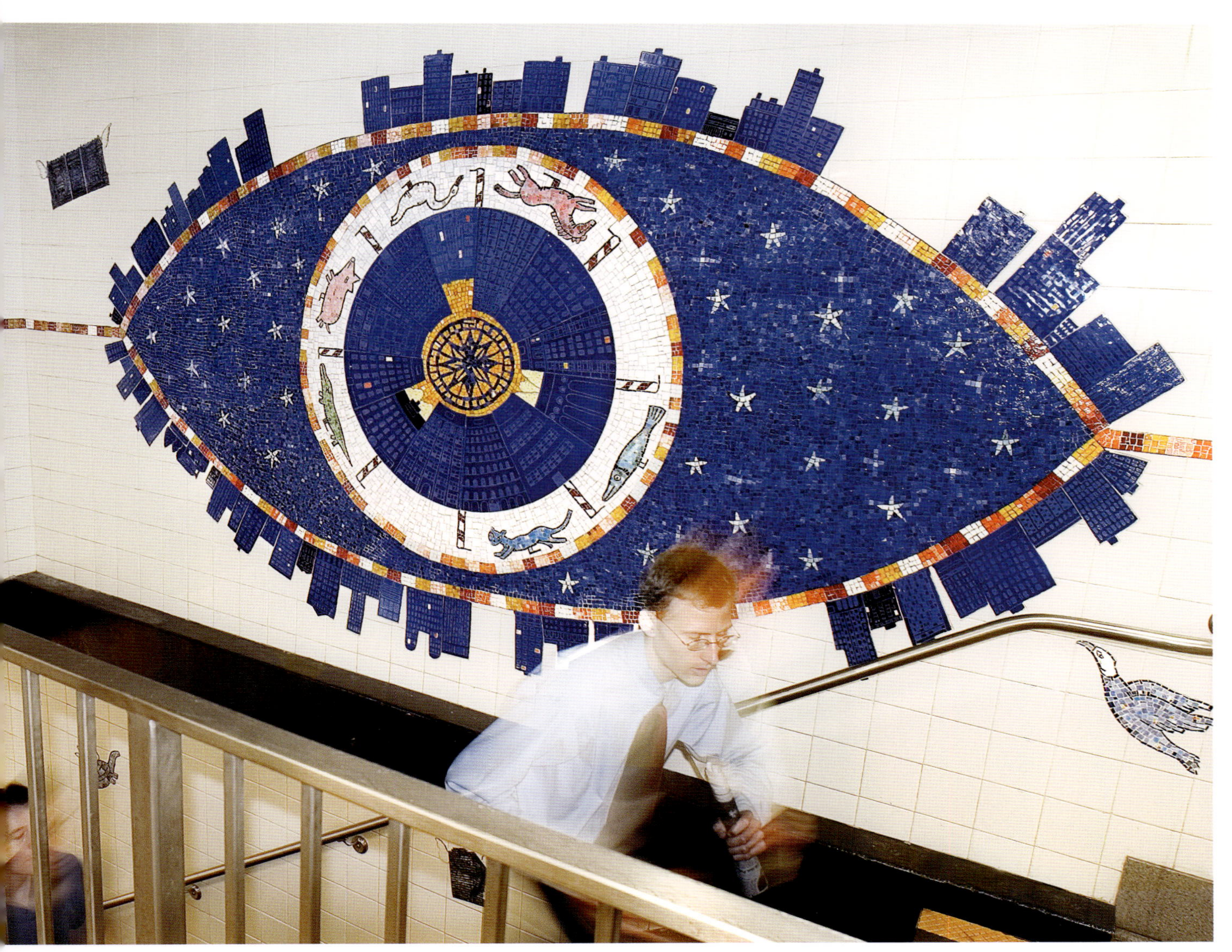

ROBERT BLACKBURN assisted by Mei-Tei-Sing Smith

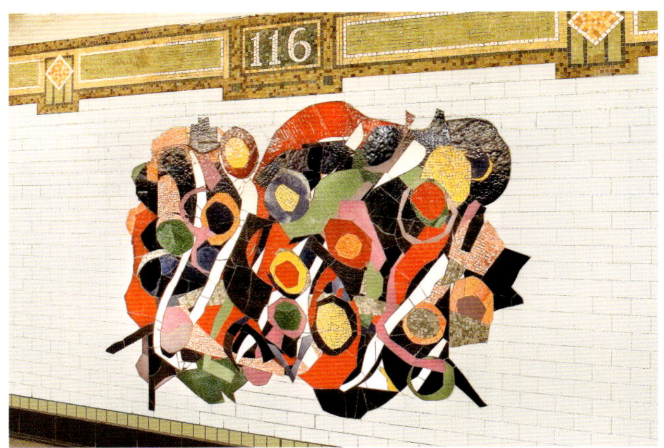

IN EVERYTHING THERE IS A SEASON, 2005

116th Street 

Glass and ceramic mosaic

PHOTOGRAPHER: ROB WILSON

Robert Blackburn's murals evoke the neighborhood through dynamic abstract patterns that suggest the color and movement of the streets above. They bring a timeless beauty into the transit environment.

The work reflects the abstract color lithographs for which Blackburn is best known. A colleague and friend of both Romare Bearden and Jacob Lawrence, Blackburn is credited for reviving interest in American printmaking, particularly through the Printmaking Workshop in Harlem, which he founded in 1948.

In failing health at the time of this commission, Blackburn chose artist Mei-Tei-Sing Smith, a Bearden Fellow at the Printmaking Workshop, to assist him on what would prove to be his last major project. Once completed, 30-by-40-inch maquettes were sent to Germany, where they were enlarged and manufactured into large ceramic and glass mosaics that today serve as a monument to Blackburn's bold use of color and masterful abstractions.

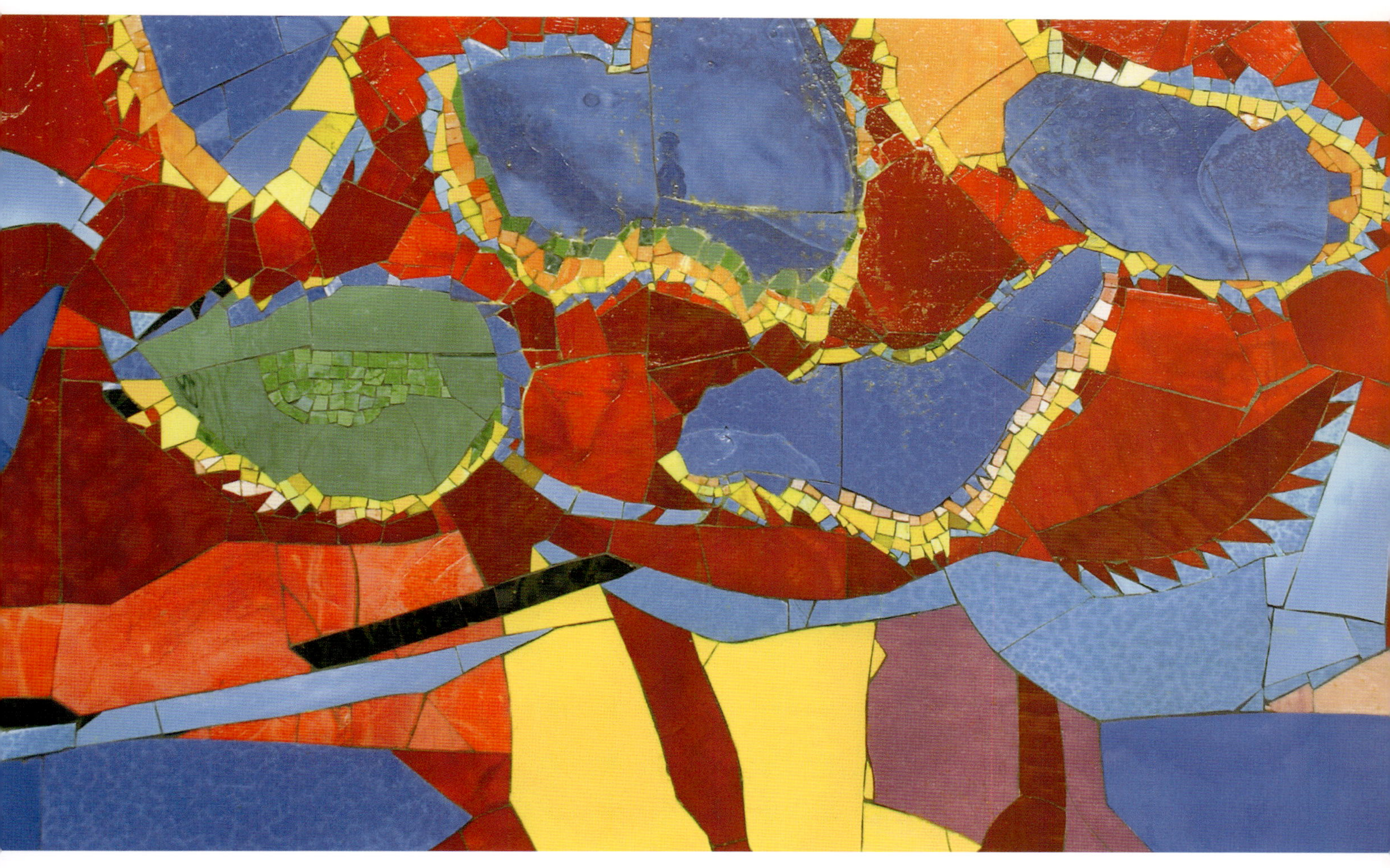

HOUSTON CONWILL

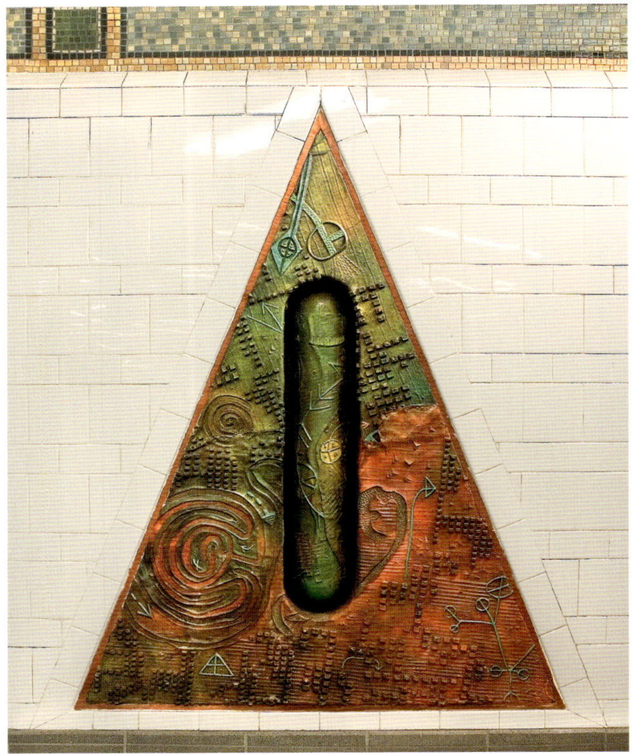

OPEN SECRET, 1986

125th Street 4 5 6

Bronze

PHOTOGRAPHER: ROB WILSON

Open Secret was the first Arts for Transit commission to be installed in the subway. The work presents various themes that had long intrigued Houston Conwill. Here, he says, he attempts "to capture the present for future generations of people through a ritual process: the creation of sacred spaces and the involvement of a community of people in bearing witness to the process and making it complete."

There is also a mysterious aspect to *Open Secret*, as its title suggests. Two of its triangular segments contain time capsules "holding information and 'secrets' about a certain place at a certain time—Harlem in the 1980s." Covered with grates so viewers can peer into them, the other two triangular elements reveal a variety of objects. As Conwill observed, "The exploration might be of a place or into our own minds where we might find eternal secrets that are saved and put in the time capsules for our children and their children."

Acknowledged as one of the pioneers of African American visual postmodernism, Conwill often works in collaboration with other artists, including his sister Estella Conwill Majozo, a poet. The themes of the works often involve the history of African Americans and their quest for freedom and equality.

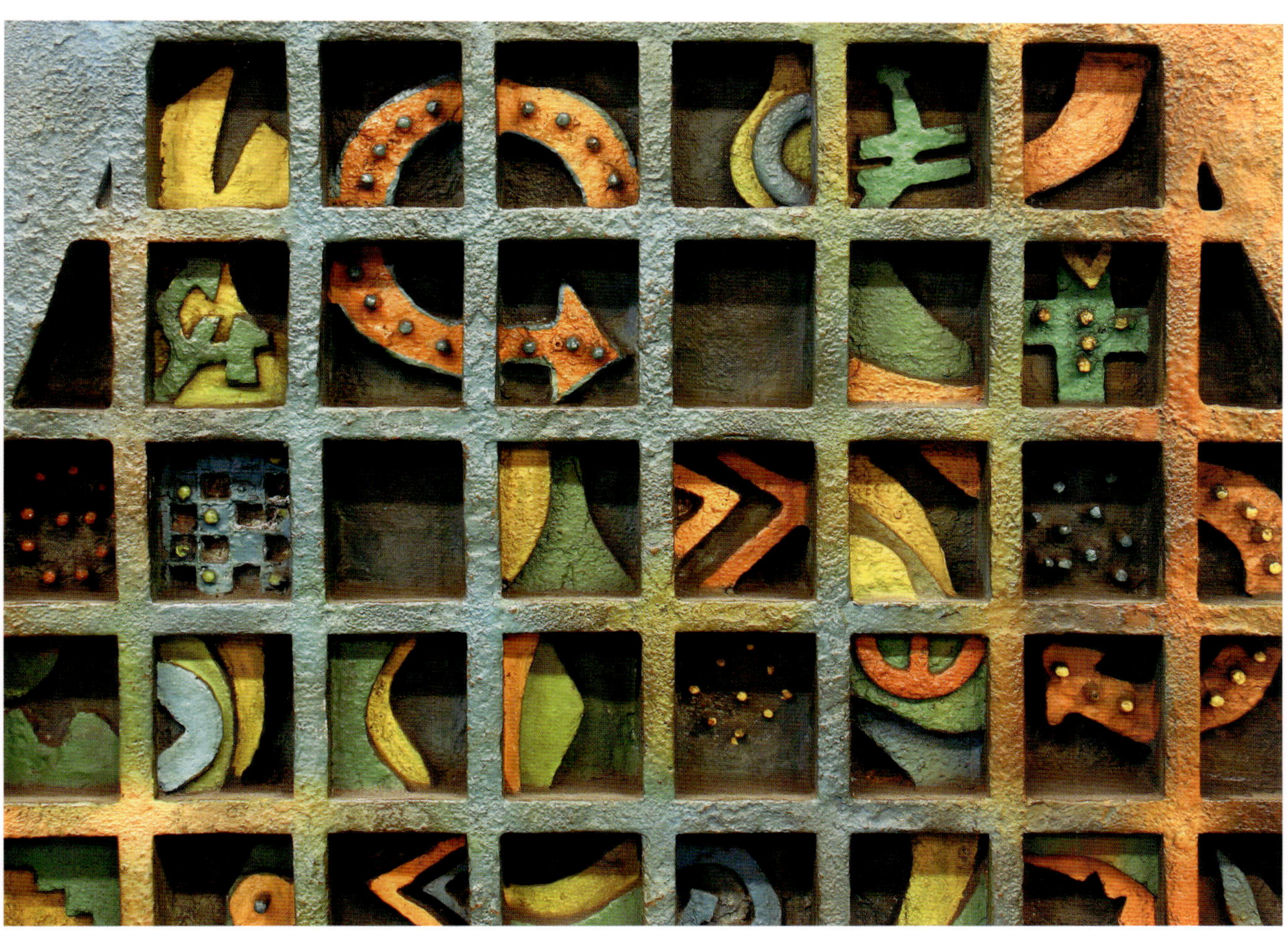

VALERIE MAYNARD

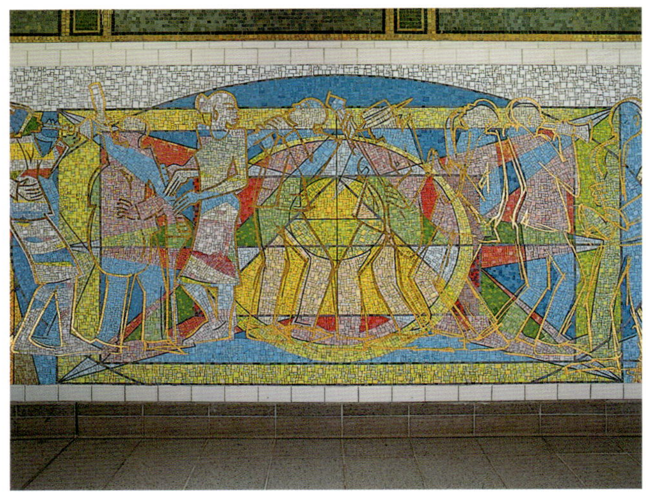

POLYRHYTHMICS OF CONSCIOUSNESS AND LIGHT, 2003
125th Street 4 5 6
Glass mosaic
PHOTOGRAPHER: PATRICK J. CASHIN

Polyrhythmics of Consciousness and Light was commissioned as part of a further renovation of the 125th Street and Lexington Avenue station, which already contained Houston Conwill's *Open Secret*. Valerie Maynard says of her work, "My living and my art are intertwined. My vision is informed by family and friends, ongoing conversations, and experiences of the spirit. This totality juxtaposes in a mélange of sights and sounds, a music that is always trying to impart a visual message that will engage the senses and hold the eyes' intelligence, while revealing much about what is seen at any given time."

The images of Maynard's translucent glass mosaic are designed to "capture the boundless energy, the beacon of light that was and is our own homegrown Mecca: the Harlem of our dreams, our imaginings and our reality. The stairwells are dedicated to the artists and visionaries whose flights of creativity, as they seek sustenance for body and soul, culminate in transcendent forms that nourish the community's consciousness and spirit."

Valerie Maynard is nationally known for her multimedia work and public art focusing on social issues. *No Apartheid Anywhere* is a particularly notable ongoing media project that explores forms of enslavement.

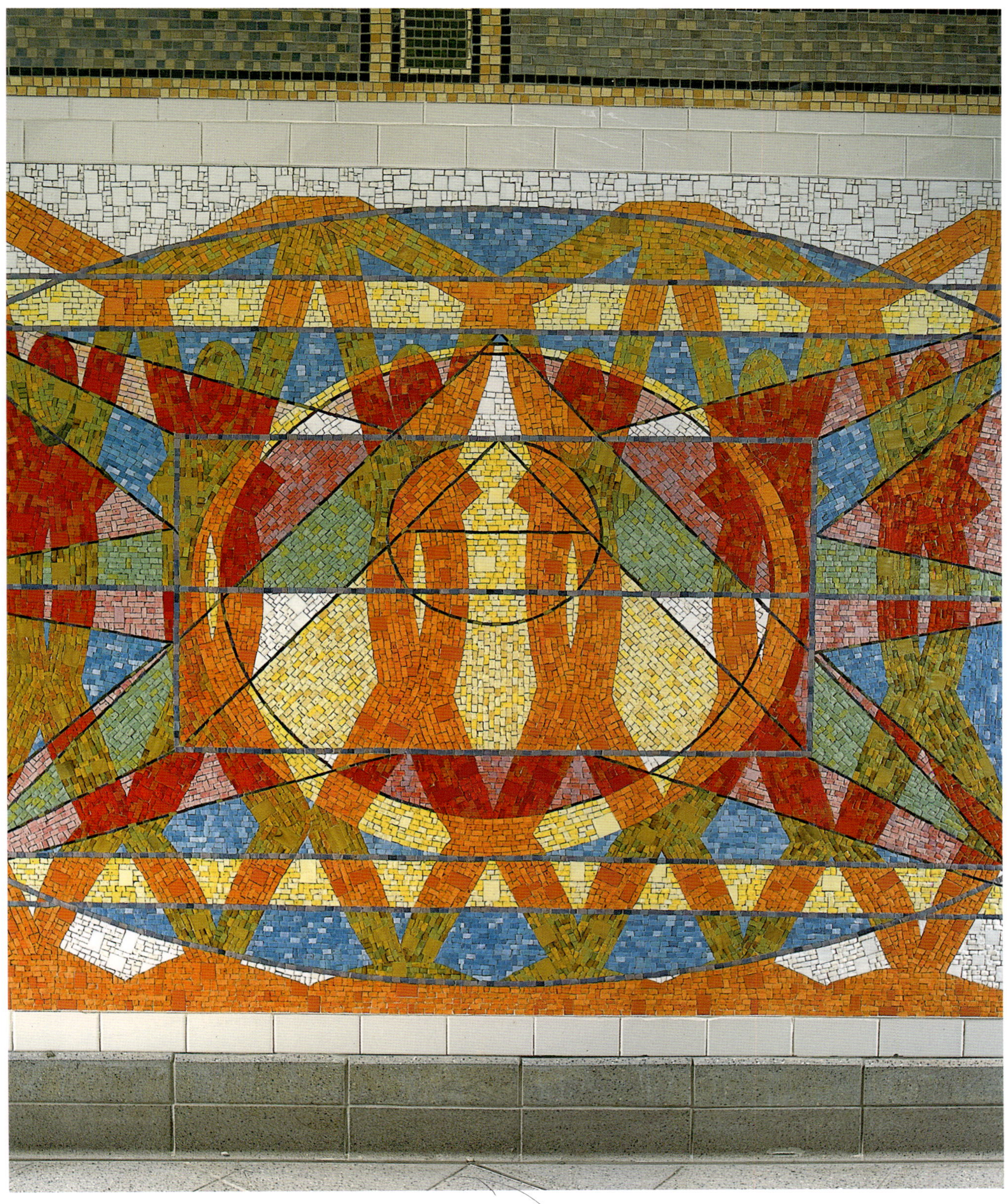

ALISON SAAR

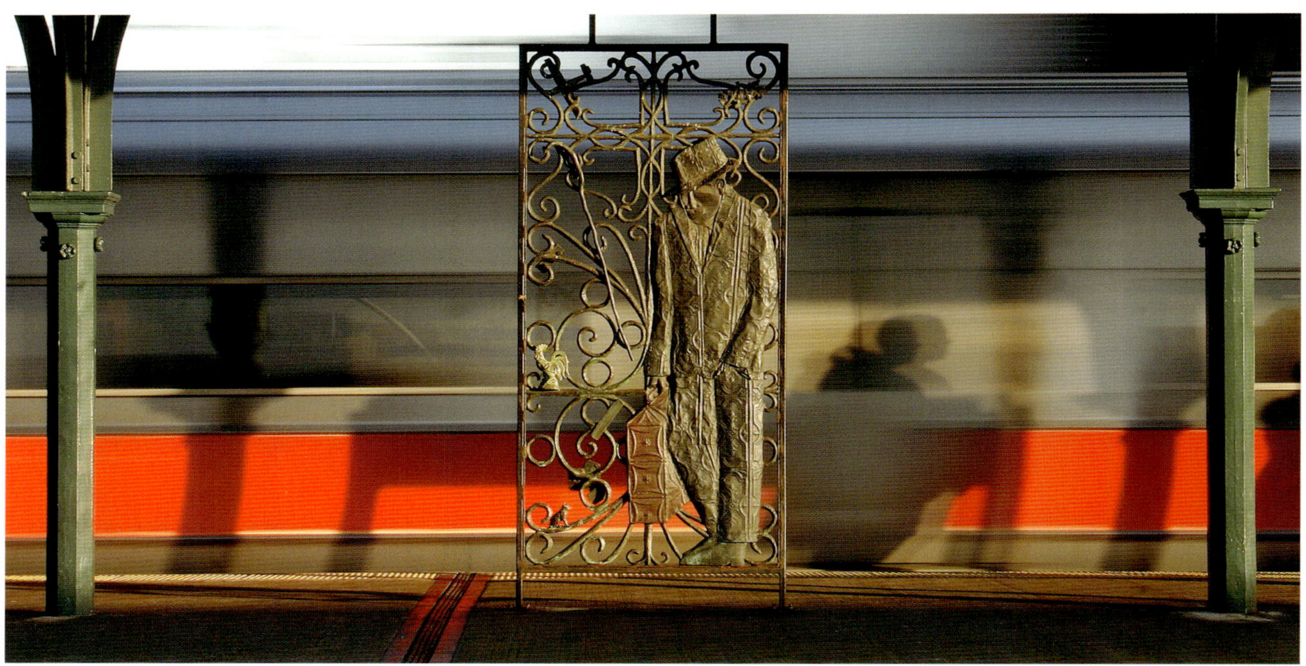

HEAR THE LONE WHISTLE MOAN, 1991
Harlem–125th Street, MTA Metro-North Railroad
Bronze
PHOTOGRAPHERS: ROB WILSON (ABOVE); DAVID LUBARKSY (OPPOSITE)

Alison Saar's *Hear the Lone Whistle Moan* consists of two figures standing against a grille as they wait for the train–a man on the northbound platform and a woman on the southbound one. The woman is arriving in town and the man is leaving New York. A third figure of a conductor stands at the top of the platform stairs.

Saar describes the work:

> The premise for these pieces was to create a simple narrative of two people. One, the young woman coming to the city in hopes of advancing her career, the other, a successful businessman leaving the city to return to his hometown. I believe these two scenarios to be examples of how many Americans have used the railroad to and from New York throughout history. Yet I also was addressing the specific and rich tradition of the role of the railroad in general in the lives of African Americans.

The title, *Hear the Lone Whistle Moan*, she continues, comes from a spiritual that uses the train as a metaphor for the passage to heaven. For African Americans, trains have strong associations with escape and with the Underground Railroad in particular, which was sometimes referred to as the Phantom Train.

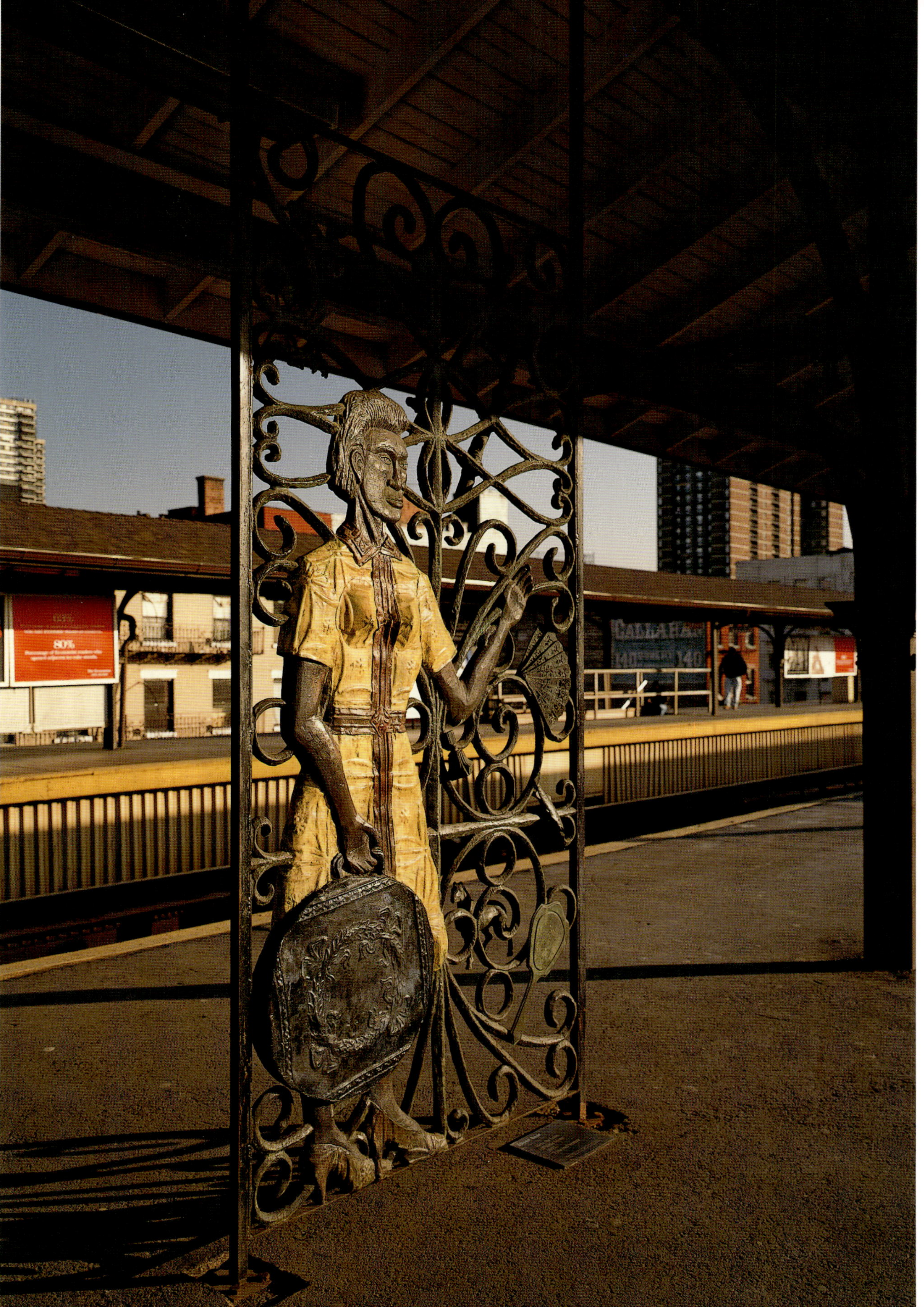
80%

TERRY ADKINS

HARLEM ENCORE, 1999
Harlem–125th Street, MTA Metro-North Railroad
Aluminum
PHOTOGRAPHER: JAMES DEE

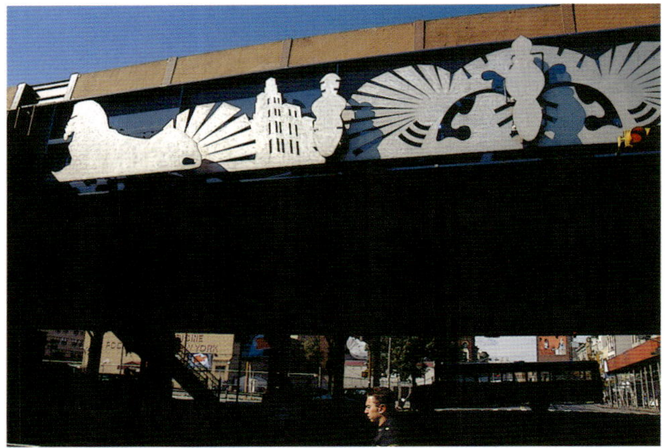

One of the largest and most imposing structures in Harlem is MTA Metro-North's Park Avenue Viaduct, which extends for two miles through the community. The massive structure is now enlivened with a bold new artwork, sculptor Terry Adkins's *Harlem Encore*. In a talk entitled "Black History Re-imagined," Adkins declared: "I try to represent people's contributions to making the world a better place. I try to right historical wrongs. I try to educate, and to give a total view of what individuals such as Sojourner Truth, Jimi Hendrix, Ralph Ellison, and Zora Neale Hurston are all about."

Harlem Encore takes the form of two aluminum relief panels, which are dramatically backlit in blue at night. On the western side of the bridge, Adkins focuses on Harlem's contribution to the arts, humanities, and science. Also included are representations of ancestors from Africa. On the opposite, eastern side of the overpass, the New York skyline is shown, with figures of people and their shadows.

On both sides of the bridge, mysterious sphinx images appear. In his narrative statement for the project, Adkins explained, "The front layers of both elevations are framed at either end by stylized sphinxes appropriated from the work of Aaron Douglas, an artist/titan of the Harlem Renaissance. I was compelled to use this image not only to pay homage to Mr. Douglas's seminal Harlem legacy, but also because through him, I personally experienced a direct connection to the Harlem Renaissance era. The sphinxes are the keystones of the work, speaking of the common Afro-Diaspora of all Harlem residents."

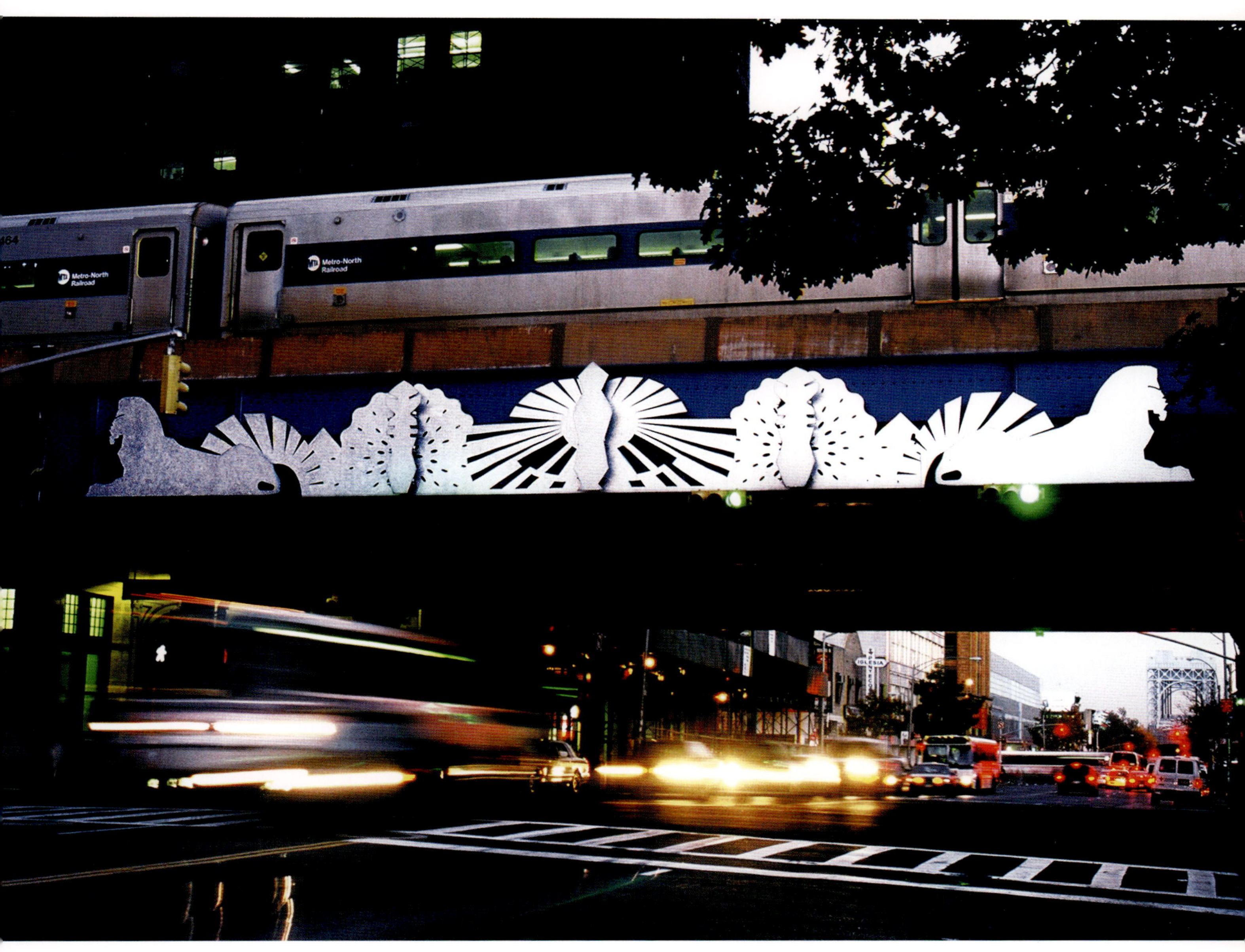
Metro-North Railroad
Metro-North Railroad
IGLESIA

VINCENT SMITH

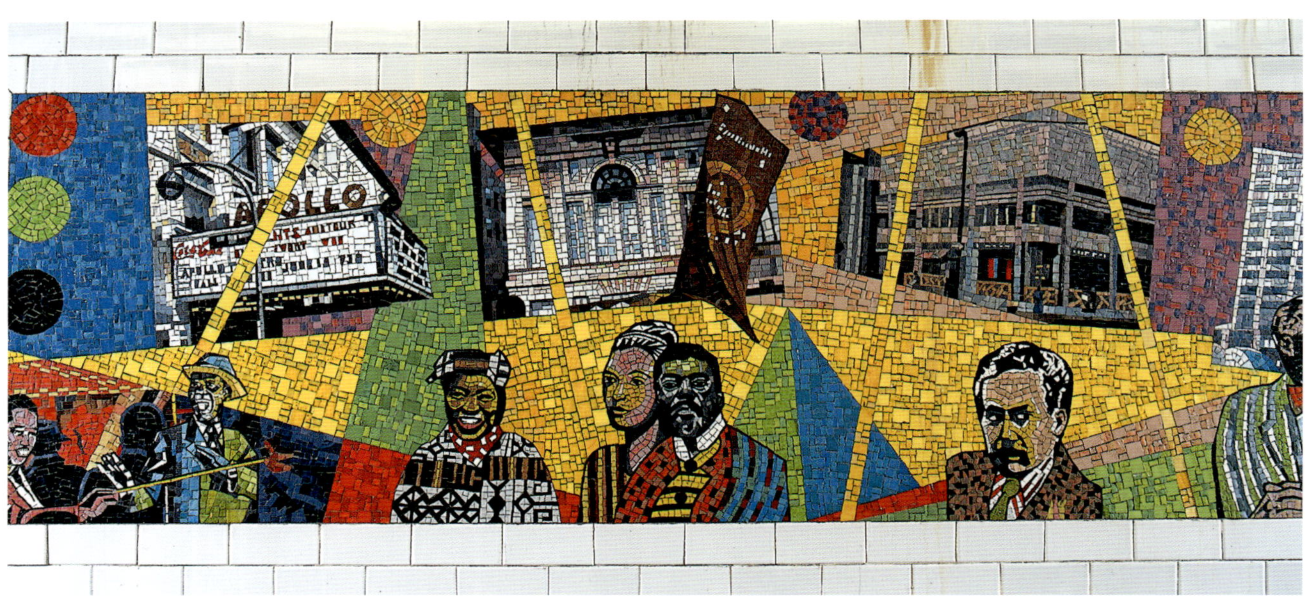

MINTON'S PLAYHOUSE/THE MOVERS AND SHAKERS, 1999
116th Street 2 3
Glass mosaic
PHOTOGRAPHER: PATRICK J. CASHIN

The Movers and Shakers celebrates and commemorates the rich history of Harlem. Renowned residents of the neighborhood are depicted in front of the places with which they are associated. Singer and actor Paul Robeson is shown at the Abyssinian Baptist Church, the poet Langston Hughes at the National Black Theatre, and the dancer Alvin Ailey and writer Zora Neale Hurston at the Studio Museum in Harlem. Thurgood Marshall is pictured as well, as is Marcus Garvey. Others include Duke Ellington and Bill "Bojangles" Robinson at the Apollo Theater and A. Philip Randolph, the influential union organizer, at Harlem Hospital.

The Minton's Playhouse portion of Smith's work salutes, in the artist's words, "old friends and new contemporaries, with juices flowing as they broke musical ground and discovered new techniques." Here, in the setting of Minton's—one of the most celebrated Harlem clubs and one that the artist frequented—a group of musicians is pictured before a brightly colored glass-tile backdrop, with motifs to suggest jazz's debt to the music of Africa and the Caribbean islands. Represented, along with a tribute to vocal music, are energetic percussion, bass fiddle, piano, saxophone, and trumpet players.

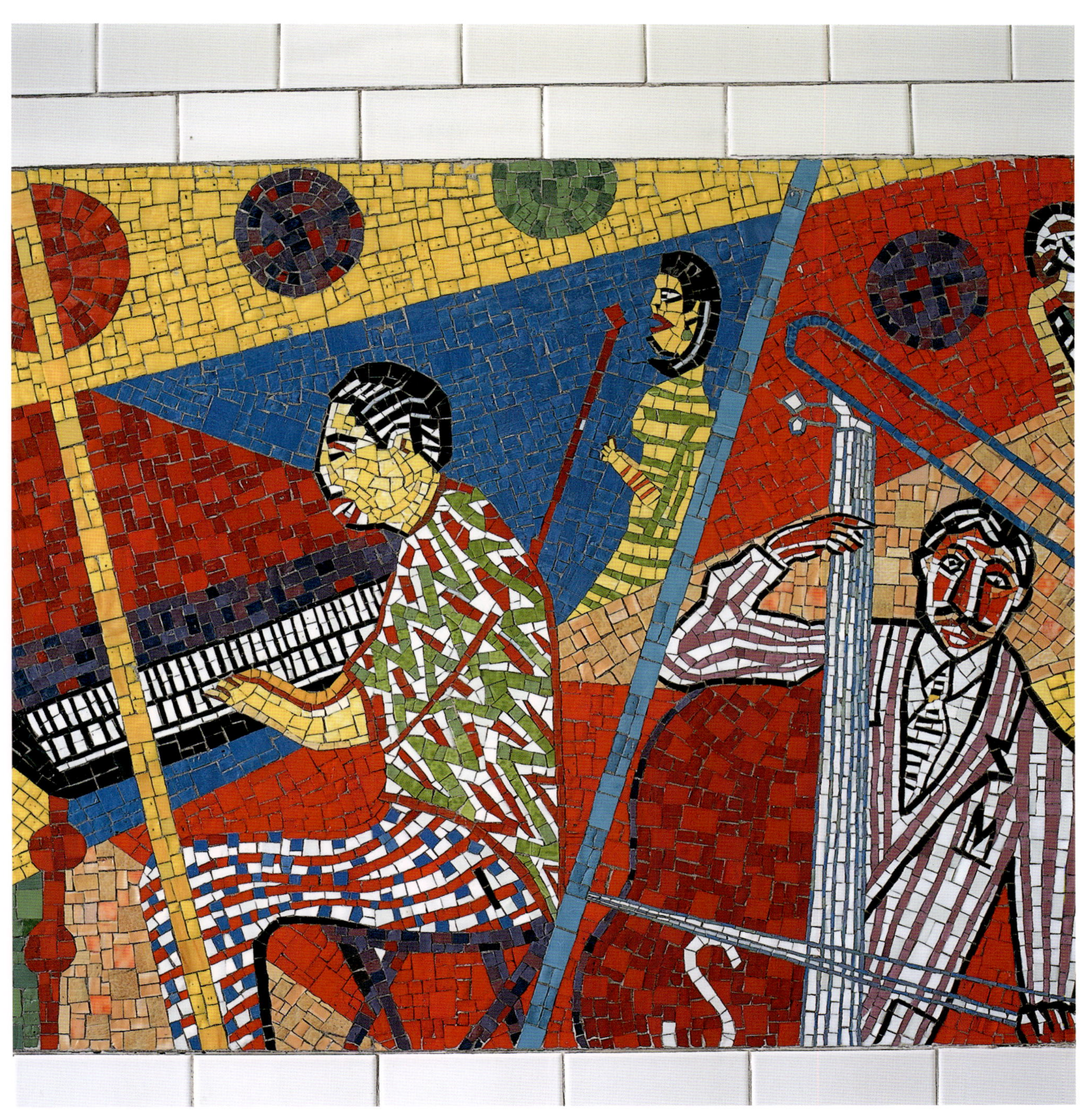

WILLIE BIRCH

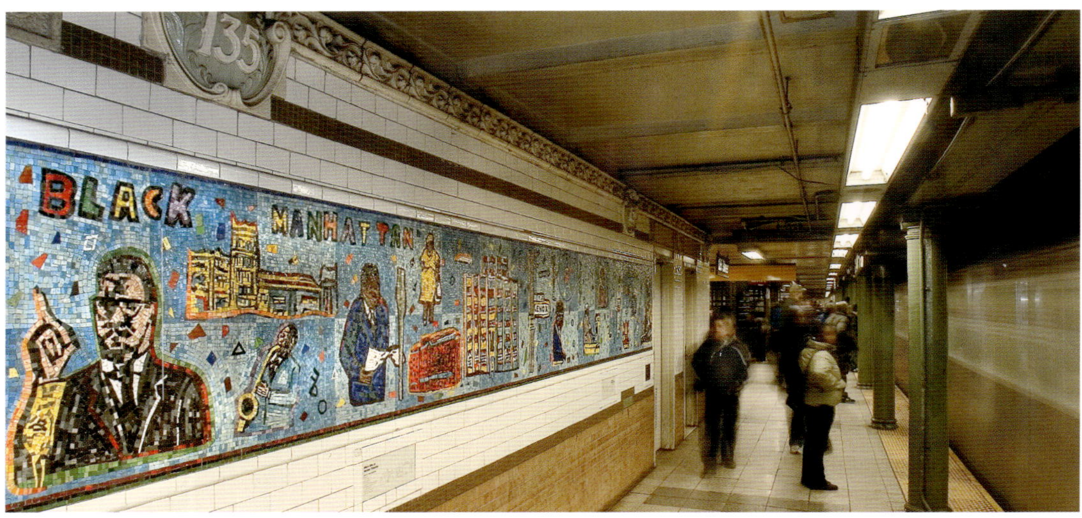

HARLEM TIMELINE, 1995
135th Street ❷❸
Glass mosaic
PHOTOGRAPHER: ROB WILSON

Harlem Timeline is part of the paean to Harlem luminaries, but the famous are shown among the ordinary people of Harlem going about their daily affairs–playing, studying, going to church. "It's about being connected," Birch says. "Harlem is a village built on global energy, infused with the histories of migrants from Africa, the American South, and the Caribbean."

Birch calls New Orleans his home, but he also maintains a studio in New York. The theme of returning to roots often permeates his artwork. According to fellow artist Robert Taplin, writing in *Art in America*, among contemporary black artists "Birch is one of the most forthright in adopting an 'Africanizing' cultural model . . . In the end, it's [his] clear sense of design that makes it all work."

In *Harlem Timeline,* on the downtown platform, along with a depiction of the Schomburg Center for Research in Black Culture, Birch shows Langston Hughes reading from his works and Reverend Adam Clayton Powell Jr. preaching to a rapt gathering. Boxing champion Joe Louis is depicted triumphing over an opponent and Charlie Parker excels on the saxophone.

Uptown riders are treated to a moving rendition of the blues, with Billie Holiday singing her heart out. Also shown are jazz greats Thelonious Monk and John Coltrane, playing away, and civil rights activists Malcolm X and Marcus Garvey. Community services are represented by Harlem Hospital and its predecessor.

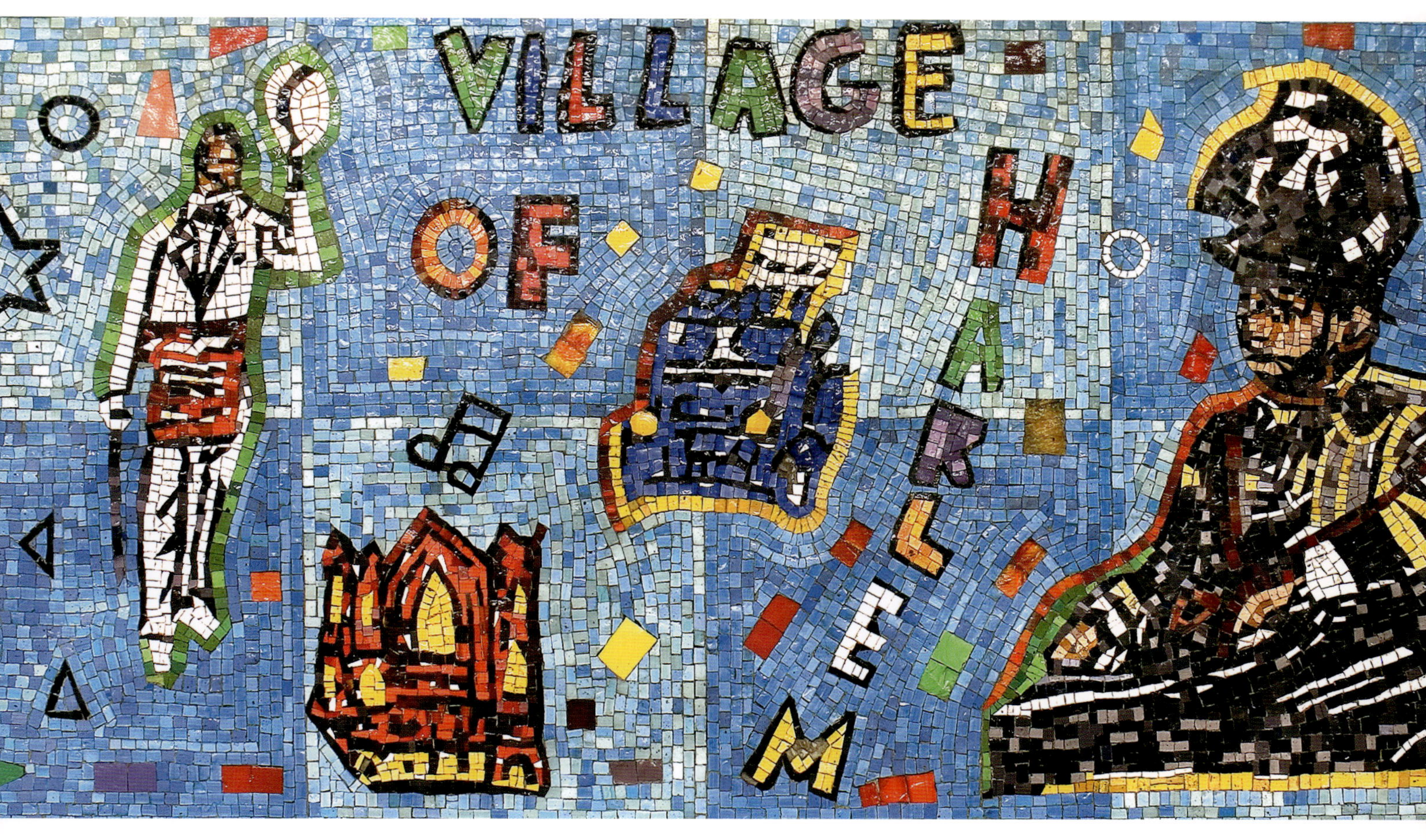
VILLAGE
OF
HARLEM

FAITH RINGGOLD assisted by Tim Tait Designs

FLYING HOME: HARLEM HEROES AND HEROINES, 1996

125th Street ❷❸

Glass mosaic

PHOTOGRAPHERS: ROB WILSON (BELOW); MICHAEL KAMBER (OPPOSITE)

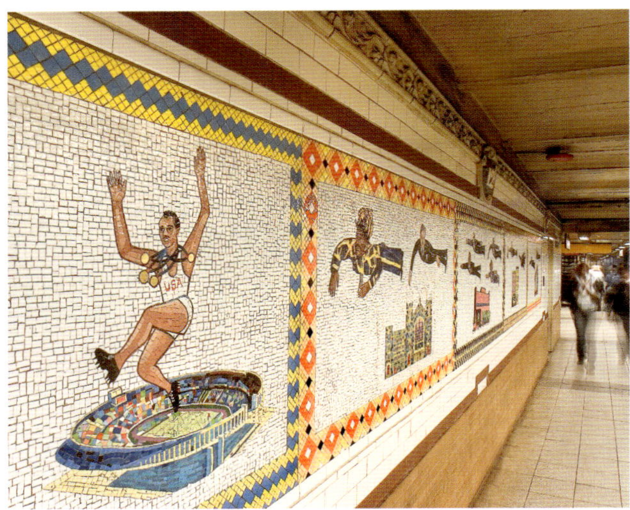

Faith Ringgold's *Flying Home* celebrates the spirit and soul of Harlem, where she was born and spent her youth. The inspiration for the work and the source of its title was a piece by Lionel Hampton, the great African American jazz composer and musician. In these ten mosaic panels, selected luminaries of the Harlem pantheon now soar joyfully on the platform walls of the station.

Harlem heroes on one platform include writers, leaders in the political and civil rights fields, and others of world fame—Zora Neale Hurston, Malcolm X, and Jesse Owens among them. On the opposite side of the tracks, sports figures and musicians are given their due—Josephine Baker, Dinah Washington, Sugar Ray Robinson—along with artists Jacob Lawrence, Romare Bearden, Aaron Douglas, Norman Lewis, and Augusta Savage, all grouped with the community's revered arts institution, the Studio Museum in Harlem.

"I love every one of these people," Ringgold says. "I grew up among them, knew some of them as neighbors. My mother took me to see Billie Holiday perform. I demonstrated with the Reverend Dr. Adam Clayton Powell Jr. We listened to Joe Louis fight on the radio and cheered when he won. And, of course, I loved the music, especially Duke Ellington. I wanted to share those memories, to give the community—and others just passing through—a glimpse of all the wonderful people who were part of Harlem. I wanted them to realize what Harlem has produced and inspired."

Since the 1960s, Faith Ringgold has concentrated largely on African American themes. She is particularly well known for her mixed-media works in the form of quilts or inspired by them. These works often ingeniously play with stereotypes of blacks, turning images usually associated with prejudice into expressions of racial pride—for instance, her *Who's Afraid of Aunt Jemima* of the 1970s.

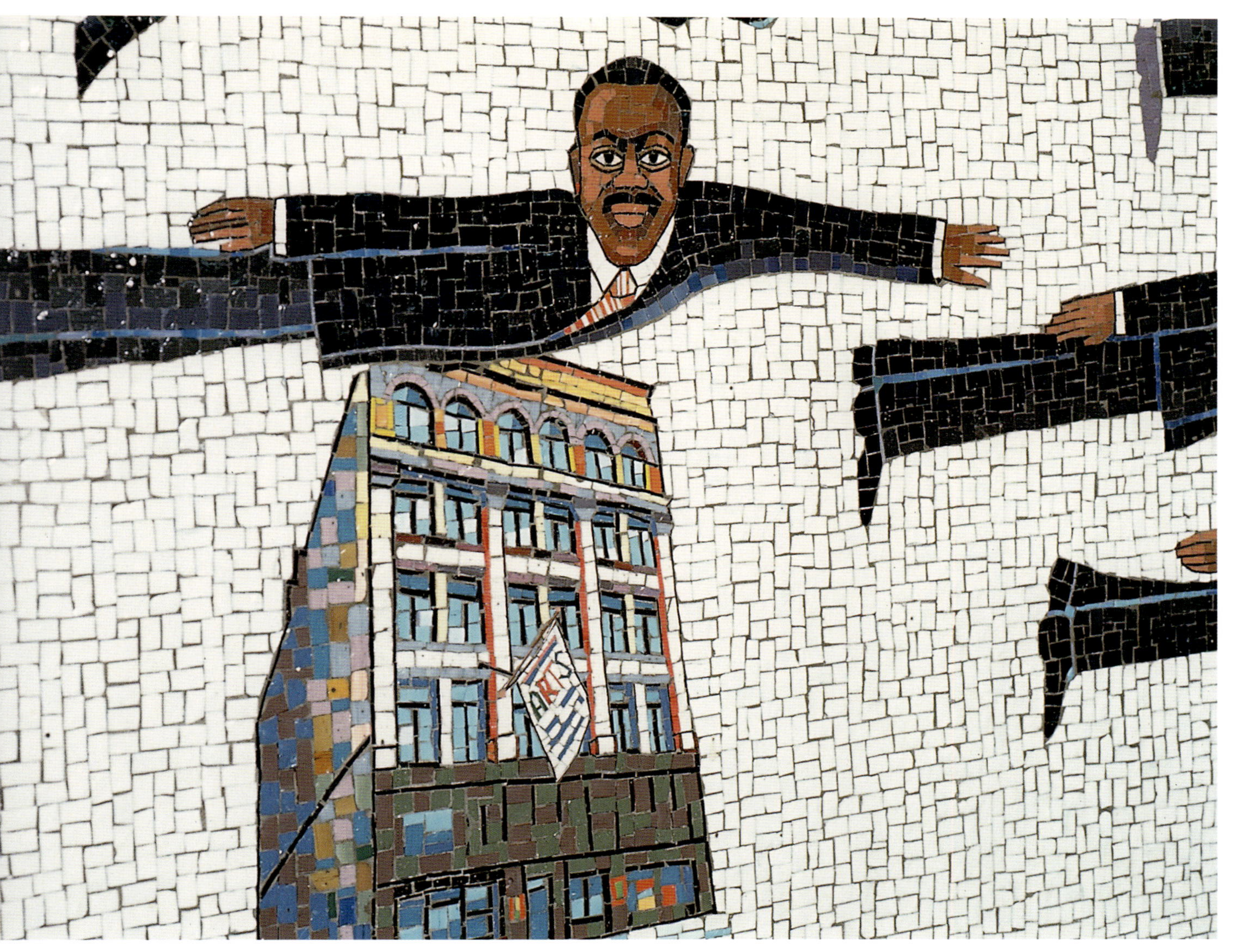
ARTS

SHEILA LEVRANT de BRETTEVILLE

in cooperation with Ehrenkrantz Eckstut & Kuhn Architects

AT THE START... AT LONG LAST..., 1999

Inwood-207th Street (A)

Glass mosaic, silkscreened tiles, etched railings, and terrazzo

PHOTOGRAPHER: ROB WILSON

Sheila Levrant de Bretteville's work celebrates the composition and history of the multinational community in and around Inwood at the northern tip of Manhattan—its multiple generations of immigrants culminating in today's new settlers and their Caribbean heritage.

In her proposal, de Bretteville wrote:

> In each of my projects I have looked for what elements could make the "hereness" of the site significant . . . I particularly enjoy imagining what could enhance a particular site, the alchemy by which the various images and pieces of texts reveal a hidden history, the plurality of voices reveal agencies and knowledge different from mine at the same time that I too am myself reflected in the experience.

In the Inwood station, a terrazzo paver marks the northernmost point of the A line, and metallic silver Murano mosaics compose the large letters that signal that this is a place of arrival and departure. White glazed ceramic tiles comment on the experience of recent immigrants to New York, and on the elevator wall are figures depicted from various present-day Latino civilizations—including a "Moco Jumbie" stilt dancer and an unorthodox-looking Uncle Sam. Flute-playing figures in terrazzo pavers on the mezzanine convey the role of music in the community. Words from Billy Strayhorn's "Take the A Train" are etched on the stainless-steel railing of the mezzanine stairwell.

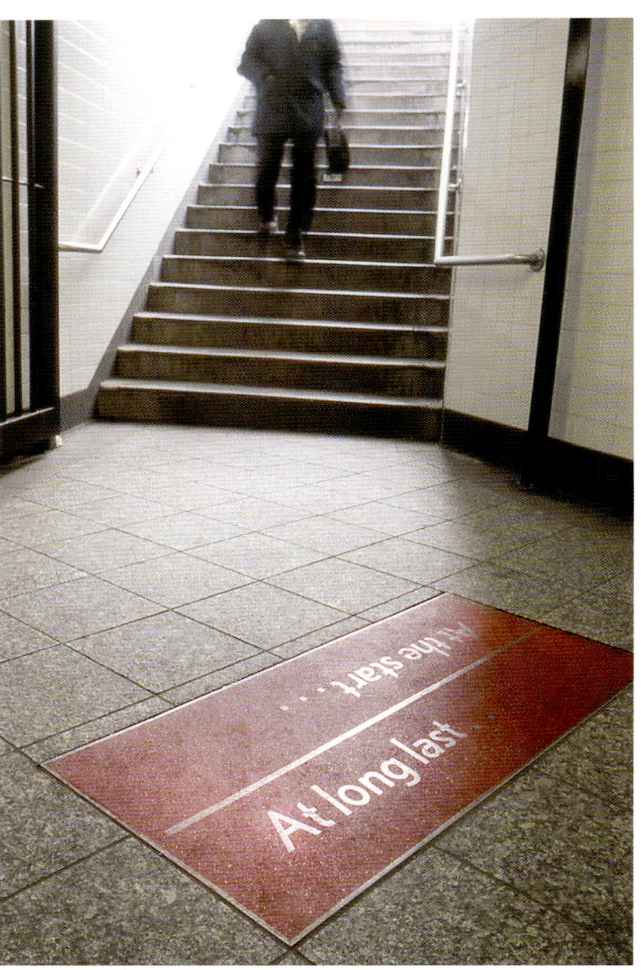

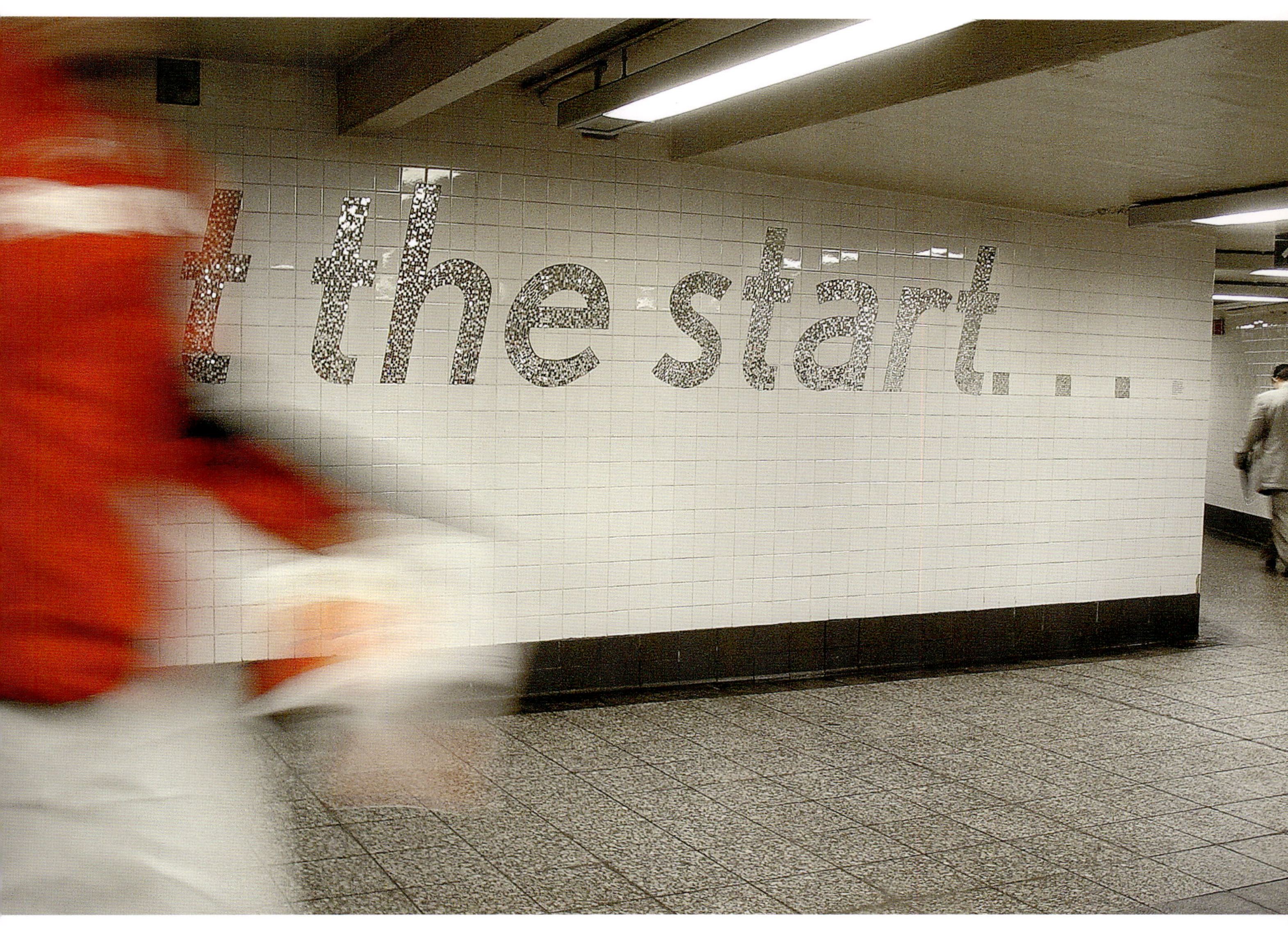
t the start. . . .

ARTS FOR TRANSIT COLLABORATIVE

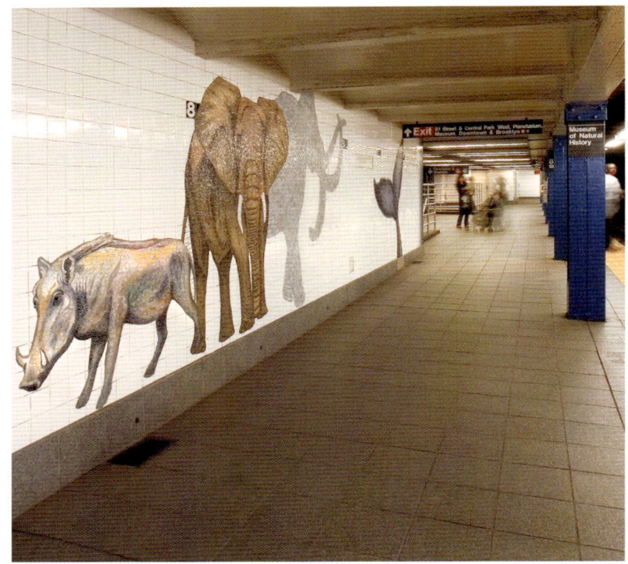

FOR WANT OF A NAIL, 2000

81st Street–Museum of Natural History 

Glass and ceramic mosaic, handmade ceramic relief tile, hand-cast glass, bronze, and cut granite

PHOTOGRAPHER: ROB WILSON

In *For Want of a Nail*, the artist team used a variety of materials to suggest the range and diversity of offerings at the American Museum of Natural History. The work is a swirling assemblage of images, from outer space to the earth's core, from the first organisms to emerge from the primeval ooze to mammals of today.

Glass mosaic, glass tile, ceramic tile, granite, and bronze relief are combined in a variety of ways to highlight the ten key fields represented at the museum: anthropology, astronomy, earth and planetary sciences, entomology, herpetology, ichthyology, invertebrates, mammalogy, ornithology, and vertebrate paleontology. The result is a compelling visual treatise on the earth, its inhabitants—both past and present—and the heavens that surround it.

For Want of a Nail, whose title is taken from a proverb, asks the viewer to ponder the way in which everything in the universe is connected and how it, the earth, and organisms have changed and continue to change over time.

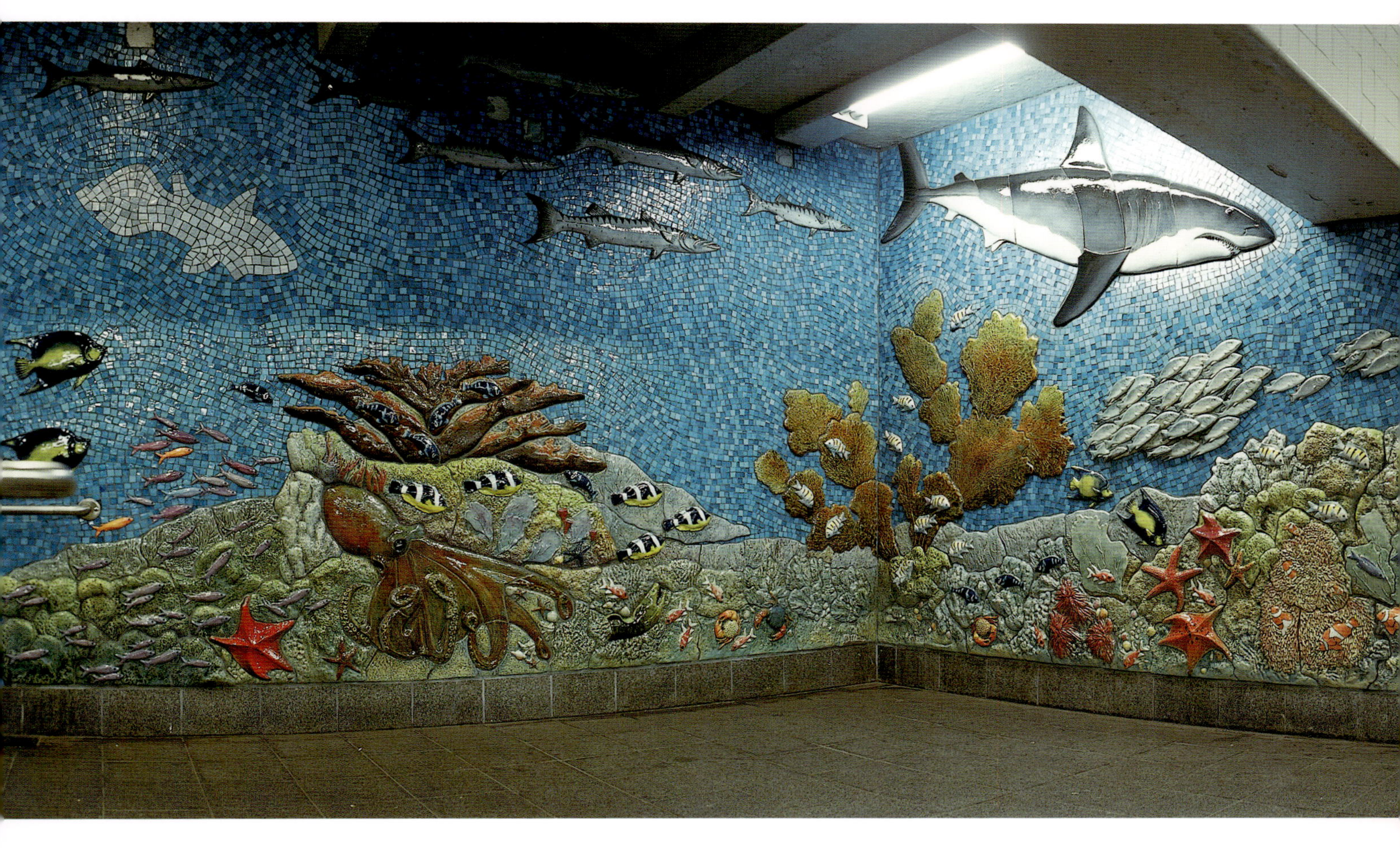

ROBERT HICKMAN in cooperation with Dattner Architects

LACED CANOPY, 2002

72nd Street 1 2 3

Mosaic glass

PHOTOGRAPHERS: JEFFREY STURGES (BELOW); ROB WILSON (OPPOSITE)

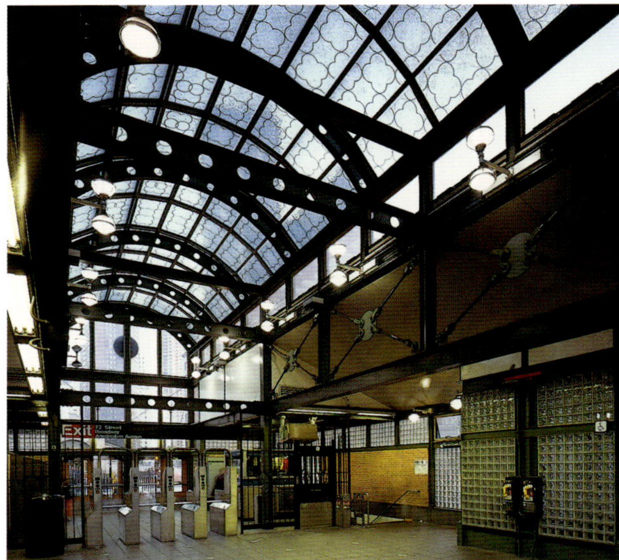

Robert Hickman's *Laced Canopy* includes over one hundred decorative mosaic glass panels—composed of more than one million fragments of glass—installed in the skylight of the new subway control house at 72nd Street and Broadway, the first aboveground station house to be built in New York in over a century. The artist achieved the light and lacy effect by trapping the mosaic fragments between two sheets of glass that he and his assistants fabricated in his studio. The depictions of knots subtly interwoven into the composition can also be read as musical notes from Giuseppe Verdi's opera *Rigoletto*, referencing Verdi Park, in which the station is located, as well as the nearby Metropolitan Opera House.

The artist describes the sparkling canopy as akin to "a delicate covering of crushed diamonds." Nineteenth-century English sources inform the work. The overall concept is based on Joseph Paxton's 1851 Crystal Palace in London; William Morris fabric and wallpaper designs—as well as classical knot patterns—are incorporated as motifs. In Hickman's words, "The fine glass filigree acts to atmospherically filter daylight into the station; surrounding buildings become distorted like impressionist paintings."

Hickman is also a filmmaker, and he sees important connections between his work in glass and the cinema: both involve the creative arrangement and rearrangement of disparate, fragmented elements; both depend for their effects on light streaming through semitransparent elements.

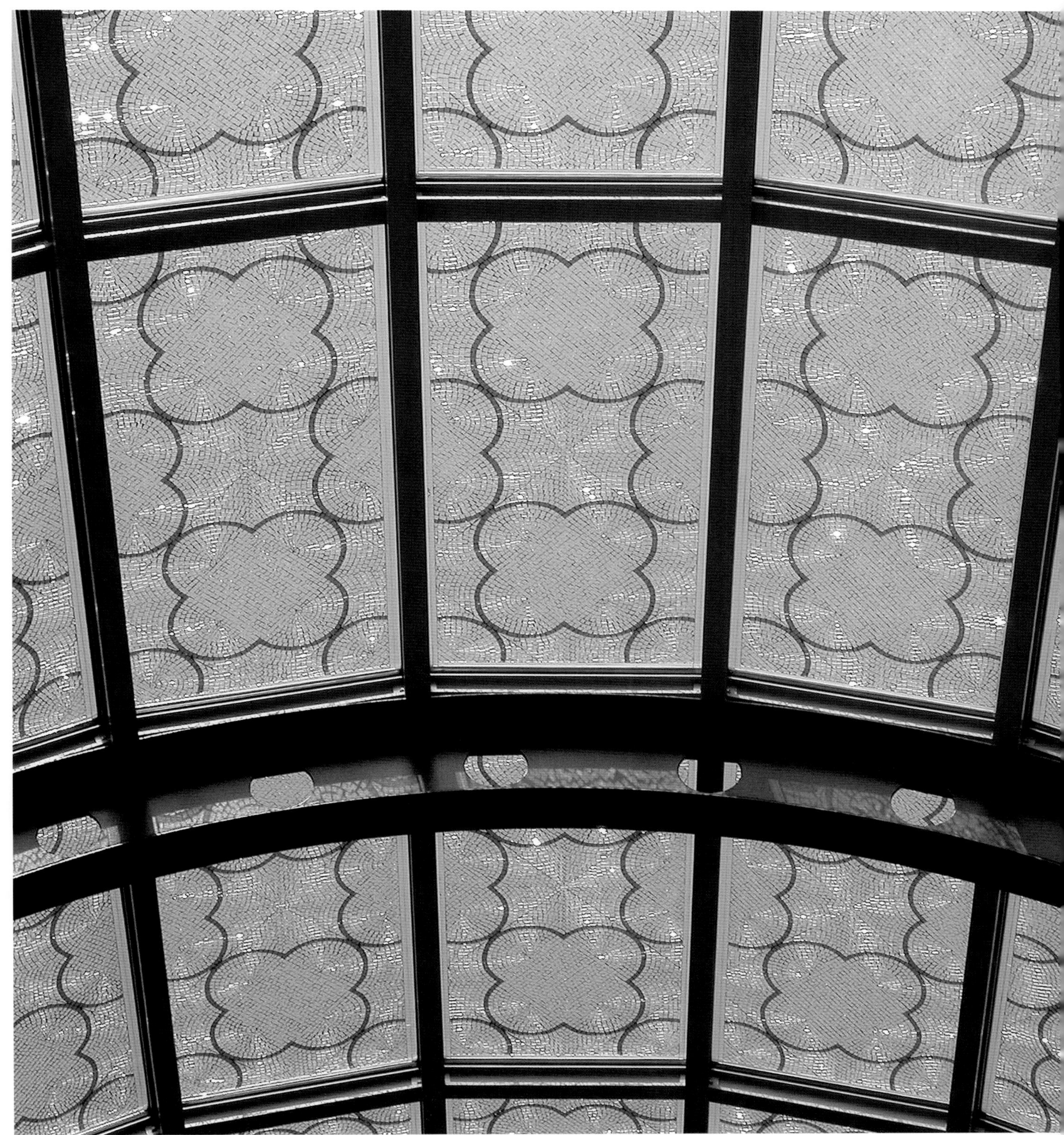

NANCY SPERO

ARTEMIS, ACROBATS, DIVAS, AND DANCERS, 2001

66th Street-Lincoln Center 1

Glass and ceramic mosaic

PHOTOGRAPHER: ROB WILSON

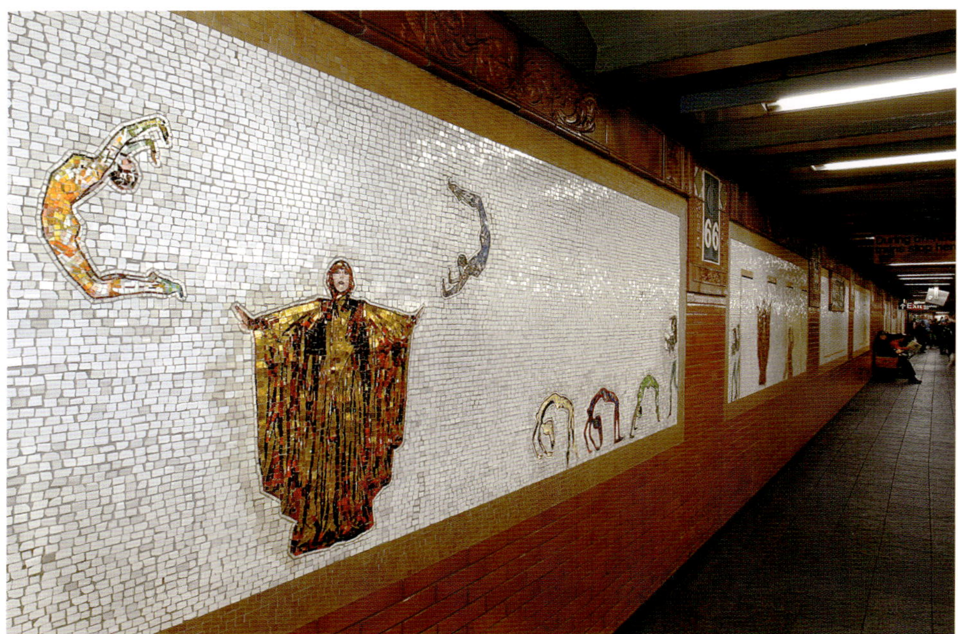

Artemis, Acrobats, Divas, and Dancers, a series of twenty-two brilliantly colored glass mosaic panels, lines the walls of the station. Spero's work evokes both Lincoln Center's performing arts institutions—opera, ballet, classical music—and the vibrant, artistic character of the Upper West Side neighborhood. She conveys this through the use of iconic images of women both real and mythical, from such varied sources as archaeology, architecture, mythology, and the contemporary world.

In her long career, Nancy Spero consistently focused her art on "challenging questions about women as artists and women as women." In the 1960s she began working as a figurative abstract painter with a political agenda. Medium has always been important to her; she has generally avoided working on canvas, preferring paper and collage. To her, these symbolize "women's liberation from traditional language into communication that seemed more pertinent." From the 1970s onward, she rejected all but female images in her work and sometimes included text with depictions of partial female forms, addressing issues of women's control over their own bodies. Her current work often reveals an element of sadness, even despair: "In many of the works now I'm trying to depict a sense of the vitality of life, but also to pose the question: what does happen after the revolution? There have to be solutions and there aren't a lot of them."

In *Artemis, Acrobats, Divas, and Dancers*, the central icon of opera, the Diva, is repeated in various forms that lead and follow riders through the station, giving the illusion of movement and change. In another area, Spero represents scenes from the subway and the city outside, the architectural backgrounds enlivened by musicians performing and athletes running.

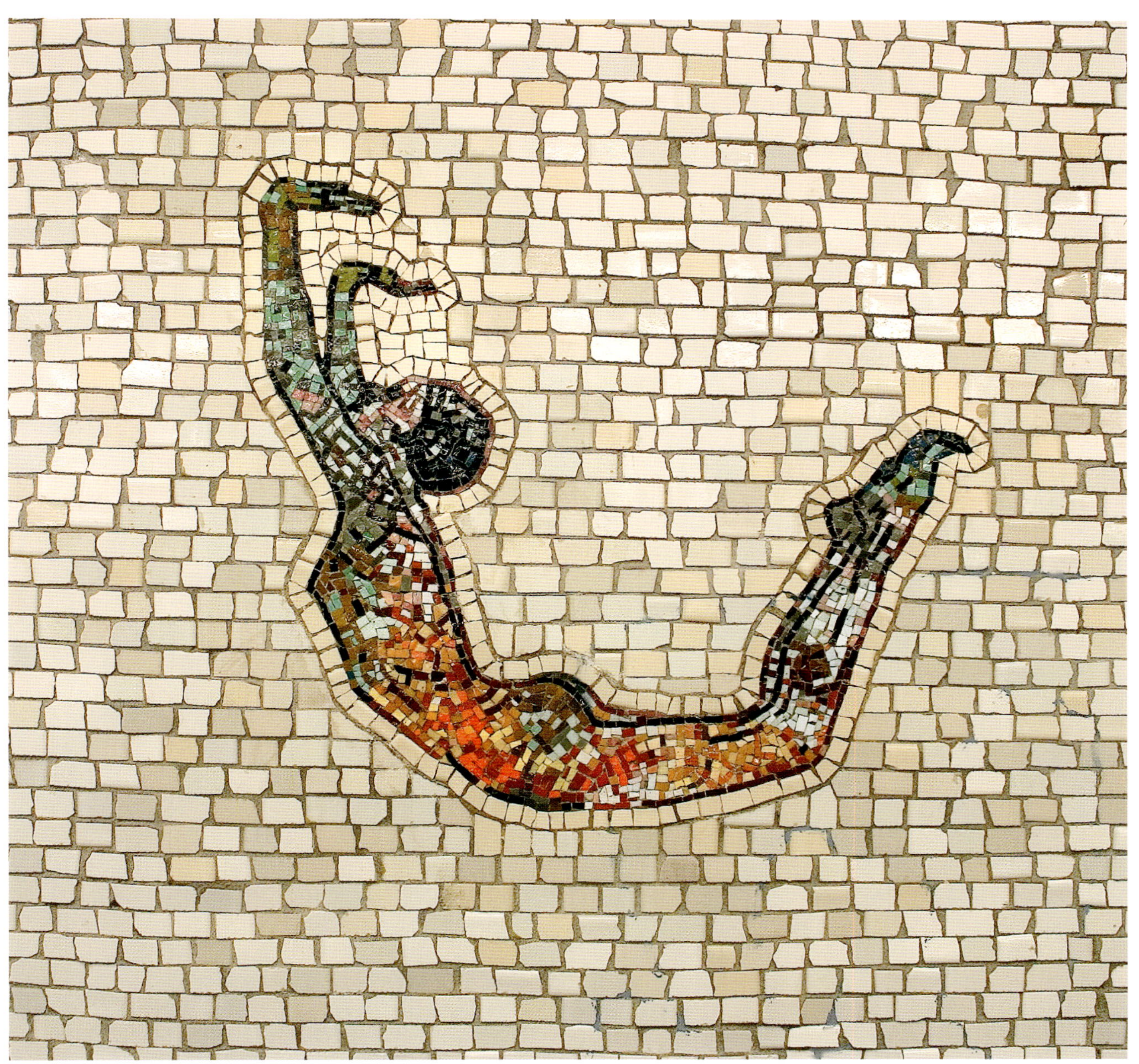

TOM OTTERNESS

in cooperation with Skidmore, Owings & Merrill

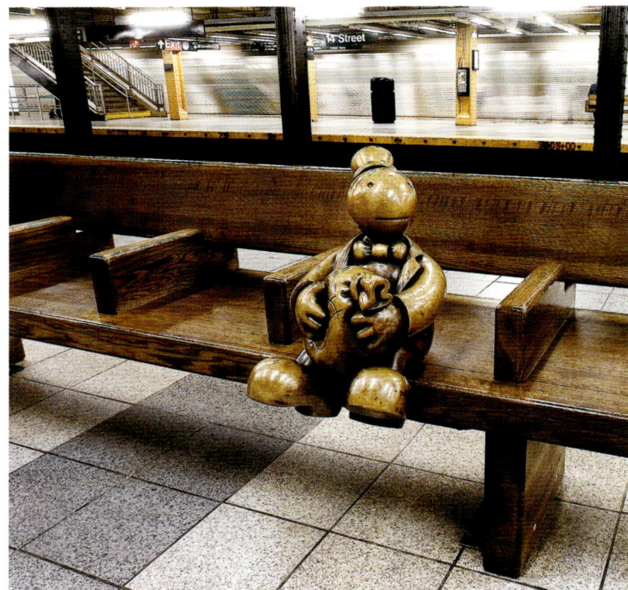

LIFE UNDERGROUND, 2001

14th Street–8th Avenue 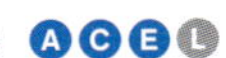

Bronze

PHOTOGRAPHERS: ROB WILSON (LEFT); PATRICK J. CASHIN (OPPOSITE)

Otterness's figures in *Life Underground* are humorous, captivating, and also a bit disconcerting. The subject he has chosen is the subway, its history and construction, and its place in the life of the city. Among the apparitions are an alligator poking its head through a sewer opening and consuming a man with a "money bag" head; colossal feet; and a totem-like sculpture whose human features are formed into the shape of a telephone. He has succeeded in invigorating an antiseptic environment and transforming it into a place of joy and whimsy. "I wanted to celebrate the monumental effort it took to create the system—an effort of both design and drudgery, of muscle and mind—and to represent the system as an underground world of its own, a subterranean cross-section of New York."

In the 14th Street station, these figures lurk in the stairwells; they dangle from the ceiling; they peer at riders from under barriers; they rest at the foot of pillars. Hints as to their meaning are given by their poses and expressions as well as the objects they carry or have with them; some are shown with tools to indicate they are subway workers and others are sidewalk superintendents, just observing. Others are intently sweeping up piles of coins, an allusion to the subject that seems to obsess New York more than any other. Indeed, the critique of money and pervasive consumer culture has often preoccupied Otterness. In all of his projects, however, as in *Life Underground*, the artist's touch is light and whimsical, making the art all the more effective for its deftness.

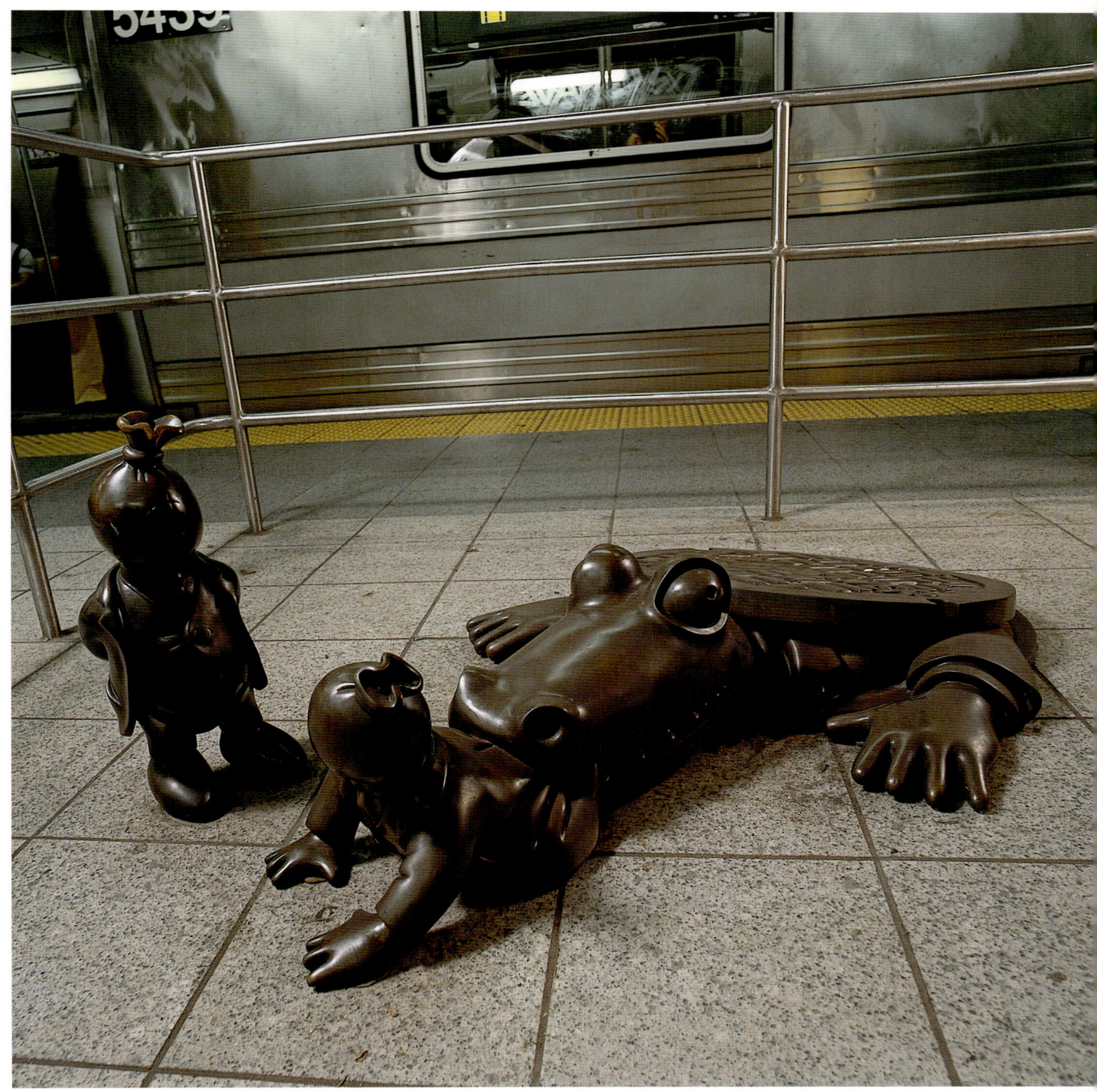

WALTER MARTIN and PALOMA MUÑOZ

A GATHERING, 2001

Canal Street 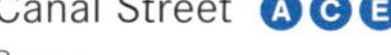

Bronze

PHOTOGRAPHER: ROB WILSON

Walter Martin and Paloma Muñoz have turned the Canal Street station into a scene that seems, at first glance, reminiscent of Alfred Hitchcock's *The Birds*. But the birds in *A Gathering* are comforting rather than menacing. There are 174 grackles and blackbirds, in a number of different poses, and seven crows, all cast in bronze and given a glossy black patinated coating. They stand in groups, like people waiting in the subway, thinking, conversing, or ignoring one another. Most of them can be found roosting on railings, watching and serving as companions to the flocks of people using the transportation system. Birds, the artists note, are very social creatures; riders may find echoes of themselves and other subway travelers in their lively, cocky, quizzical interactions.

Canal Street is a main artery of several busy neighborhoods—long-established Little Italy and Chinatown and the newer SoHo and Tribeca. But Canal Street is largely devoid of nature. The birds of *A Gathering* make up for this, enlivening the space and bringing relief from the sometimes oppressive commercialism of the area.

Walter Martin and Paloma Muñoz have collaborated for many years. As part of Arts for Transit's Lightbox Project, they installed their series of "Travelers" in the lower level of Grand Central Terminal. They created twenty sculptural vignettes and photographed them to appear to be snow globes, creating magical winter wonderlands.

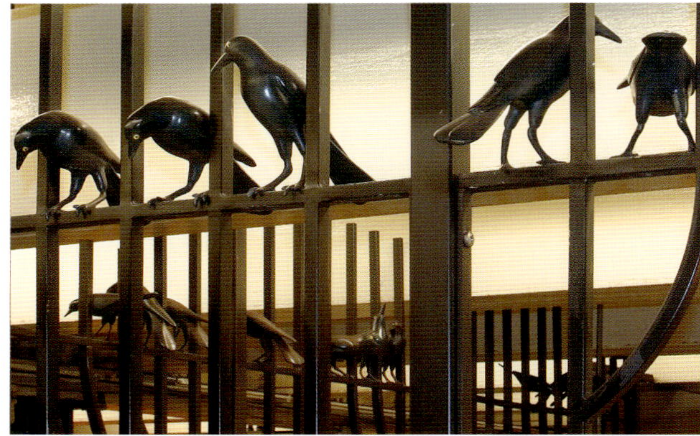

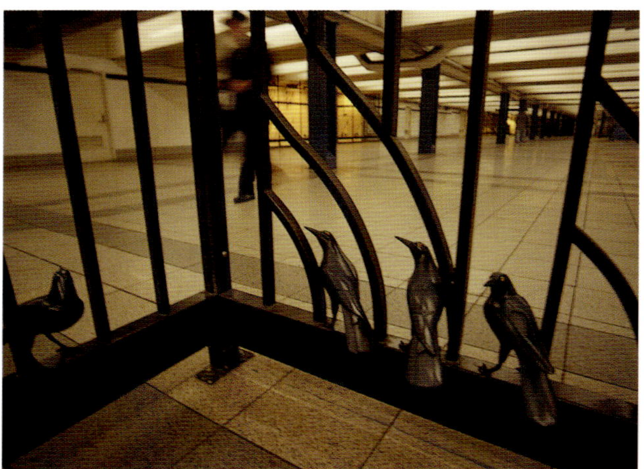

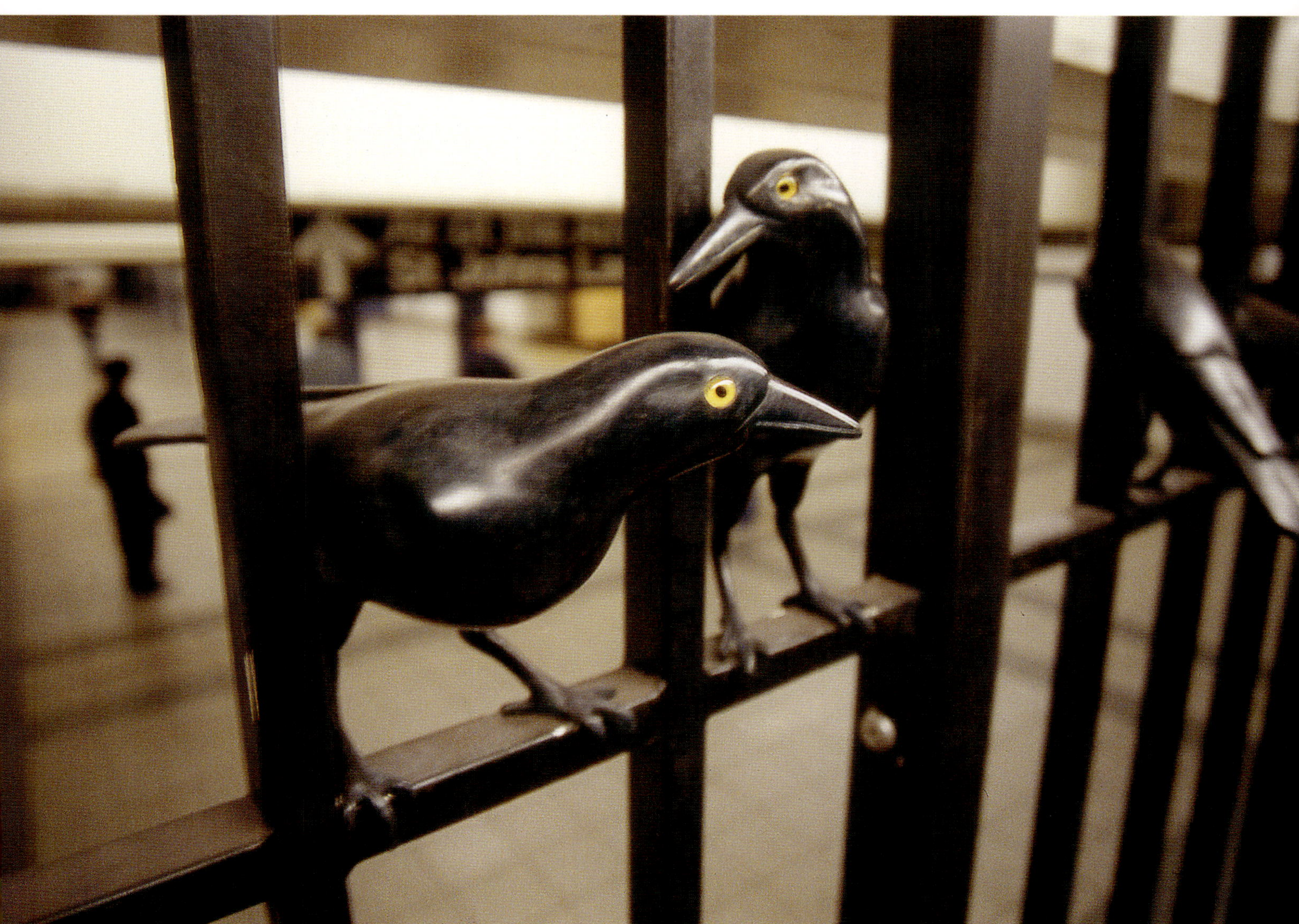

MARY MISS in collaboration with Lee Harris Pomeroy Architects

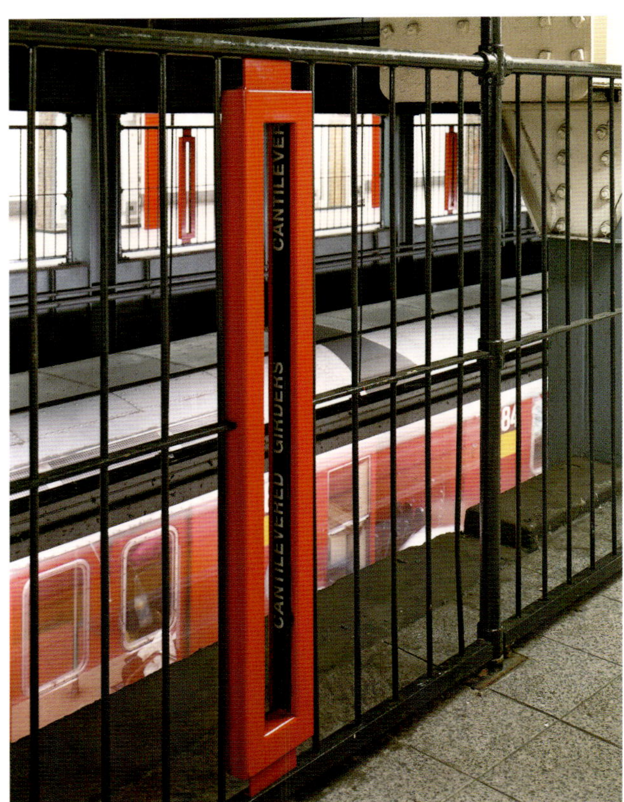

FRAMING UNION SQUARE, 1998

14th Street–Union Square L N Q R W 4 5 6

Glass, enameled steel, and aluminum

PHOTOGRAPHER: MICHAEL MORAN

Mary Miss is fascinated by the material remains of the recent past, and the oldest parts of the MTA transportation system provide an archaeological treasure trove. Working with architect Lee Harris Pomeroy, she has used the transformation of the Union Square station into a modern and efficient transit hub as an opportunity to explore, observe, learn, and teach. New construction at the site uncovered hidden wonders–structural elements, cables, and conduits–some of them still functional and others superseded by more modern improvements. Historic decorative work reappeared–mosaics, pilasters, and name plaques–including six eagles in terra-cotta dating from the 1904 station that had been out of view for decades.

Miss set out to share her findings with users of the station, drawing their attention to the previously hidden elements though a network of frames, windows, apertures, and mirrors to focus viewers' attention and invite them to ponder the changes that this environment has experienced over time. The immediacy of the bright red frames contrasts with the subtlety of the object–a bolt, a fragment of ancient-looking mosaic, a piece of rusted steel cable. A series of red slots inserted into the enameled black railings encourages travelers to look downward to the tracks, which reveal station design and technology. In her words, "I'm inviting the public to look below the surface, to see a 'slice' of the station, its structure, its history. In this most public of places, the apertures offer an intimate engagement. Looking in, you will see the station's workings–sometimes you will see layers of words and reflected images, including your own!"

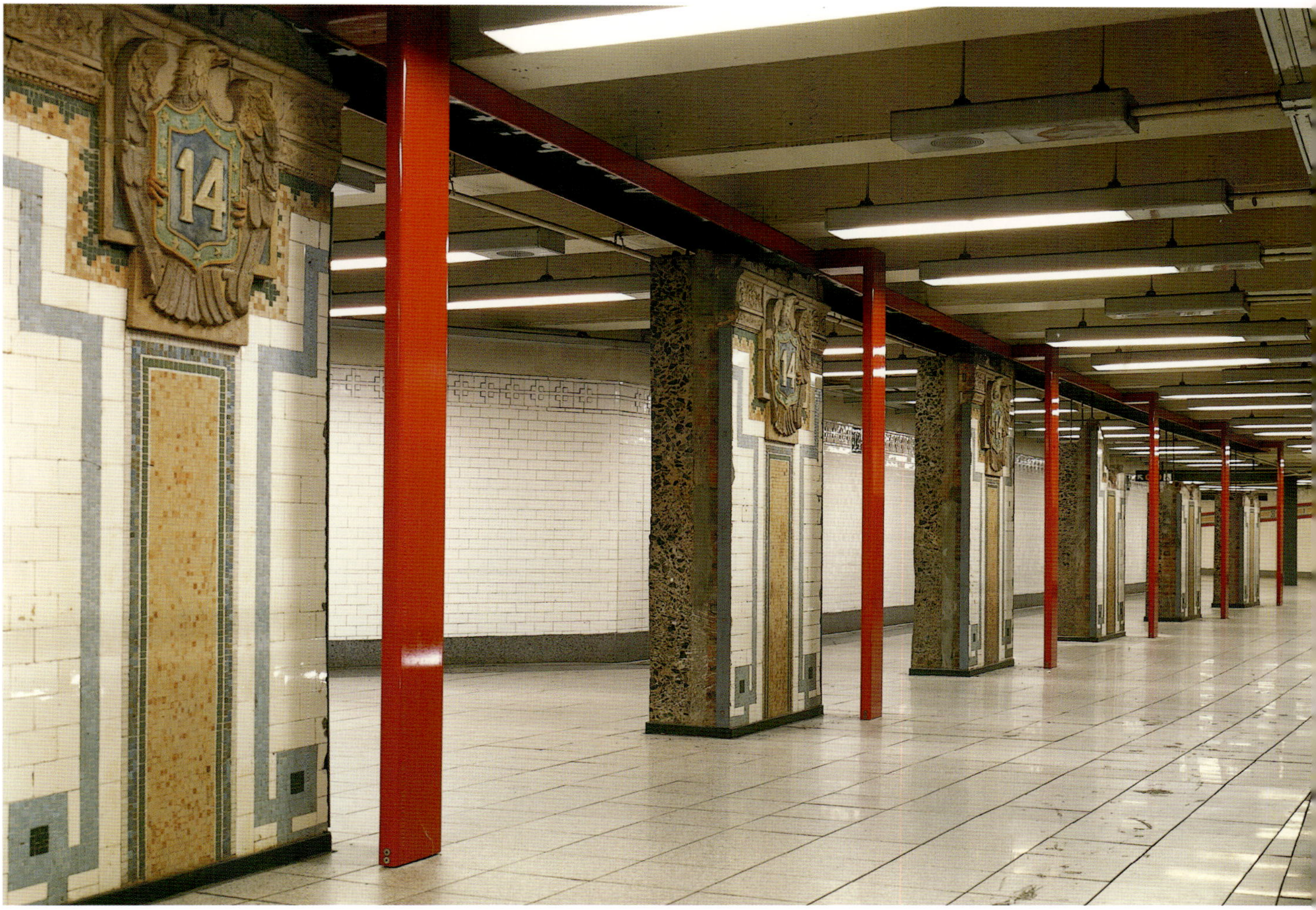

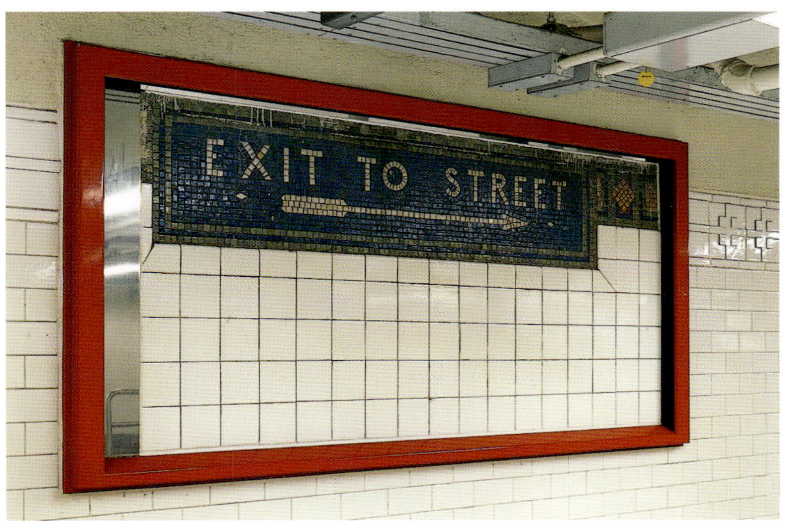
EXIT TO STREET

MILTON GLASER

in cooperation with Prentice & Chan, Olhausen Architects

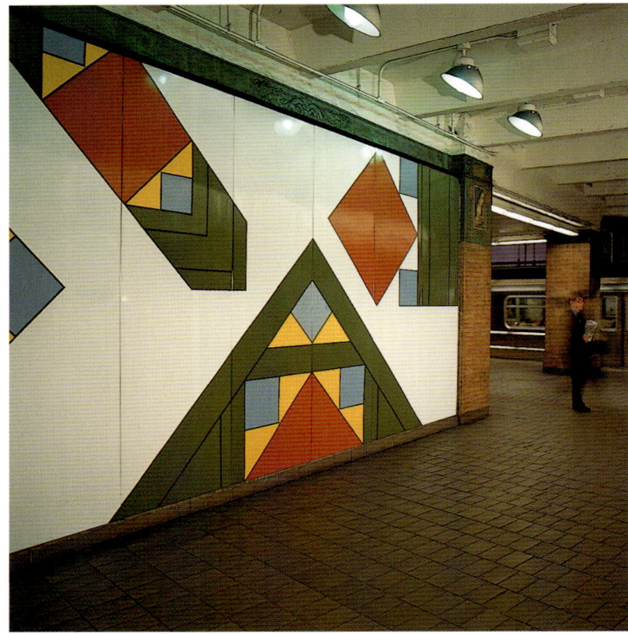

UNTITLED, 1986
Astor Place 6
Porcelain enamel
PHOTOGRAPHER: MICHAEL KAMBER

Milton Glaser, best known as a graphic designer and printmaker, was approached to complement Rolf Olhausen's architectural plans for the restoration and redesign of Astor Place station. This was an interesting challenge, since the station boasted some of the most beautiful historic terra-cotta and mosaics in the transportation system but at the same time required a large-scale redesign in order to make it function in today's world. Glaser's response was to meld the two: to use the historic Grueby Faience Company plaques (which depicted beavers, a reference to the origins of the Astor fur-trading fortune) as a springboard for his thoroughly modern design.

In the artist's words:

> The design concept . . . is basically a variation on the existing forms. By extracting fragments of the motifs on the tile panels, enlarging their scale, and placing these pieces in a random pattern, they take on the appearance of a large puzzle. Viewers may perceive these fragments and discover their relationship to the original design motifs. The resulting dialectic between the previously existing and the new panels inspires an appreciation for the original details of the station.

Glaser was born in New York and has long been at the very center of the city's cultural life. He was especially pleased to be asked to design a work for this particular station: "This was a wonderful commission, not just because of the proximity of Cooper Union, my alma mater. I lived on the Lower East Side for years, and it's good to see the old neighborhood coming back to life."

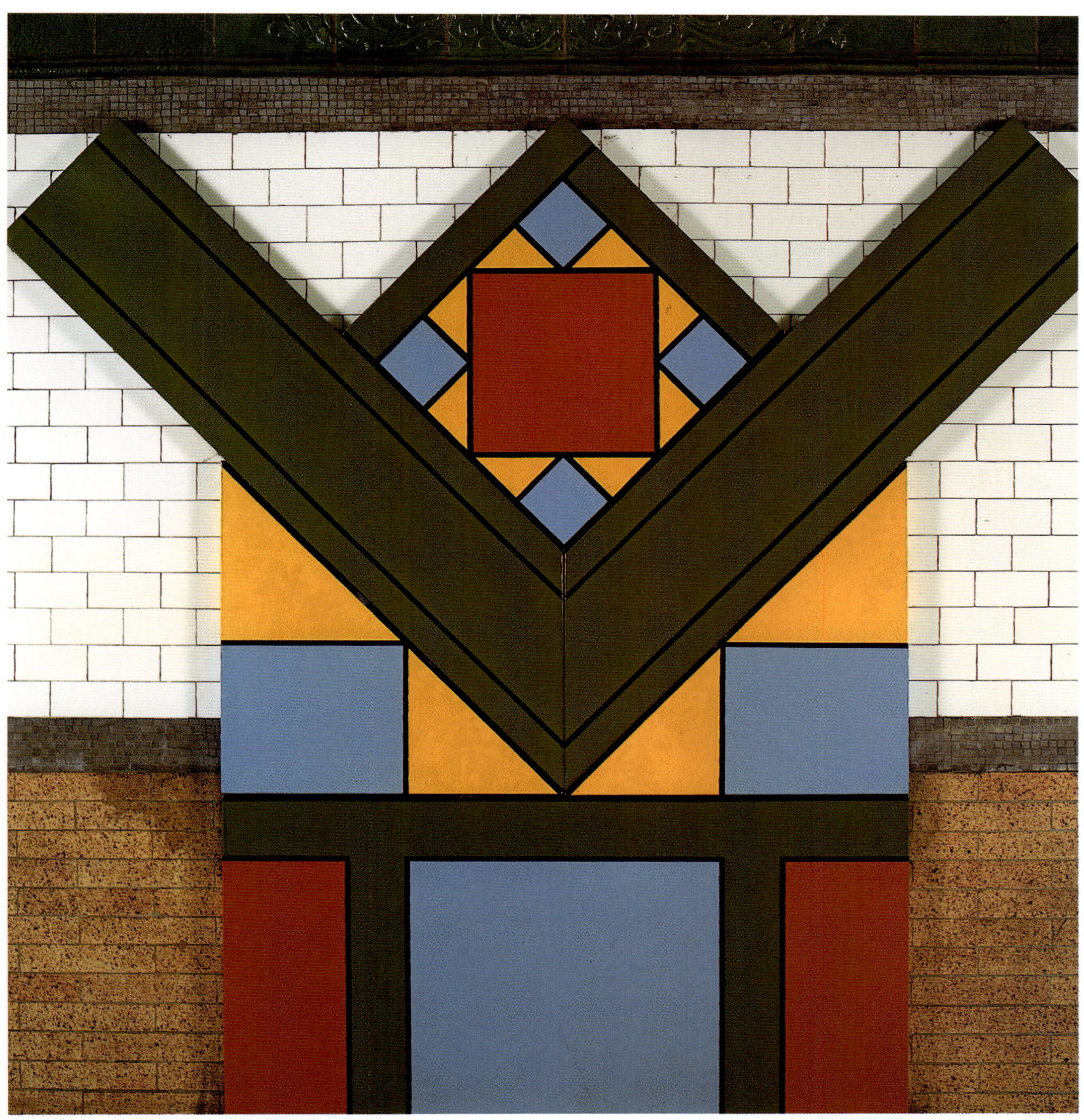

MEL CHIN

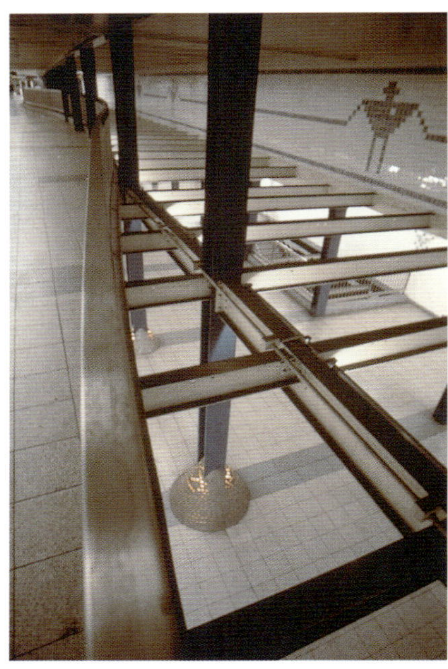

SIGNAL, 1997

Broadway-Lafayette Street B D F V

Stainless steel and glass; ceramic tile

PHOTOGRAPHER: ROB WILSON

Today Broadway and Lafayette mark an intersection of art and commerce, ringed with historic facades and glossy billboards. In *Signal*, Mel Chin, collaborating with Seneca tribe member Peter Jemison, draws upon the rich history of this crossroads, which once served as a trading route for the tribes of the Six Nations (Seneca, Cayuga, Onondaga, Mohawk, Tuscarora, and Oneida).

On the mezzanine walls are figures that represent the nations with outstretched arms reaching to one another. Below, on the main concourse, the conical forms at the bases of support pillars break up the severe geometry of the space and suggest campfires used to send signals.

Here lights within the cones brighten and dim as trains approach and depart. Patterns within the steel forms are based upon tribal badge patterns, which themselves were based upon a fusion of various cultures with which the tribes came in contact. Another historical overlay is seen in the tile patterns that surround the concourse; they evoke rising smoke while the pattern is inspired by an Iroquois message of peace.

Mel Chin is known for making art in unexpected places, including landfills and decaying buildings. He insists that art should "provoke greater social awareness and responsibility" and has been especially active in the movement to introduce art into inner-city communities.

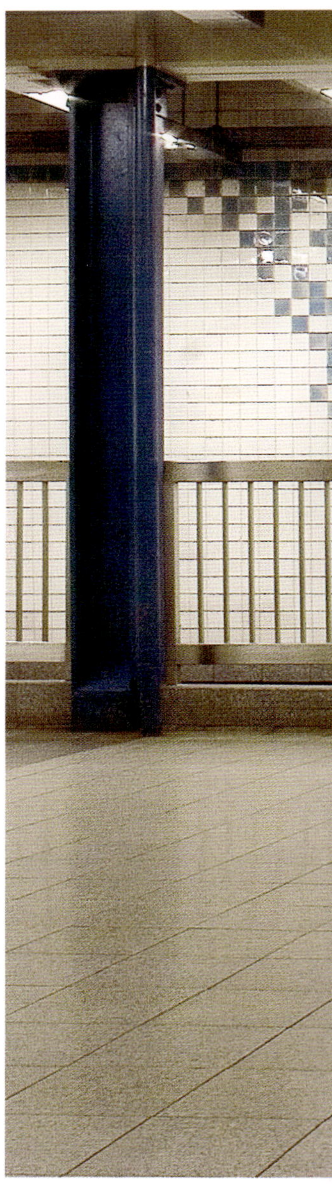

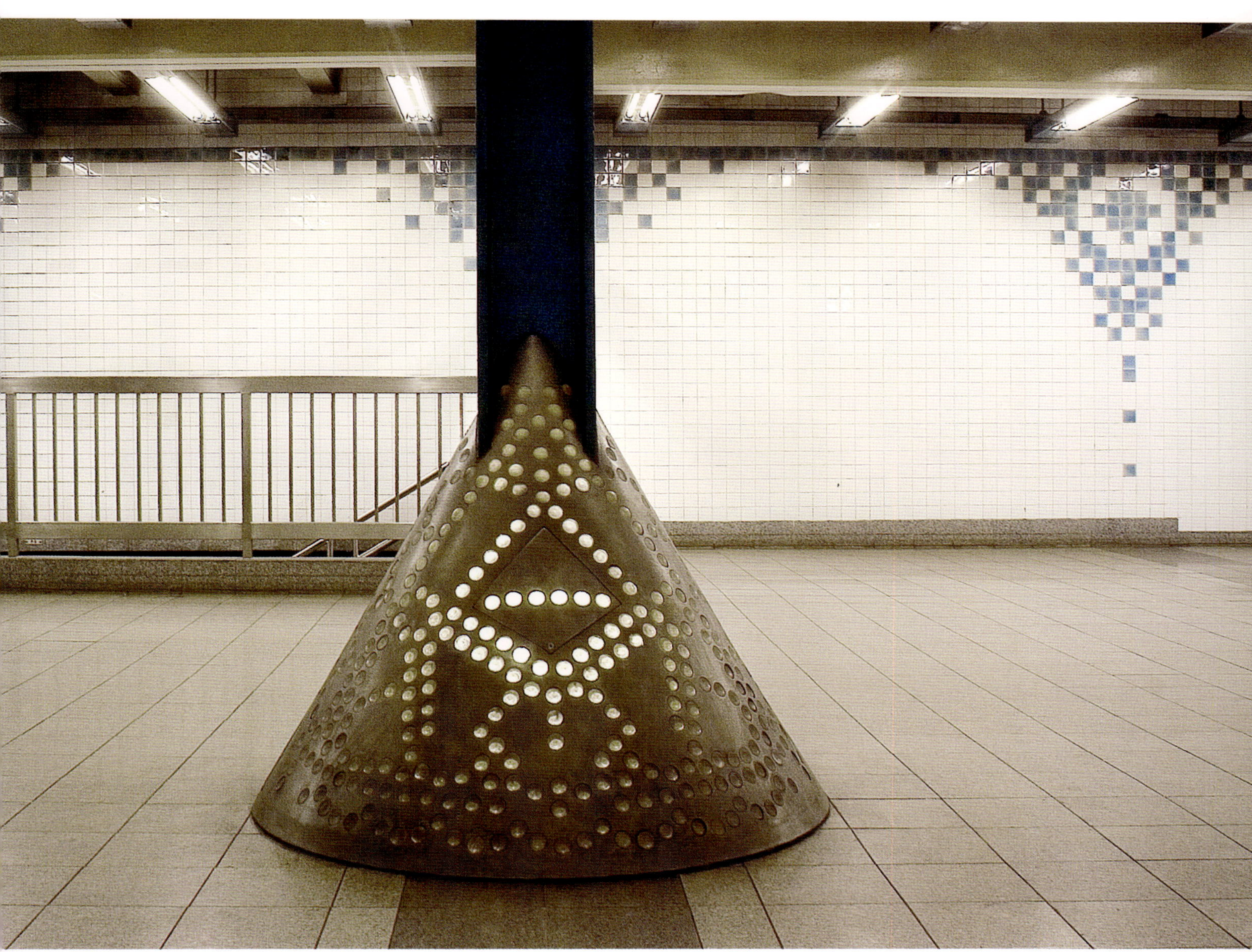

MING FAY

SHAD CROSSING, DELANCEY ORCHARD, 2004

Delancey Street–Essex Street 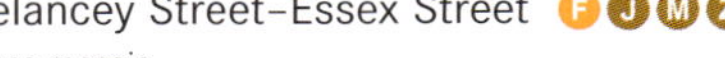

Glass mosaic

PHOTOGRAPHER: ROB WILSON

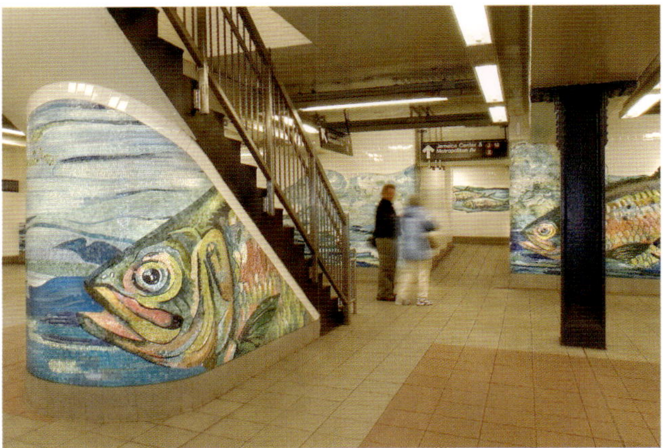

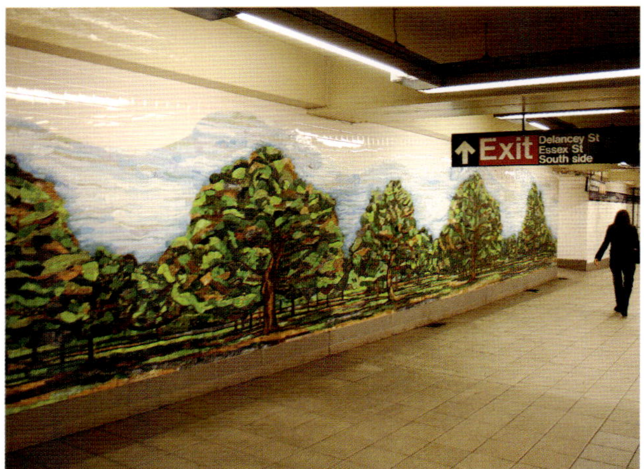

Ming Fay brings downstairs the busy marketplace that thrives in this Lower East Side neighborhood. Each mosaic has a pictorial theme; one features cherry trees and the other depicts giant shad, a fish of the herring family, swimming on a blue background. As with most of his public works, the artist undertook extensive research into the neighborhood's history—both its environmental and its man-made components.

Shad Crossing refers to the fish that were abundant in the Hudson River and familiar to new immigrants who settled on the Lower East Side in the late nineteenth century. The images celebrate the return of the shad to New York and water as a metaphor for "crossing," in this case, traveling or commuting to Brooklyn.

Delancey Orchard alludes to the DeLancey family farm, which once stretched from the Hudson River to the East River and included this area. The family's cherry grove was nearby, where Orchard Street is now located.

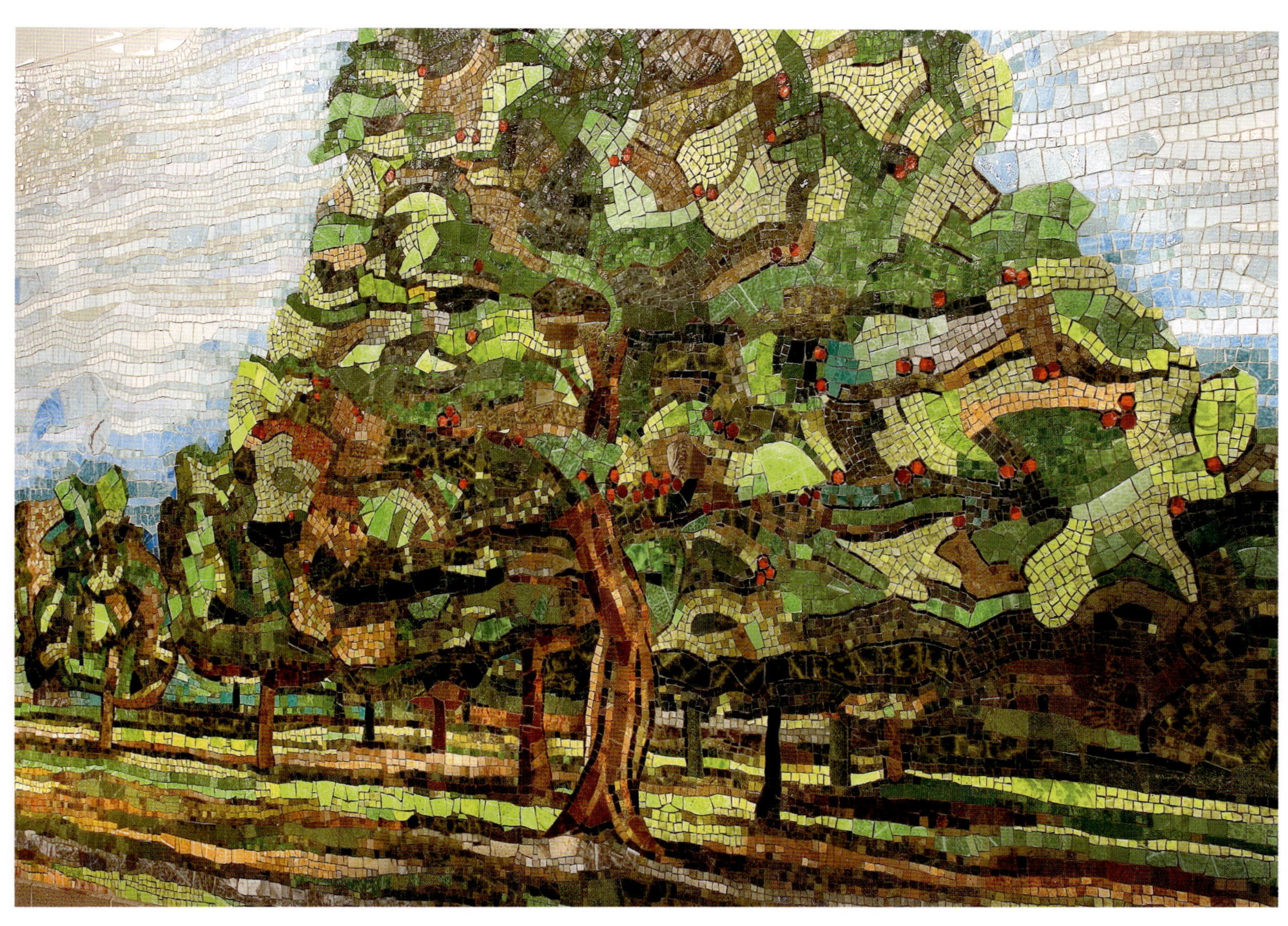

NANCY HOLT

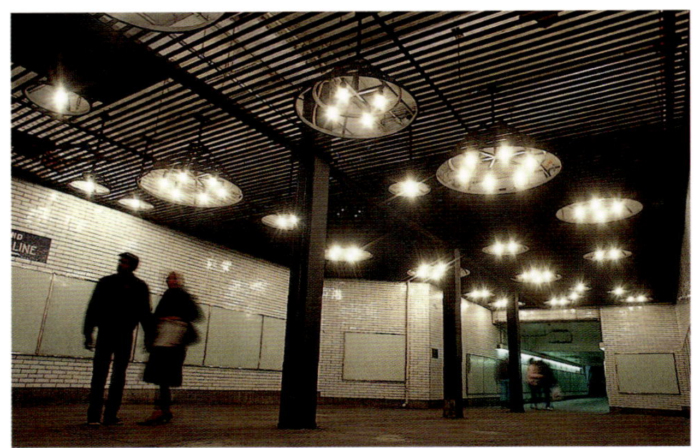

ASTRAL GRATING, 1987
Fulton Street–Broadway–Nassau A C J M Z 2 3 4 5
Steel and lighting
PHOTOGRAPHER: NANCY HOLT

An environmental artist, Nancy Holt creates art by giving physical form to universal cycles of the sun, moon, and stars. Previous work concentrating on the heavens has included her *Sun Tunnels* (Great Basin Desert, Utah, 1973–76), a site-specific work with four tunnels aligned to the rising and setting of the sun on the summer and winter solstices. Holt's *Dark Star Park* (Arlington, Virginia, 1979–84) is an urban renewal project consisting of pipes, tunnels, circular pools, and spheres that the artist thinks of as fallen stars.

In *Astral Grating*, Holt surrounded lights with graduated circular rings making domed openings in a dropped steel-grate ceiling. "The rings and light fixtures in this ceiling light sculpture are in the configuration of the stars in five constellations: Aries, Auriga, Canis Major, Cygnus and Piscis Austrinus," she explains. The number of lights in a cluster and the diameter of the domed openings vary in size according to the brightness of the stars represented.

Efforts are being made to incorporate *Astral Grating* into the reconfigured passageways in the new Fulton Street Transit Center.

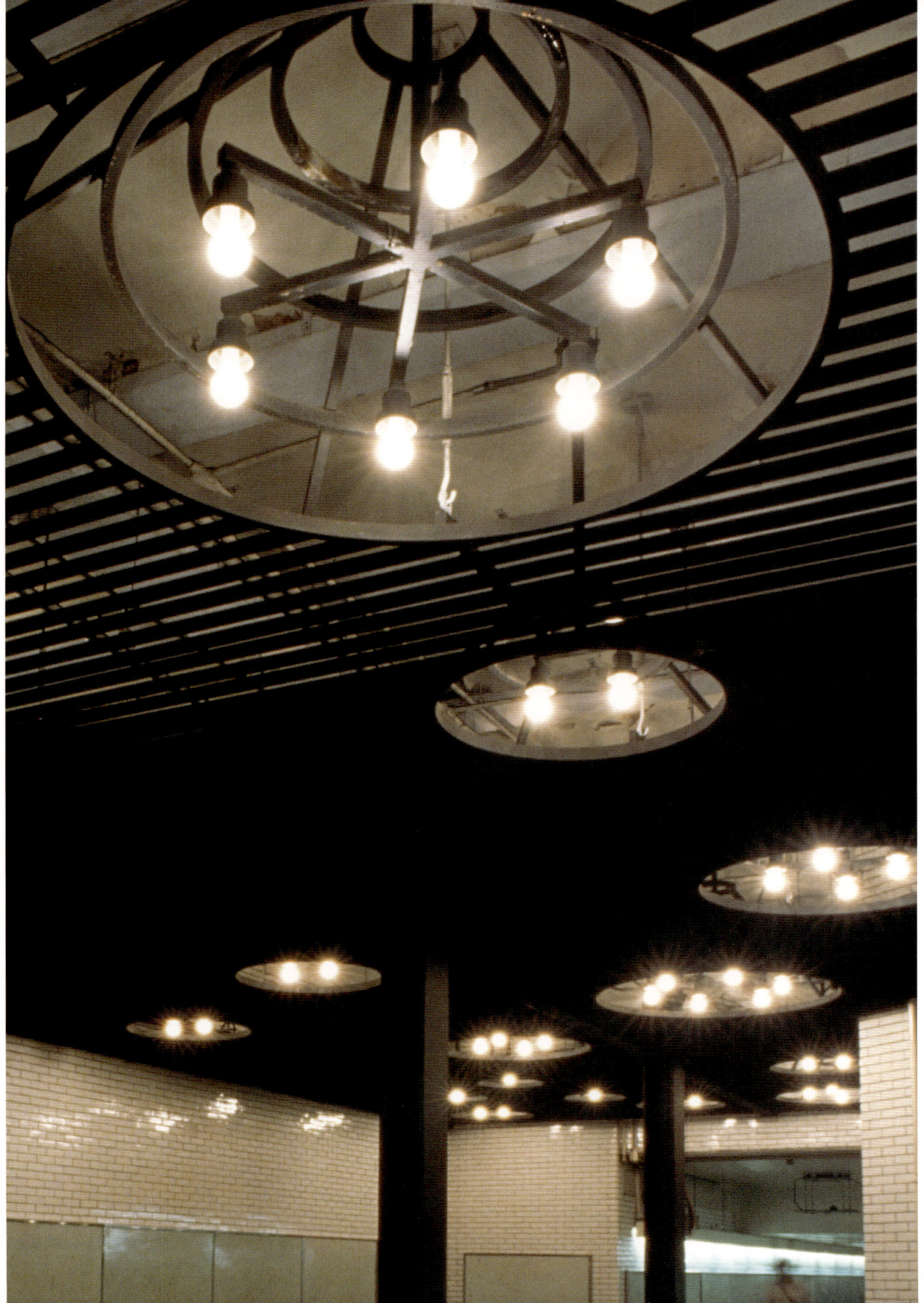

FREDERICK DANA MARSH

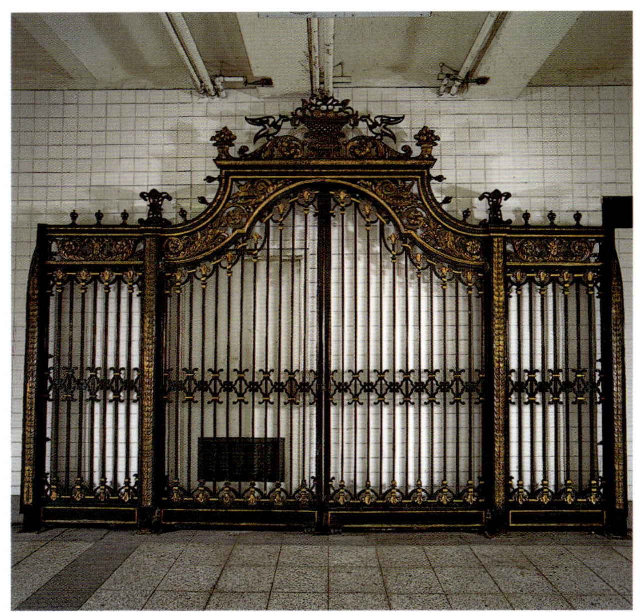

MARINE GRILL MURALS, 2000
(created 1912 for the McAlpin Hotel)
Fulton Street–Broadway–Nassau A C J M Z 2 3 4 5
Glazed terra-cotta, painted cast and wrought iron
PHOTOGRAPHER: PATRICK J. CASHIN

At the opening of the twentieth century, lavish hotels were built in New York to accommodate a prosperous new class of business travelers and tourists. The McAlpin was one of these. Located at 34th Street and Broadway, it set a new standard of luxury, becoming one of the places to see and be seen. In 1912, Frederick Dana Marsh created a series of twenty terra-cotta murals for its restaurant, all with maritime themes in celebration of the importance of New York as a seaport.

Atlantic Terra Cotta Company on Staten Island fabricated the murals. Converting Marsh's drawings to clay was a complex process that required enlarging the original art, creating a complete version in clay, and then cutting this apart to create a plaster mold for each piece, so that multiple copies of each mural could be made. Each piece was then glazed and fired a number of times, resulting in a much finer and more nuanced work than is usually the case with decorative terra-cotta.

When the hotel was converted into cooperative apartments, the murals were taken to storage, where they remained for a decade, under the guardianship of the Landmarks Preservation Commission. In 2000, six were installed at the Fulton-Broadway station along with the ironwork entrance gate from the Marine Grill. All of this blends perfectly, both aesthetically and philosophically, with the terra-cotta murals installed elsewhere in the system by the original builders of the subway.

As part of the rebuilding of the Fulton Street Transit Center, the murals will be moved to the William Street entrance.

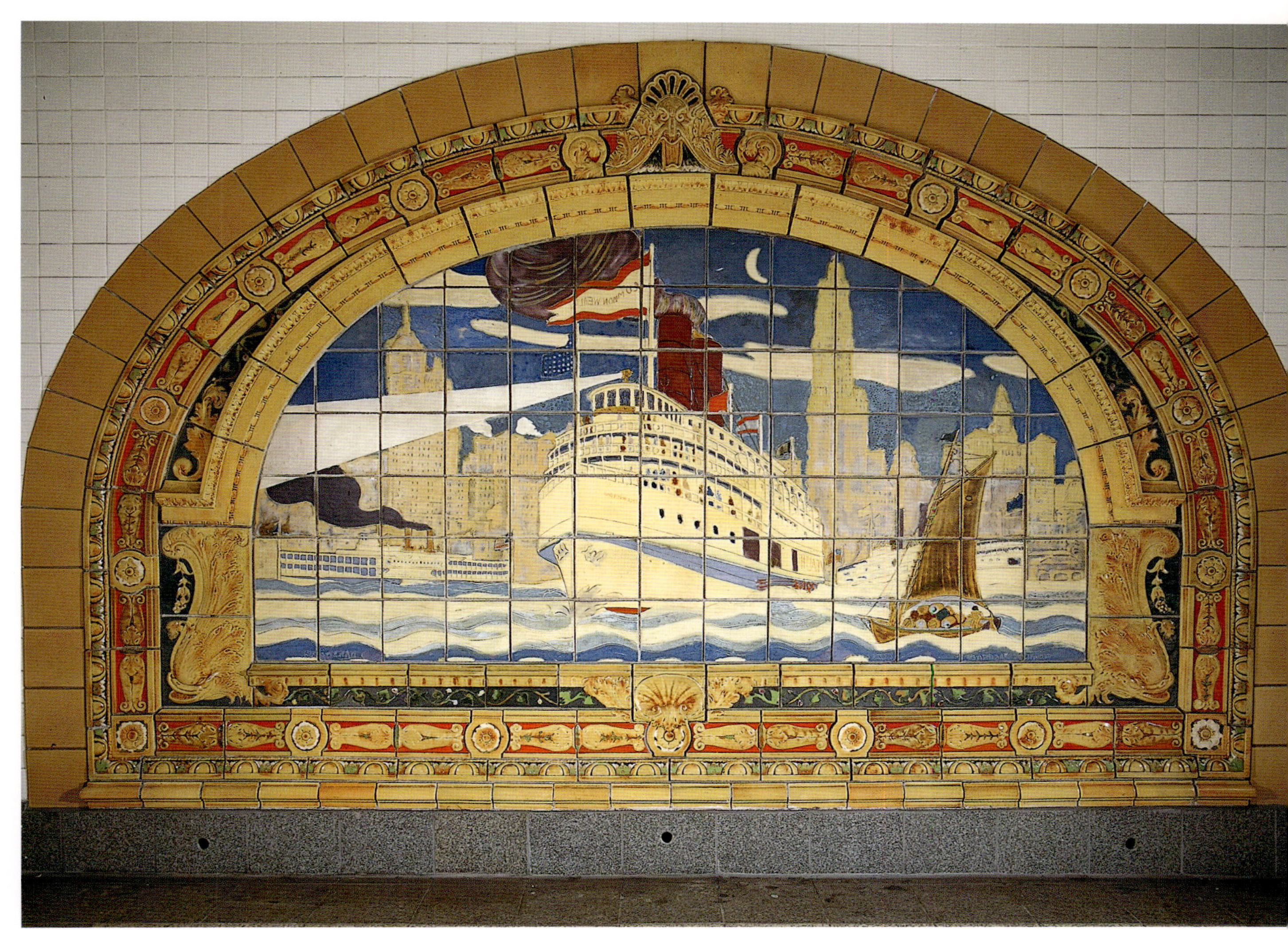

MARGIE HUGHTO

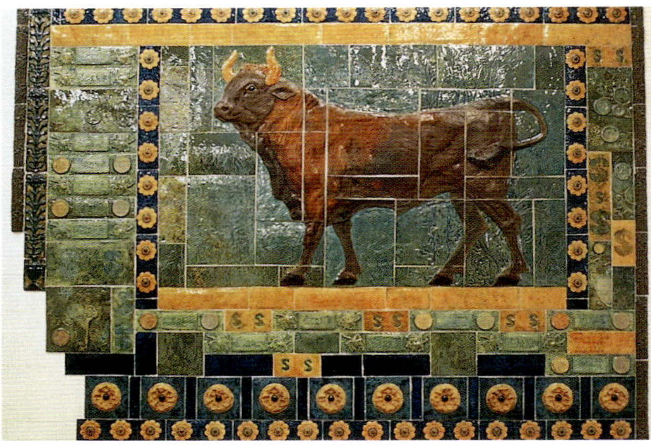

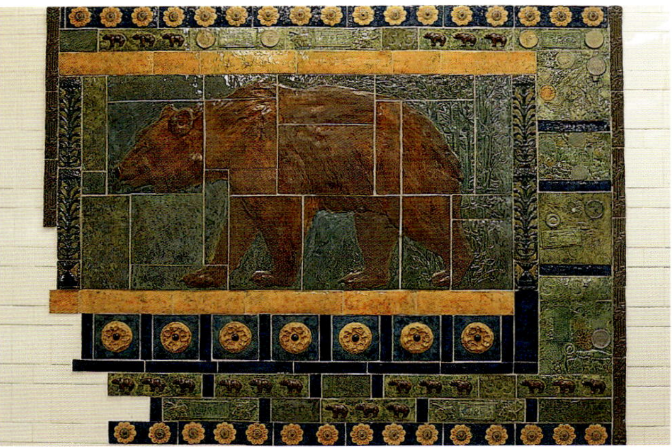

TRADE, TREASURE, AND TRAVEL, 2005
Cortlandt Street R W
Ceramic relief tiles
PHOTOGRAPHER: MICHAEL KAMBER

Margie Hughto's ceramic relief tiles survived the destruction of the World Trade Center, and they will be reinstalled in the new connecting passage between the Cortlandt Street station and the nearby Fulton Street Transit Center complex.

Trade, Treasure, and Travel recalls a much earlier time in the financial district, when Cortlandt Street ended at a busy ferry landing on the Hudson River. The artist says, "I thought about all the different peoples, products, objects and money that passed through the area, and I visualized a treasure vault filled with coins, gems, and artifacts–rich, golden, glowing, and somewhat mysterious."

The work consists of twelve separate but thematically related relief panels in ceramic tiles. In keeping with the focus on the distant past, the edges were given a rough, worn look. All sorts of objects connected with finance and trade–coins, compasses, boats, streetcars, keys, and ships–are incorporated as well as creatures connected with the sea and trade. These consist of both the real (horses, lions, tortoises, fish) and the mythical (griffins and a sphinx). A central image features a bull and a bear, the financial world's warring mascots, and a large old-fashioned compass and a chart of the stars by which mariners found their way.

The *Trade, Treasure, and Travel* reliefs were made in Hughto's studio in Jamestown, New York, by the artist, who was assisted by art students from the School of Art and Design at Syracuse University.

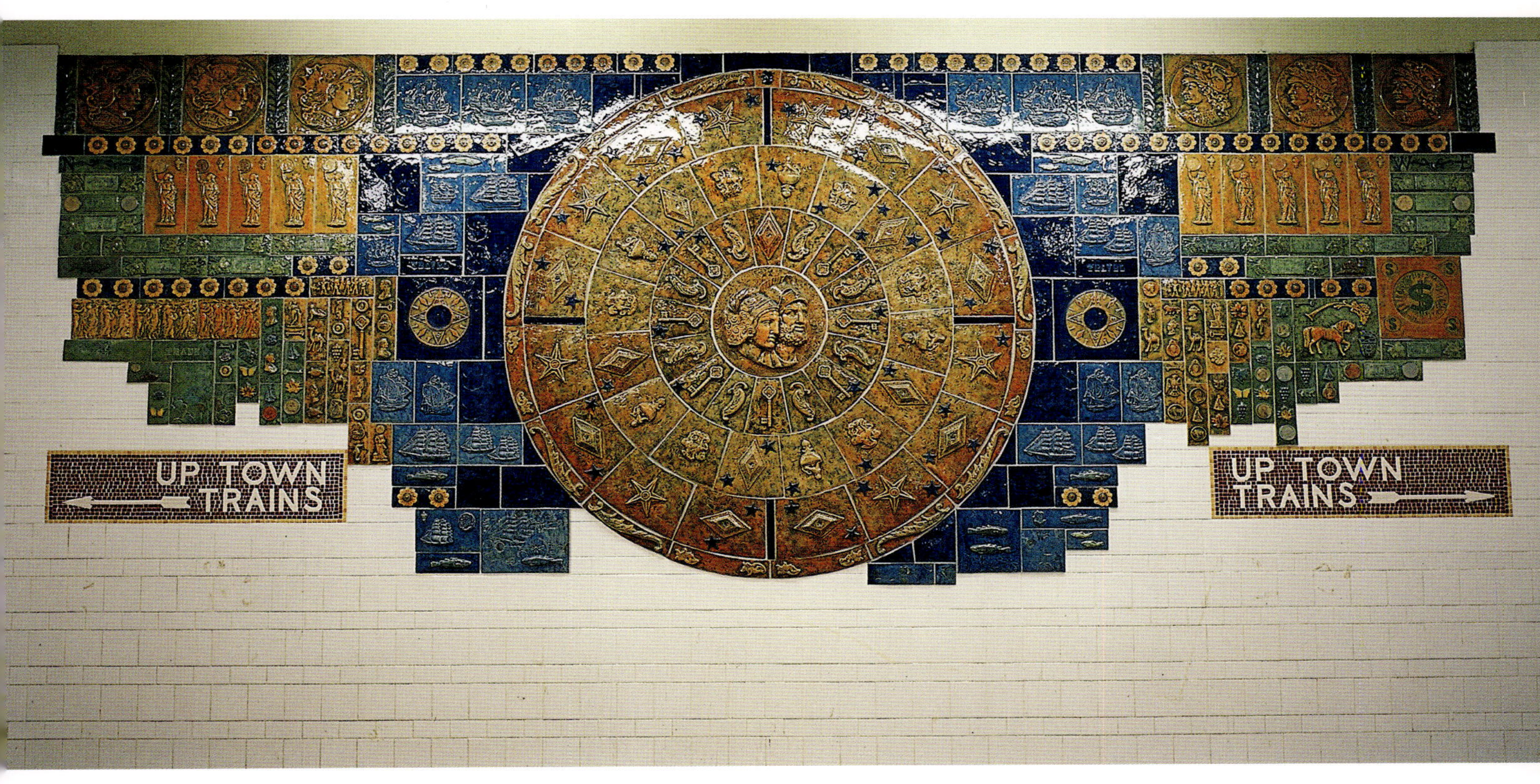
UP TOWN
TRAINS
UP TOWN
TRAINS

ANDREW GINZEL/KRISTEN JONES

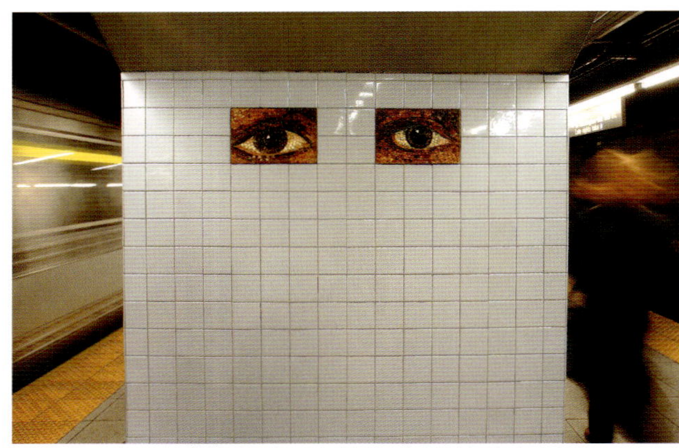

OCULUS, 1998

Chambers Street A C Park Place 2 3

Stone and glass mosaic

PHOTOGRAPHERS: ROB WILSON (LEFT); MICHAEL KAMBER (OPPOSITE)

This ambitious work, composed of more than three hundred mosaic renderings, responded to the need to make some sort of order out of the station's subterranean passages. Ginzel and Jones decided to make the oculus their central symbol. In their words, "*Oculus* was created to personalize and integrate the stations. Eyes are both subtle and strong—they engage passing individuals, allowing for meditation or inviting dialogue. People make the choice, but either way they're drawn into a dynamic and connected with the environment."

The eyes are not imaginary ones; they are derived from photographs taken in New York by the artists: "*Oculus* animates the underground world, it harmonizes and challenges, even as it reflects New York's wonderful diversity and the diversity of the larger world."

An enormous central eye grounds the composition. Set into the station floor, among circlets of stone and colored glass tiles, a map of the city is ingeniously incorporated into the design. And the eyes radiating out from it are seemingly omnipresent. Travelers making their way through the maze are never alone; there is always a reassuring eye to keep them company, note the artists. Or, as Ginzel says, "Because there is always a mosaic image within immediate view the public senses a continuity throughout the station environment."

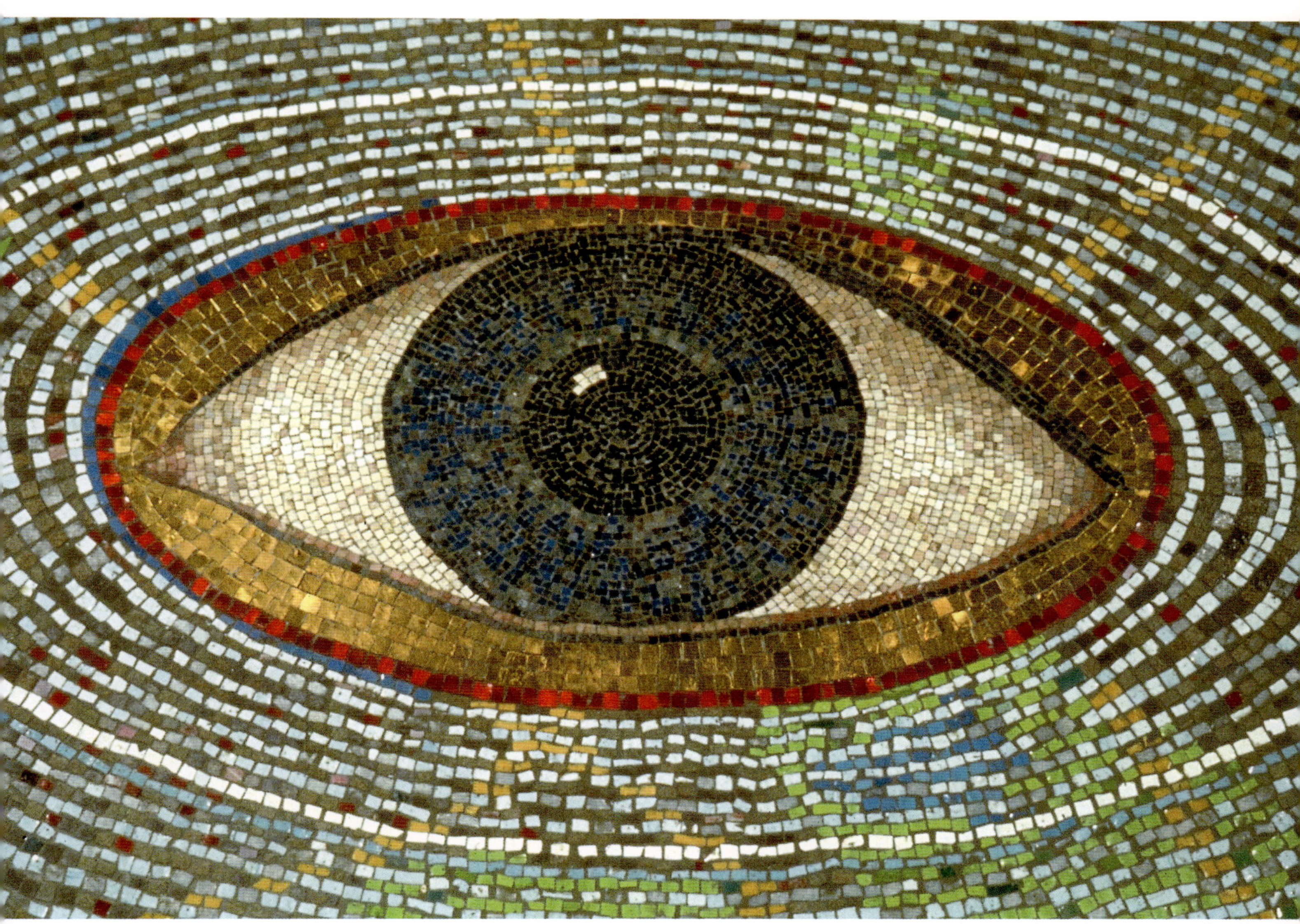

R. M. FISCHER

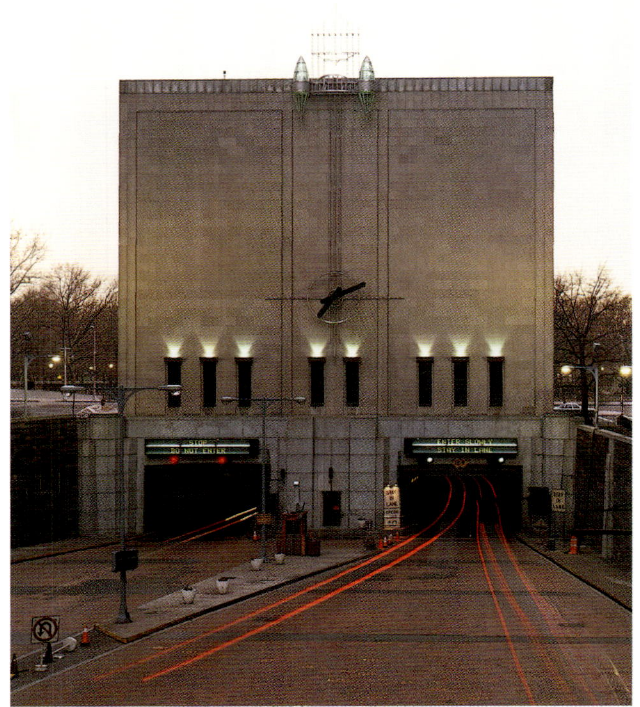

BROOKLYN-BATTERY TUNNEL CLOCK, 1992
Brooklyn Battery Tunnel, MTA Bridges and Tunnels
Stainless steel and aluminum, lighting
PHOTOGRAPHER: PAUL WARCHOL

The neo-deco forms of this wall sculpture respond to the architectural character of the tunnel ventilation building on which it is installed. In the artist's words, the clock's "traditional form and function offer a sense of anticipation, and its sculptural presence instills a sense of wonder by day and at night." Commissioned to mark the tunnel's fortieth anniversary, the sculpture announces the time and offers a glowing welcome.

In the 1970s, R. M. Fischer began working on assemblages of industrial objects, transforming them into sculptures with a futuristic look. Many of these were made from scavenged, salvaged, and reused metal parts. In the words of a critic writing in *Art in America*, "At once nostalgic and futuristic, his wacky inventions transform the mundane and prefabricated into the unique and fantastic." Clocks were often incorporated in these earlier works; in *Brooklyn-Battery Tunnel Clock* Fischer achieves the same result, if in a more serious vein, but here he has used new materials.

"Tunnels are also processional gateways, and my work celebrates the passage from one New York City borough to another," Fischer explains. The sculptures seen by drivers entering the tunnel on their way to Brooklyn evoke Coney Island and its famous amusement parks. Through the choice of materials, scale and design of the installation, and the lighting treatment, the sculpture and the architecture become a single, unified composition.

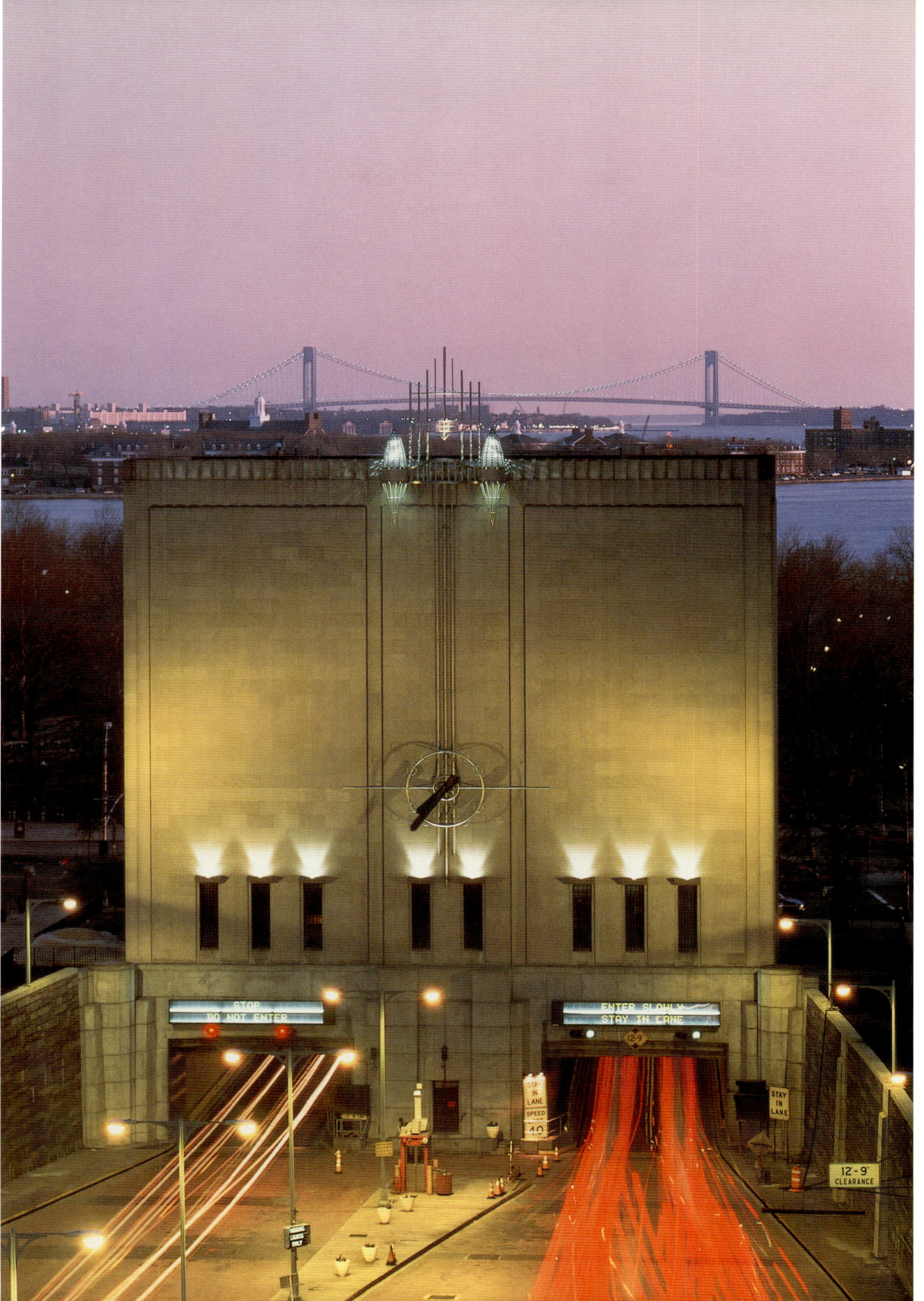
STOP
DO NOT ENTER
ENTER SLOWLY
STAY IN LANE
12-9
STAY IN LANE
SPEED
40
STAY IN LANE
12'-9"
CLEARANCE

ELLEN HARVEY in cooperation with William Nicholas Bodouva + Associates

LOOK UP, NOT DOWN, 2005
Queens Plaza E G R V
Glass mosaic
PHOTOGRAPHER: JAN BARACZ

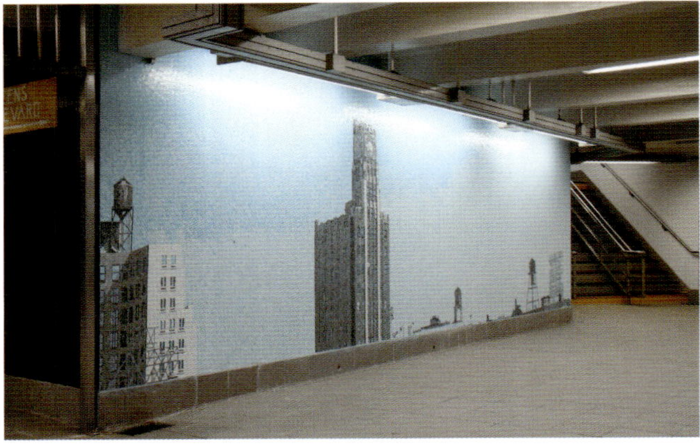

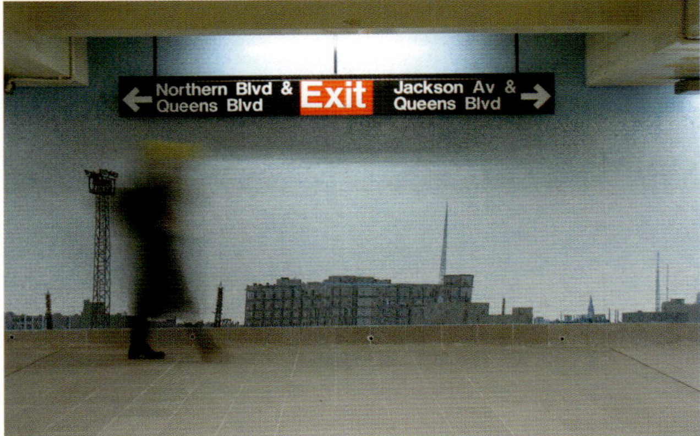

In *Look Up, Not Down* Ellen Harvey asks riders to pretend that they are gazing skyward, to imagine the panorama that they would see if they could hover immediately above the station and look up. Her mosaics represent the New York skyline as a thin, almost insignificant edge at the bottom of each mural that is otherwise filled with sky; human accomplishments are dwarfed by the immensity of nature.

For many Queens riders, Long Island City is at least as important as Grand Central. In a way, Harvey's artwork can be seen as a counterpart of the terminal's famous ceiling. And it is more practical since the landmarks in the mosaics help subway riders to orient themselves in the station and in the city.

Queens is portrayed as an important focal point from which the city's looming silhouette can be viewed. At a time when images of the skyline can be associated with tragedy, *Look Up, Not Down* tries to reclaim the skyline as an image of hope and beauty. The sun marks the former location of the World Trade Center, reminding us that nothing is absolute. In years to come, as the city continues to reinvent itself, the mosaics will serve as a view of a vanished moment in time.

Harvey's work includes video, installation art, and painting. It is, she says, "generally concerned with the theoretical and social implications" of art. In her 2001 *New York Beautification Project* she explored these concerns in the streets, in a transgressive way but with redeeming social virtue; at forty sites throughout the city, she painted oval-shaped traditional landscape paintings–but all on top of defaced surfaces.

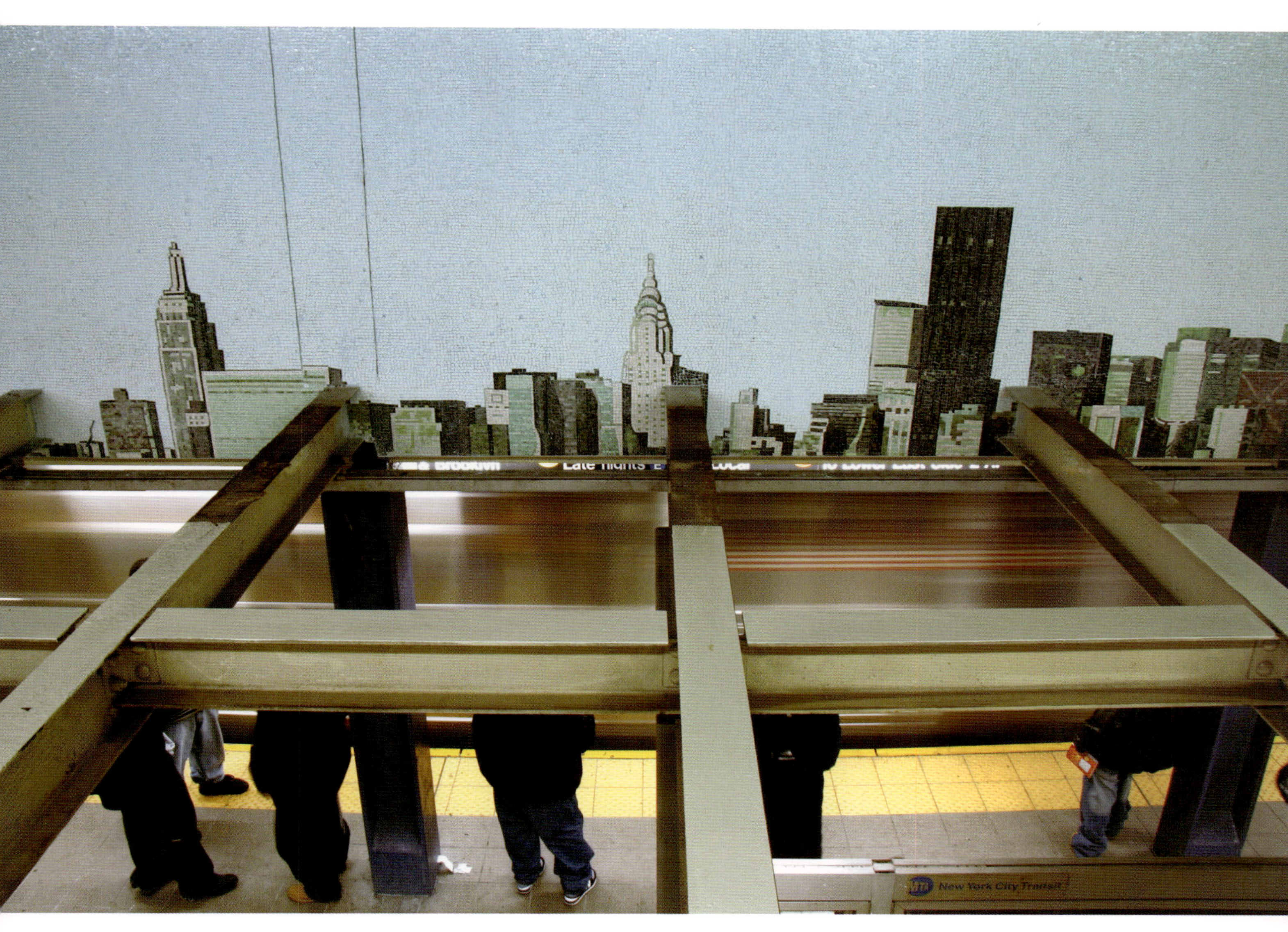
New York City Transit

ELIZABETH MURRAY

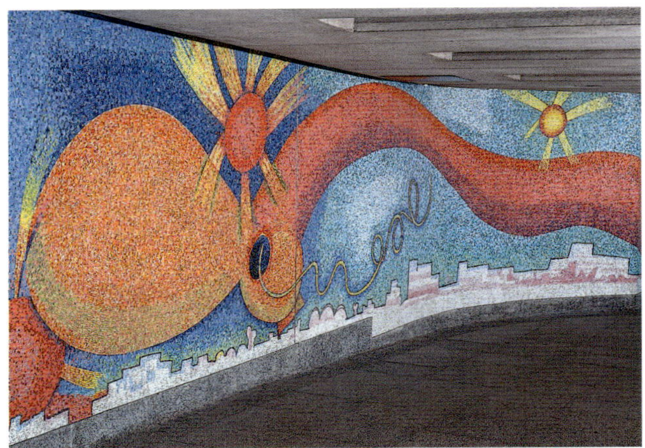

STREAM, 2001

23rd Street-Ely Avenue, Long Island City-Court Square 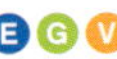 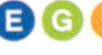

Glass mosaic

PHOTOGRAPHERS: JEFFREY STURGES (LEFT); DAVID ALLISON (RIGHT)

A giant foot rests on a skyline view of Long Island City; accompanying images evoke a storm, as well as the sun after the storm. Feet follow riders everywhere throughout the Court Square subway station. Elizabeth Murray intends the title *Stream* to evoke feet as they stream out along the passageway. Initially the artist had planned to create a totally abstract work, but she eventually decided to use imagery related to her earlier mural, *Blooming* (see page 44).

This is not the first time Murray has moved from total abstraction to representation. Her early work included simple, colorful abstract forms and lines, but she soon introduced familiar shapes and forms as well. For the subway pieces, Murray kept her audience in mind as she created these magical forms that connect spaces as people travel through them. They also connect viewers with the spirit of the artist as mosaic tesserae in vibrant colors fill the walls. Murray has said that she embraces the changes that occur during her process, that in fact change is integral to her working method. The changes that occur are part of the art. What could be more fitting in a space that is constantly changing throughout the day with the sea of people passing by?

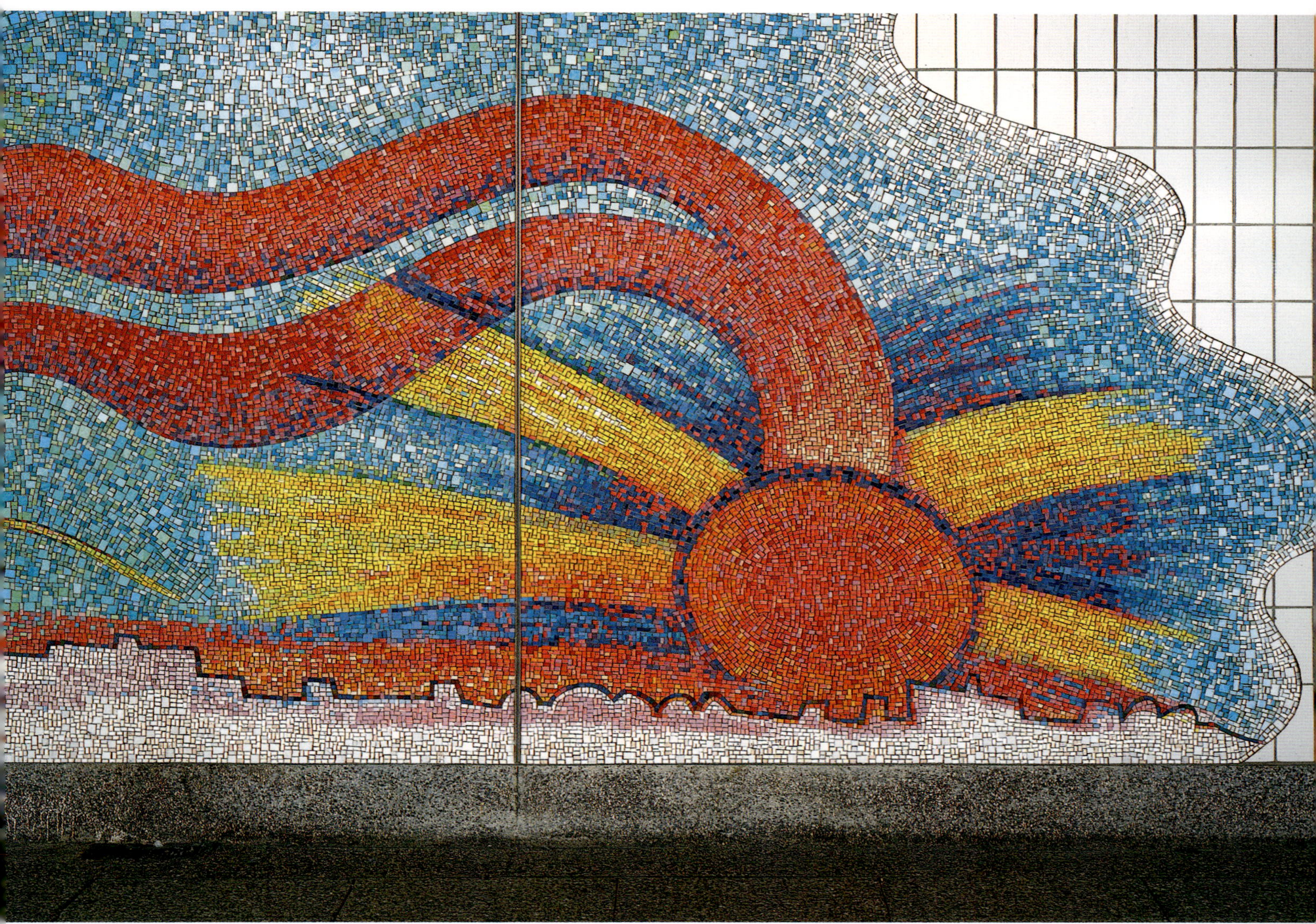

TOM PATTI in cooperation with FXFOWLE

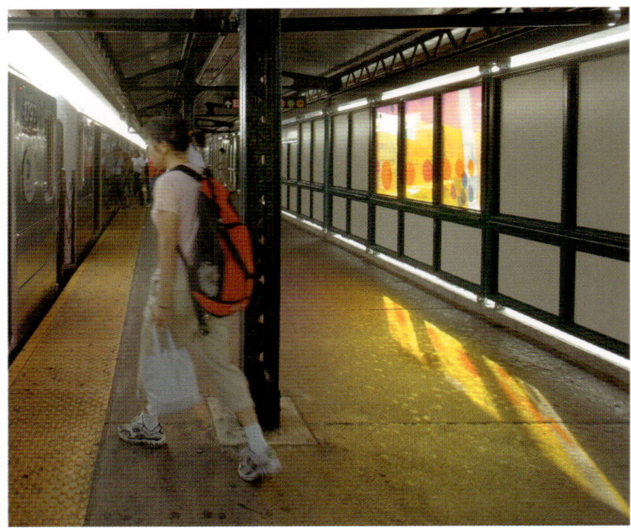

PASSAGE, 2004
74th Street–Broadway–Jackson Heights–Roosevelt Avenue
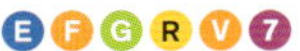

Glass
PHOTOGRAPHERS: DAVID SUNDBERG/ESTO (LEFT AND OPPOSITE BOTTOM); PAUL ROCHELEAU (OPPOSITE TOP)

Passage presents a unique view of a bustling, diverse community. As Patti has observed, *Passage* complements its neighborhood, and vice versa, its design influenced by the markets, flowers, and colors on the streetscape above.

The windowlike work was designed in tandem with the architects FXFOWLE to be seen as an integral part of the curved station wall. The trapezoidal windows are operable, admitting fresh air into the subway forty-five feet below.

Tom Patti is widely acknowledged as a pioneer for his integration of industrial and architectural glass into works of art. "The ability of glass to occupy several physical states—transparent, opaque, dense, solid, weightless, all altering our spatial boundary—challenges me," he says.

All of *Passage*'s components were handmade in Patti's studio. The laminated, impact-resistant security glass is layered with a plasma composite material to break up light into the colors of the spectrum.

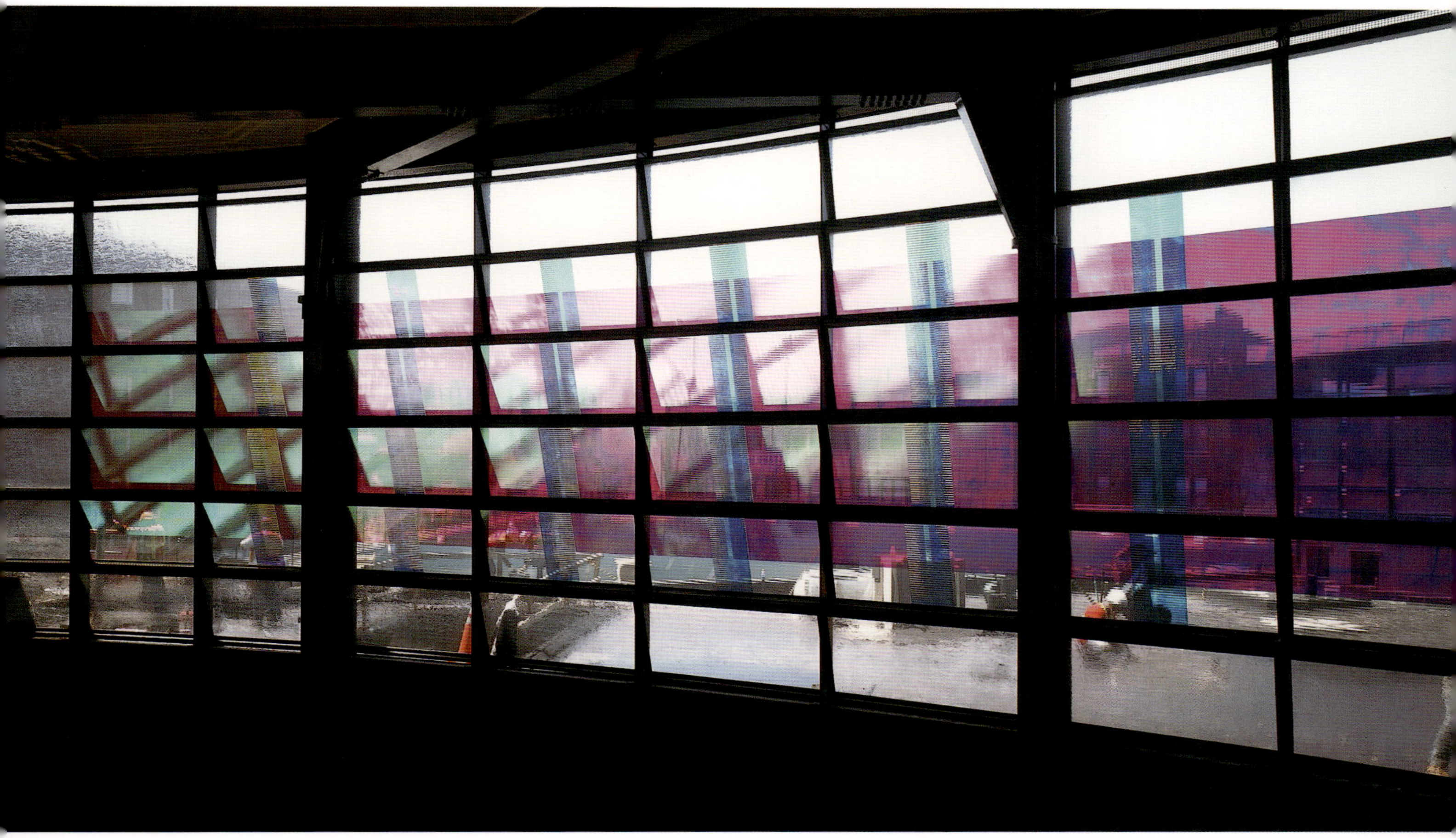

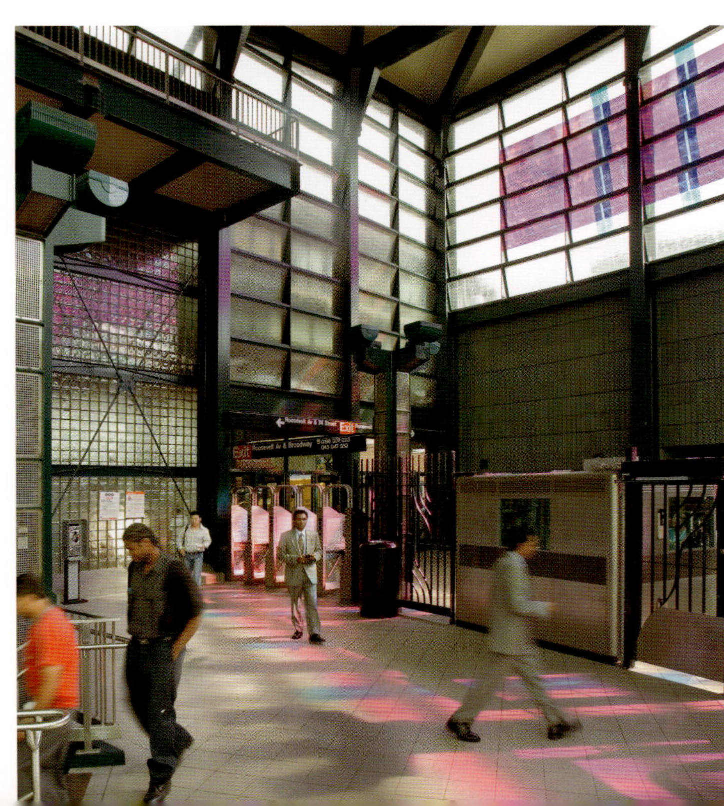
Roosevelt Av & 74 Street
Exit
Exit
Roosevelt Av & Broadway

IK-JOONG KANG

HAPPY WORLD, 1999

Flushing-Main Street 7

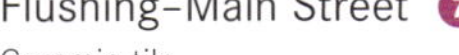

Ceramic tile

PHOTOGRAPHER: ROB WILSON

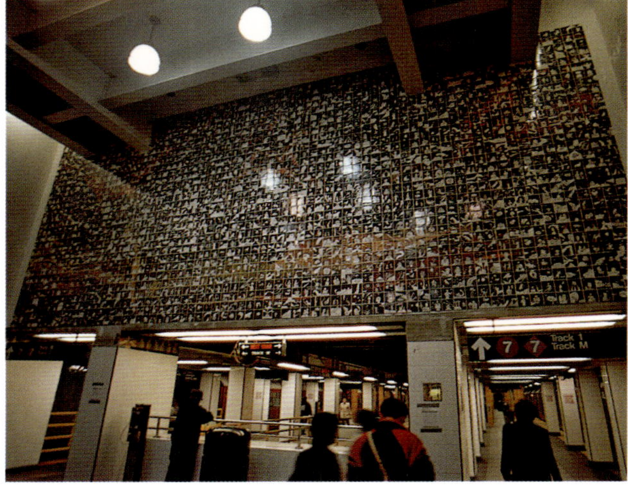

Ik-Joong Kang's *Happy World* celebrates Flushing, one of New York City's most ethnically diverse neighborhoods. The mural is composed of more than two thousand ceramic tiles, and no two of them are alike. They show community events and city views, familial gatherings, people at work and children at play—everything from the humblest backyard to highly recognizable buildings such as the Guggenheim Museum.

For his proposal, Kang carefully worked out the arrangement of the images in the context of the station: "As subway passengers get on the escalator, they will get a glimpse of a world map on the wall facing them. As the escalator descends, they will get a closer look at the images on each tile. Each ceramic tile will function as part of a puzzle."

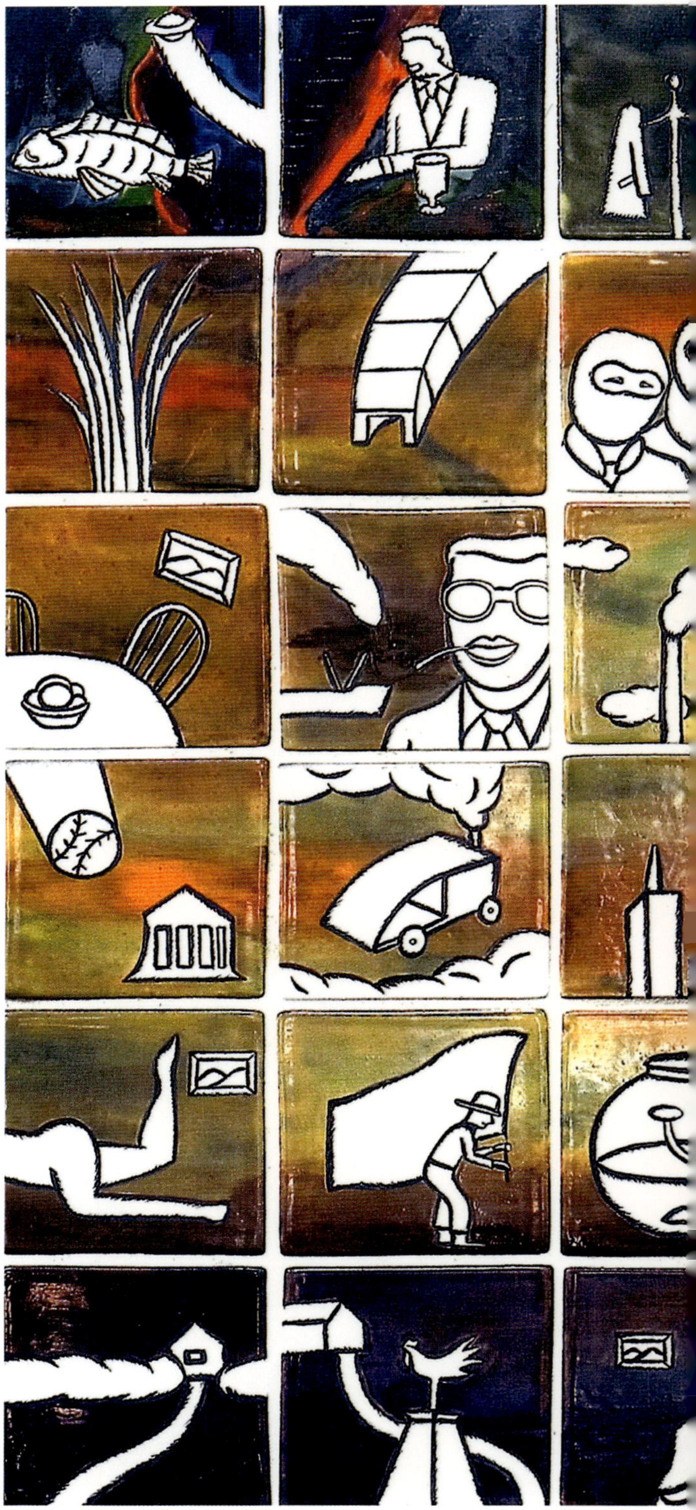

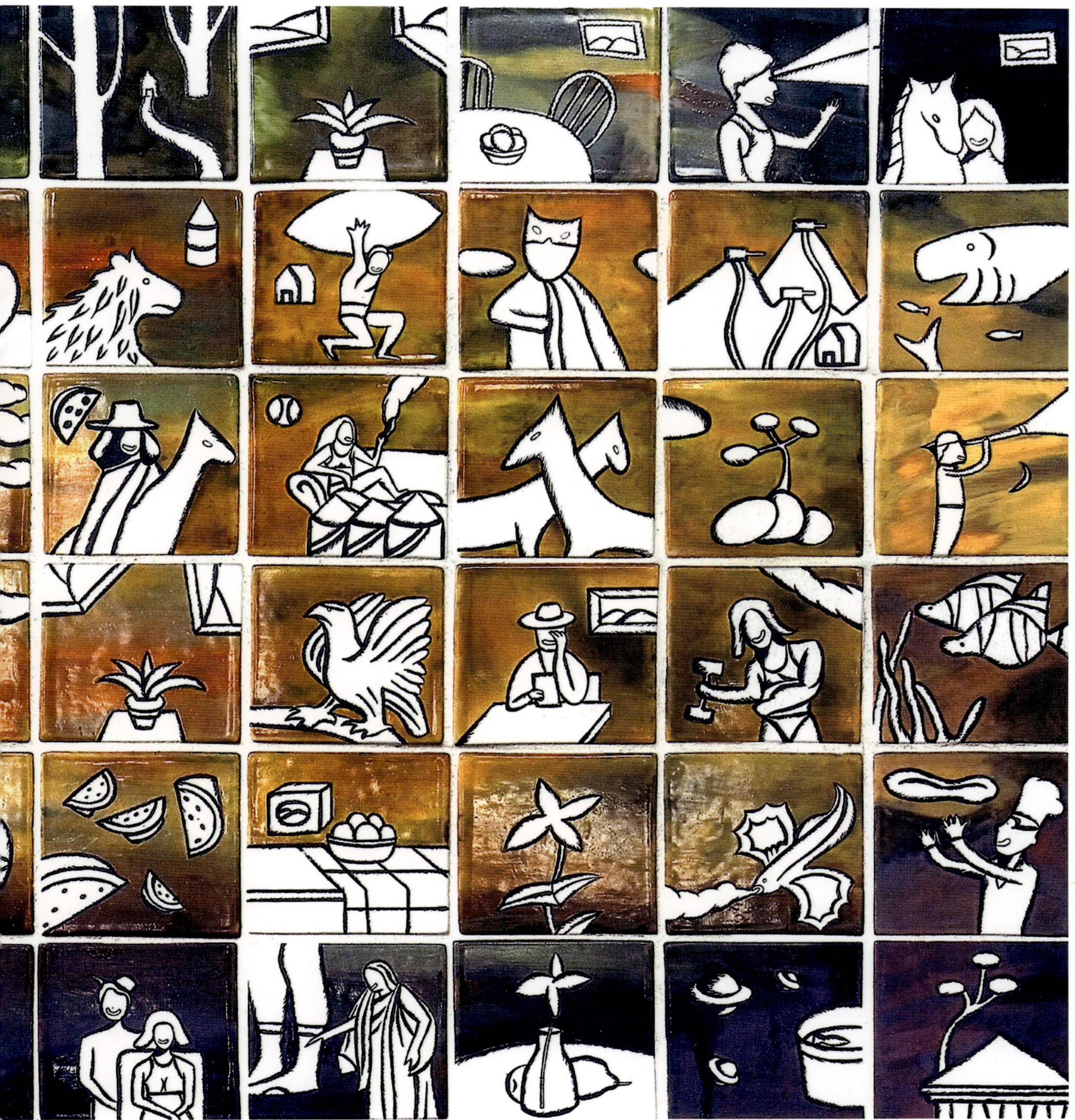

SAM GILLIAM

JAMAICA CENTER STATION RIDERS, BLUE, 1991
Jamaica Center–Parsons/Archer E J Z
Painted aluminum
PHOTOGRAPHER: DAVID LUBARSKY

Jamaica Center Station Riders, Blue is composed of two elements: a large ellipse and an armature to which the ellipse is attached, constructed of aluminum plate with deep welds.

In Gilliam's words, the work is "complex in its simplicity":

> It calls to mind: movement, circuits, speed, technology and passengership. The fact that this is a very modern sculpture places it in contemporary life as well as the future . . . The colors used in the piece. . . refer to colors of the respective subway lines. The predominant use of blue provides one with a visual solid in a transitional area that is near subterranean.

Sam Gilliam is referred to as a third-generation "Washington Color School" artist. Over the years, his works became more sculptural and theatrical, more interactive with space. Eventually, Gilliam literally took the canvas off the frame and attached it to the wall and used the draped canvas as painting in space.

The color-filled draped canvases led directly to Gilliam's public works, including *Jamaica Station Riders, Blue,* where aluminum has replaced canvas as the medium.

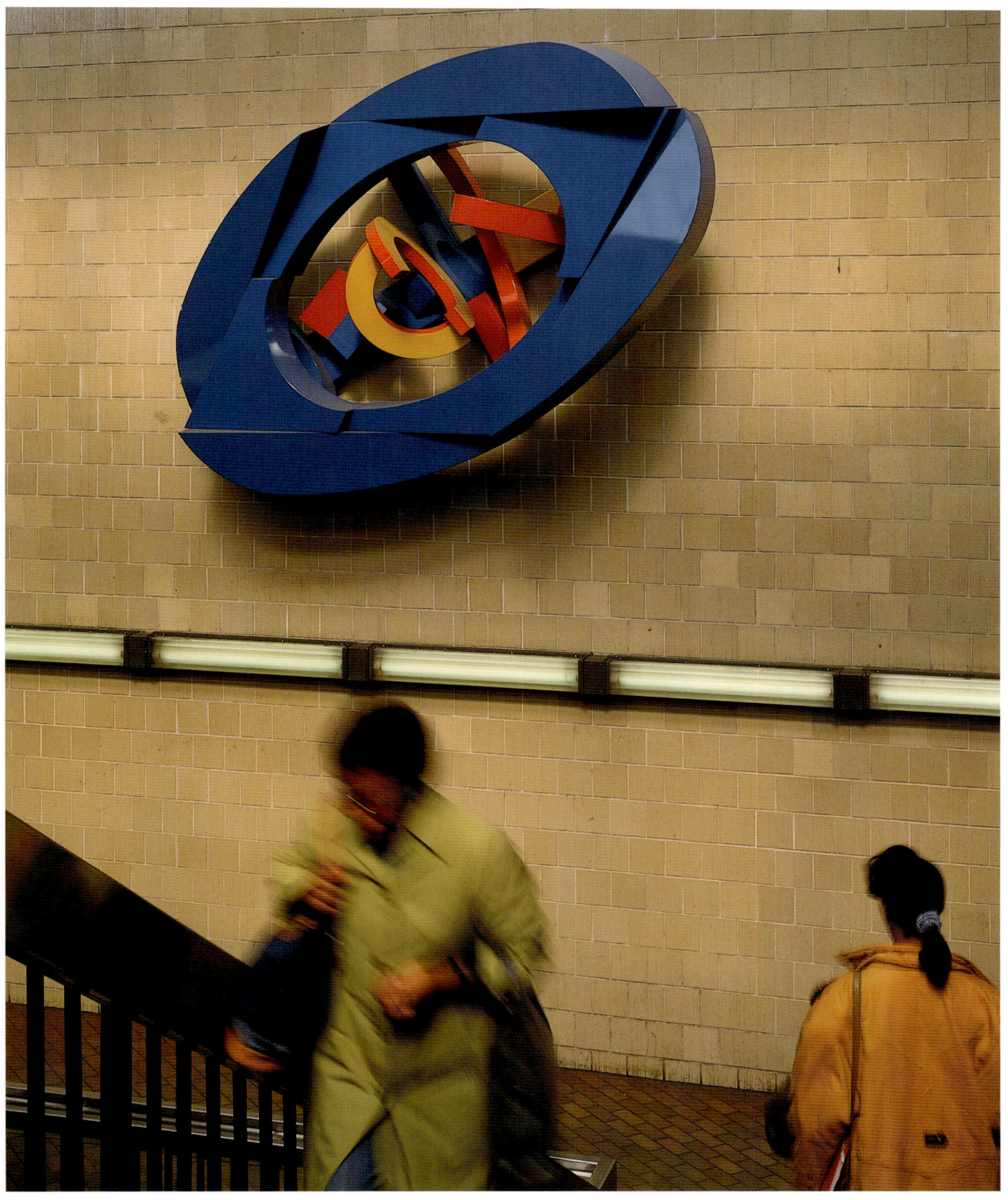

ED McGOWIN

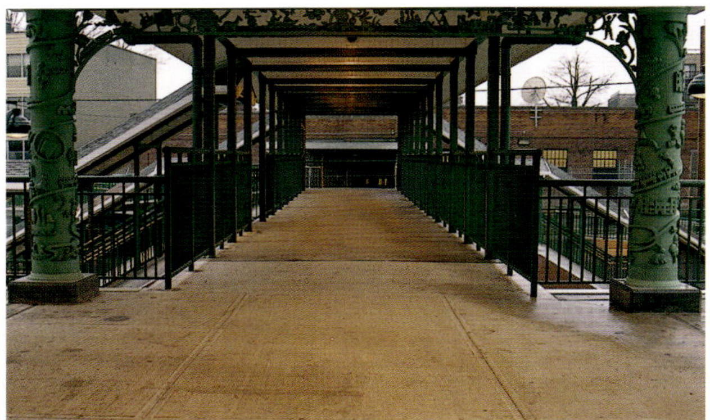

BAYSIDE STORY, 1999
Bayside Station, MTA Long Island Rail Road
Bronze
PHOTOGRAPHER: PATRICK J. CASHIN

Commenting on *Bayside Story,* Ed McGowin said, "Community history can so easily be lost or forgotten. I wanted the work to give the public a sense of pride about Bayside's noble past. I consulted with the Bayside Historical Society and the community to choose significant local events and people, and I worked in bronze to reinforce a sense of the town's permanency."

Bayside was originally the home of the Native American Matinecock people, who were later largely replaced by English colonists. In the 1890s, the wealthy of the Gilded Age built estates there. Then in the early twentieth century, before the center of the movie industry moved to Hollywood, it was the home of some of film's most illustrious celebrities, the likes of John Barrymore and Gloria Swanson.

Indians paddling a canoe are given a central position in *Bayside Story*. Around them are shown an early settler's homestead, a soldier from the American Revolution, a farm vista, and a representation of Fort Totten, a stronghold built during the Civil War. A train locomotive prominently appears as well, denoting the importance of the Long Island Rail Road to the area. Finally, boxer "Gentleman Jim" Corbett represents local heroes, and other sporting events are included as well, with a yacht for sail races and a checkered flag.

In addition, *Bayside Story* features spiral friezes that wrap around the station's supporting columns, bearing animal and floral motifs to call attention to the natural glories of the area. And a modern train makes the point that the railroad remains an important part of the community's way of life.

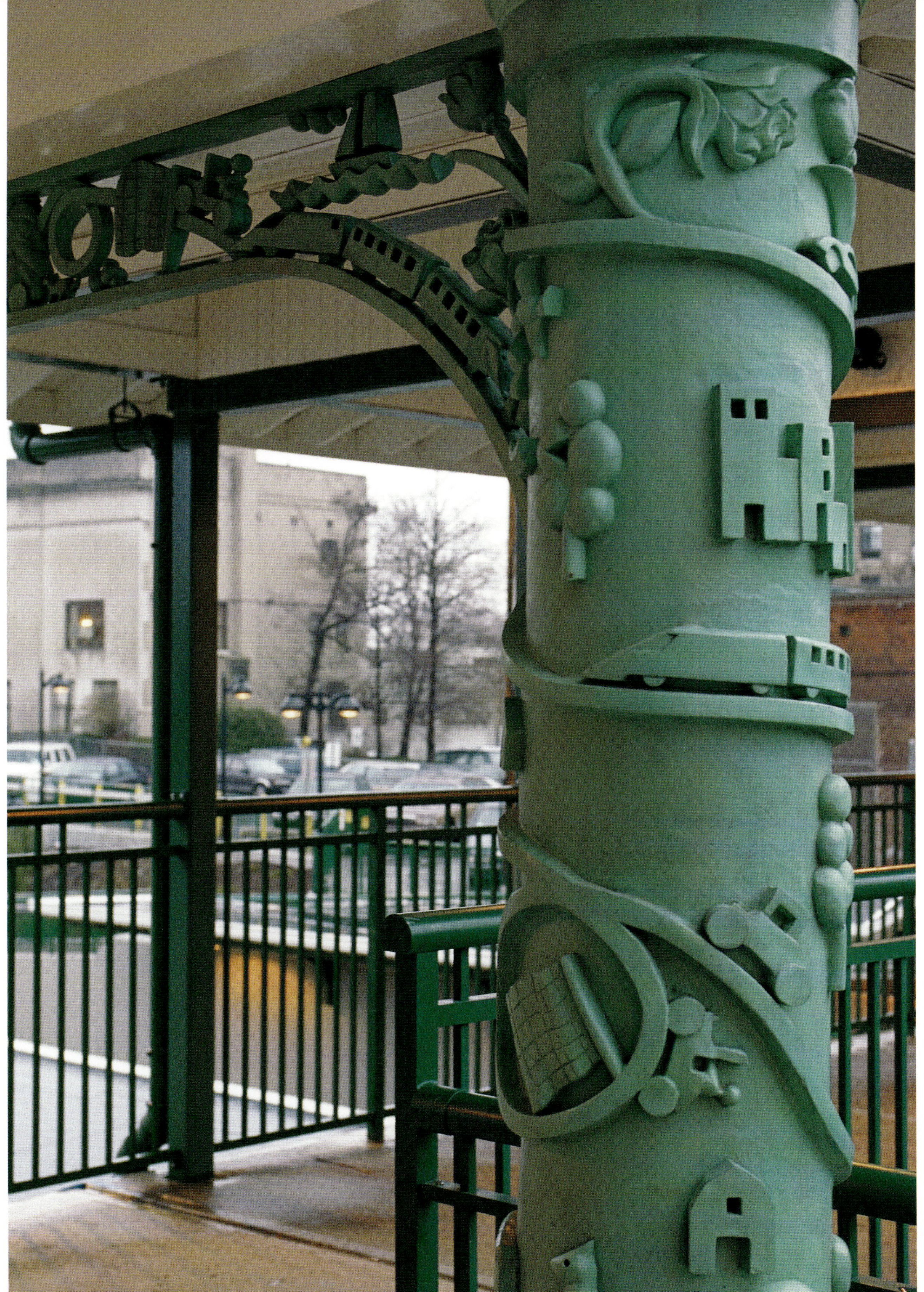

GEORGE TRAKAS in collaboration with di Domenico + Partners

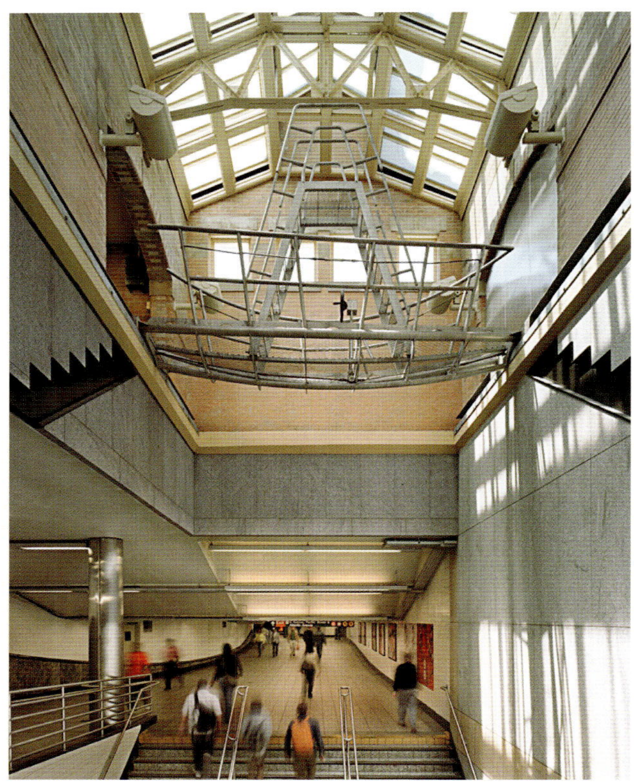

HOOK (ARCHEAN REACH), LINE (SEA HOUSE), AND SINKER (MINED SWELL), 2004

Atlantic Avenue–Pacific Street B D M N Q R 2 3 4 5

Polished granite, brushed steel, limestone, and Rockville granite

PHOTOGRAPHER: JONATHAN WALLEN

The bewildering junction of subway lines at the Atlantic Avenue Terminal Complex presented a perfect opportunity to explore the concept of collaboration—the artist and architect working within a shared vision. The architectural goal was to bring together a myriad of passages and stairways to create a functional space with a unified feeling. Trakas's ideas are melded with the equally clear vision of the architects di Domenico + Partners to create forms and spaces that underscore both the efficiency and beauty of the cavernous space.

The title combines fishing parlance with terms that refer to the materials and subterranean location of the work. The Archean is the period when Earth began to form; a sea house is a mythical underwater dwelling; and the mined swell describes the effect on water of underground excavation.

Trakas selected the stone pavers and bollards incorporated into the traffic island above the station. The architects designed a skylight for the historic station kiosk to help illuminate the platform below. The former entry building now includes a brick-sized opening equipped with a fish-eye lens that focuses directly on the sculptural gantry beneath the skylight.

A granite "wave" sited at the point where the Atlantic and Pacific stations intersect clarifies the circulation between them. Playing on the names *Atlantic* and *Pacific*, the idea is to suggest a place of landing and departure—functions that both subway stations and seaports share. To complete the metaphor, the central kiosk is constructed in the form of a lighthouse, which helps guide travelers through the mazelike complex.

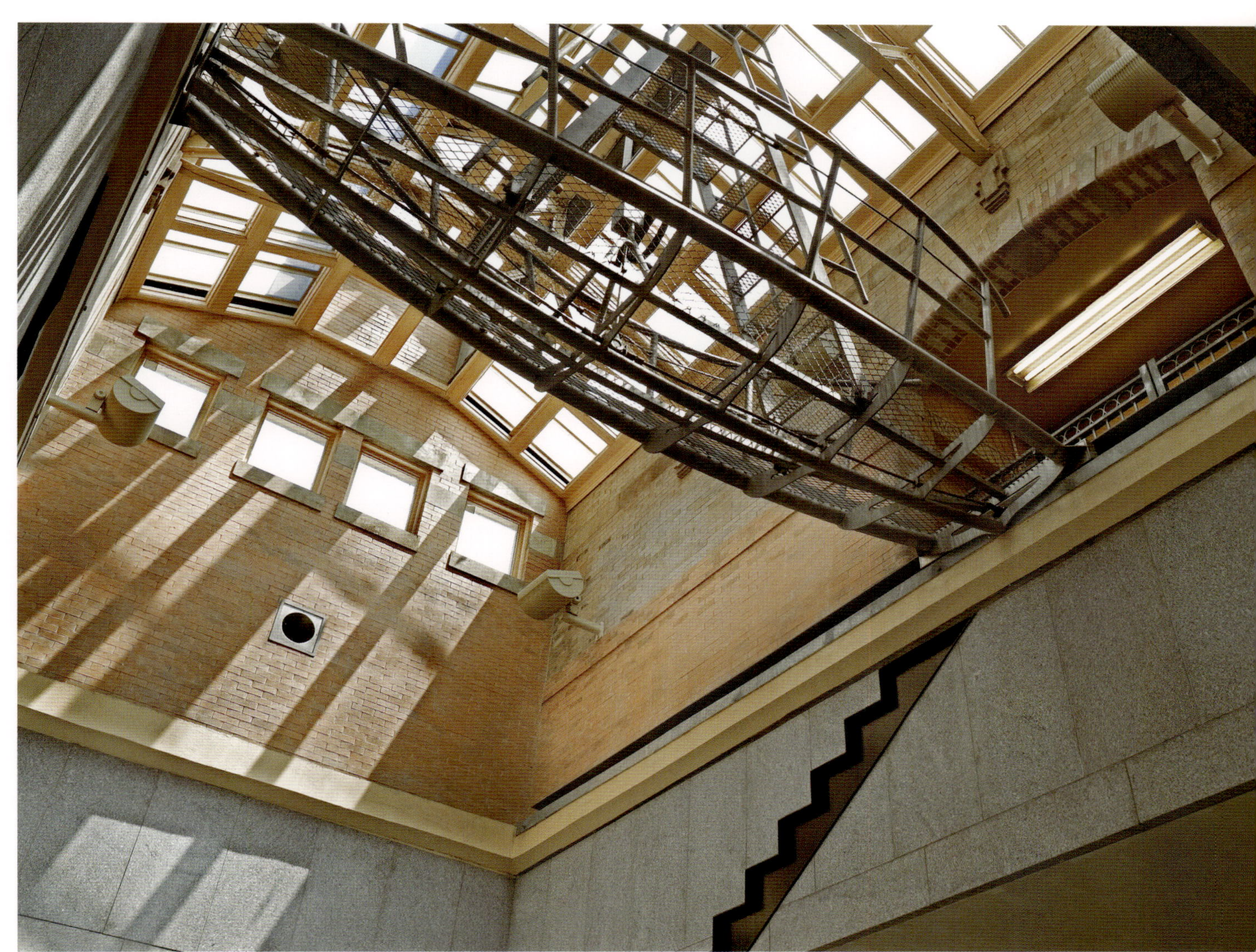

ARTS FOR TRANSIT COLLABORATIVE

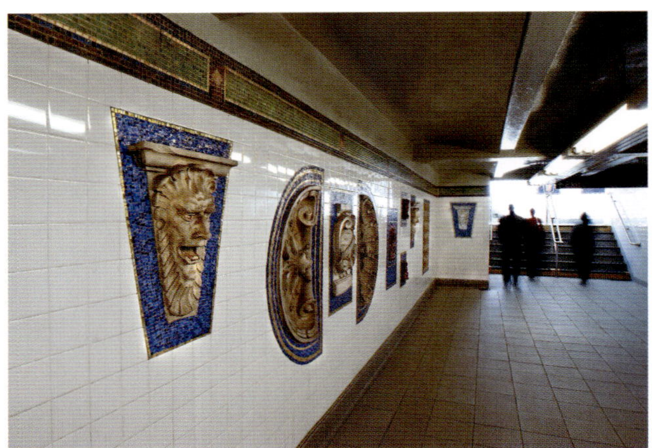

NEW YORK CITY ARCHITECTURAL ARTIFACTS FROM THE COLLECTION OF THE BROOKLYN MUSEUM, 2004

Eastern Parkway–Brooklyn Museum 2 3

Terra-cotta and glass mosaic

PHOTOGRAPHER: ROB WILSON

For many years, the Brooklyn Museum has been the repository for ornamental architectural forms salvaged from significant New York City buildings. Seventy-eight of these artifacts have been installed in the Eastern Parkway-Brooklyn Museum station to enrich the environment and to create an introduction to the museum above.

The entrance to the station was redesigned as part of an enormous and ambitious project to improve the appearance and public access to the Eastern Parkway side of the museum. Emerging passengers—many are visiting schoolchildren—have a welcoming view of the new museum entry structure and public plaza designed by the Polshek Partnership. The salvaged and repositioned architectural elements add to the experience, drawing attention to the classical facade of the original McKim, Mead & White structure where similar elements appear.

The project is an outstanding example of institutional collaboration. The Brooklyn Museum, working with MTA Arts for Transit and Vel Riberto Consulting, selected the artifacts and donated them to the project. New mosaic designs were added to set off the objects and to make connections with the architecture of the station.

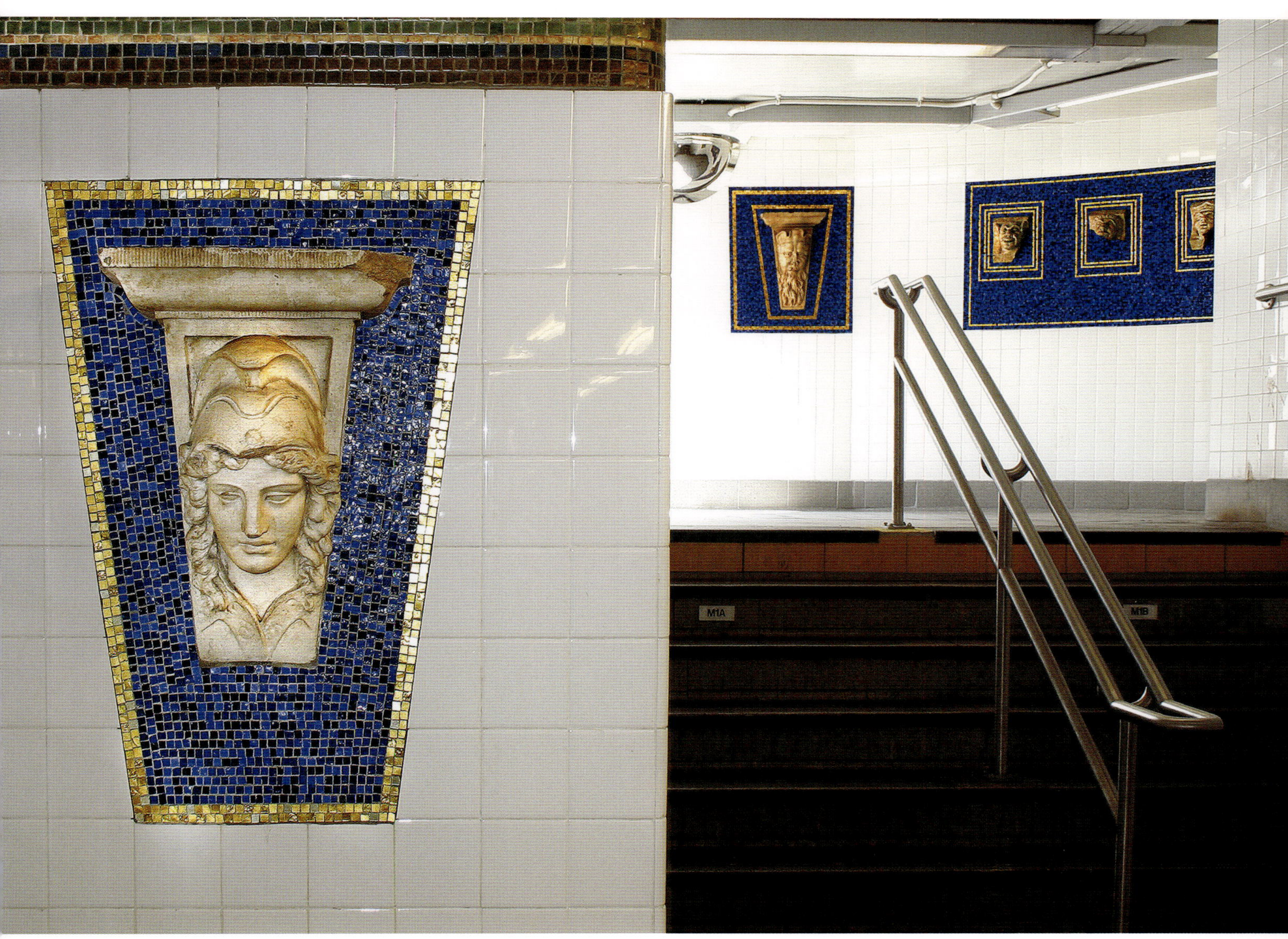

OWEN SMITH

AN UNDERGROUND MOVEMENT: DESIGNERS, BUILDERS, RIDERS, 1998

36th Street D M N R

Ceramic mosaic

PHOTOGRAPHERS: ROB WILSON (BELOW); DAVID LUBARSKY (OPPOSITE)

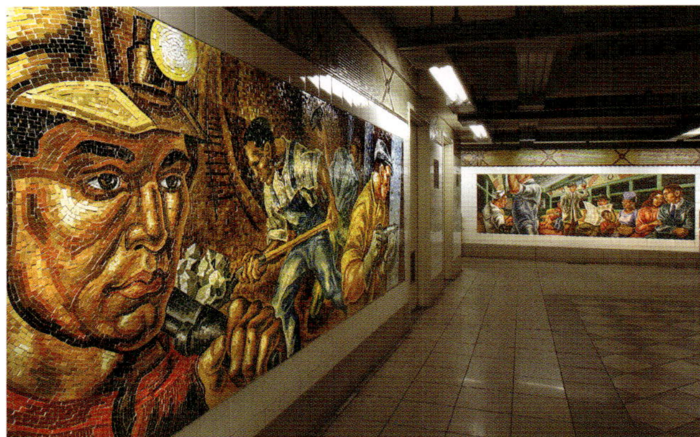

Owen Smith designed his brilliantly colored mosaic work *An Underground Movement: Designers, Builders, Riders* specifically for Brooklyn commuters as "a celebration of the working people who have made the subway what it is today."

The murals focus on the story of the subway's creation and trumpet its importance. The artist describes the expansive works: "The west wall depicts the designers and engineers who achieved this great engineering feat. The panel on the north wall pays tribute to the workers who dug the tunnels and laid the 722 miles of track. And the third panel represents the people who use the subway every day and whose lives are improved by it." In his stylized cityscapes, Smith highlights popular pastimes and haunts for New Yorkers and those who visit here. On the Manhattan-bound side, the Rockettes are shown in all their high-kicking splendor, while the Brooklyn-bound side depicts a classic brownstone stoop with Coney Island in the background.

Muralists of the Mexican Social Realist school, particularly Diego Rivera, influenced Smith in both his style and his choice of subject matter. "Rivera taught many of the artists who produced public art under the WPA and the Federal Art Project of the 1930s and 1940s," he explains. "I was attracted to the strength and accessibility of their style and the educational as well as aesthetic quality of their art. It told a story about the lives of the working people. These mosaic panels were designed in the same spirit."

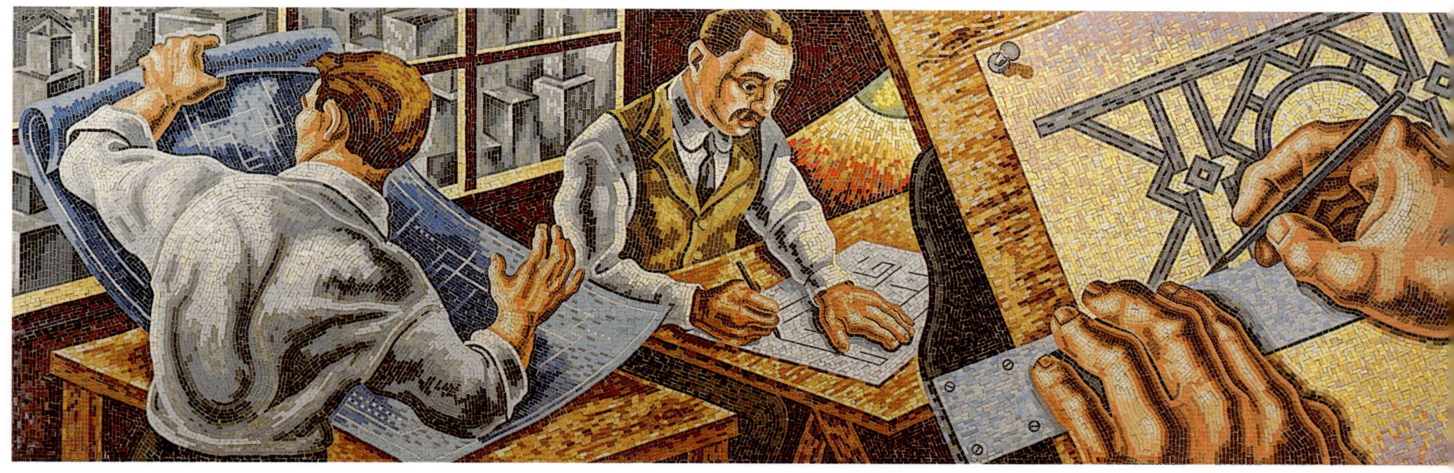

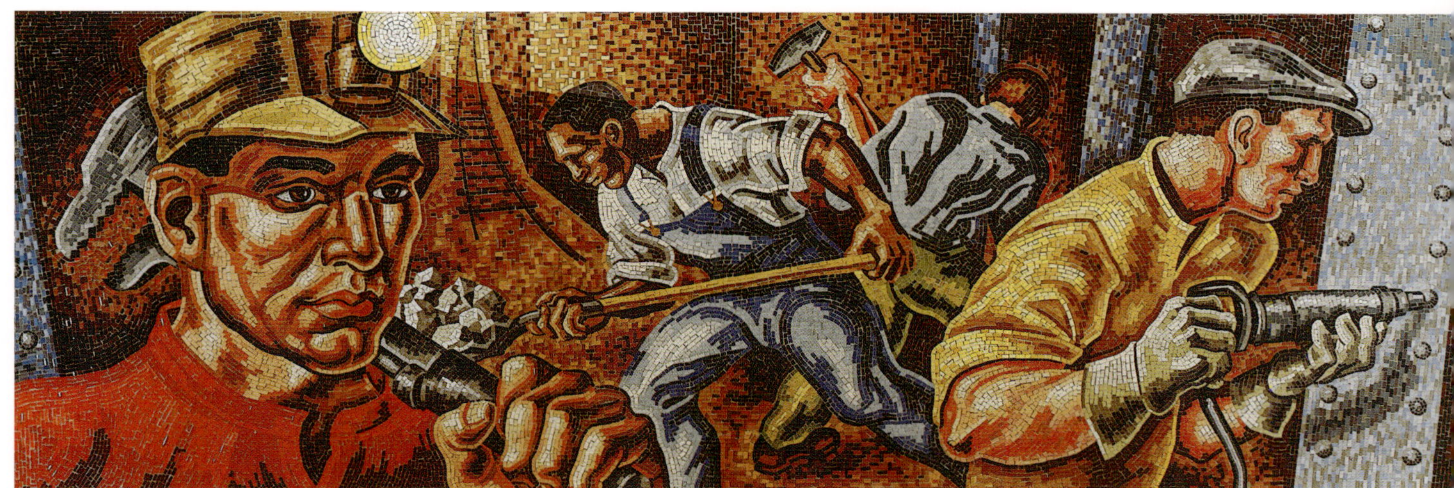

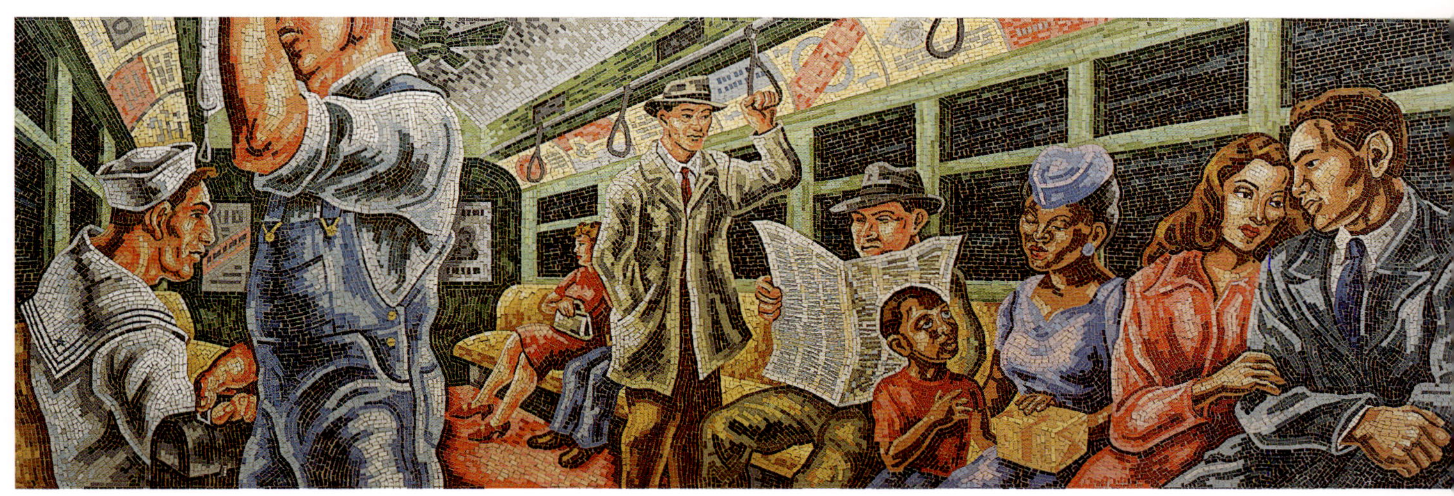

AL LOVING

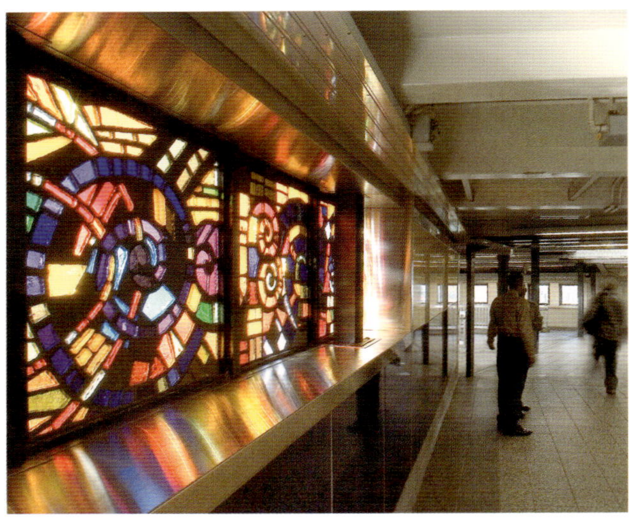

BROOKLYN, NEW MORNING, 2001

Broadway Junction 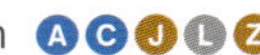

Glass mosaic and faceted glass

PHOTOGRAPHER: ROB WILSON

Brooklyn, New Morning consists of seventy-five faceted-glass panels, which are arranged into a series of murals throughout the complex, as well as a seven-by-ten-foot glass mosaic mural wall. According to Al Loving:

> Faceted glass is an opportunity to work with real light . . . In ancient Chinese culture the spiral was the tip of the flame. In contemporary time it is a symbol of continuity. I have tried to bring a spirit of inclusiveness to this project.

He felt that *Brooklyn, New Morning* expressed a "spirit of interdependence and interconnection as an important aspect of the American experience," reflecting the fact that this large station is literally a cultural crossroad. Working with natural light, the artist aimed to "fuse human animism with intellectual visual consciousness." The overall effect of the work is to bring a new liveliness into the station; its vividly colorful and energetic forms introduce a sense of optimism and well-being.

Throughout his career, Loving was fascinated with the shape of the spiral and spent much of his life exploring this form and studying the properties of bright and bold colors. In 1974, in the *New York Times*, he described his multilayered, painted constructions as "dynamically composed reliefs, wall pieces that energize the space around them, seemingly almost to be caught in the act of moving across the wall." This dynamic quality infuses *Brooklyn, New Morning* as well, but this time in faceted glass and glass mosaic.

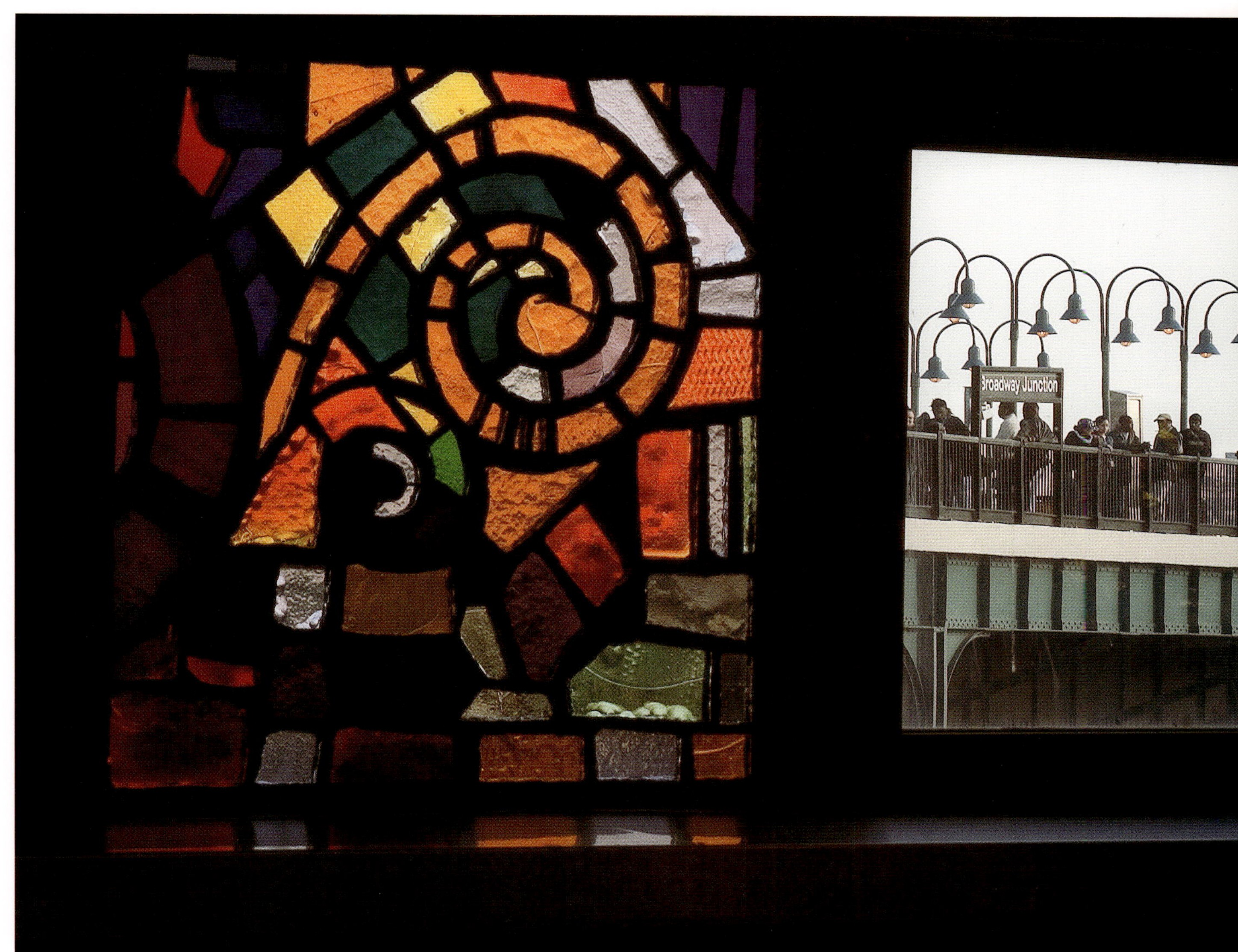
Broadway Junction

ELLSWORTH AUSBY

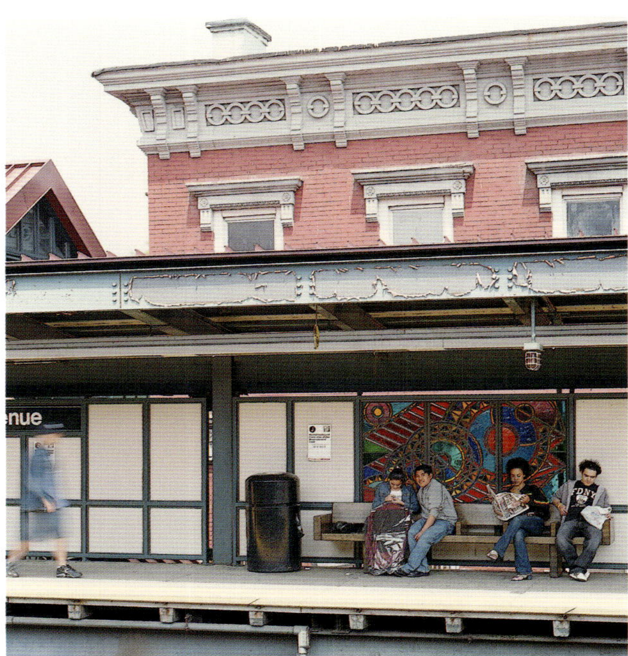

SPACE ODYSSEY, 2004

Marcy Avenue 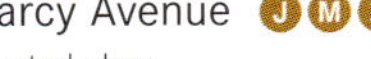

Faceted glass

PHOTOGRAPHER: JEFFREY STURGES

For the Marcy Avenue station, Ellsworth Ausby created eight triptychs, inserted into the windscreens on the elevated platforms, that explore the relationship of man to the universe as well as the spirit of the bustling metropolis. In a subtle way, the brilliantly colored forms evoke the feeling of the swirling cosmos. For this commission, the artist produced a series of drawings to fit the window openings, carefully considering the component shapes and colors and the fact that the drawings would later be translated into a new and different medium, faceted glass.

Ausby says he is particularly attracted by "the idea of traveling in infinite space, which is as a passenger on the Earth Express line, experienced through the cycle of the seasons." *Space Odyssey* provided "a new and exciting medium for me to work with, faceted glass," he explains. "These windows have allowed me to expand my understanding of the possibilities that this concept has as public art, also what and how different mediums expand the impact that a work of art has on the public."

"My art has always been informed by my interest in African art and music, the African American experience, the Cubist school, and contemporary American painters," Ausby says. "The connection between art and spirit, or rather how visual art becomes a voice for religious or spiritual belief, intrigues me. It is my hope that these windows express what I feel is the spirit of New York, the hustle and bustle, the fast pace of the city."

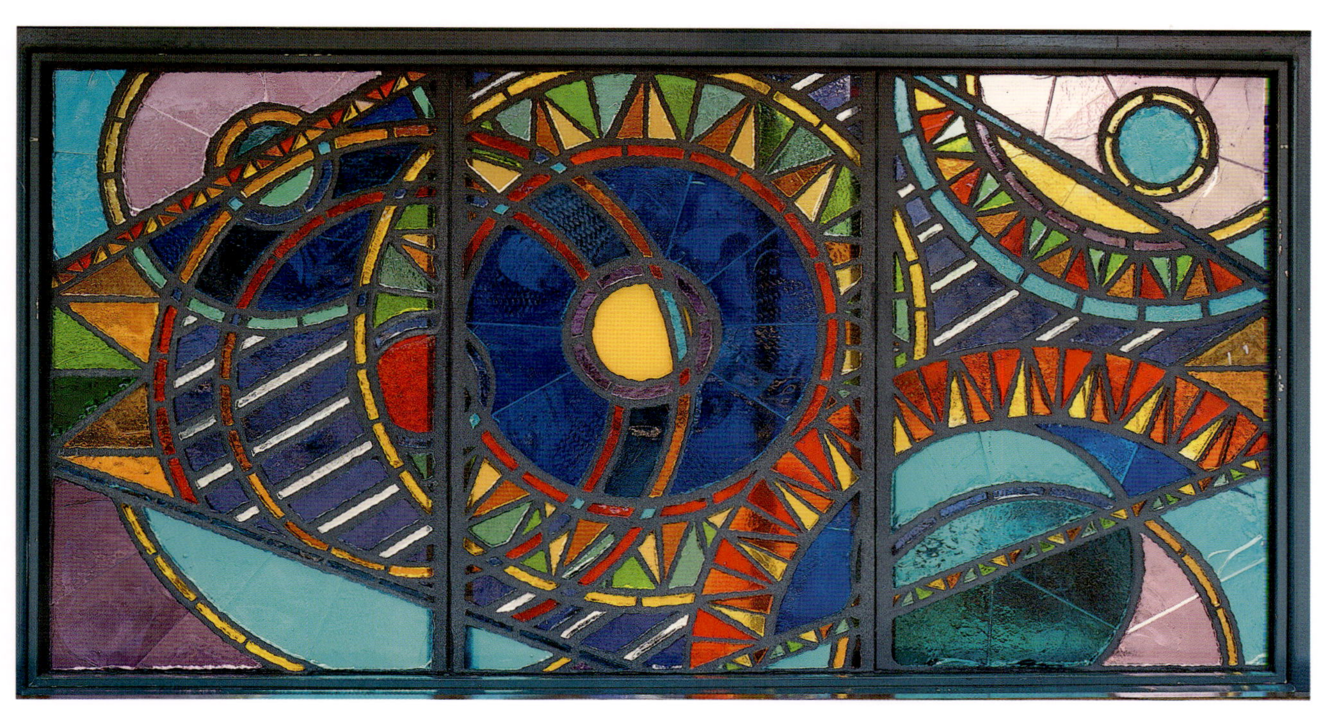

ACCONCI STUDIO in collaboration with Daniel Frankfurt

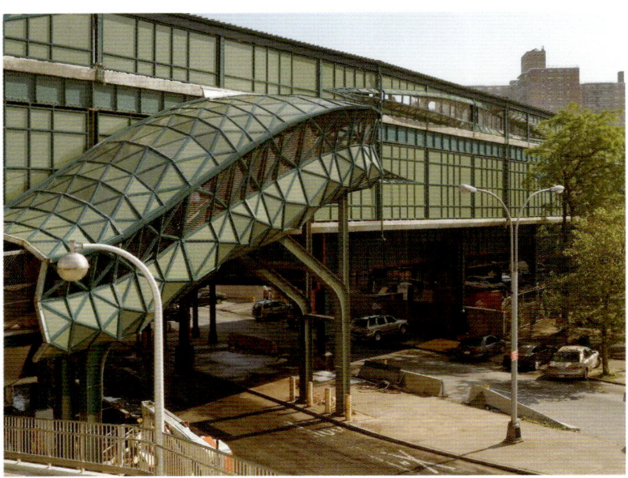

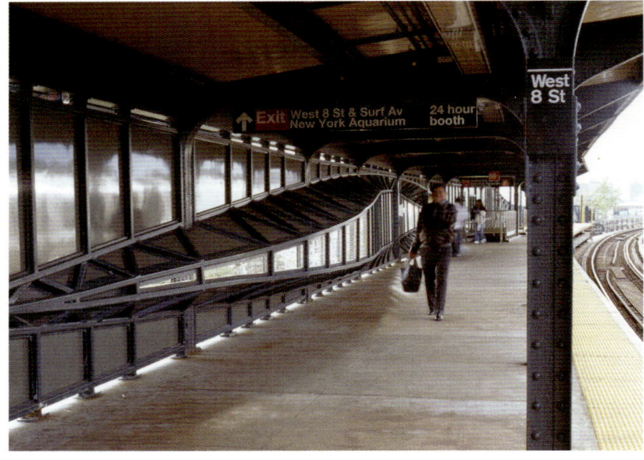

FACADE FOR WEST 8TH STREET SUBWAY STATION, 2005

West 8th Street–New York Aquarium 

Platform windscreens and seating

PHOTOGRAPHERS: JONATHAN WALLEN (LEFT); DANIEL WILLNER AND TAEWON JANG (BOTTOM LEFT AND OPPOSITE)

The concept of these windscreens was influenced by local sites—the Coney Island boardwalk and beaches, the aquarium, the Cyclone roller coaster—and the history of the area, which was formerly a part of the famous Luna Park Amusements. The station is on the approximate site of a roller coaster.

Acconci and architect James McConnell of Daniel Frankfurt worked in tandem on the project. Acconci touched on this aspect, as well as the elements of the design, in his unorthodox proposal, the language of which suggests a wave approaching, breaking, and then receding:

> The architect started a wave; we came in later and tried to make a wave, break a wave.
>
> Like a wave of the ocean, like the sand in waves. The program is: that the station has views to the beach. Use the wave, then, to make a view—the force of the wave—the wave forces a view.
>
> Not a picture of a wave, not a wave in two dimensions. A wave in all directions. The facade itself should be a wave, like a wave in the ocean, like a wave of sand.

Before rehabilitation, the windscreens blocked all views from this elevated vantage point; the new windscreens open up the platform to reveal the Atlantic Ocean to the passengers as they arrive and depart Coney Island. The south side presented the additional opportunity to be creative with the design of the windscreen itself. "The normally horizontal and vertical steel windscreen tubes and panels have been transformed into a more sinuous form that evokes the notion of a wave, or that of motion as in the Cyclone or the subway itself," says Acconci.

West 8th Street is Acconci's second MTA Arts for Transit project. In contrast to this investigation of the outer shell, *Wall-Slide* at Yankee Stadium (see p. 140) is concerned with what is below the surface.

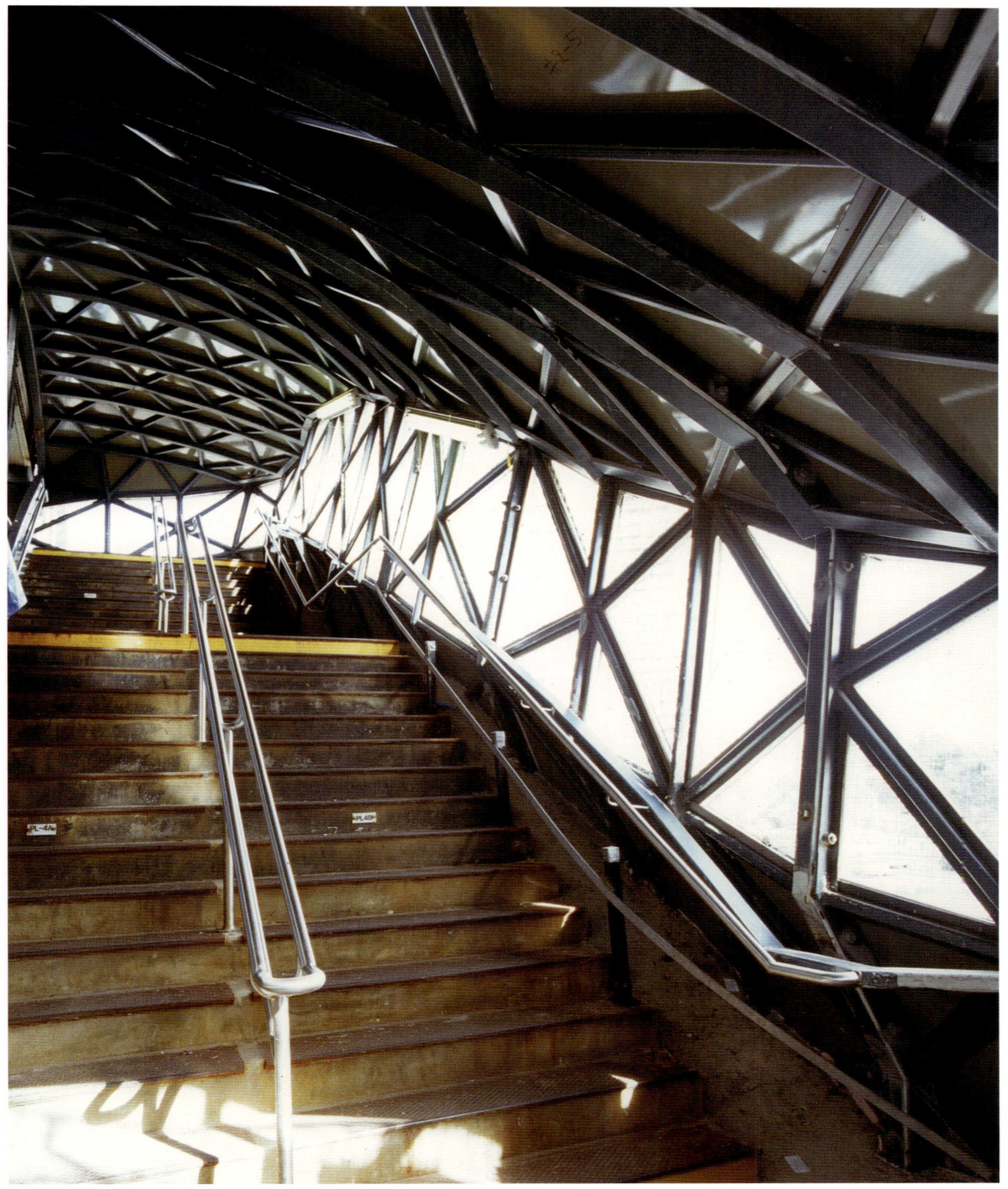

ROBERT WILSON

MY CONEY ISLAND BABY, 2004
Coney Island–Stillwell Avenue 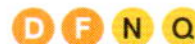
Painted and laminated Vista glass brick
PHOTOGRAPHER: ROB WILSON

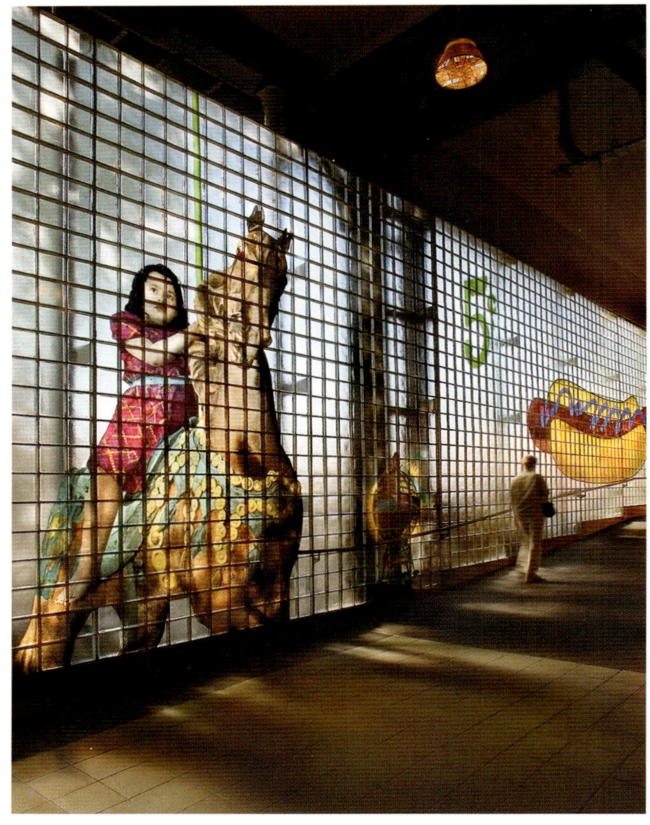

Robert Wilson's *My Coney Island Baby* is big, bold, and attention-grabbing, as befits a featured attraction in the area that was once the nation's most famous amusement park. Vivid images have been silk-screened onto glass bricks and then joined together to form part of a colossal 370-foot glass-brick wall. Wilson describes the concept:

> I see a glass wall built as a celebration of life and joy containing all sorts of different images relating to the history of one of the greatest landmarks in the city, Coney Island. It's a place forever associated with optimism and entertainment and where people from all over the world gather for the same destination: fun.

As light conditions change, *My Coney Island Baby* does as well. It responds equally well to sunlight during the day and to artificial light at night, from both inside and outside. In daylight, with the sun streaming in from outside, its images and colors are boldly delineated. At nighttime it glows mysteriously, adding an ephemeral quality to the surroundings.

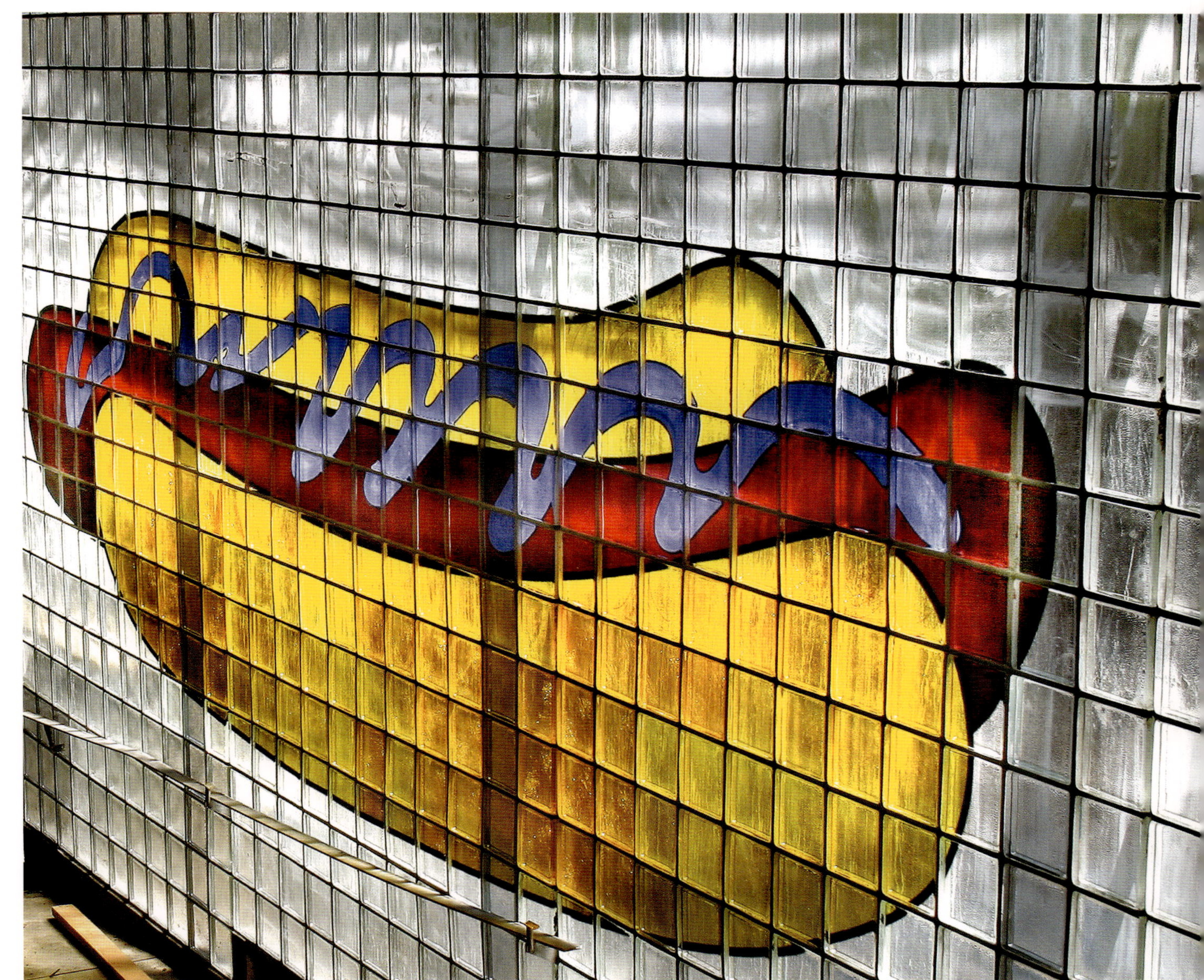

ROMARE BEARDEN

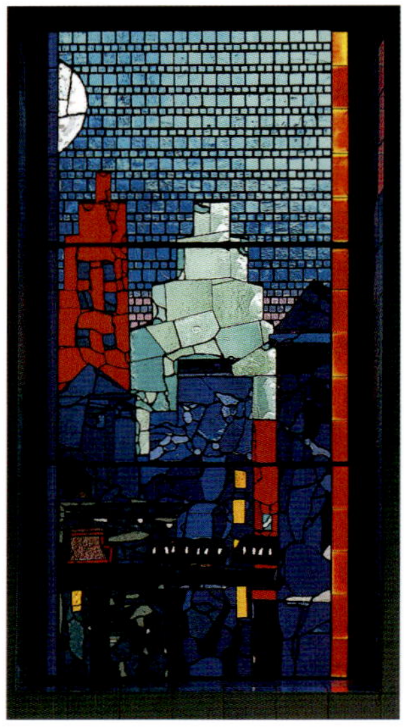

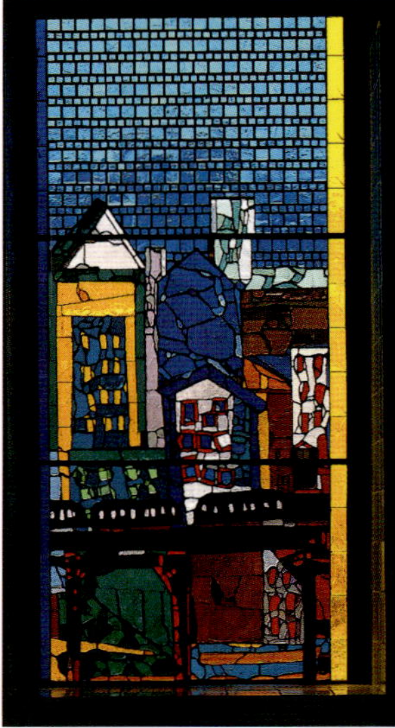

UNTITLED ("CITY OF LIGHT"), 1993
(proposal created by artist, 1982)
Westchester Square–East Tremont Avenue 6
Faceted-glass triptych
PHOTOGRAPHER: DAVID LUBARSKY

The hundreds of brilliant facets of Romare Bearden's glass triptych throb with life, woven together by the heavy black thread of a subway train wending its way from tenements to skyscrapers. The work began as a collage maquette; this was then faithfully and skillfully enlarged, and transformed into a glowing work in jewel-like colored glass.

Bearden consistently maintained that his concern was with universal human themes, not just those pertaining only to African Americans: "I work out of a response and need to redefine the image of man in the terms of the Negro experience I know best." Or, as Ralph Ellison wrote, "Bearden's art is not only an evaluation of his own freedom and responsibility as an individual and artist, it is an affirmation of the irrelevance of the notion of race as a limiting force in the arts. These are works of a man possessing a rare lucidity of vision."

City of Light is classic Bearden as it skillfully weaves together the spirit found in his beloved music, social concerns, and his interest in trains. Rendered in his characteristically bright colors, the work was the result of a long collaboration between Romare Bearden and the fabricators, Benoit Gilsoul and Helmut Schardt. Following the artist's death in 1988, they were able to complete the work from the preparatory studies and instructions he had left behind.

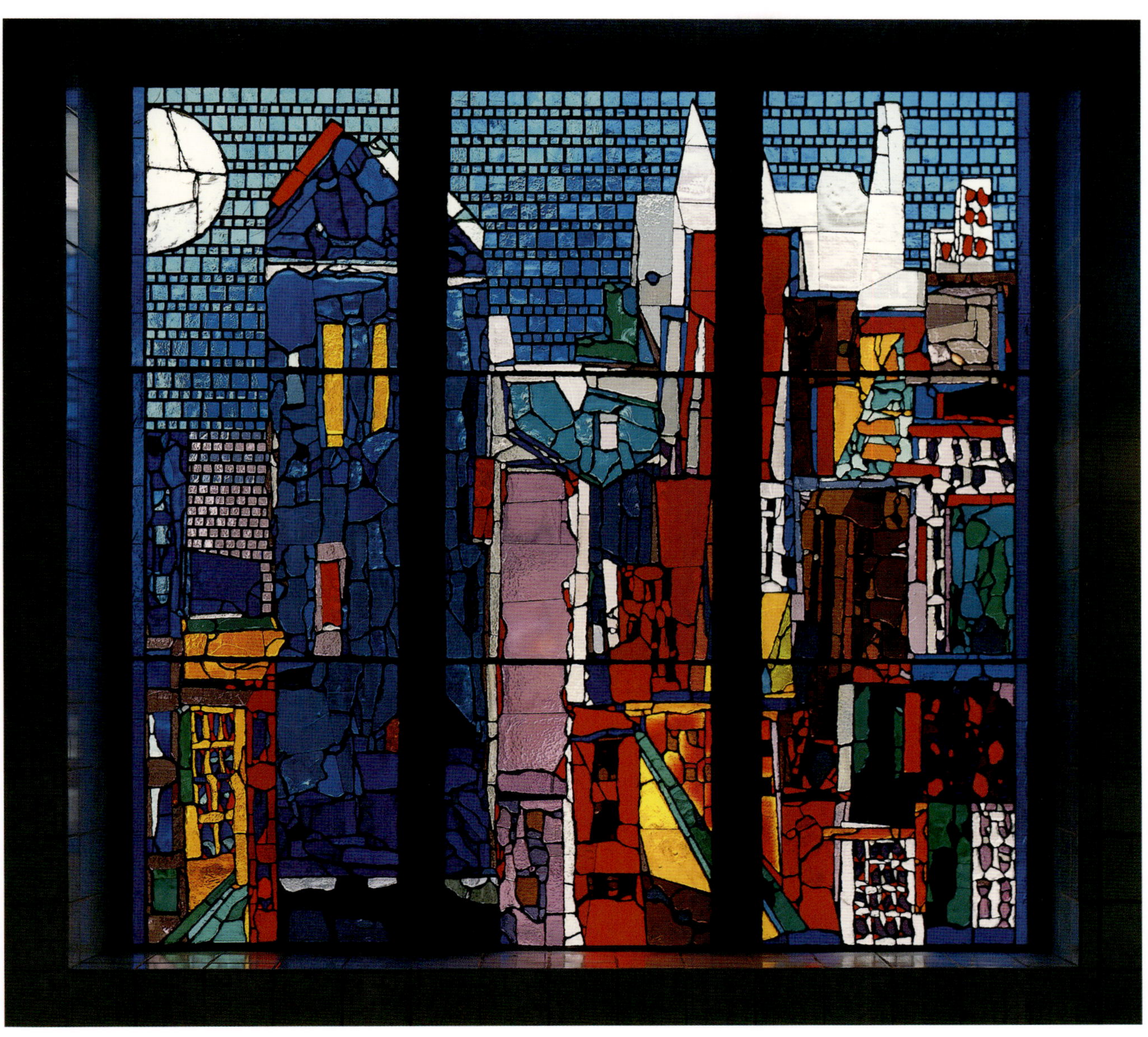

ACCONCI STUDIO in collaboration with di Domenico + Partners

WALL-SLIDE, 2002

161st Street–Yankee Stadium 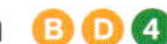

Stone, tile, and fiberglass

PHOTOGRAPHER: ROB WILSON

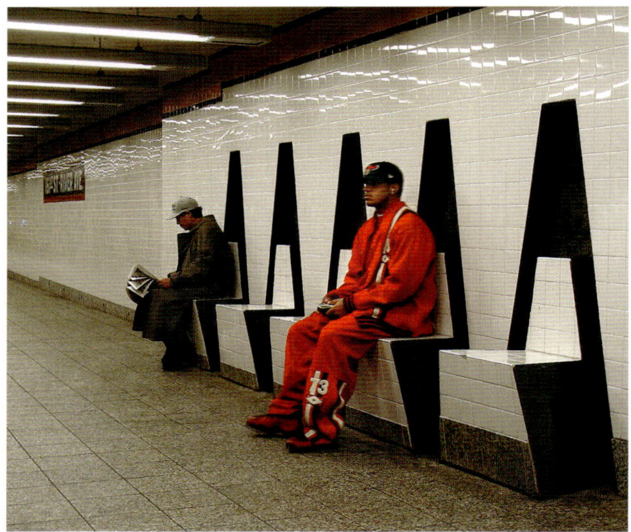

Wall-Slide asks subway riders to think of the 161st Street station as an archaeological site. Tongue-in-cheek dislocations of its walls allow the curious to "see" the stone and steel underneath. Elsewhere, protruding and receding walls magically provide seating for people waiting for the train. Parts of the project thrust through floors and ceilings and at one point even project aboveground. The overall effect suggests that the station has been pushed and pulled in various directions to accentuate the relationship of the building to the earth into which it has been inserted.

The architectural goal of the project—opening up the lower levels to admit natural light—provided a unique opportunity for collaboration between architect and artist. Vito Acconci, who grew up in the Bronx, was a logical choice. He began his career as a poet and in the late 1960s and early 1970s was a well-known performance artist. In recent projects he has joined with architects and landscape designers to visualize and build ambitious constructions that meditate on and meld the meeting of private and public spaces. At the Yankee Stadium station, his illusion of walls being opened to the outside led to the opportunity to include Helene Brandt's *Room of Tranquility*, a work that is revealed as the walls in the elevated station slide up on the ceiling and down through the floors.

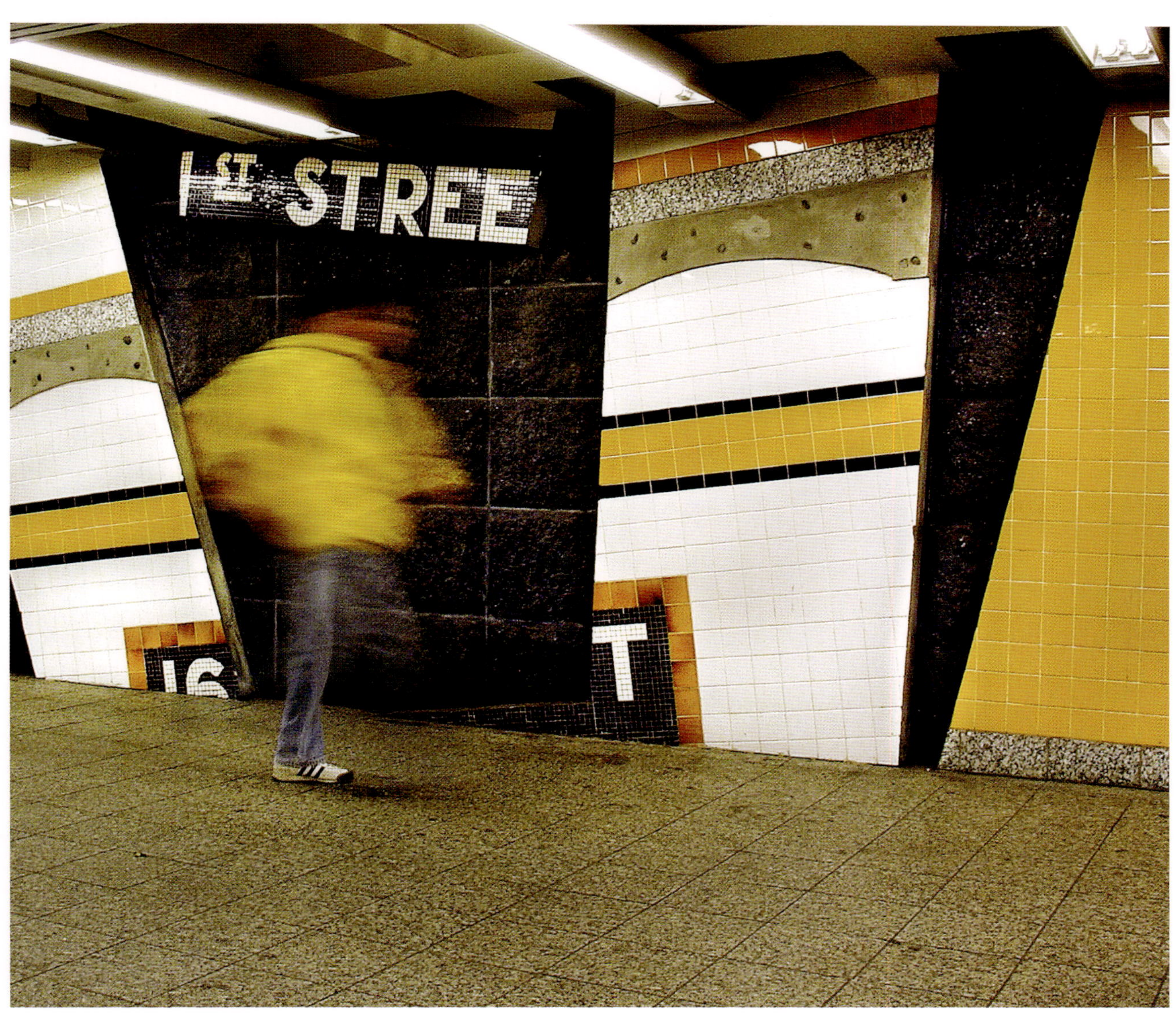
1ST STREE
16
T

HELENE BRANDT

in cooperation with Acconci Studio
and di Domenico + Partners

ROOM OF TRANQUILITY, 2002

161st Street-Yankee Stadium B D 4

Glass, stone, and marble mosaic

PHOTOGRAPHER: ROB WILSON

In the Yankee Stadium elevated station, walls that open in Vito Acconci's shifting architectural forms reveal Helene Brandt's *Room of Tranquility,* where all is peaceful, still, and reassuring. Trees and sky seem eerily real; the space appears to expand and depth is convincingly suggested. In the artist's words, "I envisioned an imaginary room revealed behind the sliding tile walls—a quiet, restful space with a radiant view to the outside, a room of tranquility. I wanted the room to have illusionary windows that would seem to let the outside world penetrate into the station."

Brandt rose to the challenge of responding to the site with a work that relates to Acconci's in counterpoint. As she stated, "I want my *Room of Tranquility* to look as if it has always existed and is only now exposed to view by the sliding tile walls." Her site-specific response to the Acconci Studio and di Domenico + Partners collaboration achieves a place of serenity close to the roar of the stadium crowds.

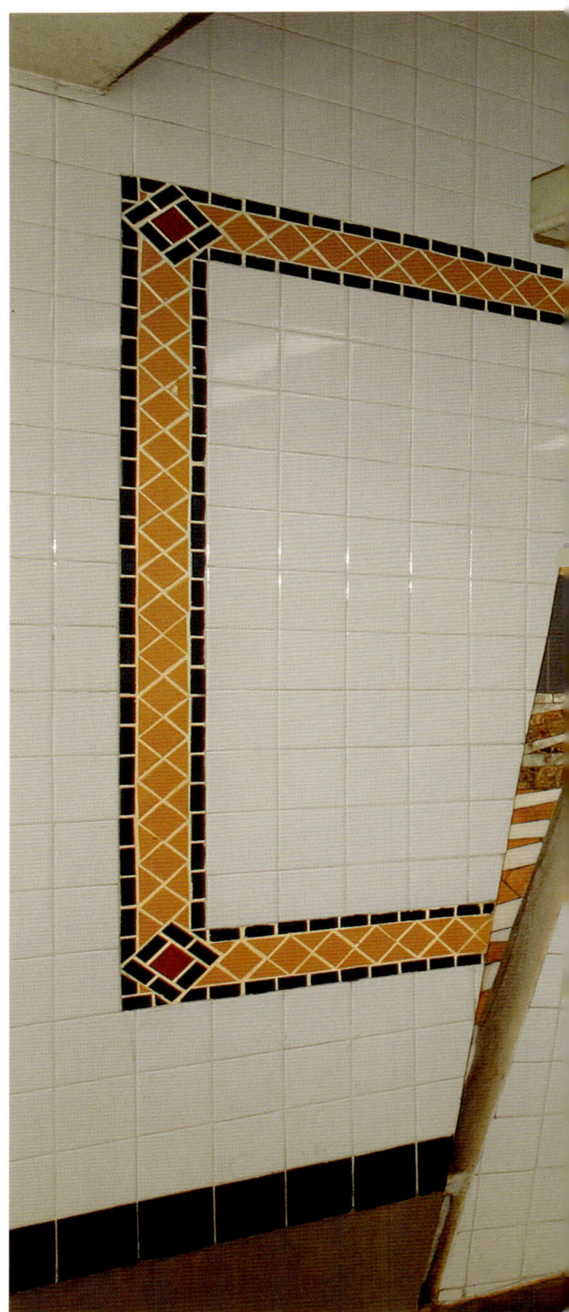

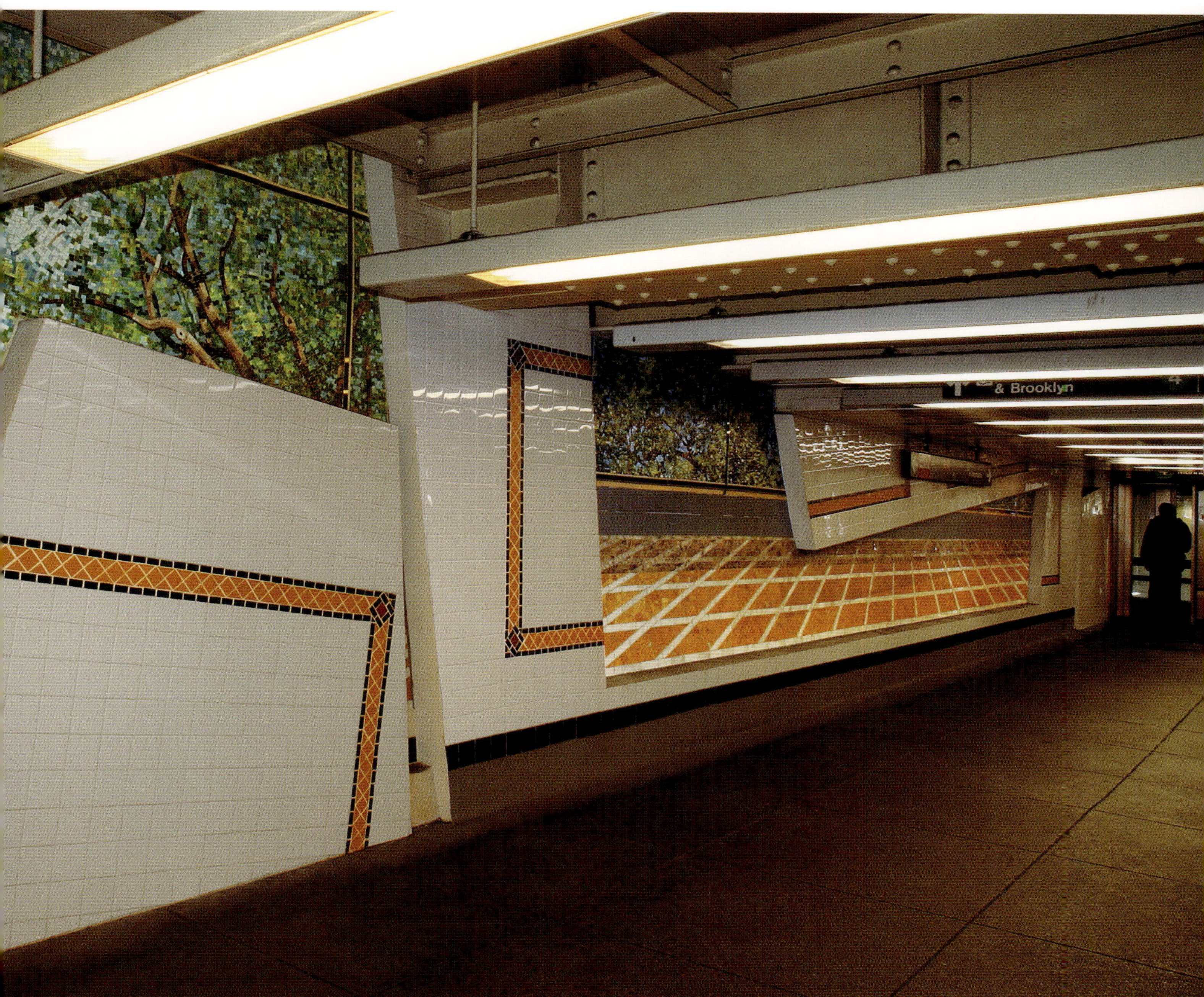
& Brooklyn

BARBARA SEGAL

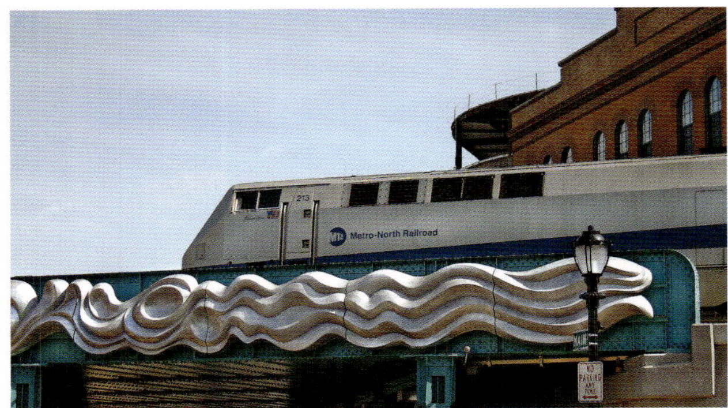

MUHHEAKANTUCK (The River That Flows Two Ways), 2005
Yonkers Station, MTA Metro-North Railroad
Cast aluminum
PHOTOGRAPHERS: ROB WILSON (LEFT); BARBARA SEGAL (OPPOSITE)

Muhheakantuck (The River That Flows Two Ways) is composed of two overscaled metal reliefs installed on the east and west faces of the bridge that elevates the tracks at the Yonkers Station. The American Indian word *muhheakantuck* refers to the fact that at this point the Hudson River can flow upstream as well as down, depending on tidal conditions.

Barbara Segal, a Yonkers resident, consulted both art-historical and scientific sources to evoke the river's past. She has said of her approach:

> As a public artist, I am especially interested in the biography of a specific location, the history and nature of a place, unearthing that history and telling its story through sculpture. I want to link the past that gave way to the present and expose the connection between the community we know and share and what must have come before.

She describes *Muhheakantuck* as an abstract representation of the river: "The sun and moon will constantly change the lighting on the sculpture, and the shadows will change with the sunrise and sunset." The sculpture is installed at a spot where the river's original shoreline was situated before landfill and development of the riverfront.

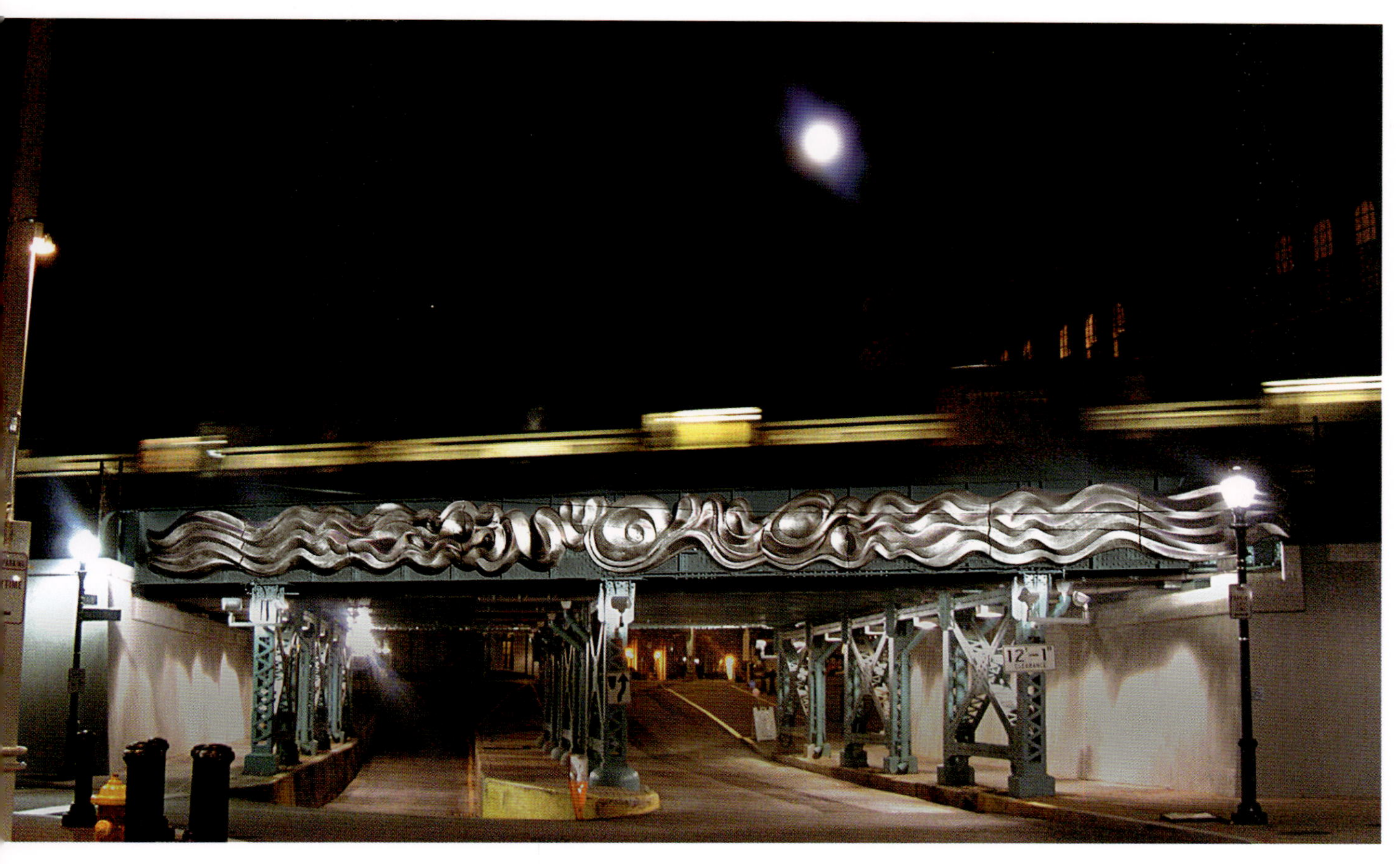
12'-1"

KANE CHANH DO/JANE GREENGOLD

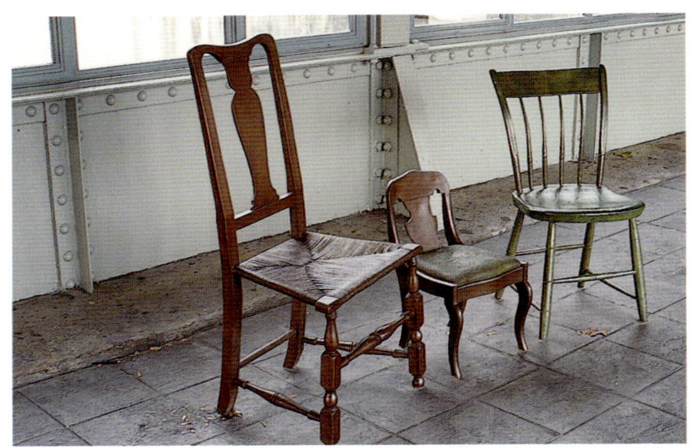

ALMOST HOME, 2002
Pleasantville Station, MTA Metro-North Railroad
Bronze
PHOTOGRAPHER: JANE GREENGOLD

Twenty-two cast-bronze sculptural chairs surprise and delight those who use or visit the Pleasantville station. The artists Kane Chanh Do and Jane Greengold explain the concept:

> In this suburb of New York City, we have re-created, in bronze, chairs likely to be found in the homes of the commuters who use the station, bringing some of the comforts of home out to meet the riders, making the station almost like home, and reminding riders that they, too, are almost home. Because the chairs look so life-like, so much like wood and upholstery fabric, they create a humorous, trompe l'oeil effect.

The components of *Almost Home* were cast from six types of chairs in a variety of styles. They are arranged in clusters throughout the interior and exterior of the station overpass and waiting area. And, for good measure, two of them are child-size. The chairs were cast by using a special molding wax, with great care taken not to damage or mar the originals. Then the castings were finished by hand to ensure that each is a perfect replica. Finally, a custom finish and patination ensure that each echoes its prototype in color as well as form.

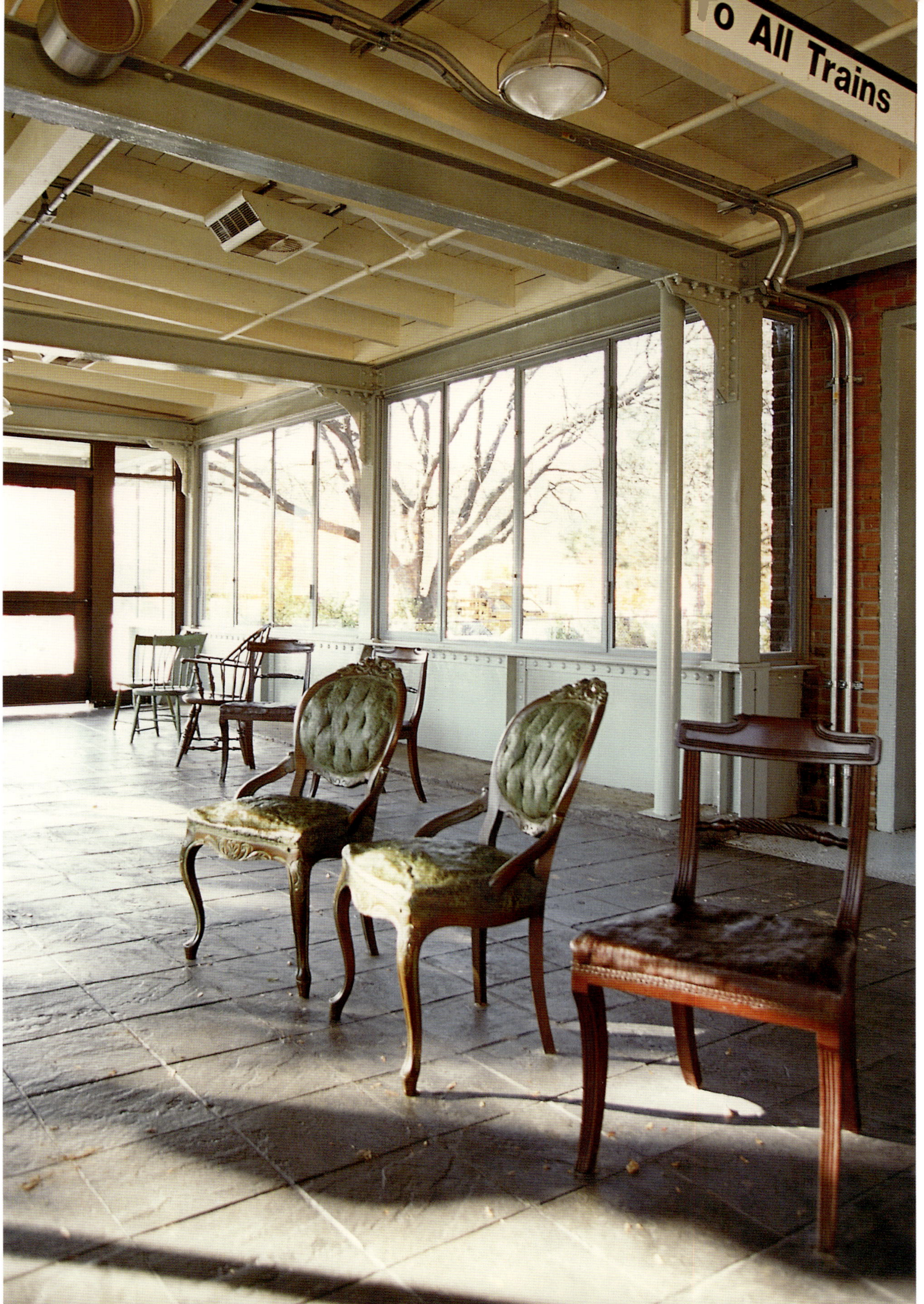
o All Trains

ROBERT TAPLIN

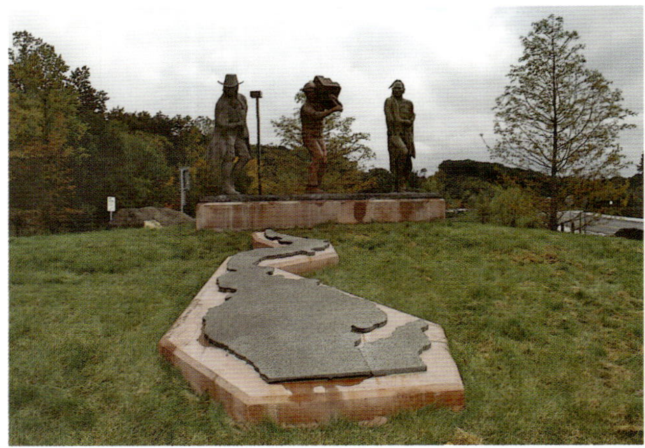

THREE STATUES (A SHORT HISTORY OF THE LOWER HUDSON VALLEY), 1996
Cortlandt Station MTA Metro-North Railroad
Bronze and granite
PHOTOGRAPHER: ROB WILSON

Robert Taplin's *Three Statues (A Short History of the Lower Hudson Valley)* might be taken for ghosts from the area's storied past. One is a Native American rendered in earth tones; another, in gray, is a prosperous Dutch landowner of the seventeenth or eighteenth century; and the third, in dull reddish hues, is an industrial worker, perhaps from the nineteenth century. Taplin says, "Each figure presents a moment in the history of this place." And together, they symbolize the sweeping changes the surrounding area has experienced over the past three centuries.

The figures, each seven feet tall, were cast in bronze and then patinated to give the effect of varied surfaces and colors. They stand proudly on a knoll, raised on a platform as if contemplating the green granite representation of the Hudson River spread in front of them, silently reflecting on the advantages and disadvantages of progress. They are archetypal historic figures—even stereotypes—that suggest that we too might profitably ponder the past.

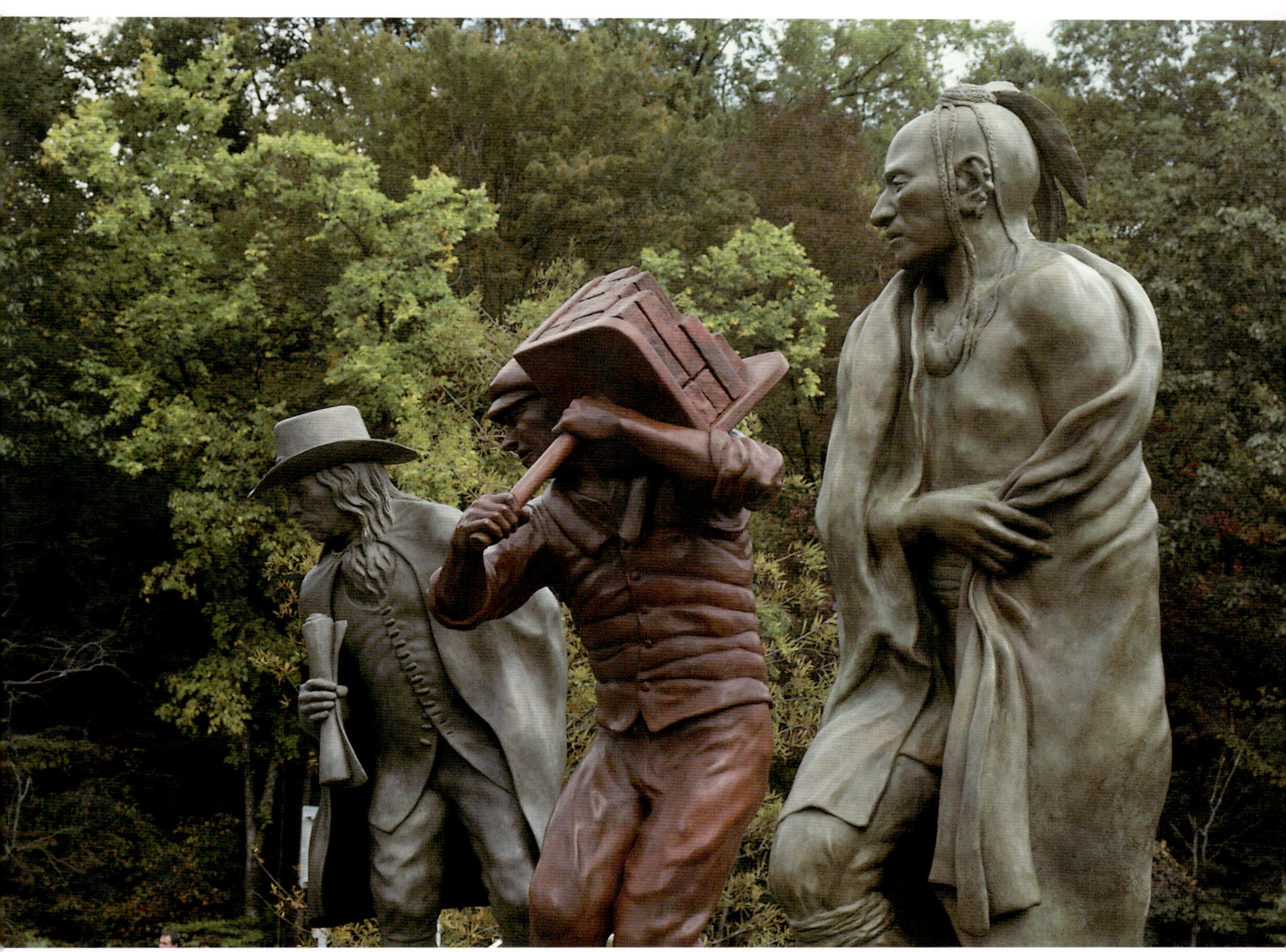

RON BARON in cooperation with DMJM Harris

LOST AND FOUND: AN EXCAVATION PROJECT
2005
Hempstead Station, MTA Long Island Rail Road
Bronze
PHOTOGRAPHER: IRIT BANIEL STUDIOS

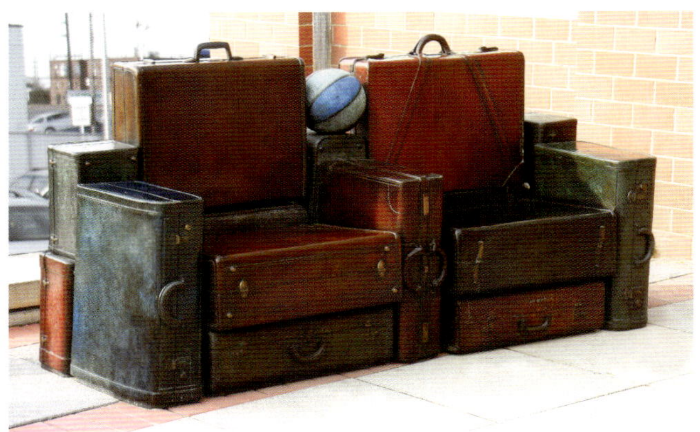

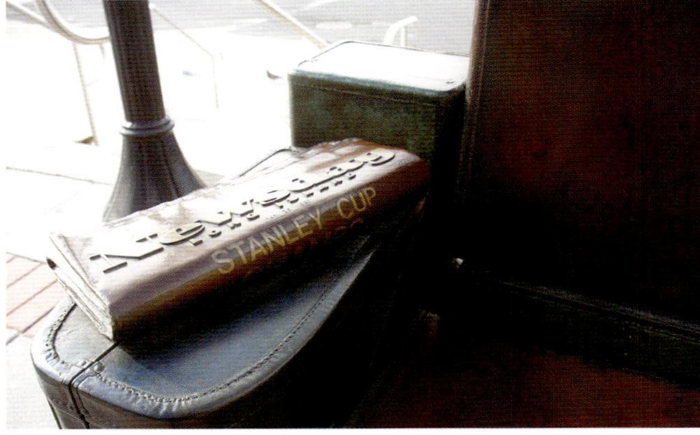

Lost and Found is part of a public plaza designed to engage commuters as they arrive and depart. These piles of luggage—old-fashioned trunks, suitcases, and briefcases interspersed with ephemera—cast in bronze and realistically painted, are intended to remind riders of the community's rich history. Ron Baron refers to himself as a "cultural archaeologist"; he amasses seemingly mundane objects from streets and sidewalks, thrift shops and garage sales. He then forms his monuments, "geological" constructs of his finds, which transform the objects into something completely new, commenting on our collective past.

Among the Long Island-related treasures to be found in *Lost and Found* are an edition of *Newsday* featuring the Islanders winning the Stanley Cup, an NBA basketball (Julius Erving was from nearby Roosevelt), a Jets football reflecting the team practices at Hofstra University, and yearbooks from Hempstead High School highlighting community events, such as Martin Luther King's address to students of the high school in 1968. For good measure, and to enliven the work, *Lost and Found* also includes a miniature scene showing a Hempstead station vignette, with a train at the station, railroad personnel on the platform, and people boarding the train or waiting for another.

The station plaza had been designed by architect Peter Hopkinson of DMJM Harris with the idea that art would be added later; Baron's response was a perfect fit, as if it had been there from the beginning.

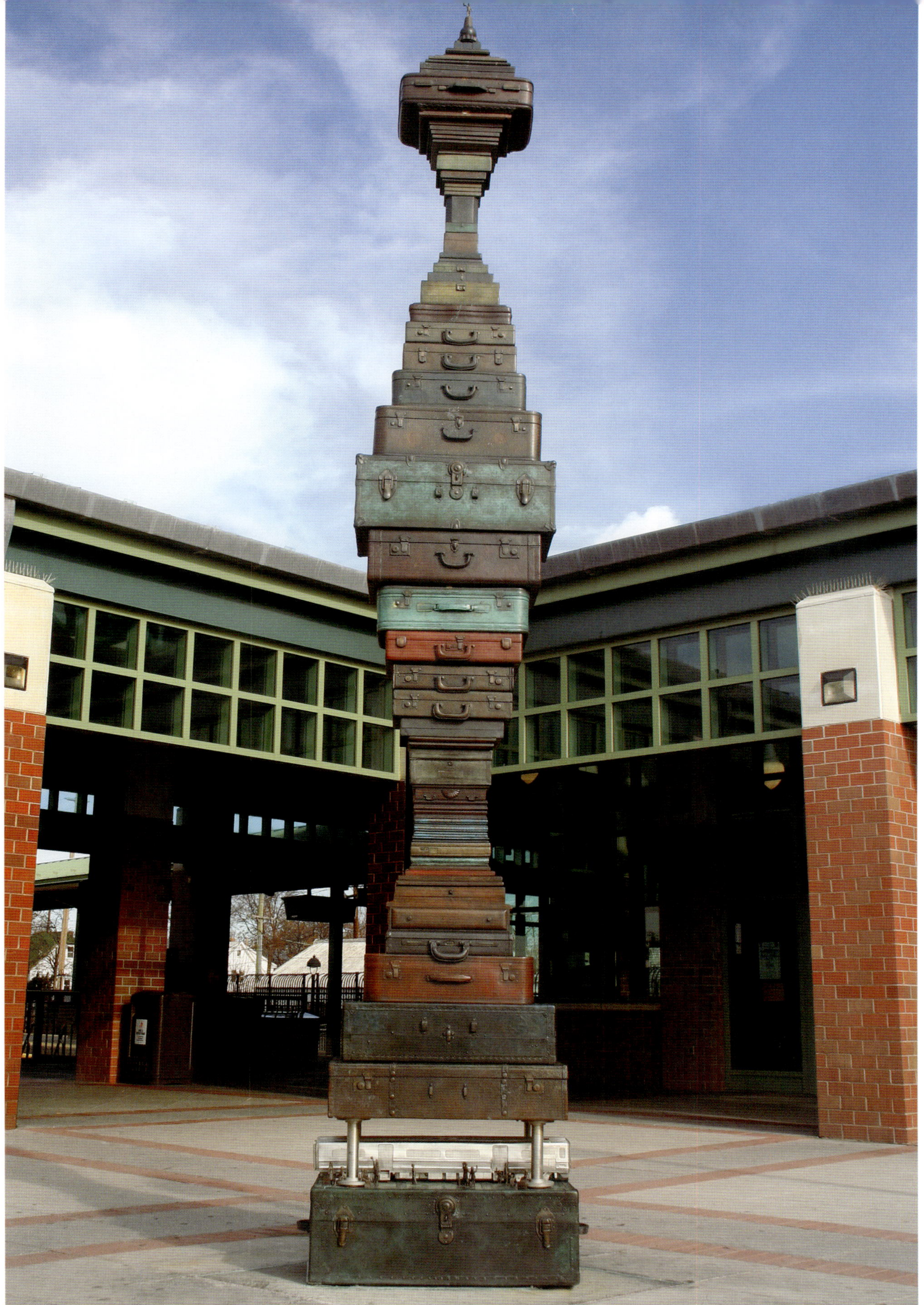

ROY NICHOLSON

MORNING TRANSIT, HEMPSTEAD PLAIN
EVENING TRANSIT, HEMPSTEAD PLAIN, 2001
Hicksville Station, MTA Long Island Rail Road
Glass mosaic
PHOTOGRAPHER: PATRICK J. CASHIN

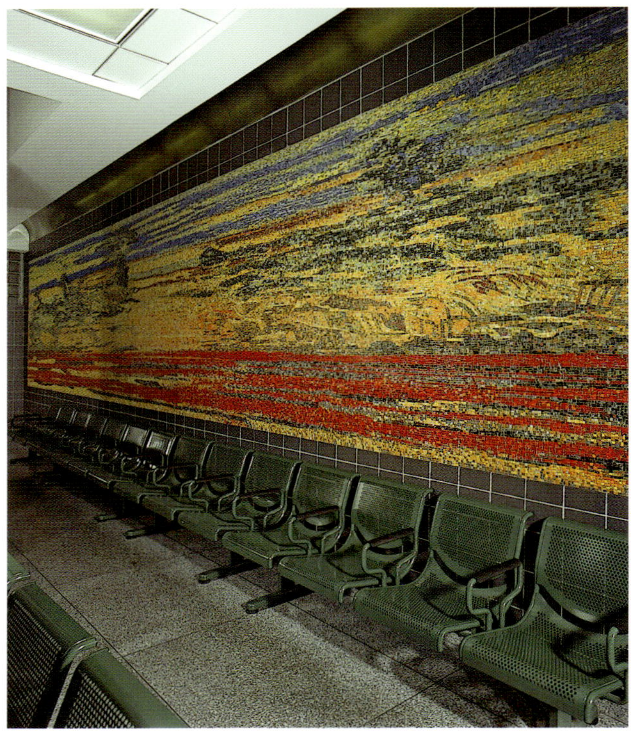

In *Morning Transit, Hempstead Plain* and *Evening Transit, Hempstead Plain*, Roy Nicholson has set out to take viewers back to another time in this Long Island community. The area around Hicksville was once a prairie, a landscape now associated with the Midwest but once also characteristic of this part of Long Island. Here Nicholson recaptures that setting, in both look and spirit, as if it were being seen from a train speeding through it. The colors vary according to the time of day depicted–soft greens and blues for sunrise in *Morning Transit*, and reds and blues for sunset in *Evening Transit*. "Each commuter imagines his or her own personal scenery," Nicholson said in a 2000 interview. "One can look at it over and over again and discover new images."

The Hempstead Plain murals are sensitively integrated into the station waiting room. Special lighting emanating from the tops of nearby columns is used to show them to their best advantage. This contemplative meditation on landscape is an affectionate look back at Long Island before the postwar housing boom forever altered the land.

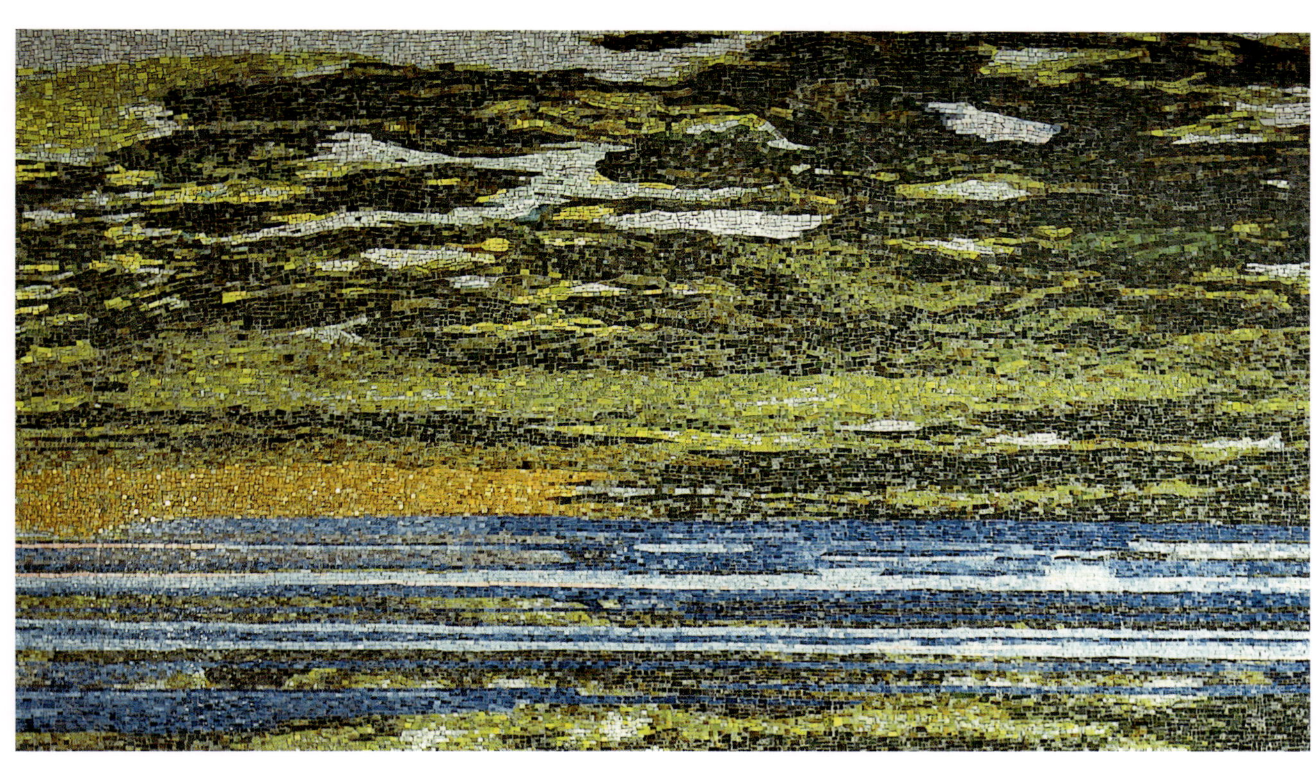

ALICE ADAMS in collaboration with Richard Henry Behr

PLANTING (DEDICATED TO LONG ISLAND TREE FARMERS), 1995
Ronkonkoma Station, MTA Long Island Rail Road
Brick, concrete, aluminum, and plantings
PHOTOGRAPHER: BILL GORDY

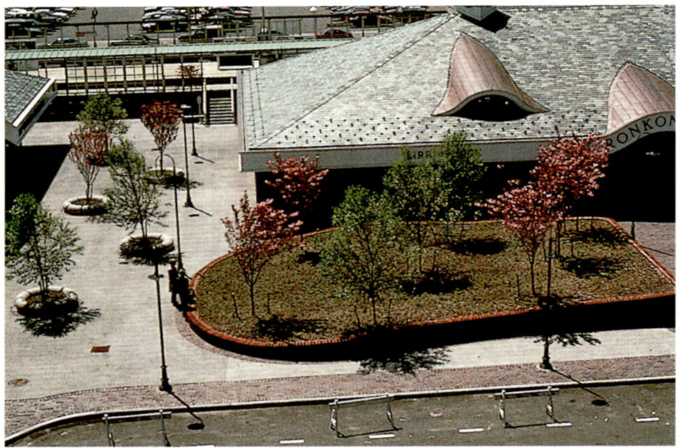

Planting is composed of a variety of planters and trees, using paving, plantings, and curving brick walls to define the outdoor space. Adams's intention was "to create an ensemble of functional and sculptural forms that is unique and specific to the region and together with the architectural structures makes a place that is memorable over time." She continues:

> The planting of trees in rows in the "islands" and the placement of the "tree ball" planters in the paved areas of the central plaza symbolizes and pays homage to a familiar and historic enterprise on Long Island. One of the first tree farms in the United States was started on Long Island and the nursery business has always been a thriving Long Island enterprise. Old Long Island nursery catalogs offer specific photo documentation of the tree moving process with large trees shown as they were being moved on the Long Island Rail Road.

To ensure that the planters would suggest tree balls but, at the same time, allow the trees to be planted directly into the ground, Adams came up with an ingenious solution: a pre-cast concrete ring simulating burlap-wrapped tree balls surrounds each planting space, and metal support elements in the form of ropes extend upward from them.

Adams designed *Planting* in consultation with the planners and architects who were building a new station to replace a much smaller and outmoded facility. Her work helps to articulate the placement of the buildings and platforms in relation to one another and to ensure a seamless, functional overall statement.

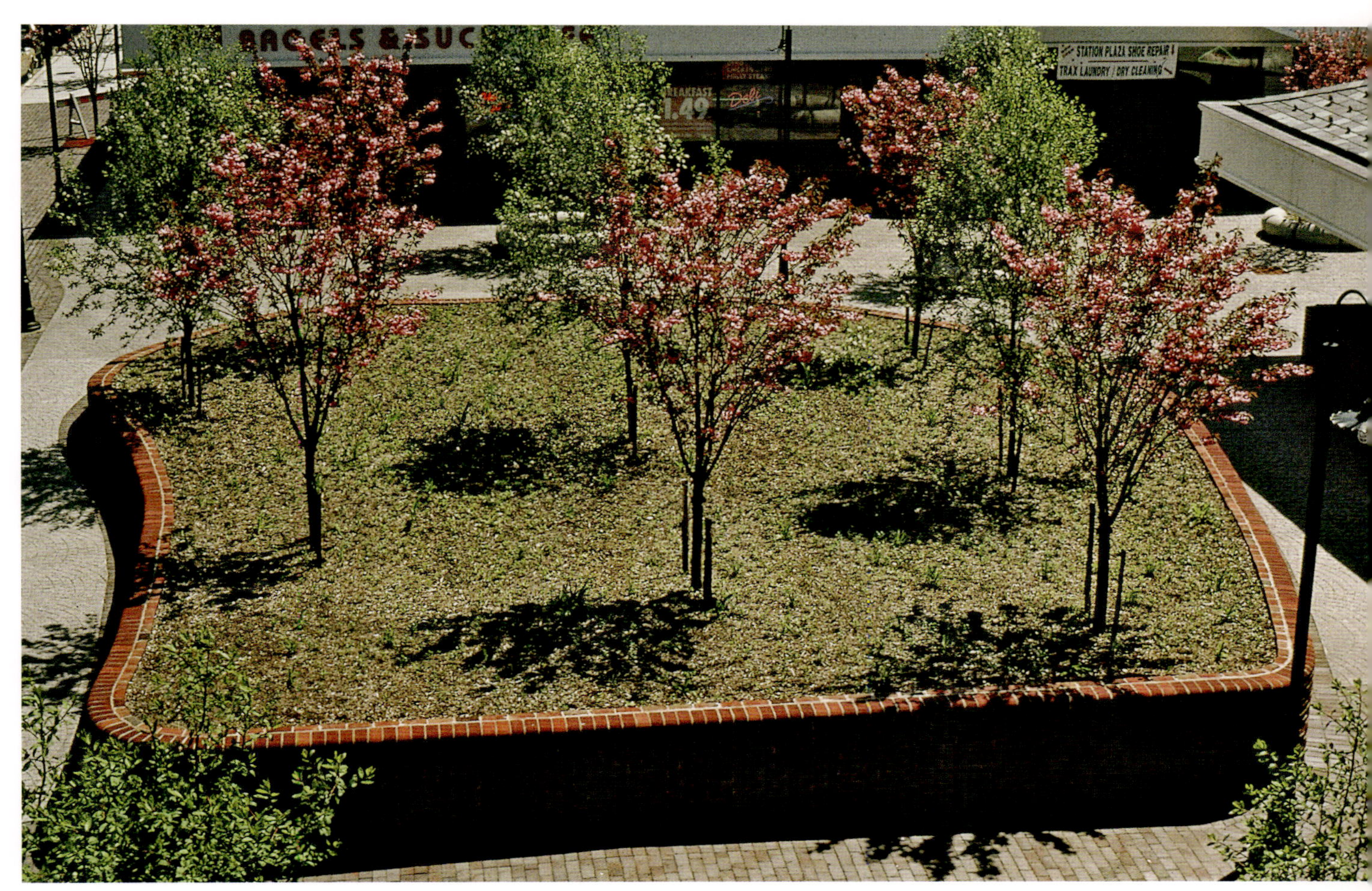
STATION PLAZA SHOE REPAIR
TRAX LAUNDRY / DRY CLEANING
Deli

JOE ZUCKER

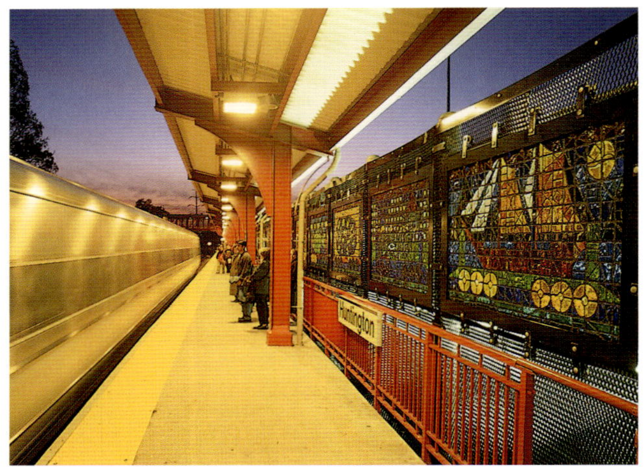

FOR MY GRANDFATHER NOYE PRIDE, A LOCOMOTIVE ENGINEER, 1998
Huntington Station, MTA Long Island Rail Road
Faceted glass
PHOTOGRAPHER: MICHAEL KAMBER

At the Huntington station, Joe Zucker's 130-foot fantasy train cheerfully chugs down the platform, brightening riders' days and at the same time protecting them from the force of cross-track winds. The cartoonlike flatcars are shown carrying all manner of Long Island–related objects, one prize specimen to a car. Products of Long Island's fields and waters are represented by a giant lobster, a gargantuan duck (the famed Long Island Flanders), the king of all potatoes, and a monster bluefish. Tourist attractions are there too—the Montauk lighthouse, a sailboat. The images are delightfully wacky and bizarrely colored; why, for instance, is the bluefish green and the potato blue?

Zucker designed his images to be rendered in faceted glass, in such a way that they are equally powerful day and night and are effective when viewed from either side. During daylight hours, they respond to the path of the sun. At night, lights shining on the faceted glass give commuters a glowing welcome back home.

"The railroad is simultaneously a metaphor for movement and stability," says Zucker. "It is restless and powerful, gliding across the continent." But mainly it is meant to be just fun: "I hope that this piece brings travelers enjoyment, that it gives them memories of Long Island and moments of pleasure."

As the title indicates, members of the artist's family were employed on the railroad: "It is in memory of my grandfather and uncles who served as engineers and firemen on the trains of a distant past."

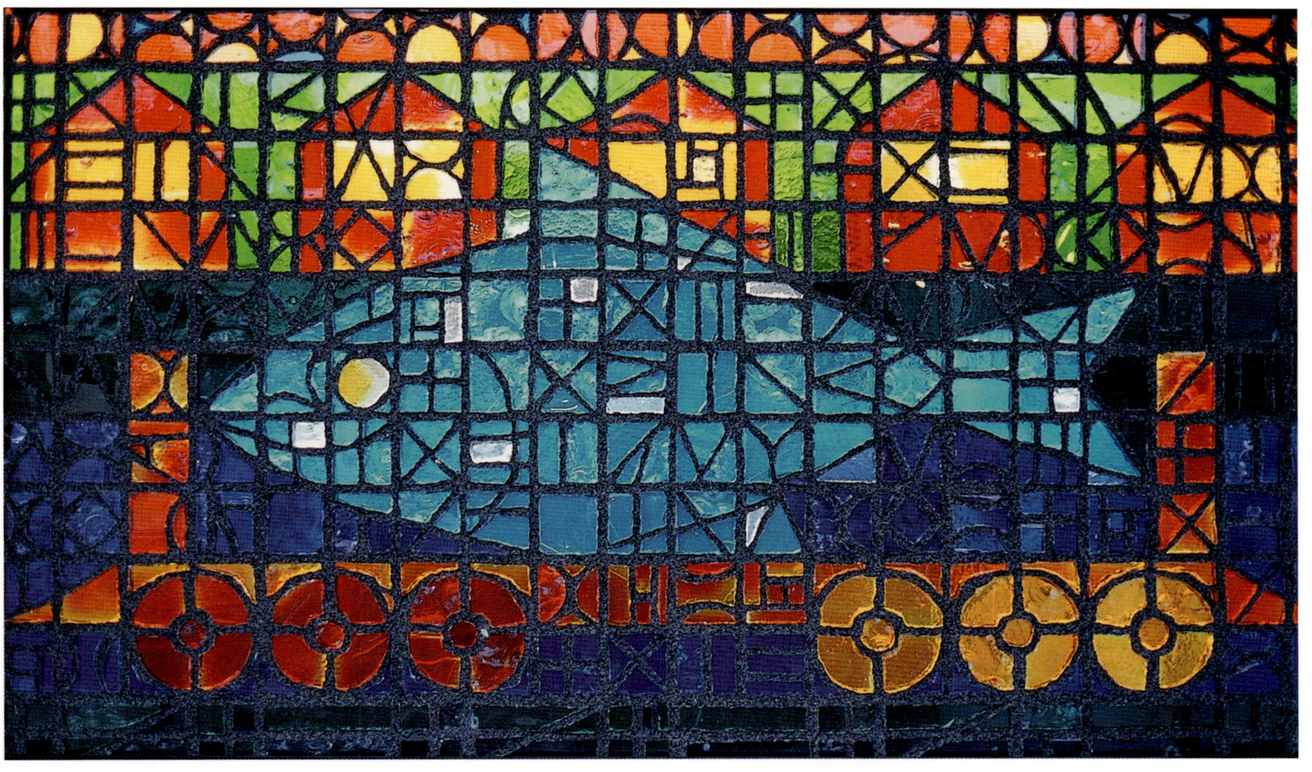

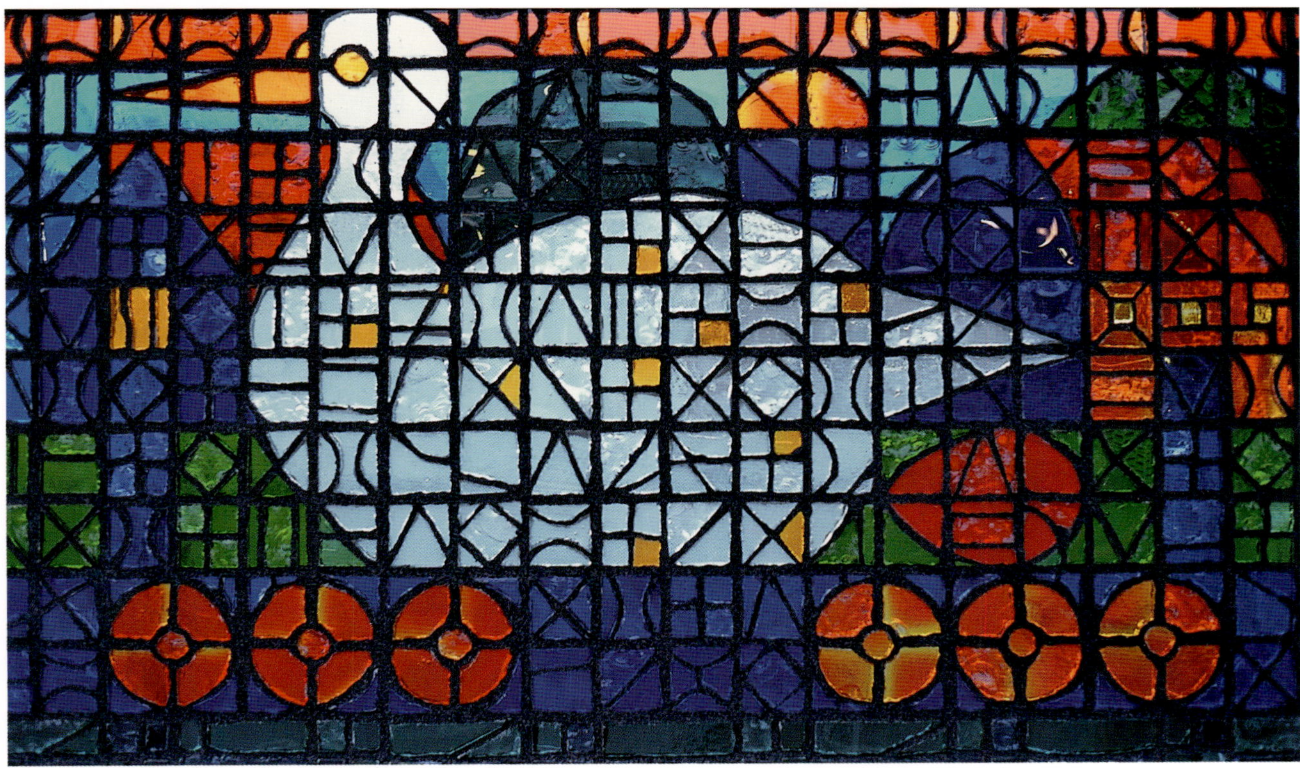

ANITA THACHER

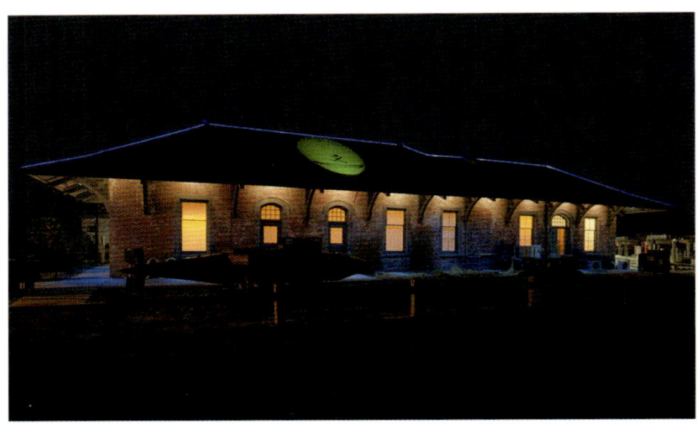

ILLUMINATED STATION, 2005
Greenport Station, MTA Long Island Rail Road
Lighting and projection
PHOTOGRAPHER: PETER MAUSS/ESTO

Illuminated Station evokes the era when most of the people in Greenport and the entire North Fork were farmers, fishermen, storekeepers, and railroad workers. Today Greenport is the hub of an ever-growing population boom of year-round and seasonal residents, as well as a place known for its encouragement of artistic expression.

Anita Thacher is noted for her evocative light-works. Here the stationhouse roof is outlined with LED illumination in blue, and the area immediately surrounding the building is imbued with deeper blue light. From inside comes a yellow glow suggesting candlelight. Images of an American Indian pictograph are projected on the walls and roof to emphasize the importance of the first people to live on Long Island. The man-and-canoe pictograph was taken from a plaster cast of an American Indian artifact discovered in nearby Orient by a local family.

The project was executed with the support of the East End Seaport Museum and Marine Foundation.

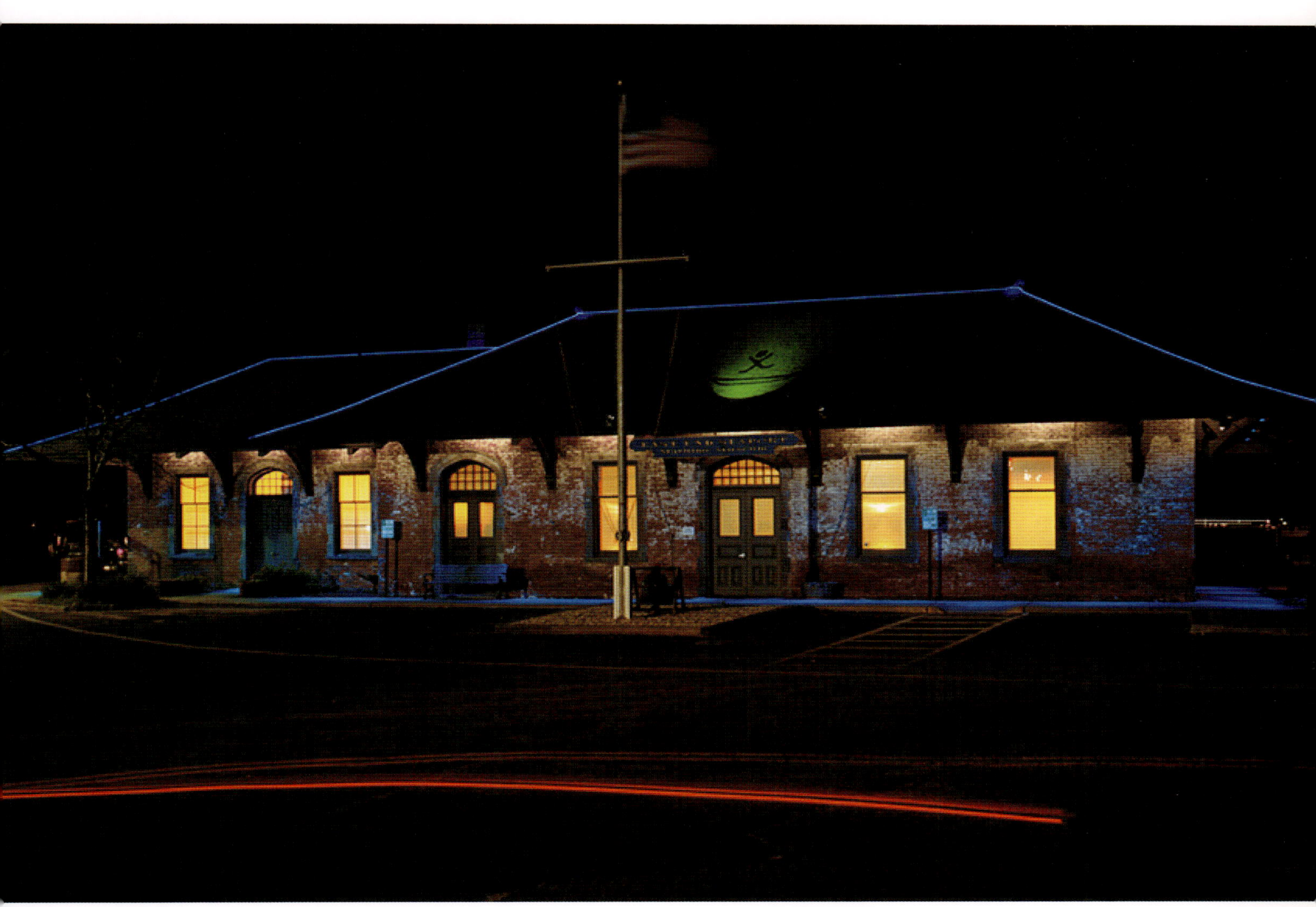

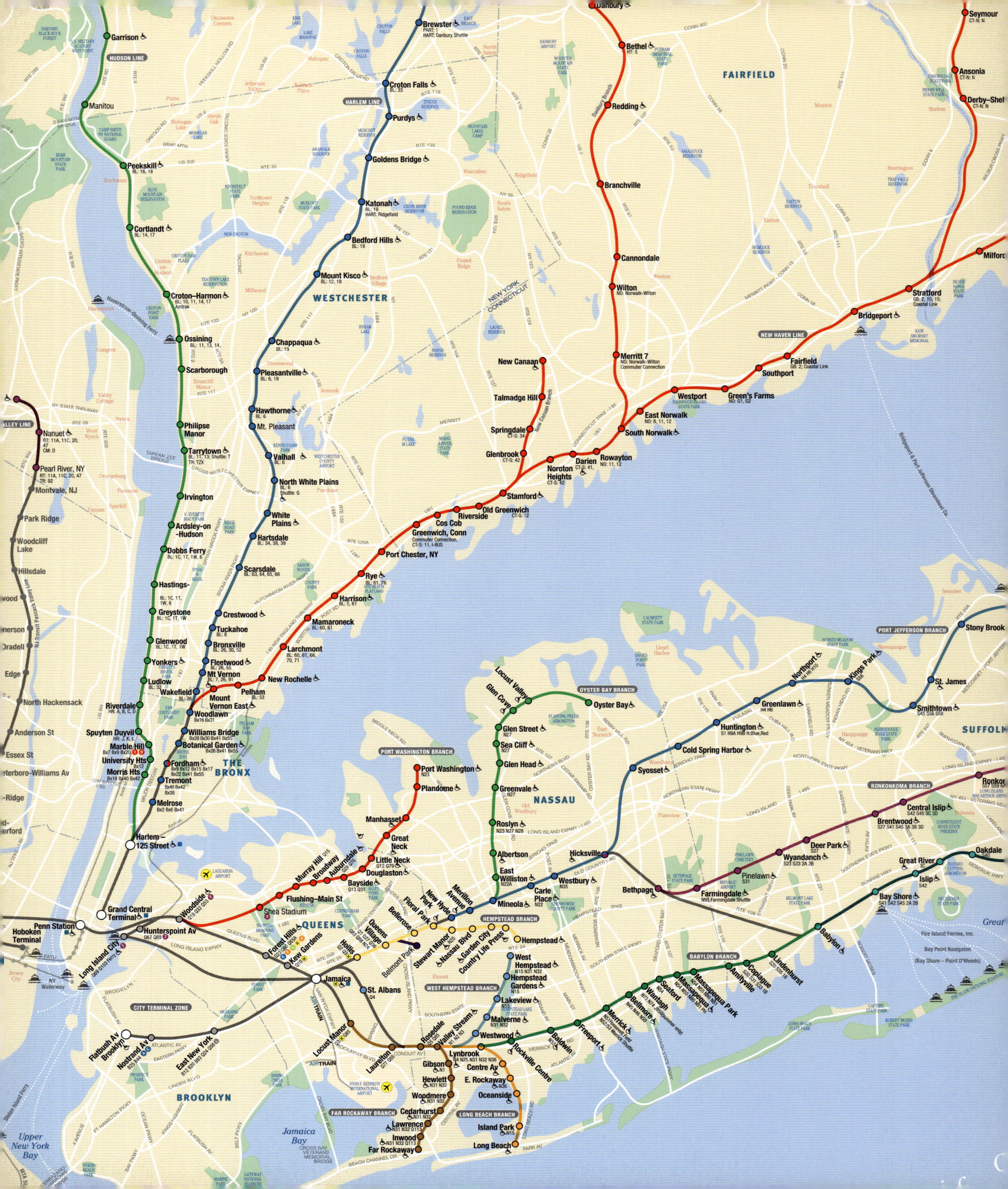

HUDSON LINE
HARLEM LINE
NEW HAVEN LINE
FAIRFIELD
WESTCHESTER
NASSAU
QUEENS
THE BRONX
BROOKLYN
SUFFOLK
PORT JEFFERSON BRANCH
OYSTER BAY BRANCH
PORT WASHINGTON BRANCH
RONKONKOMA BRANCH
HEMPSTEAD BRANCH
WEST HEMPSTEAD BRANCH
BABYLON BRANCH
FAR ROCKAWAY BRANCH
LONG BEACH BRANCH
CITY TERMINAL ZONE
Garrison
Manitou
Peekskill
Cortlandt
Croton–Harmon
Ossining
Scarborough
Philipse Manor
Tarrytown
Irvington
Ardsley-on-Hudson
Dobbs Ferry
Hastings-on-Hudson
Greystone
Glenwood
Yonkers
Ludlow
Riverdale
Spuyten Duyvil
Marble Hill
University Hts
Morris Hts
Harlem – 125 Street
Brewster
Croton Falls
Purdys
Goldens Bridge
Katonah
Bedford Hills
Mount Kisco
Chappaqua
Pleasantville
Hawthorne
Mt. Pleasant
Valhalla
North White Plains
White Plains
Hartsdale
Scarsdale
Crestwood
Tuckahoe
Bronxville
Fleetwood
Mt Vernon
Wakefield
Woodlawn
Williams Bridge
Botanical Garden
Fordham
Tremont
Melrose
Danbury
Bethel
Redding
Branchville
Cannondale
Wilton
Merritt 7
New Canaan
Talmadge Hill
Springdale
Glenbrook
Stamford
Old Greenwich
Riverside
Cos Cob
Greenwich, Conn
Port Chester, NY
Rye
Harrison
Mamaroneck
Larchmont
New Rochelle
Pelham
Mount Vernon East
Noroton Heights
Darien
Rowayton
South Norwalk
East Norwalk
Westport
Green's Farms
Southport
Fairfield
Bridgeport
Stratford
Milford
Seymour
Ansonia
Derby–Shelton
Nanuet
Pearl River, NY
Montvale, NJ
Park Ridge
Woodcliff Lake
Hillsdale
North Hackensack
Anderson St
Essex St
Teterboro-Williams Av
Grand Central Terminal
Penn Station
Hoboken Terminal
Long Island City
Hunterspoint Av
Woodside
Shea Stadium
Flushing–Main St
Murray Hill
Broadway
Auburndale
Bayside
Douglaston
Little Neck
Great Neck
Manhasset
Plandome
Port Washington
Forest Hills
Kew Gardens
Jamaica
St. Albans
Hollis
Queens Village
Bellerose
Floral Park
New Hyde Park
Merillon Avenue
Mineola
Carle Place
Westbury
Hicksville
Bethpage
Farmingdale
Pinelawn
Wyandanch
Deer Park
Brentwood
Central Islip
Ronkonkoma
Syosset
Cold Spring Harbor
Huntington
Greenlawn
Northport
Kings Park
St. James
Smithtown
Stony Brook
East Williston
Albertson
Roslyn
Greenvale
Glen Head
Sea Cliff
Glen Street
Glen Cove
Locust Valley
Oyster Bay
Stewart Manor
Nassau Blvd
Garden City
Country Life Press
Hempstead
West Hempstead
Hempstead Gardens
Lakeview
Malverne
Westwood
Belmont Park
Flatbush Av
Nostrand Av
East New York
Locust Manor
Laurelton
Rosedale
Valley Stream
Lynbrook
Gibson
Hewlett
Woodmere
Cedarhurst
Lawrence
Inwood
Far Rockaway
Centre Av
E. Rockaway
Oceanside
Island Park
Long Beach
Rockville Centre
Baldwin
Freeport
Merrick
Bellmore
Wantagh
Seaford
Massapequa
Massapequa Park
Amityville
Copiague
Lindenhurst
Babylon
Bay Shore
Islip
Great River
Oakdale
Fire Island Ferries, Inc.
Bay Point Navigation (Bay Shore – Point O'Woods)
Bridgeport & Port Jefferson Steamboat Co.
Upper New York Bay
Jamaica Bay
NEW YORK CONNECTICUT

CATALOG

1986

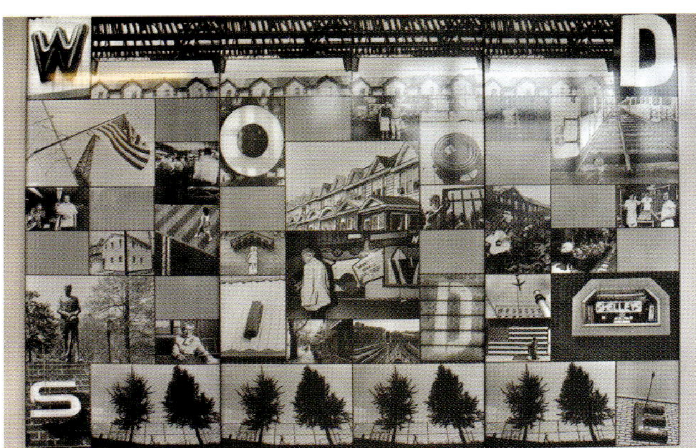

JOHN CAVANAGH

COMMUTING/COMMUNITY, 1986
Woodside–61st Street (7)
Porcelain enamel
PHOTOGRAPHER: ROB WILSON

Commuting/Community reflects John Cavanagh's impressions of Woodside, a neighborhood where the Long Island Rail Road and a major subway line intersect. Constructed as two separate but related photomontage murals, the work echoes the pace of Woodside life and the people who reside there. Both murals spell out "Woodside" using individual letters from neighborhood sites. The murals are about dichotomies. In one, the artist contrasts the loud, rushing train overhead with the bucolic street life below. In the other, he juxtaposes scenes of young children playing in the park with adults commuting into the city. The images in the work, says Cavanagh. "are ordered and chaotic, busy and quiet, joyous and reflective. They are offered to the community to provoke, stimulate, console, strengthen, and enjoy."

HOUSTON CONWILL

OPEN SECRET, 1986
125th Street (4)(5)(6)
Bronze
Fabricator: Modern Art Foundry
Station Design: Castro-Blanco, Piscioneri & Associates
See page 68

MILTON GLASER

UNTITLED, 1986
Astor Place (6)
Porcelain enamel
Fabricator: Cherokee Porcelain Enamel
Station Design: Prentice & Chan, Olhausen
See page 96

1987

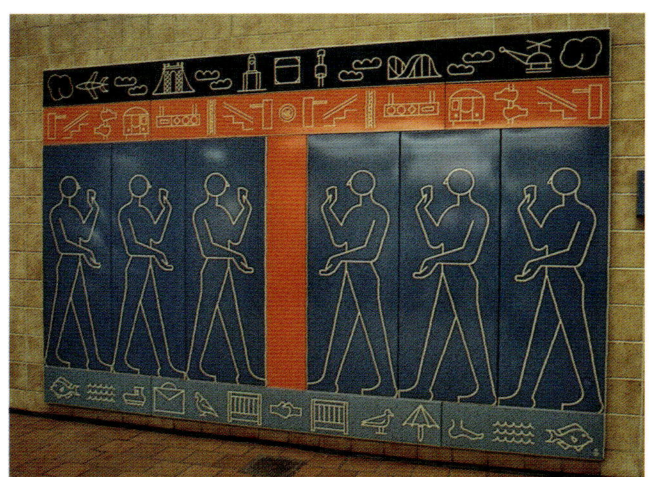

RHODA ANDORS

KINGS HIGHWAY HIEROGLYPHS, 1987
Kings Highway (B)(Q)
Porcelain enamel
Fabricator: ELB Associates (with Pefco, Inc.)
Station Design: Perkins + Will
PHOTOGRAPHER: ROB WILSON

According to Rhoda Andors, "If public art is elegantly and permanently crafted, it will delight audiences of the present and the future, in the way the wall paintings of ancient civilizations delight us today, thousands of years after their creation . . . Like the ancient pyramids, the subway is a great monument, with underground caverns, and like them, decorated with art. It is no accident, then, that the style of these murals is hieroglyphs. I wanted the cool dignity, the symbolism full of messages, the cordial sense of humanity in the figures that are found in the Valley of the Kings . . . Perhaps some future archaeologist will dig through the layers of Brooklyn, discovering who knows what relics of our civilization, and find these murals, for after all they are forged in enamel, an art form as permanent and enduring as any. And perhaps he or she will be able to glimpse in them what daily life was like here, in 1987. I hope so."

NANCY HOLT

ASTRAL GRATING, 1987

Fulton Street–Broadway–Nassau A C J M Z 2 3 4 5

Steel and lighting

Fabricators: Tallix; McPhilbin

Station Design: Lee Harris Pomeroy Architects

See page 102

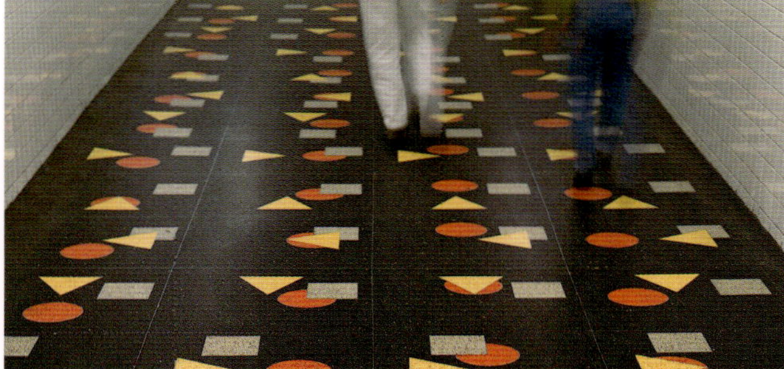

RAY RING

CLARK STREET PASSAGE, 1987

Clark Street 2 3

Terrazzo

Fabricator: Expert Terrazzo Co., Inc.

Station Design: Castro-Blanco, Piscioneri & Associates

PHOTOGRAPHER: DAVID LUBARSKY

Brooklyn-born artist Ray Ring points out, "The *Passage* uses three geometric shapes—a circle, a square, and a triangle—that turn in four different directions. The floor of the subway corridor is divided into large black squares. As people walk down the passage, they experience all the possible combinations of these elements. The study of ever-changing geometric patterns comes out of my earlier work from the 1970s. Today, I continue to work in variations of geometric shapes."

1988

VALERIE JAUDON

LONG DIVISION, 1988

23rd Street 6

Painted steel

Fabricator: A&T Iron Works

Station Design: Perkins + Will

See page 60

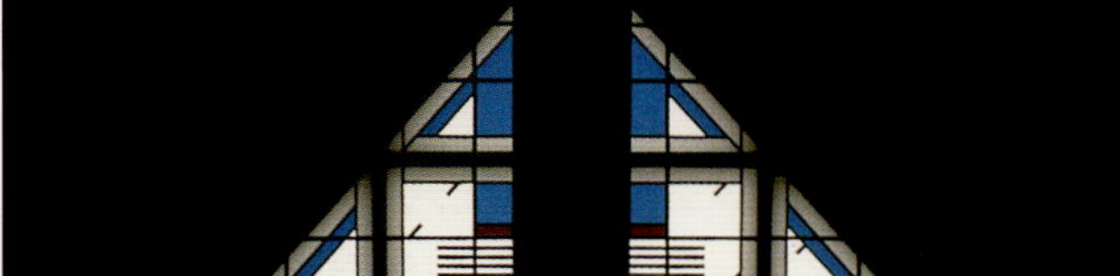

DAVID WILSON

TRANSIT SKYLIGHT, 1988

Newkirk Avenue B Q

Zinc-glazed polycarbonate

Station Design: Perkins+Will

PHOTOGRAPHER: DAVID WILSON

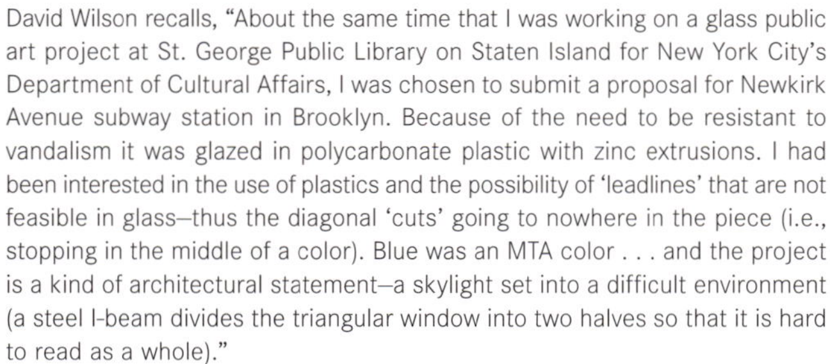

David Wilson recalls, "About the same time that I was working on a glass public art project at St. George Public Library on Staten Island for New York City's Department of Cultural Affairs, I was chosen to submit a proposal for Newkirk Avenue subway station in Brooklyn. Because of the need to be resistant to vandalism it was glazed in polycarbonate plastic with zinc extrusions. I had been interested in the use of plastics and the possibility of 'leadlines' that are not feasible in glass—thus the diagonal 'cuts' going to nowhere in the piece (i.e., stopping in the middle of a color). Blue was an MTA color . . . and the project is a kind of architectural statement—a skylight set into a difficult environment (a steel I-beam divides the triangular window into two halves so that it is hard to read as a whole)."

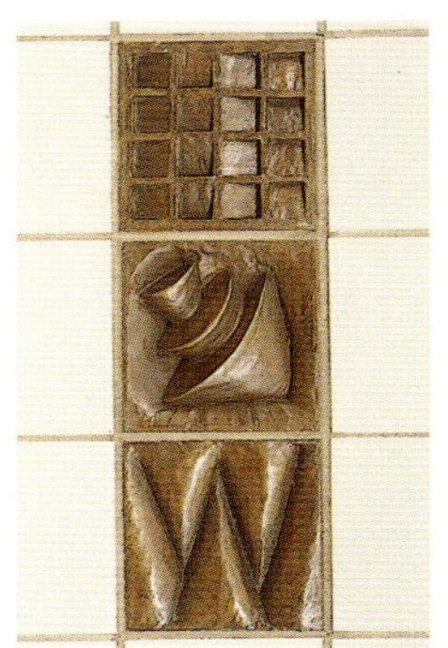

STEVE WOOD

FOSSILS, 1988
137th Street–City College 1
Bronze
Fabricator: Modern Art Foundry
Station Design: Stull and Lee Associates
PHOTOGRAPHER: ROB WILSON

Steve Wood's piece consists of 160 bronze relief tiles embedded in the platform walls, 80 on each side. Each represents the fossilized remains of a biological form. As he explains, "The idea behind *Fossils* is simple: the subway is underground, fossils are found in the earth . . . I wanted these reliefs to be 'scattered' over the walls of the northbound and southbound platforms in such a way that both children and adults would see them personally and close-up. They are meant to be looked at, touched, talked about, and remembered."

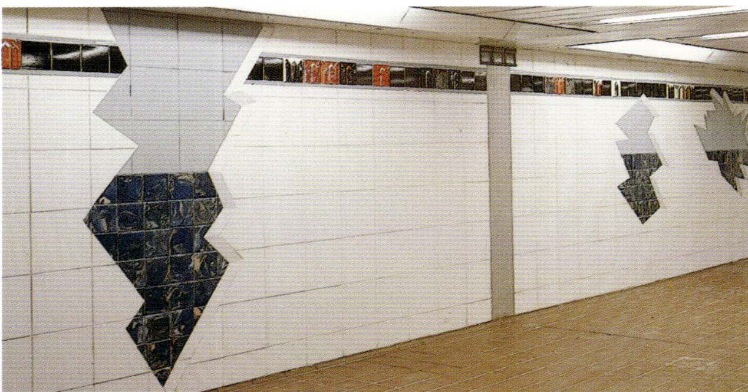

NINA YANKOWITZ

TUNNEL VISION, 1988
51st Street 6
Ceramic tile
Station Design: Mayers & Schiff
PHOTOGRAPHER: JOSEPH COSCIA JR.

Nina Yankowitz explains her concept: "I approached this project with a desire to make the underpass feel wider, brighter, and more expansive. With ceramic mosaic inlays, I created faux shadow and color shading to establish a series of 'openings' in the walls, which allow the traveler/viewer to peer through to the third dimension. The view through these 'torn' windows is of carefully constructed seascapes. A ceramic relief architectural frieze of the New York City skyline in red, black and white wraps around the top portion of the walls, and ceramic columns appear to be holding up the ceiling."

1989

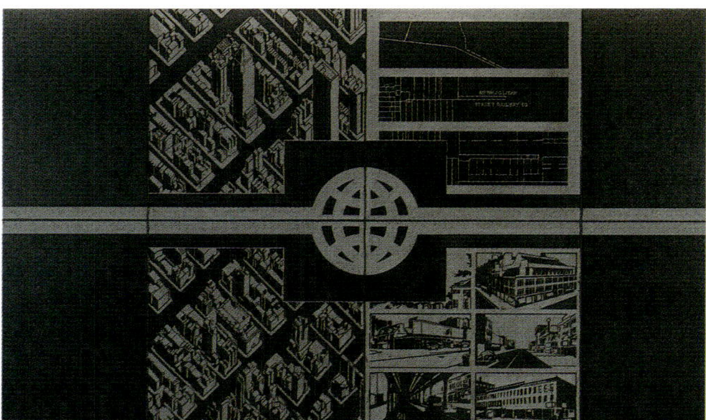

MATT MULLICAN

UNTITLED, 1989
50th Street C E
Etched granite
Sponsored by New York Communications Center Associates
Fabricator: Carved by Shefts
Station Design: Skidmore, Owings & Merrill
PHOTOGRAPHER: DAVID LUBARSKY

The Zeckendorf Company's Worldwide Plaza provided new station entrances accessible to the mobility impaired, wells that bring natural light into the underground platform areas, and a sandblasted granite mural by Matt Mullican, which he describes as a timeline of the site. "It was once countryside, once had a cabin, and it was also a previous site of Madison Square Garden," said Mullican. "Referencing the iconography of the subway map, the artwork interprets the history of this location through using elements that take you back in time."

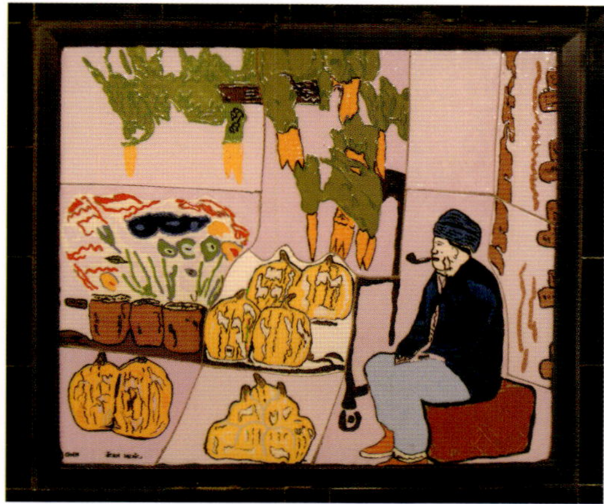

NITZA TUFIÑO in collaboration with Grosvenor Neighborhood House student muralists

WESTSIDE VIEWS, 1989
86th Street (1)
Ceramic plaques
PHOTOGRAPHER: PATRICK J. CASHIN

Westside Views is an unusual project that began when the local community board suggested that amenity funds from the Bromley Company be applied to a youth-opportunity community improvement project to upgrade the 86th Street station. Artist and teacher Nitza Tufiño worked with seventeen young people, most of whom attended or were graduates of the high school equivalency program at Grosvenor Neighborhood House. Students photographed notable sites in the neighborhood, and their work was translated into forty ceramic tiles that speak volumes about the place and time in which they were created. Guided by Pedro Pietri, whose poetry expresses what it is like to be a Puerto Rican in New York, the students also wrote a poem to capture the spirit of the neighborhood, its multiethnic character, its parks, the foods–the flavor of the community. The poem is captured in tile and installed in the station.

1990

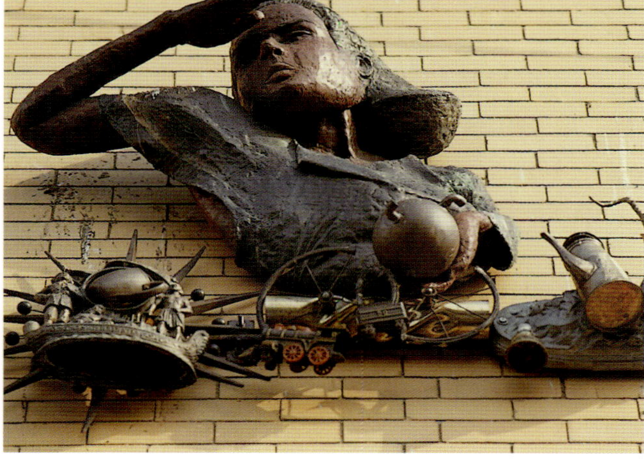

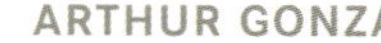

ARTHUR GONZALEZ

THE FINDER/THE SEEKERS, 1990
Tuckahoe Station, MTA Metro-North Railroad
THE DISCOVERY, 1990
Crestwood Station, MTA Metro-North Railroad
TIME CATCHER, 1990
Fleetwood Station, MTA Metro-North Railroad
Bronze and mixed-media
Fabricators: Tallix; Dennis Cobb
Station Design: MTA MNR Architects/Engineers
PHOTOGRAPHER: FRANK ENGLISH

The themes of time and travel are central to Arthur Gonzalez's monumental figurative bronze sculptures. *The Finder/The Seekers* at Tuckahoe (the first project in the Arts for Transit program to be completed and installed at a Metro-North station) includes images of speed and travel in the forms of children's toys below each sculptural representation of explorers and settlers. At Crestwood, *The Discovery* is a bronze figure of a girl in a boat, holding a compass, evoking themes of travel and exploration. *Time Catcher* at Fleetwood is a polychrome bronze featuring a worker with his tools and a historic map of the region, an homage to the railroad workers.

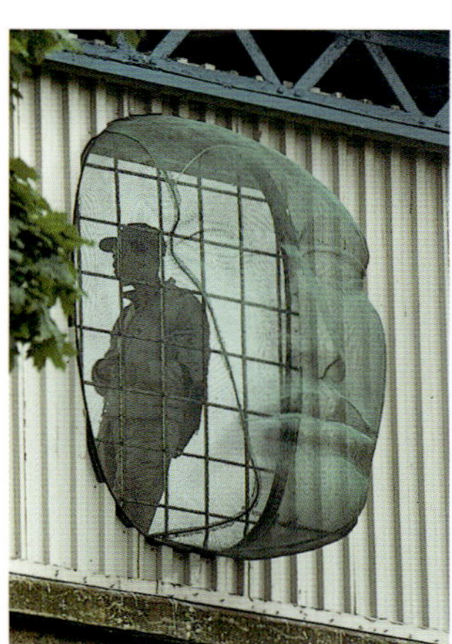

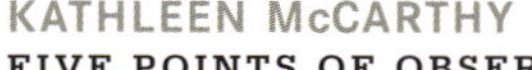

KATHLEEN McCARTHY

FIVE POINTS OF OBSERVATION, 1990
111th Street, Cypress Hills, Woodhaven Boulevard, 75th Street, and 104th Street (J) (Z)
Copper wire mesh and stainless steel
Station Design: Fritz Johnson Architect
PHOTOGRAPHER: KATHLEEN MCCARTHY

Five Points of Observation, sited on the walls of five adjacent elevated stations in Queens, is composed of five copper-mesh heads, each inserted into the windscreen walls, opening views from the platforms to the streets below. From behind the heads, riders can look out onto the world through the eyes of the sculptural forms. Kathleen McCarthy created the faces to be both multiethnic and androgynous, leaving room for viewers to construct their own stories about the haunting forms and what they might signify. The faces are protected on the platform side with stainless-steel armatures and a wire-mesh grid, which also add to the aesthetic experience. The position of the forms is different from station to station, adding further variety to their expressions.

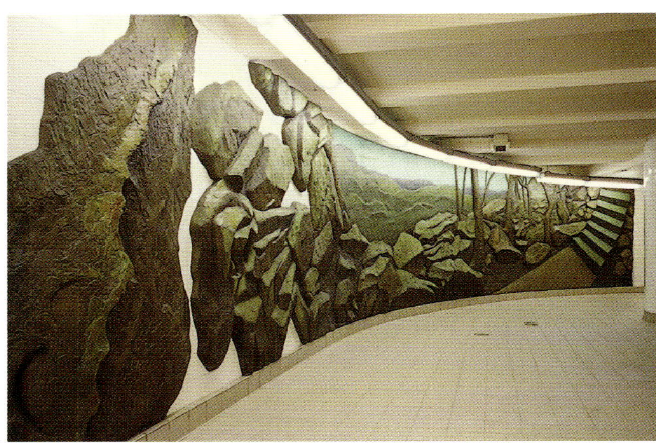

HARRY ROSEMAN

SUBWAY WALL, 1990
Wall Street 2 3
Bronze
Sponsored by JP Morgan
Fabricator: Tallix
Station Design: Kevin Roche John Dinkeloo and Associates
PHOTOGRAPHER: DOUG BAZ

As Harry Roseman notes: "[This site] is underground, in the 'earth,' under an urban setting . . . Rocks are interspersed among tiles. The rocks in this situation could actually have been a part of the excavation process for the subway tunnel . . . [and they] thus become a symbol for the process of building the tunnel and for being underground . . . The path and stairs as well as the tiles . . . intermingle nature with the man-made. The built aspect of the stairs also alludes to the built environment, the city. The landscape could be the kind of place that was here before this was an urban center . . . The curve [of the tunnel] . . . was also the perfect opportunity to twist the perspective of the staircase to reiterate the curve and suggest going from one type of environment to another. Aside from the layers of references and meaning, I tried to create a work that would be visually pleasing and could be enjoyed instinctually."

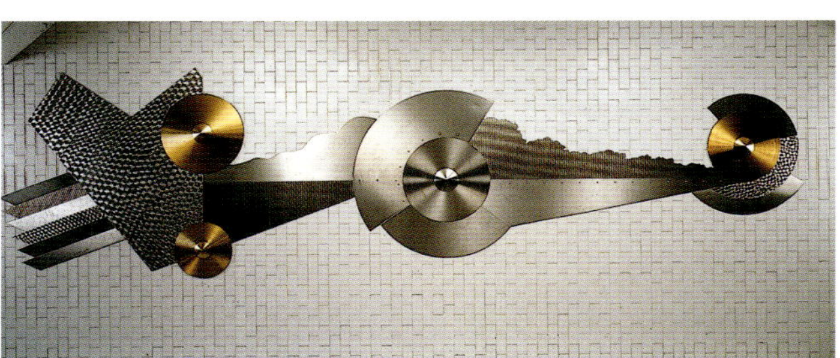

DAN SINCLAIR

FAST TRACK AND SPEEDWHEELS, 1990
Grand Central–42nd Street S 4 5 6 7
Brass, aluminum, stainless steel, and copper
Station Design: TAMS Consultants
PHOTOGRAPHER: DAVID LUBARSKY

Dan Sinclair's sculptures are exuberant assemblages of metal parts including wavy aluminum sheets, steel wheels, brass disks, and copper springs and wires. *The New Yorker* observed on March 25, 1991, that the pieces "seem to have grown on the site," in their homes at the ends of the long underground passage for the shuttle to Times Square. Curious riders are invited to make associations and to read varied meanings into the metal collages. They might suggest antiquated machinery, photograph records, or birds in flight. "I want my sculpture to make people think of the power of the engines that drive the trains, the speed and efficiency of them . . . the sculptures also reflect the architectural elements of Times Square and the Art Deco glamour of Radio City Music Hall," says the artist. Or as the writer of the *New Yorker* piece commented, "They remind me of what a hankie would look like if you fluttered it out of a subway-car window."

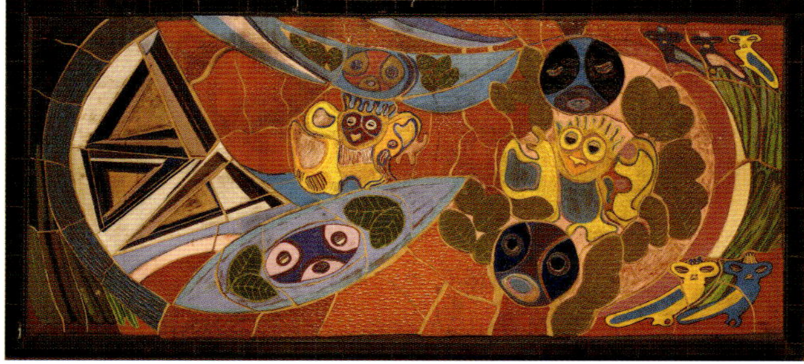

NITZA TUFIÑO

NEO-BORIKEN, 1990
103rd Street 6
Ceramic tile
Station Design: Castro-Blanco, Piscioneri & Associates
PHOTOGRAPHER: PATRICK J. CASHIN

Nitza Tufiño's murals refer to people from her native Puerto Rico and other parts of the Caribbean and Latin America who have, in her words, "transplanted themselves from the tropical jungles into New York." The title of the mural derives from the pre-Columbian Taíno Indian name for the island of Puerto Rico, "Boriken" or "Boricua." The ancient Taínos also designed the petroglyphs that the murals allude to, accompanying Aztec and Mayan forms. Tufiño's art is informed by her connections to the people of Latin America, their history and culture, as well as her training as a teacher.

1991

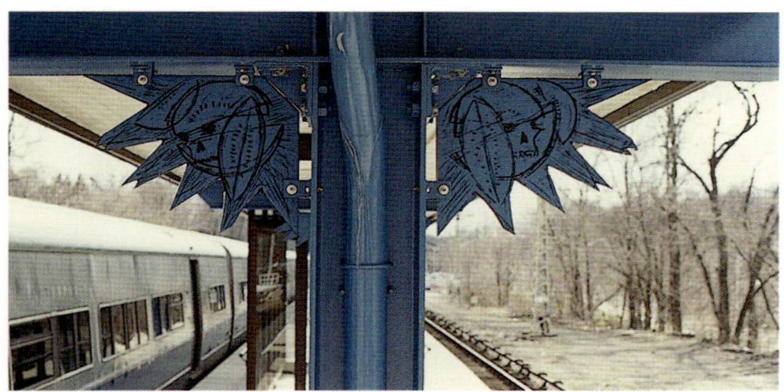

ROLANDO BRISEÑO

AT THE TABLE, 1991
North White Plains Station, MTA Metro-North Railroad
Painted cast aluminum
Fabricator: Fundición Baf
Station Design: MTA MNR Architects/Engineers; Goodkind & O'Dea
PHOTOGRAPHER: DAVID LUBARSKY

Rolando Briseño's *At the Table* is a series of cast-aluminum capitals on the canopy columns along the platforms. Starting at the stairway and moving down the platform, this piece complements the architecture of the station while presenting a variety of witty everyday objects etched into the capitals. Pieces that combine these symbols in black architectonic culminations of the capitals are under six of the station signs.

MICHELE OKA DONER

RADIANT SITE, 1991
34th Street-Herald Square B D F N Q R V W
Handmade bronze-colored tiles
Fabricator: Pewabic Pottery
Station Design: William Nicholas Bodouva + Associates
See page 56

SAM GILLIAM

JAMAICA CENTER STATION RIDERS, BLUE, 1991
Jamaica Center-Parsons/Archer E J Z
Painted aluminum
Fabricator: Modern Metalsmiths
Station Design: MTA NYCT Architects/Engineers
See page 120

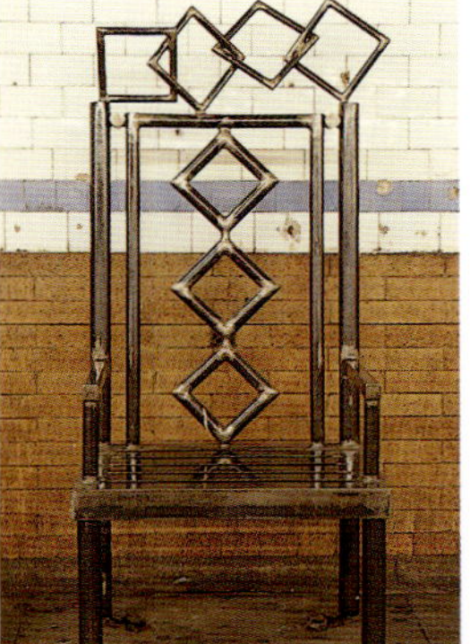

MICHELLE GREENE

RAILRIDER'S THRONE, 1991
116th Street-Columbia University 1
Steel
PHOTOGRAPHER: MICHELLE GREENE

Michelle Greene's *Railrider's Throne* introduces humor into the station. The artist says, "I wanted to create a whimsical environment that allows the commuter to feel special as opposed to alienated. I believe that art in a public space has the potential to stir people from their daily routine." And it works. As reported by *Art News* in January 1992, a frequent user of the station commented, "What's weird about that chair is that when you sit in it everyone stares at you. It feels royal." Another rider reported, "There's a musician who plays his violin [in the chair]. At first, I thought he brought the chair with him. I think he makes more money when he sits there." Elements of the chair's design were influenced by the historic tile pattern in the station, reiterating the credo of the original subway designers that ornamental additions to the stations should make the subway a more pleasant place to be.

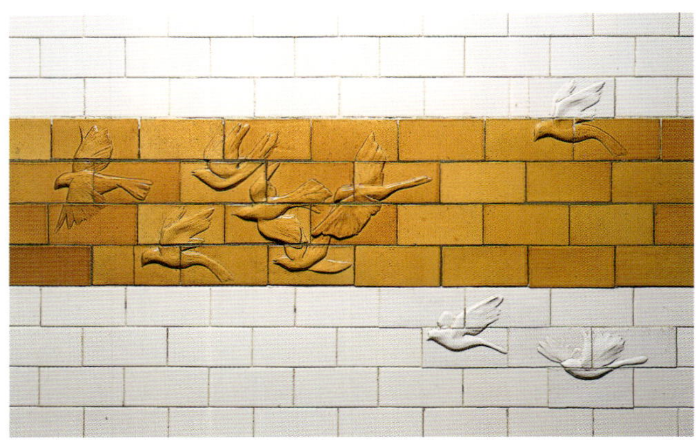

WOPO HOLUP

FLIGHT, 1991

Dyckman Street 1

Ceramic relief tiles

Station Design: MTA NYCT Architects/Engineers

PHOTOGRAPHER: DAVID LUBARSKY

As Wopo Holup notes, "How a work of public art is integrated into its site and the interplay of ideas with the use of the site are of primary importance. I like to think about how people will participate with the work, how they will move by, around, through or over it. With this movement in mind, I have made works using several sculptural elements linking areas of a site into a single concept. I looked at the station's existing tile frieze and continued the frieze as a relief tile band. The relief shows a flight of birds—gold when they fly through the gold band and white as they travel over the white tile of the stairwells. I thought of the birds as flying along with the people as both ascend the stairs to the train's elevated platform."

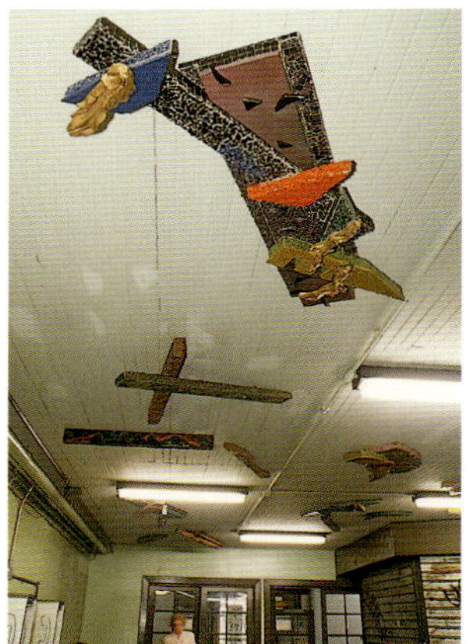

MARTHA JACKSON-JARVIS

TRAVELIN' TIME, 1991

Mount Vernon West Station, MTA Metro-North Railroad

Glass and ceramic mosaic

Station Design: MTA MNR Architects/Engineers

PHOTOGRAPHER: ROB WILSON

Martha Jackson-Jarvis began experimenting with the qualities of fired clay as a child. Since then, she has worked with hundreds of clay bodies, kiln types, and glazes, continuing to test the various possibilities that the medium presents. Along with her experimentation, Jackson-Jarvis welcomes surprise and chance occurrences that may unexpectedly alter her work. Of this piece, the artist says, "Conceptually, *Travelin' Time* occupies transitional space. It is a space between points, a place of resting, of waiting, of new beginnings and departures. Though Mount Vernon station is indeed public space, it still remains an intimate space where human scale and pace are slowed momentarily. It is a space in which we are asked to wait . . . and while waiting contemplate traveling through time and space to distances unknown, yet familiar."

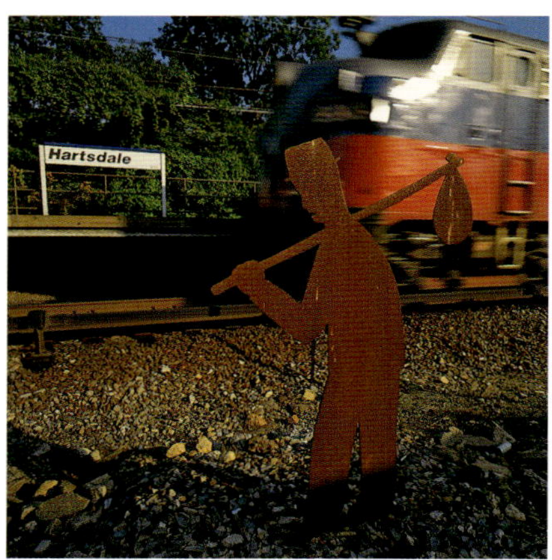

TOM NUSSBAUM

TRAVELERS, 1991

Scarsdale Station, MTA Metro-North Railroad

WORKERS, 1991

Hartsdale Station, MTA Metro-North Railroad

COR-TEN® steel

Station Design: MTA MNR Architects/Engineers

PHOTOGRAPHER: MICHAEL KAMBER

In these silhouetted figures, Tom Nussbaum pays his respects to the people most likely to view his work—commuters and railroad workers. At the Hartsdale station, twenty-one life-size figures in the track bed are busy guiding trains, maintaining the track, and throwing switches. At the Scarsdale station is a group of flattened iron travelers carrying all manner of things. *Travelers* also includes three-foot figures standing along the roofline of the station canopies. Nussbaum says, "My approach to this kind of figurative work reflects an on-going interest in American folk sculpture of all kinds, especially whirligigs and weather vanes."

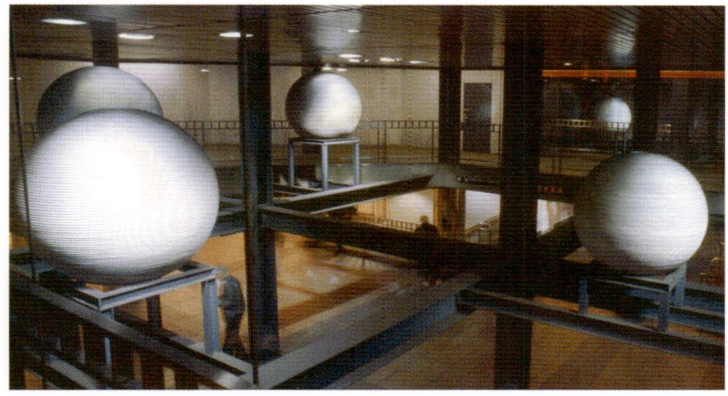

NICHOLAS PEARSON

HALO, 1991
34th Street–Herald Square B D F N Q R V W
Hand-coiled aluminum
Station Design: William Nicholas Bodouva + Associates
PHOTOGRAPHER: NICHOLAS PEARSON

Halo offers a contrast to the utilitarian aesthetic of the station and creates what the artist describes as "an unexpected serenity." Made of bent aluminum rods that are fashioned in a way similar to coiling a ceramic pot, the spheres are suspended on a framework of small beams from the larger steel structural components of the station. Pearson explains, "It was my aim to create an enigmatic distribution of objects that would stand in sharp contrast to the rectilinear nature of the site, and in doing so, to establish an oasis of visual language amid an otherwise functional environment."

ALISON SAAR

HEAR THE LONE WHISTLE MOAN, 1991
Harlem–125th Street, MTA Metro-North Railroad
Bronze
Fabricator: Dennis Cobb
Station Design: MTA MNR Architects/Engineers;
Wormser + Associates, Architects; BTA Architects
See page 72

1992

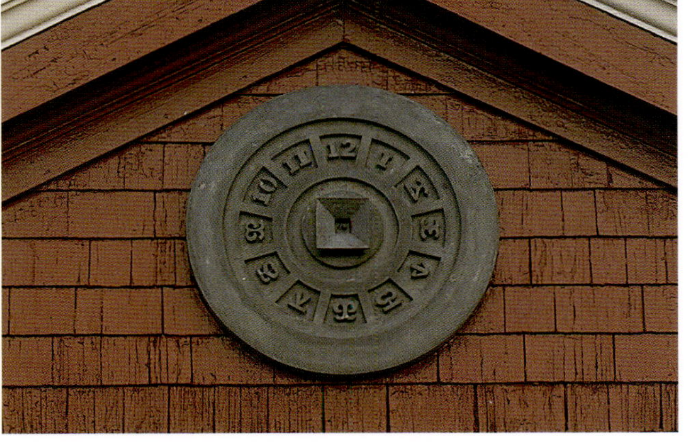

BRIT BUNKLEY

BAY SHORE ICONS, 1992
Bay Shore Station, MTA Long Island Rail Road
Cast stone
Station Design: MTA LIRR Architects/Engineers
PHOTOGRAPHER: BRIT BUNKLEY

The disks in Brit Bunkley's architectural fantasy *Bay Shore Icons* are oblique abstractions of clocks and calendars, and the digits are primarily mirror images of numbers. To highlight the advantages of public transportation, the artist created a cast-stone frieze portraying cars in a traffic jam. "Since I thought the architecture of the waiting areas looked somewhat like a Prairie Style Doric temple, I designed the extended lintel as a Prairie Style window-like structure (which also mimics the LIRR train windows)," says Bunkley. "The images within it are a sort of 'system of icons' that refer to transportation and aspects of Bay Shore and Fire Island. They include a mirror image pleasure boat, a beach umbrella/arrow with egg (a reference to the egg and dart molding), and a Fire Island lighthouse as a chess piece."

R. M. FISCHER

BROOKLYN-BATTERY TUNNEL CLOCK, 1992
Brooklyn Battery Tunnel, MTA Bridges and Tunnels
Stainless steel and aluminum
Fabricators: Tallix; Mariano Brothers, Inc.
See page 110

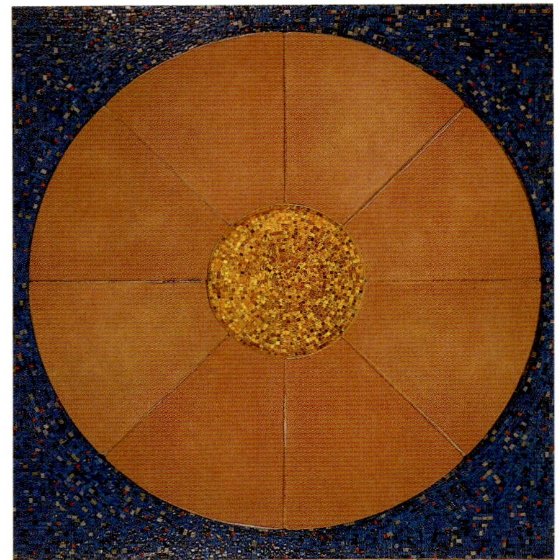

FRANK OLT

TEMPLE QUAD RELIEFS, 1992

23rd Street–Ely Avenue E V

Ceramic tile with glass mosaic

Fabricators: The artist; Miotto Mosaic Art Studios

Station Design: MTA NYCT Architects/Engineers

PHOTOGRAPHER: BRIT BUNKLEY

Temple Quad Reliefs consists of four ceramic murals with large terra-cotta-colored ceramic tiles set in architectural formations on a mosaic background. Olt explains that the reliefs "relate to the architecture that surrounds them, to the ebb and flow of humanity that will engulf them and to one another, for a unified design approach to the station. The Archways represent a symbol of welcome, strength, and beauty. Their compelling form and rich color draw upon Romanesque architecture, augmenting the theme of welcome and adding the theme of continuance in the daily life and work of New Yorkers. The Gothic Circle component is a symbol of endurance, renewal and perpetuity, and will lend inspiration to daily commuters, spent from their days' toil. The Greek Temple Quad, a series of four house-shaped pieces, reinforces the theme of welcome and comfort, but itself resembles a cityscape or place of commerce with all the societal vitality that it implies."

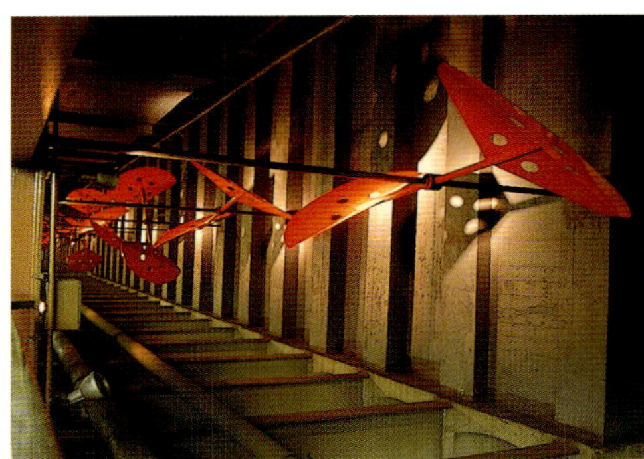

DAVID PROVAN

YAB-YUM, 1992

34th Street–Herald Square B D F N Q R V W

Aluminum

Station Design: William Nicholas Bodouva + Associates

PHOTOGRAPHER: MICHAEL KAMBER

Yab-Yum is a series of fourteen red paddle-like forms, each twelve feet long, suspended between the east wall of the platform and the columns that run the length of it. David Provan intended that the delicately balanced paddles would spin and flutter in the wind generated by approaching and departing trains. "It's my interest to build and install a series of subway 'wind paddles' that will utilize and make visible these subterranean breezes," he explains. "The varying amounts of wind will set the brightly colored paddles floating, tilting, and spinning in descriptive patterns."

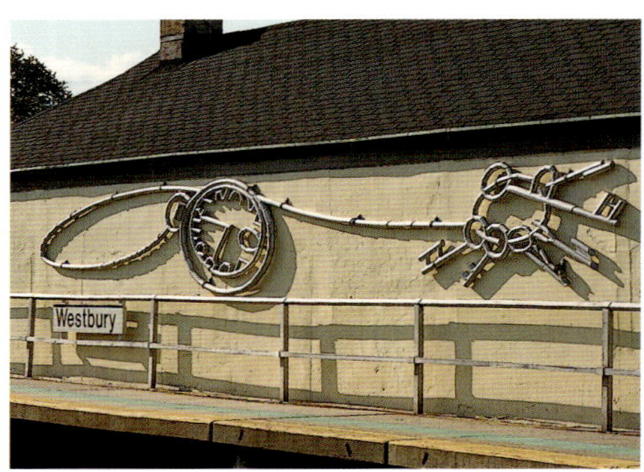

DAVID SAUNDERS

CONDUCTOR'S WATCH AND KEY CHAIN, 1992

Great Neck Station, MTA Long Island Rail Road

(relocated from Westbury Station, 2001)

Aluminum

PHOTOGRAPHER: MICHAEL KAMBER

To capture the romance and excitement of historic train travel, David Saunders immortalized the conductor's watch and key chain. The tubular design forms complement and blend into architectural components of the station, particularly its handrails and exposed pipes. "The chain mimics the movement of the Long Island Rail Road's long silver trains that take commuters to and from their destinations," says Saunders. "Those speedy back and forth movements are echoed in the long swooping gestures of the sculpture's silver lines."

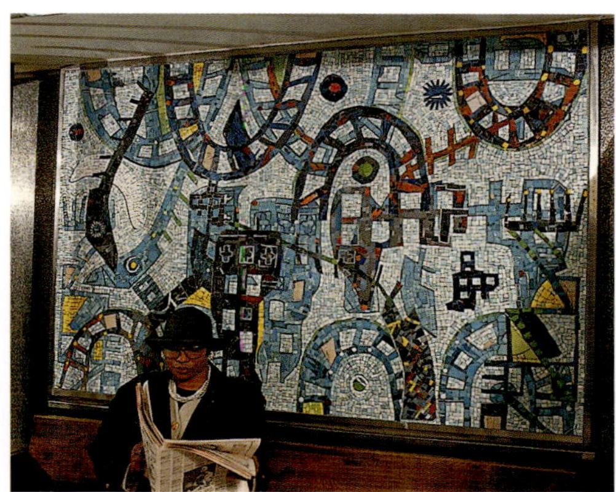

MICHAEL KELLY WILLIAMS

EL 2 AND EL 5, 1992
Intervale Avenue 2 5
Glass mosaic
Fabricator: Miotto Mosaic Art Studios
Station Design: MTA NYCT Architects/Engineers
PHOTOGRAPHER: MICHAEL KAMBER

According to Michael Kelly Williams, *El 2* "features a snake motif, seen in the track patterns, as well as symbols representing elevated structures and the signal lights in the subway. *El 5* suggests the movement of elevated trains throughout the city. Light is a major theme of the piece, especially the burst of light that envelops a subway train when it leaves an underground tunnel and becomes elevated. African and Native American influences are integral to the work, as are arch shapes suggested by tunnels and 'els.' Charged with energy, color and music, reflecting myth and dance, these fulfill my wish to continue the tradition of mosaics in NYC's subway system."

1993

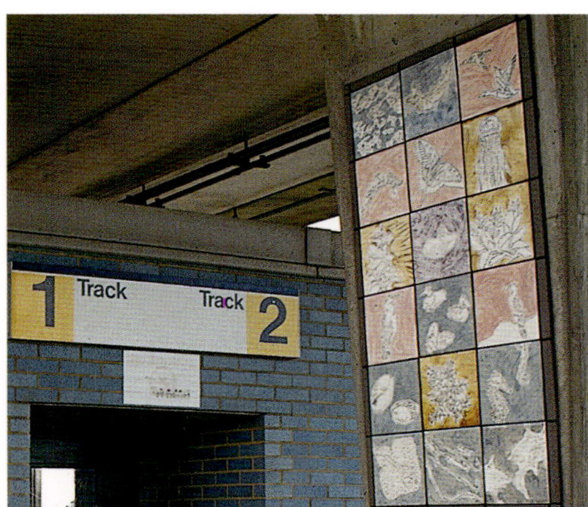

ALAN SONFIST

THE NARRATIVE HISTORY OF MERRICK, 1993
Merrick Station, MTA Long Island Rail Road
THE NARRATIVE HISTORY OF BELLMORE, 1993
Bellmore Station, MTA Long Island Rail Road
Hand-painted porcelain tile
Station Design: LIRR Architects/ Engineers
PHOTOGRAPHER: ROB WILSON

Alan Sonfist describes his concept: "I will create a series of tiles tracing the history of Long Island, beginning in the Ice Age, through paintings of rocks and plant life. The next stage would show how the Native Americans interacted with plants and sea life, followed by the first Europeans, who settled in Long Island and established farms and a seafaring industry. Later, a tourist industry developed, as well as several advanced industries. The early history of Merrick describes developed grain farms with cows and sheep. At the same time, Bellmore was developing a fishing industry. The railroad eventually became a bridging device to bring together the surrounding communities and contributed greatly to the development of contemporary Long Island."

ROMARE BEARDEN

UNTITLED ("CITY OF LIGHT"), 1993 (proposal created by artist, 1982)
Westchester Square–East Tremont Avenue 6
Faceted-glass triptych
Fabricators: Benoit Gilsoul and Helmut Schardt Master Craftsman
Station Design: MTA NYCT Architects/Engineers
See page 138

1994

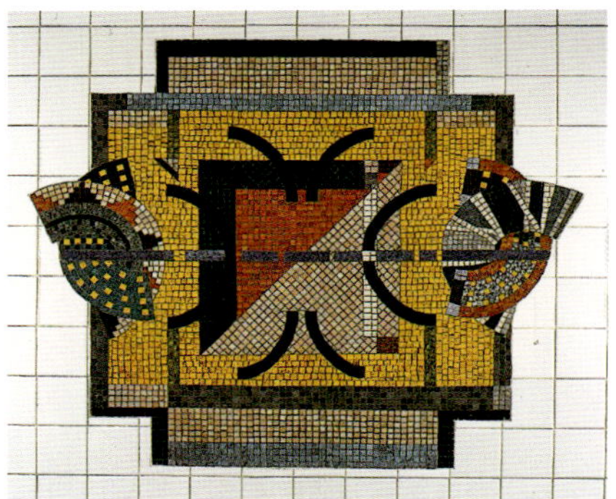

LAURA BRADLEY

CITY SUITE, 1994
96th Street 6
Marble mosaic
Station Design: MTA NYCT Architects/Engineers
PHOTOGRAPHER: DAVID LUBARKSY

Laura Bradley's *City Suite* is composed of a first "movement" in a terrazzo square that surrounds a column on the station's mezzanine, and two large mosaic medallions that form the visual centerpiece of the work. Bradley also created new signage tablets that resemble the originals but incorporate her medallion design, adding new elements that complement the historic patterns. The *City Suite* mosaics were the inspiration for the designs that were translated into the metalwork forms at 96th Street and subsequently adapted for use throughout the system.

DEBORAH BROWN

PLATFORM DIVING, 1994
Houston Street 1
Glass mosaic
Fabricator: Miotto Mosaic Art Studios
Station Design: MTA NYCT Architects/Engineers
PHOTOGRAPHER: ADAM REICH

Deborah Brown's *Platform Diving* shows realistically rendered marine animals doing oddly human things. A manatee patiently anticipates the arrival of the next train while a whale reads a newspaper over a commuter's shoulder and turtles dive off a station platform. "I wanted to explore the analogy between subway travel and the movement of our fellow creatures through their natural environment," Brown says. "Underwater creatures navigate a complex spatial array of undersea passageways, much as we maneuver through our own man-made systems. I thought it would be provocative to portray them in a part of our world most closely resembling their own, but involved in activities familiar to us."

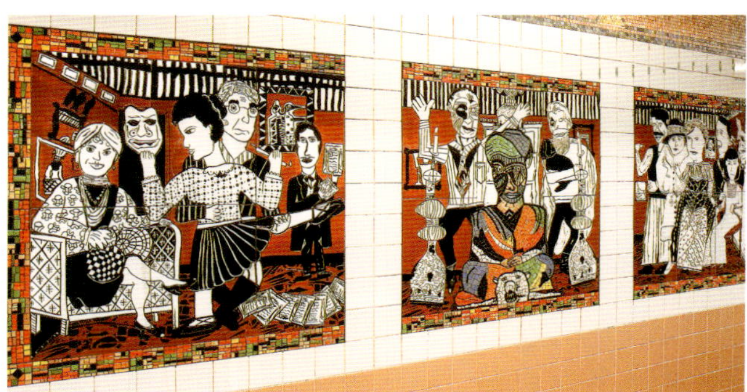

LEE BROZGOLD

THE GREENWICH VILLAGE MURALS, 1994
Christopher Street–Sheridan Square 1
Ceramic mosaic
Fabricators: Sherle Wagner; Miotto Mosaic Art Studios
Station Design: MTA NYCT Architects/Engineers
PHOTOGRAPHER: ROB WILSON

The Greenwich Village Murals are amalgamations of children's drawings assembled and arranged by Lee Brozgold. He first set out only to commemorate a few famous people, "but the Village is so rich in amazing characters who shaped America that picking only twelve was impossible." The figures are arranged in four groups: Founders, Providers, Bohemians, and Rebels. Student artists from P.S. 41 in Greenwich Village assisted Brozgold, and Deborah Lewis, a teacher at the school, selected the final images.

ANDREW LEICESTER

GHOST SERIES, 1994
Penn Station, MTA Long Island Rail Road
Terra-cotta and porcelain enamel on steel
Fabricator: LDDK Studios
Station Design: TAMS Consultants
See page 50

MAYA LIN

ECLIPSED TIME, 1994

Penn Station, MTA Long Island Rail Road

Sandblasted etched glass, aluminum, stainless steel, and fiber optics
Fabricators: Treitel/Gratz; Starfire
Station Design: TAMS Consultants

See page 52

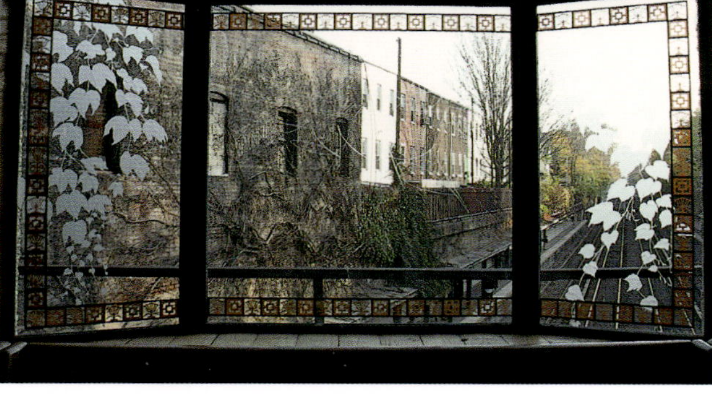

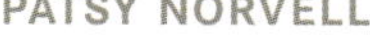

PATSY NORVELL

GARDEN STOPS, 1994

Beverley Road and Cortelyou Road (Q)

Sandblasted glass windows; iron stair railing and exterior fence
Fabricators: The artist; Cesar Color
Station Design: William Nicholas Bodouva + Associates
PHOTOGRAPHER: MICHAEL KAMBER

In these historic elevated stations, the railings on both the entrances and the stairwells suggest trellises from neighborhood gardens. The floral motif continues in columns adorned with abstracted flowers and decorative inserts in the railings that hark back to the original fences. Large windows trimmed with floral patterns repeated from the fencing look onto the tracks below. Patsy Norvell explains *Garden Stops*: "It is an environment that surrounds you rather than something you stop to look at. As viewers pass through, elements evoke the history of the stations, trigger people's own memories, and spark a kind of inner dialogue about space, nature, and change."

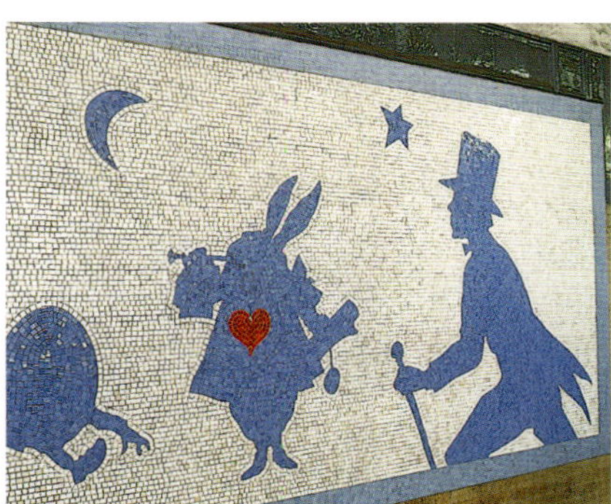

LILIANA PORTER

THE WAY OUT, 1994

50th Street (1)

Ceramic mosaic
Fabricator: Miotto Mosaic Art Studios
Station Design: MTA NYCT Architects/Engineers
PHOTOGRAPHER: DAVID LUBARSKY

Liliana Porter's silhouetted figures illustrate characters from Lewis Carroll's *Alice in Wonderland*. Creating a conceptual link to the many Broadway theaters near the station, the artist subtly evokes the theatrical and playfully connects it with the underground by showing Alice pulling back a curtain to reveal a dramatic scene. Porter, an Argentinian artist living in the United States, prefers to let the viewer's imagination fill in the details of her shadowy figures, playing on their varying views of reality.

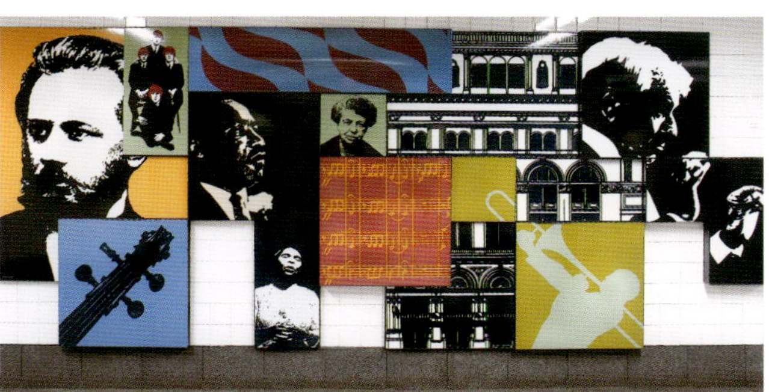

JOSH SCHARF

CARNEGIE HALL MONTAGE, 1994

57th Street–Seventh Avenue (N) (Q) (R) (W)

Ceramic tiles and porcelain enamel
Fabricators: Enamel-Tec; Wirth-Salander
Station Design: MTA NYCT Architects/Engineers
PHOTOGRAPHER: ROB WILSON

In *Carnegie Hall Montage*, Josh Scharf explores the vast range of illustrious figures who have graced the world-renowned stage. The work consists of two parts: a mural collage of large, vivid images showing some of the greats who have appeared there—Tchaikovsky, Eleanor Roosevelt, Leonard Bernstein, Martin Luther King Jr., and the Beatles—and dozens of small white tiles in the entryways. The tiles are inscribed with the dates of appearances of still others, ranging from Alexander Graham Bell to Helen Keller.

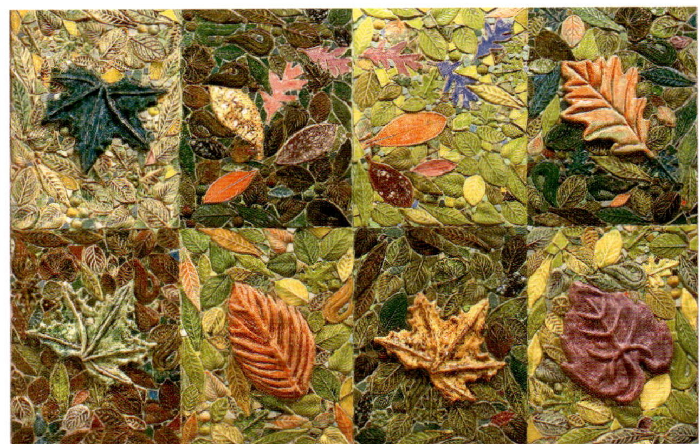

SUSAN TUNICK

BRIGHTON CLAY RE-LEAF NOS. 1–4, 1994
Prospect Park B Q S
Parkside Avenue Q
Ceramic tile
Fabricator: Lisa Portnoff
Station Design: William Nicholas Bodouva + Associates
PHOTOGRAPHER: ROB WILSON

Dating from 1919, the Prospect Park and Parkside Avenue stations on the Brighton Beach line feature distinctive "head houses"—covered entrance structures located above the stations. Their wall tiles and ceramic borders are characteristic of the Arts and Crafts movement that was influential at that time. In newly reconfigured areas of the stations, Susan Tunick designed ceramic murals and borders reminiscent of this earlier style. The leaf motifs of these works derive, she says, from childhood memories of the nearby Brooklyn Botanic Garden and Prospect Park, as well as her deep interest in ceramic history and modern artistic expressions in fired clay. Tunick has long been involved as a leader of Friends of Terra Cotta, which is dedicated to restoring ceramic architectural forms on significant buildings and monuments in New York and across the country.

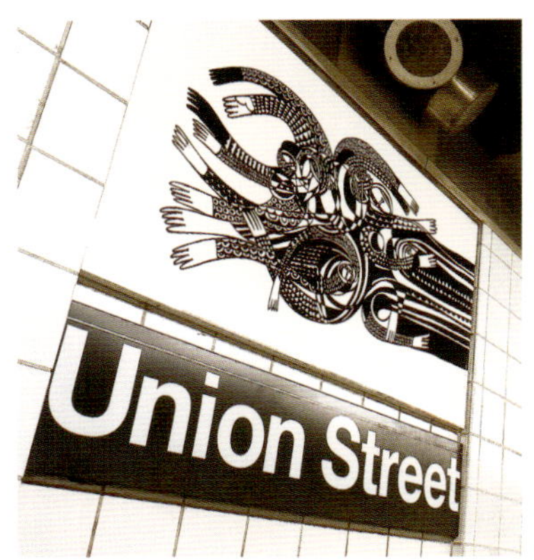

EMMETT WIGGLESWORTH

COMMUNION, 1994
Union Street M R
Porcelain enamel and ceramic tile
Fabricator: Fireform Porcelain
Station Design: MTA NYCT Architects/Engineers
PHOTOGRAPHER: ROB WILSON

In this series of twenty-two panels located in a recessed area above the station signs, symbolic figures move about and interact with one another. Although the panels are separated by space, they are linked by their graphic quality. The artist explains the concept: "As a unit they form a composite to symbolically show, as in a 'Union,' the best of each part of racial, religious and cultural life . . . The community above the Union Street station is mirrored in these panels because they are successfully working at making their community into this reality." Additionally, the artist designed a series of tiles on the station track walls in red, yellow, blue, green, and orange.

1995

ALICE ADAMS in collaboration with Richard Henry Behr

PLANTING (DEDICATED TO LONG ISLAND TREE FARMERS), 1995
Ronkonkoma Station, MTA Long Island Rail Road
Brick, concrete, aluminum, and plantings
Fabricators: H. Eberhard Nurseries; Johnson Atelier; Londino Stone Company
Station Design: Richard Henry Behr
See page 154

WILLIE BIRCH

HARLEM TIMELINE, 1995
135th Street 2 3
Glass mosaic
Fabricator: Miotto Mosaic Art Studios
Station Design: Urbahn Architects; MTA NYCT Architects/Engineers
See page 78

RALPH FASANELLA

SUBWAY RIDERS, 1995 (created by artist, 1950)

Fifth Avenue–53rd Street E V

Oil on canvas

Subway Riders was presented to New York's transit customers as a gift from the artist and his wife, Eva, through Public Domain, an initiative to place Fasanella's paintings in museums and public institutions. The painting is on permanent loan from the American Folk Art Museum, New York.

See page 46

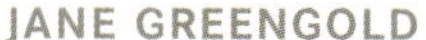

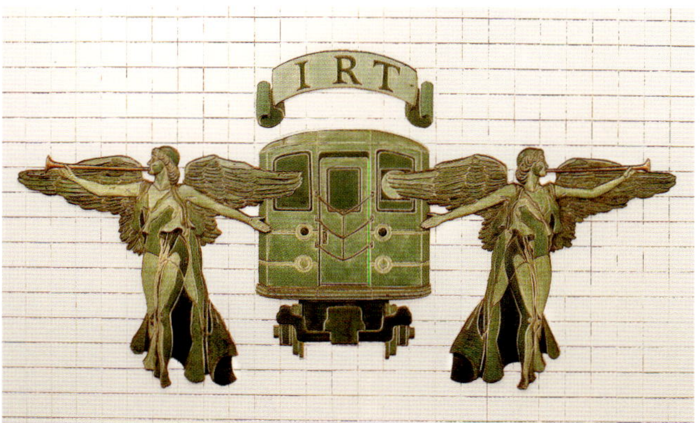

JANE GREENGOLD

WINGS FOR THE IRT: THE IRRESISTIBLE ROMANCE OF TRAVEL, 1995

Grand Army Plaza 2 3

Bronze and terra-cotta

Fabricators: LDDK Studios; Patrick Mahoney; Tallix

Station Design: MTA NYCT Architects/Engineers

PHOTOGRAPHER: ROB WILSON

Directly above the Grand Army Plaza subway station is the Soldiers and Sailors Memorial Arch, erected after the Civil War to commemorate the victory of Union forces. The ornate monument is surmounted by a sculptural group composed of two Winged Victories and four charging steeds pulling the figure of Columbia in her chariot. Jane Greengold has turned the Winged Victory figures to another use; they now also serve as companions and guides to riders in the subway station below. Two Victories at the bottom of the stairways welcome riders into the station and see them off as they exit; Victories in bas relief above the downstairs platform usher in the subway cars. The initials IRT in the title of the work reference the former name of the subway line that serves the station.

1996

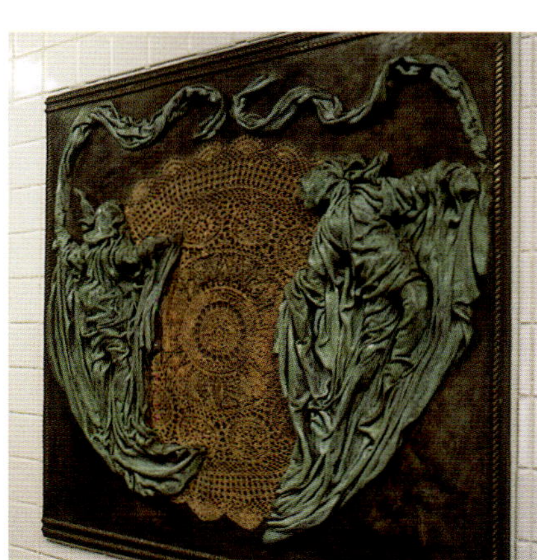

MURIEL CASTANIS

FLATBUSH FLOOGIES, 1996

Brooklyn College–Flatbush Avenue 2 5

Bronze reliefs

Fabricator: Paul King Foundry

Station Design: Breenan Beer Gorman/Architects

PHOTOGRAPHER: ROB WILSON

In *Flatbush Floogies*, frolicking sprites and nymphs accompany participants in the neighborhood's history—Native Americans, the pirate Captain Kidd, and the Brooklyn Dodgers. Memorialized on plaques in the station's entry and on the train platform, these figures create shell-like shapes that suggest human forms but also create haunting emptiness. It is as if these people have suddenly vanished from sight, leaving only the clothing they were wearing as traces of their existence. This effect was achieved by draping mannequins with fabric that had been saturated with epoxy resin, which allowed the clothes to be further shaped before they dried. Later, the human forms were removed and the hardened fabric was cast in bronze.

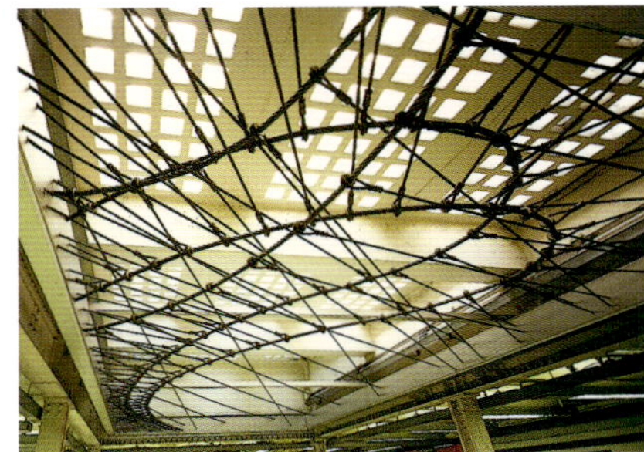

MARK GIBIAN

CABLE CROSSING, 1996
Brooklyn Bridge–City Hall 4 5 6
Steel cable
Station Design: Conklin Rossant Architects
PHOTOGRAPHER: CATHY CARVER

Cable Crossing specifically references the Brooklyn Bridge's pioneering use of steel cables and a suspended roadway. According to Mark Gibian, the lacy curves of the barrier panels "echo the beauty of the bridge's cross-hatched cables and the feeling of flight as it springs across the East River," while the tensile strength of the work suggests "the controlled power of the subway and its network of metal and concrete that undergirds the city."

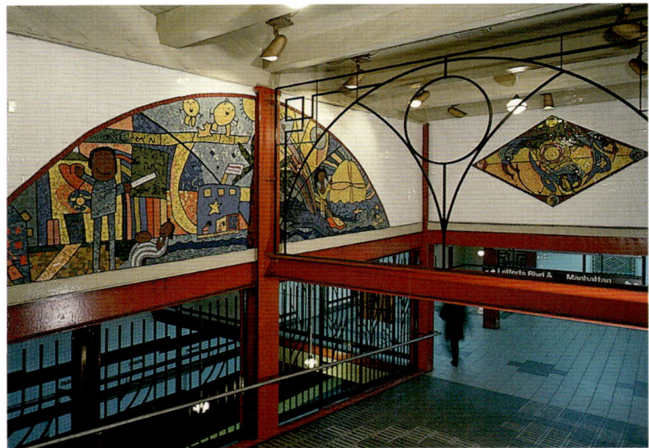

JIMMY JAMES GREENE

CHILDREN'S CATHEDRAL, 1996
Utica Avenue A C
Ceramic mosaic and iron grillwork
Fabricators: Peter Columbo Artistic Mosaics; A & T Iron Works
Station Design: Brennan Beer Gorman/Architects
PHOTOGRAPHER: MICHAEL KAMBER

In *Children's Cathedral*, Jimmy James Greene set out to capture the hopes and ambitions of the young people of the neighborhood. "At first," he says, "I talked with the kids about how they play, learn, pray, and celebrate. Then they drew." The result was an amazing variety of work with certain recurrent subjects—local stores and other buildings, school scenes, people going about their daily lives on the street, trees, flowers, and the children themselves involved in all sorts of activities. Greene then culled and sorted the images, trying them out in various combinations, to create the final eight assemblages. The original drawings were in pencil, so Greene added color and also enlarged them. However, he maintains that the youngsters are the real artists. "They were the soloists," he says. "I was the orchestra leader."

ELIZABETH MURRAY

BLOOMING, 1996
Lexington Avenue–59th Street 4 5 6
Glass mosaic
Fabricator: Miotto Mosaic Art Studios
Station Design: Prentice & Chan, Olhausen
See page 44

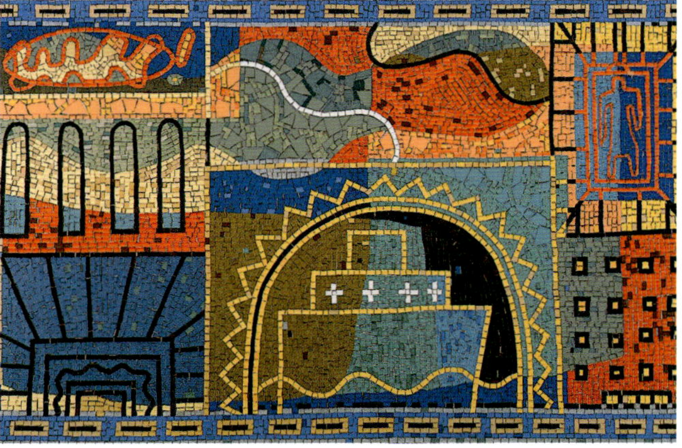

JOSÉ ORTEGA

UNA RAZA, UN MUNDO, UNIVERSO
(One Race, One World, One Universe), 1996
Third Avenue–149th Street 2 5
Ceramic mosaic
Fabricator: Peter Columbo Artistic Mosaics
Station Design: Urbahn Architects
PHOTOGRAPHER: DAVID LUBARSKY

For this group of seven murals, José Ortega took as his inspiration the lively street life just above, where neighborhood residents gather to talk, shop, do business, or just hang out. He used curved forms because the messages he wanted to convey are universal ones. As he explains, "The circle is a powerful symbol. It connotes infinity, implies wholeness. It has no beginning and no end." The brightly colored murals focus on three circular images– "the sun as the provider of energy and the center of our universe, the earth as the sustainer of our humanly developed and natural worlds, and the face as the translator, both receptor and interpreter of the human and natural worlds."

FAITH RINGGOLD assisted by Tim Tait Designs

FLYING HOME: HARLEM HEROES AND HEROINES, 1996
125th Street 2 3
Glass mosaic
Fabricator: Miotto Mosaic Art Studios
Station Design: Urbahn Architects; MTA NYCT Architects/Engineers
See page 80

ROBERT TAPLIN

THREE STATUES (A SHORT HISTORY OF THE LOWER HUDSON VALLEY), 1996
Cortlandt Station, MTA Metro-North Railroad
Bronze
Fabricator: Argos Art Foundry
Station Design: MTA Metro-North Railroad Architects/Engineers; Lev Zetlin Associates
See page 148

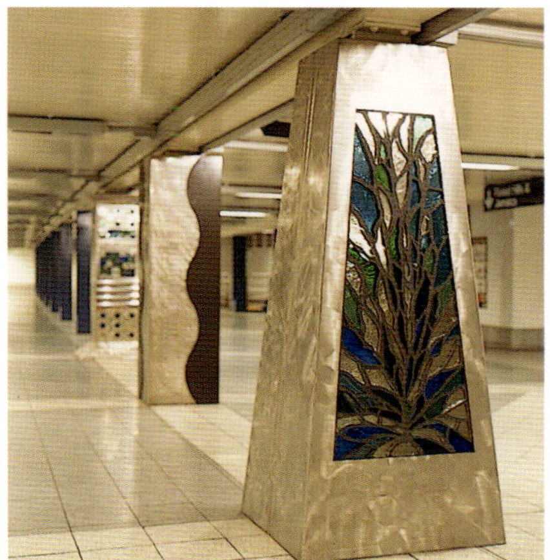

PABLO TAULER

IN MEMORY OF THE LOST BATTALION, 1996
Woodhaven Boulevard G R V
Stainless steel and faceted glass
Fabricators: Helmut Schardt Master Craftsman; Metalworks
Station Design: MTA NYCT Architects/Engineers
PHOTOGRAPHER: MICHAEL KAMBER

The Lost Battalion was a group of soldiers, most of them from New York, who were killed in battle in World War I. Pablo Tauler's sculptural forms honor their sacrifice. *In Memory of the Lost Battalion* uses nine station support beams to undergird the memorial, wrapping them in iron, steel, and glass. The artist combines and manipulates the materials to evoke the terrain of the battlefield in France where the men perished. Trees and guns are suggested in the shapes of the metal forms, and light is refracted by the glass elements, giving it further dimension. Tauler says the bent metal forms remind him of his childhood forays into the marshlands near his home. He adds, "I am profoundly aware of the importance of the environment to my art . . . Especially interesting to me is the manipulation of light through the use of texture and reflective materials."

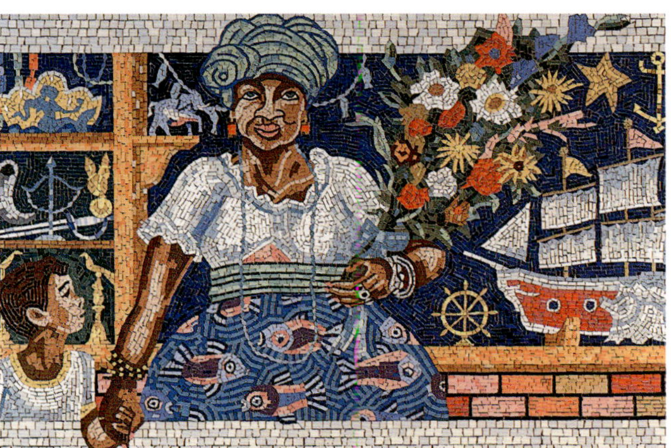

MANUEL VEGA

SÁBADO EN LA CIENTO DIEZ (Saturday on 110th Street), 1996
110th Street 6
Ceramic mosaic
Fabricator: Peter Columbo Artistic Mosaics
Station Design: MTA NYCT Architects/Engineers
PHOTOGRAPHER: DAVID LUBARSKY

In *Sábado en la Ciento Diez*, Manuel Vega recalls memories from his childhood in Puerto Rico and also captures the ambience of the 110th Street neighborhood. The work is divided into four panels–*Earth*, *Air*, *Fire*, and *Water*–a reference to the four elements once thought to make up the world. In *Earth*, a street vendor sells the fruits of the soil–bananas, plantains, papayas, avocados, and coconuts. *Fire* features Shangó, a divine being in the Yoruba culture, to acknowledge the African heritage of many community residents. In *Water*, a woman holding a child by the hand represents motherhood. *Air* shows children enjoying the chance to be outdoors in the summertime, soaking under a fire hydrant on the street.

1997

MEL CHIN

SIGNAL, 1997
Broadway–Lafayette Street B D F V
Stainless steel and glass; ceramic tile
Fabricator: Baron Brown
Station Design: MTA NYCT Architects/Engineers
See page 98

JAMES GARVEY

LARIAT SEAT LOOPS, 1997
33rd Street 6
Hand-forged bronze
Fabricators: The artist; Koenig Iron Works
Station Design: Conklin Rossant Architects
See page 58

MARGIE HUGHTO

TRADE, TREASURE, AND TRAVEL, 1997
Cortlandt Street R W
Ceramic relief tiles
Deinstalled for construction, to be reinstalled in R W station
Station Design: MTA NYCT Architects/Engineers
See page 106

ROBERTO JUAREZ

A FIELD OF WILD FLOWERS, 1997
Grand Central Terminal Waiting Room, MTA Metro-North Railroad
Mixed media
Station Design: Beyer Blinder Belle Architects and Planners
See page 40

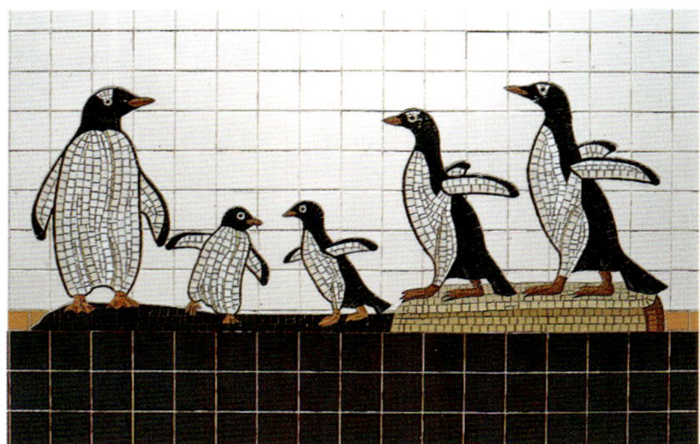

ANN SCHAUMBURGER

URBAN OASIS, 1997
Fifth Avenue–59th Street N R W
Glass mosaic and terrazzo
Fabricator: Miotto Mosaic Art Studios
Station Design: MTA NYCT Architects/Engineers
PHOTOGRAPHER: DAVID LUBARSKY

Ann Schaumburger used photographs of the nearby Central Park Zoo as well as images of the park's statues as the basis of *Urban Oasis*. The creatures are arranged in family groupings, depending upon their natural habitat—an Arctic scene, one set in the tropics, and one in a city park. "We chose glass rather than ceramic for the mosaics because of its greater translucency and color gradation," she explains. "And I selected a palette that echoes the colors in the station's original tile work, much of which has been retained."

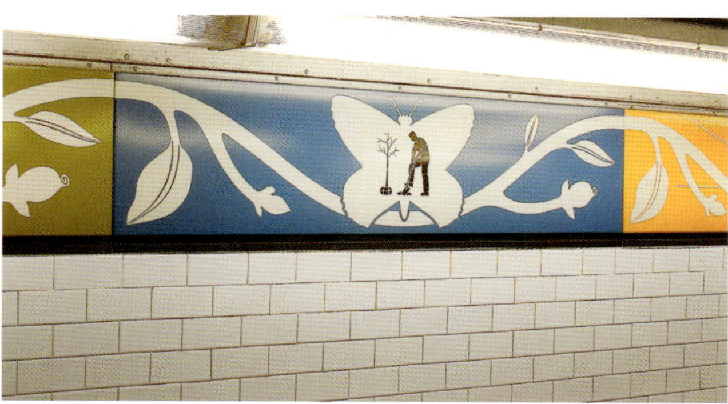

ANTON VAN DALEN

WORK & NATURE, 1997
Nevins Street 2 3 4 5
Porcelain enamel
Fabricator: Windsor
Station Design: MTA NYCT Architects/Engineers
PHOTOGRAPHER: ROB WILSON

Anton Van Dalen used the Nevins Street station's original turn-of-the-century decorative mosaic patterns, once water damaged and on the brink of permanent loss, as a springboard for the project. Capitalizing on "the station's olden elegance and grand beauty," Van Dalen created porcelain enamel murals in the same colors as the historic mosaics and fashioned them in a complementary style. Van Dalen depicts individuals—an architect, a sewing machine operator, a mother and child, a female executive, and blues musician Furry Lewis, a local hero—engaged in their occupations. For him, the overall theme is "the pride, dignity, and beauty surrounding all work."

1998

ELLEN DRISCOLL

AS ABOVE, SO BELOW, 1998
Grand Central North, MTA Metro-North Railroad
Glass, bronze, and mosaic
Fabricators: Franz Mayer of Munich; Julie Nathanson Glass; Paul King Foundry; Architectural Glass
Station Design: Beyer Blinder Belle Architects and Planners
See page 42

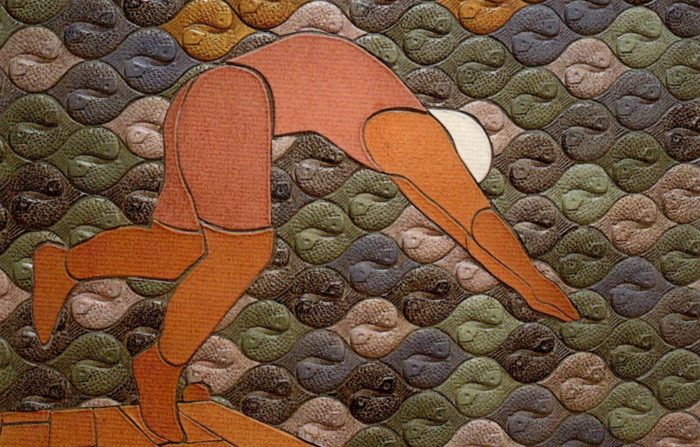

DEBORAH GOLETZ

POSTCARDS FROM SHEEPSHEAD BAY, 1998
Sheepshead Bay B Q
Ceramic tile
Station Design: MTA NYCT Architects/Engineers
PHOTOGRAPHER: MICHAEL KAMBER

At the end of the nineteenth century, Sheepshead Bay was a popular destination for sightseers. Neighborhood historic sites and scenes from its past are evoked in *Postcards from Sheepshead Bay*. The large outside mural is a gigantic replica of an antique postcard portraying a couple fishing, a jockey on horseback, and a summer home—as well as a sheepshead, the fish for which the village is named. Deborah Goletz comments that she created holes in place of the couples' faces, allowing people to "stick their heads through for souvenir photos, just like the old boardwalk props." Inside the station a second large mural shows a cast of turn-of-the-century people, and two smaller ones capture quiet moments on the bay. Goletz's Escher-like pattern of tiles, with color gradations from green to blue and back to green, create patterns that mimic the texture of the nearby water.

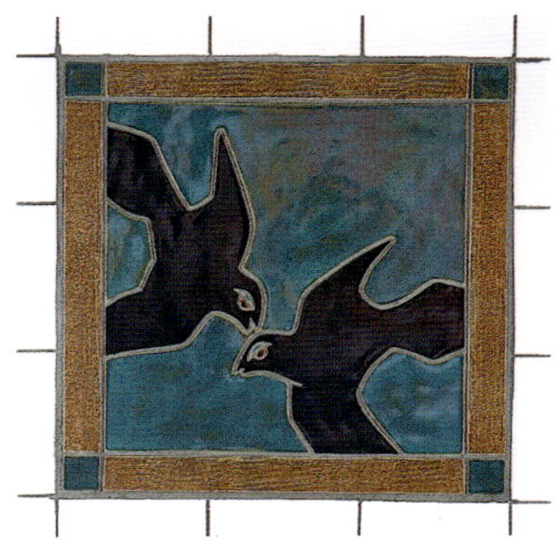

ELIZABETH GRAJALES

WHEN THE ANIMALS SPEAK . . ., 1998
34th Street–Penn Station 1 2 3
Ceramic mosaic murals; handmade ceramic relief tiles
Fabricator: Peter Columbo Artistic Mosaics
Station Design: Vollmer Associates; Claude Samton
PHOTOGRAPHER: PATRICK J. CASHIN

When the animals speak . . . shows wild animals in their habitats. One mural shows a pair of lions happily coexisting with playful birds in a familiar landscape; a stream flowing nearby (the Hudson) and cliffs behind (the Palisades) form the backdrop. Another depicts a bear contentedly observing a doe and her young. "As a child on shopping trips I found the station dull and colorless," says Elizabeth Grajales. "I wanted to give people something cheerful but also calming–a refuge in the city. That's why I used gentle colors like golden ochre and pale blues and greens for these idyllic Garden of Eden scenes."

ANDREW GINZEL/KRISTEN JONES

OCULUS, 1998
Chambers Street A C N Park Place 2 3
Stone and glass mosaic
Fabricators: Rinaldo Piras; Sectile
Station Design: MTA NYCT Architects/Engineers
See page 108

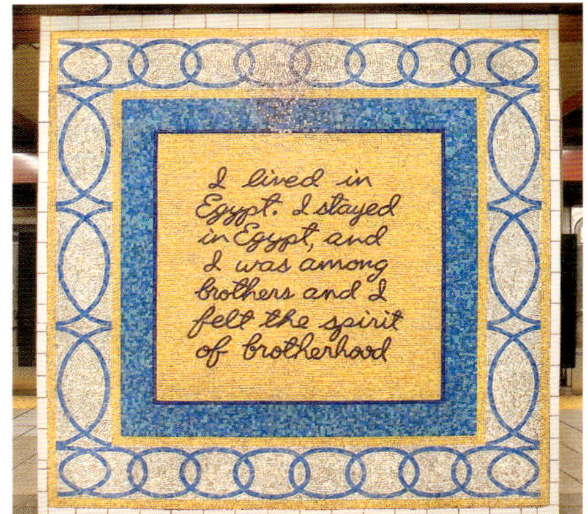

MAREN HASSINGER

MESSAGE FROM MALCOLM, 1998
Central Park North (110th Street) 2 3
Glass mosaic
Fabricators: Peter Columbo Artistic Mosaics; Miotto Mosaic Art Studios
Station Design: Urbahn Architects
PHOTOGRAPHER: ROB WILSON

Maren Hassinger explains her work: "Basically, I wanted to make something that behaved very physically with the site, while also honoring the memory of Malcolm X (through his speeches and words) and empowering the community that uses the station." Among the quotations used are "I believe in a society in which people can live like human beings on the basis of equality" and "Nobody's going to straighten out Harlem but us." Hassinger adds, "The messages also recognize Malcolm's spirituality. The upright wall within the station also contains images/symbols of prowess on one side and Malcolm's words on the reverse side. Here the idea of power, leadership and spiritual support are linked. Malcolm X believed that we as African Americans have the power to determine our destinies. This station is a reminder of that truth."

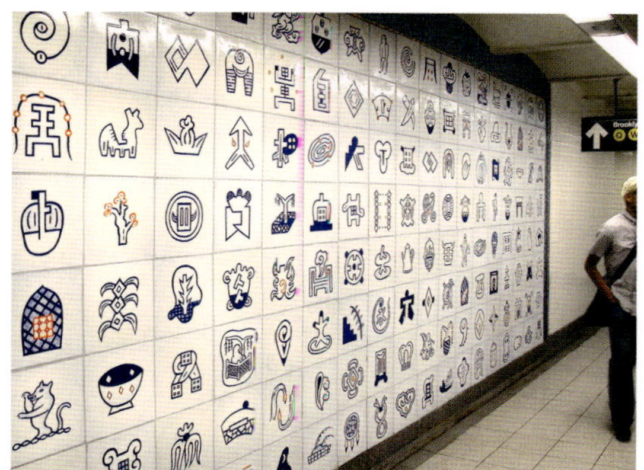

BING LEE

EMPRESS VOYAGE 2.22.1794, 1998
Canal Street J M N Q R W Z 6
Ceramic tile and mosaic banding
Fabricators: Miotto Mosaic Art Studios; Sherle Wagner
Station Design: MTA NYCT Architects/Engineers
PHOTOGRAPHER: ROB WILISON

Empress Voyage commemorates and celebrates the pioneering expedition of the American merchant ship *Empress of China*, which in 1794 returned to New York harbor laden with silk, tea, and porcelain. Through Bing Lee's light-hearted allusions to Chinese iconography, the tiles illustrate aspects of the then-new trade with Asia and celebrate life in today's Chinatown. On the platforms, interlocking teapots incorporate the Chinese character for "good life." Other symbols are variations on the characters for "Asia," "quality," and "cycle." As trains arrive, disembarking passengers see both "Canal Street" in English and the Chinese characters for "Chinatown."

DONALD LIPSKI in cooperation wtih Beyer Blinder Belle

SIRSHASANA, 1998
Grand Central Terminal Market, MTA Metro-North Railroad
Aluminum and polyester resin with crystals
Fabricator: Jonquil LeMaster with Promotion Products
Station Design: Beyer Blinder Belle Architects and Planners
See page 38

MARY MISS in collaboration with Lee Harris Pomeroy Architects

FRAMING UNION SQUARE, 1998
14th Street–Union Square L N Q R W 4 5 6
Glass, enameled steel, and aluminum
Station Design: Lee Harris Pomeroy Architects
See page 94

OWEN SMITH

AN UNDERGROUND MOVEMENT: DESIGNERS, BUILDERS, RIDERS, 1998
36th Street D M N R
Ceramic mosaic
Fabricator: Peter Columbo Artistic Mosaics
Station Design: MTA NYCT Architects/Engineers
See page 128

JOE ZUCKER

FOR MY GRANDFATHER NOYE PRIDE, A LOCOMOTIVE ENGINEER, 1998
Huntington Station, MTA Long Island Rail Road
Faceted glass
Fabricator: Helmut Schardt Master Craftsman
Station Design: MTA LIRR Architects/Engineers; Urbahn Architects
See page 156

1999

TERRY ADKINS

HARLEM ENCORE, 1999
Harlem–125th Street, MTA Metro-North Railroad
Aluminum
Fabricator: Polich Art Works
Station Design: di Domenico + Partners
See page 74

SHEILA LEVRANT de BRETTEVILLE in cooperation with Ehrenkrantz Eckstut & Kuhn Architects
AT THE START... AT LONG LAST..., 1999
Inwood-207th Street (A)
Mirror mosaic text, silk-screened tiles, etched railings, and terrazzo pavers
Fabricators: Miotto Mosaic Art Studios; Wirth Salander Studios; Giordano Monuments
Station Design: Ehrenkrantz Eckstut & Kuhn Architects
See page 82

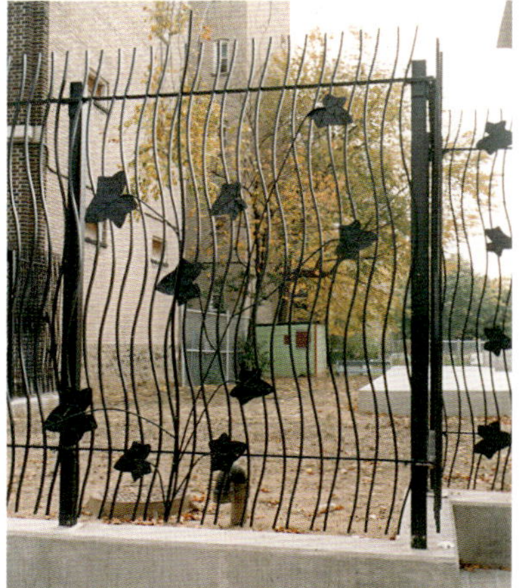

MILLIE BURNS
IL7/SQUARE, 1999
Botanic Garden (S)
Wrought iron
Fabricator: Judlau Contracting
Station Design: STV Group; Roberta Washington Architects
PHOTOGRAPHER: MILLIE BURNS

At the Brooklyn Botanic Garden station, the collaborative efforts of community representatives, the architectural team, and artist Millie Burns have created a visual transition from the street to the mini park surrounding the entrance, and finally into the transit facility itself. The fences and railings were designed to make the change of scene seem logical and effortless. The tall fences echo the trees and stately apartment buildings lining Eastern Parkway and also harmonize with the modern lines of the station house. "The communities that border Eastern Parkway and the Botanic Garden are blessed with a rich natural bounty," Burns says. "We are surrounded by trees, shrubs, plants, and vines. The fences and railing designs are drawn from what I see in this neighborhood. *IL7/Square* is about growth, a reaching toward the sun."

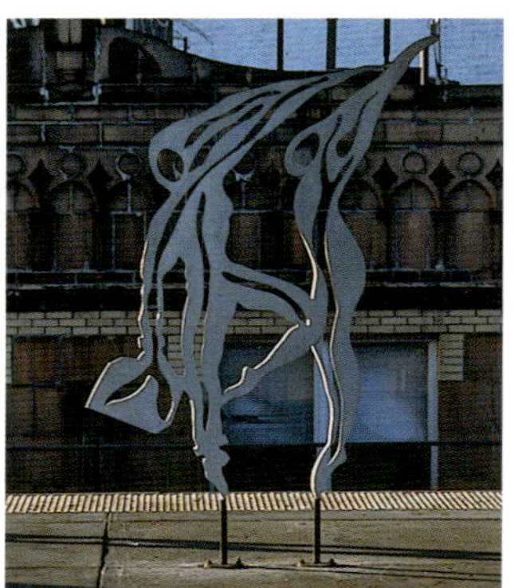

DAN GEORGE
MERMADE/DIONYSUS AND THE PIRATES, 1999
Brighton Beach (B) (Q)
Aluminum
Station Design: William Nicholas Boudova + Associates
PHOTOGRAPHER: DAN GEORGE

Brighton Beach, near Coney Island, was once one of New York City's prime seaside entertainment and recreation areas. "The sea is ancient, rich, and mysterious," says Dan George. "I wanted Dionysus to intrigue people and to remind them of the sea's mythic history and thereby spark the creation of their own dreams and fantasies." The artist used dolphins—six pairs and a singleton—to depict the metamorphosis from human to animal. They have a light and supple appearance, belying the material from which they are made—thick aluminum plate. Natural light reflects off the water and plays on the polished finish and varied planes, creating a buoyant effect.

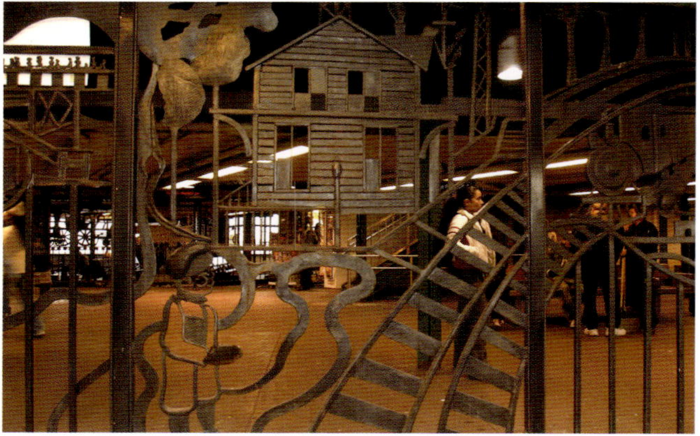

DIMITRI GERAKARIS
WOODSIDE CONTINUUM, 1999
Woodside-61st Street (7)
Hand-forged steel and stainless steel
Station Design: Urbahn Architects
PHOTOGRAPHER: PATRICK J. CASHIN

"The challenge and opportunity of the Woodside station is in its relationship to the past and to the future," Dimitri Gerakaris says. "In designing art for it, I wanted to create a continuum, to link generations starting centuries ago with wilderness, farms, country lanes, and abundant woods, to today. People rushing by may become aware of this now-vanished town and, upon reflection, realize that they are the link to the future . . . I wanted *Woodside Continuum* to present history accurately but in an engaging way. My aim was to encourage people to think about the continuity and to see the ways Woodside has changed and is changing—and the powerful role transportation has played in that process."

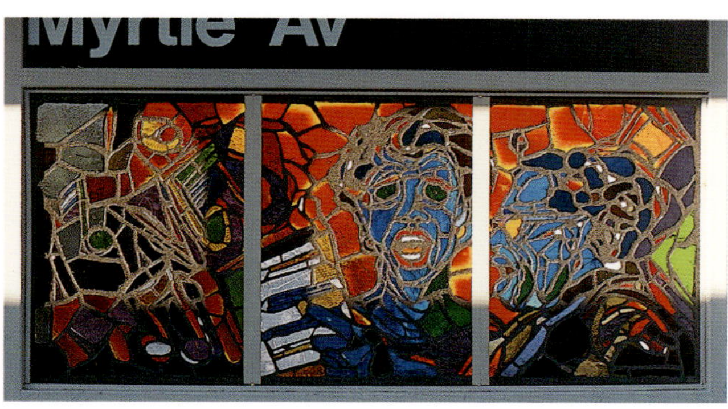

VERNA HART

JAMMIN' UNDER THE EL, 1999
Myrtle Avenue J M Z
Faceted glass
Fabricator: Helmut Schardt Master Craftsman
Station Design: Beyer Blinder Belle Architects and Planners
PHOTOGRAPHER: PATRICK J. CASHIN

Verna Hart's imaginary jazz combo captures drums, piano, guitar, and bass as well as flutes, saxophones, trombones, and trumpets, which add brassy accents. The sounds of percussion instruments are powerfully suggested and jiving vocalists complete the picture. Hart says that *Jammin' under the EL* is "a kind of jam session of the mind. A little imagination is all that's needed to enjoy a dozen solo performances in the panels. You can board the jazz express and take a jazz, rock, funk, or salsa journey of your choice."

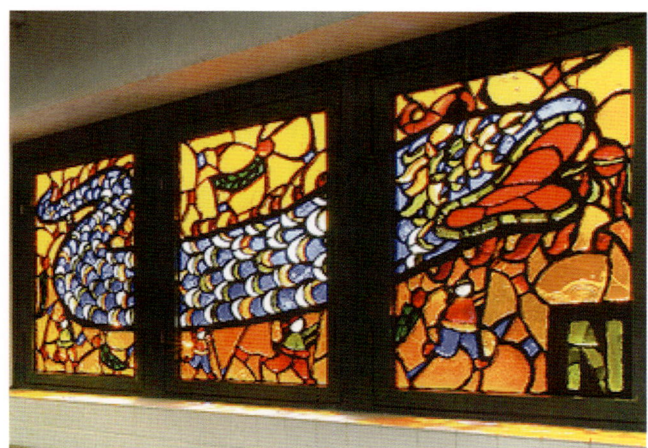

YUMI HEO

Q IS FOR QUEENS, 1999
33rd Street-Rawson Street, 40th Street-Lowery Street, 46th Street-Bliss Street 7
Faceted glass
Fabricator: Helmut Schardt Master Craftsman
Station Design: MTA NYCT Architects/Engineers
PHOTOGRAPHER: ROB WILSON

When the 7 train emerges from the ground near the East River going into Queens, it travels through a series of stations in one of the most ethnically diverse areas of the city. The renovation of this line included a major work of art to be shared by these stations, celebrating the borough and its diversity. Illustrator Yumi Heo designed thirty faceted-glass panes that have been installed along the mezzanines and platforms. Collectively titled *Q is for Queens*, the component panels successively highlight different aspects of the adjacent neighborhoods—public events, stores, food, and landmarks. The artist employs the alphabet—A is for Aqueduct racetrack . . . Z is for Zoo—to point out the enormous range of experiences that the area offers.

IK-JOONG KANG

HAPPY WORLD, 1999
Flushing-Main Street 7
Ceramic tile
Fabricator: Sherle Wagner
Station Design: Stull and Lee
See page 118

ED McGOWIN

BAYSIDE STORY, 1999
Bayside Station, MTA Long Island Rail Road
Bronze
Fabricator: Bryant Art Casting
Station Design: MTA LIRR Architects/Engineers; Urbahn Architects
See page 122

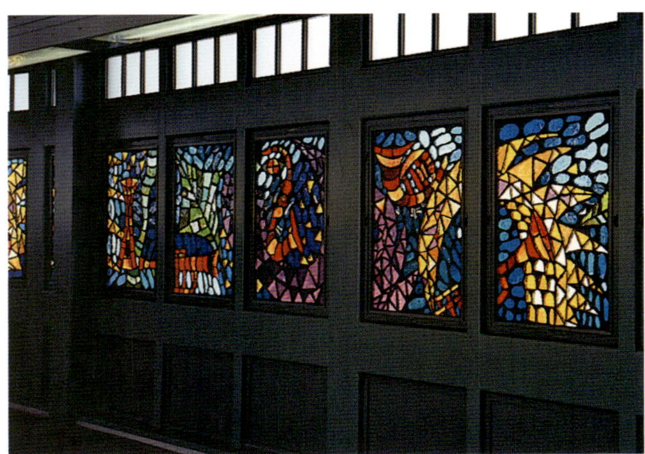

ERIC PRYOR

LIFE AND CONTINUED GROWTH, 1999

Franklin Avenue Ⓒ Ⓢ

Faceted glass

Fabricator: Gordon Stained Glass Studios

Station Design: STV Group; Roberta Washington Architects

PHOTOGRAPHER: ROB WILSON

Eric Pryor uses both traditional African and contemporary African American imagery in the twenty-nine faceted-glass windows that compose *Life and Continued Growth*. Symbols such as antelope horns suggest movement and material prosperity while butterflies represent the life cycle. The importance of music and rhythm are shown through African drums, a saxophone, and trumpets, all rendered in vivid tones of red, gold, and purple against shades of green, blue, and turquoise. "The area's rich African American heritage is being reborn," says Pryor. "Change and opportunity are arriving, and the shuttle both encourages and reflects the community's new optimism. *Life and Continued Growth* emerges from a spirit that is rooted in traditional African American culture and the new energy that is making it soar again."

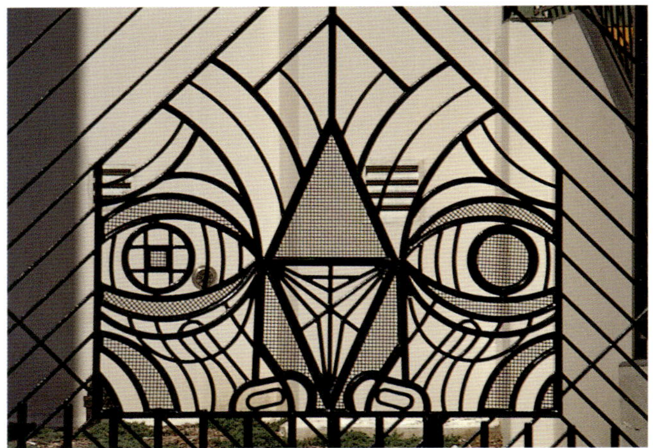

ISHA SHABAKA

UNITS OF THE FREE, 1999

Park Place Ⓢ

Wrought iron

Fabricator: Judlau Contracting

Station Design: STV Group; Roberta Washington Architects

PHOTOGRAPHER: ROB WILSON

Railings are by nature functional, but they can also be powerfully expressive, as shown by *Units of the Free*. Here Isha Shabaka uses railings to show the station as an important neighborhood site. The large-scale image of an African mask is boldly designed in open metalwork. Its nose is a starkly geometric triangle, which symbolizes power and movement in some traditional cultures. The thin, elegant diagonals used in the construction of the fence help to visually integrate the subway and the community. Other shapes in the mask are the changeable curving lines, which allow the forms to appear either awake or asleep, vigilant or distracted. "Just like commuters," Shakaba says, "sometimes they may be aware and thinking when waiting for the train, or just relaxing for a moment. I'm showing both states."

VINCENT SMITH

MINTON'S PLAYHOUSE/THE MOVERS AND SHAKERS, 1999

116th Street ② ③

Glass mosaic

Fabricator: Miotto Mosaic Art Studios

Station Design: Urbahn Architects; MTA NYCT Architects/Engineers

See page 76

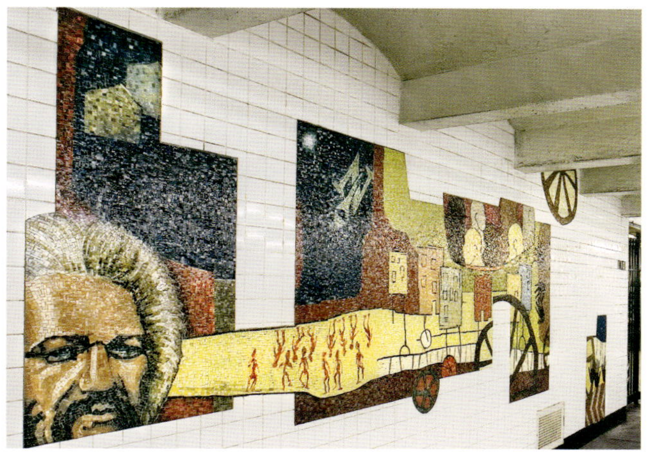

CHRISTOPHER WYNTER

MIGRATIONS, 1999
Cathedral Parkway (110th Street) B C
Ceramic mosaic
Fabricator: Miotto Mosaic Art Studios
Station Design: MTA NYCT Architects/Engineers
PHOTOGRAPHER: ROB WILSON

Three large murals enliven the station at Cathedral Parkway, Harlem's southern boundary. "Overall, the panels present the ideas of uprooting, migration, and progress in symbolic form," says Christopher Wynter. The blocks of color represent various African ancestral homelands and a circular symbol, the n'kisi, or sacred place concept, of the Nkongo people. The motifs continue with houses on stilts suggesting Central African building forms and horizontal bands of color denoting village paths. Wheels and walking feet describe faraway destinations, and are meant to recall the mass movements of Africans—both forced and voluntary—throughout history. The station is located below Frederick Douglass Circle, and Douglass himself is depicted, reinforcing the themes of movement and progress. The work was created in memory of Athie L. Wynter.

2000

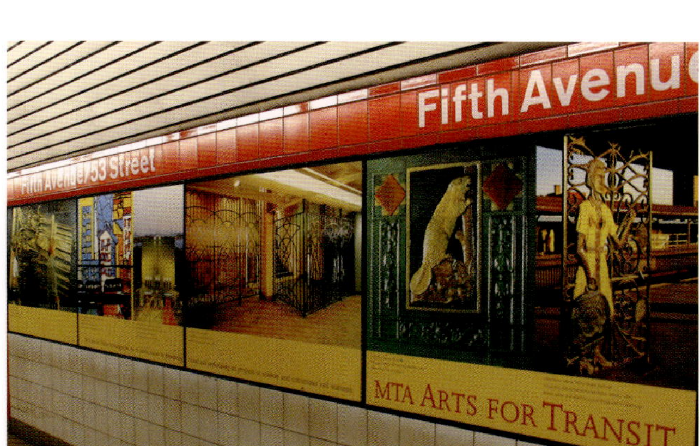

DRENTTEL DOYLE PARTNERS

53RD STREET ART STOP, 2000
Fifth Avenue–53rd Street E V
Porcelain enamel
Fabricator: Alliance International
Station Design: Lee Harris Pomeroy Architects
PHOTOGRAPHER: ROB WILSON

The cultural riches of midtown Manhattan are the subject of *Art Stop*. Seventy-three porcelain enamel panels enliven the station platform and invite arriving riders to sample the area's offerings. The cultural cornucopia includes the Museum of Television and Radio, the Municipal Art Society, the American Folk Art Museum, the Museum of Arts and Design, the Donnell Library Center of the New York Public Library, and the Museum of Modern Art. Selected Arts for Transit projects are also spotlighted. *Art Stop* shows how good design can serve both to beautify the station environment and to convey practical information for the benefit of transit users.

ARTS FOR TRANSIT COLLABORATIVE

FOR WANT OF A NAIL, 2000
81st Street–Museum of Natural History B C
Glass and ceramic mosaic, handmade ceramic relief tile, hand-cast glass, bronze, and cut granite
Fabricators: Research Casting; Surbeck Waterjet; Julie Nathanson; Margie Hughto; Mary Didoardo; Dennis D'Amelio; Miotto Mosaic Art Studios
Station Design: MTA NYCT Architects/Engineers
See page 84

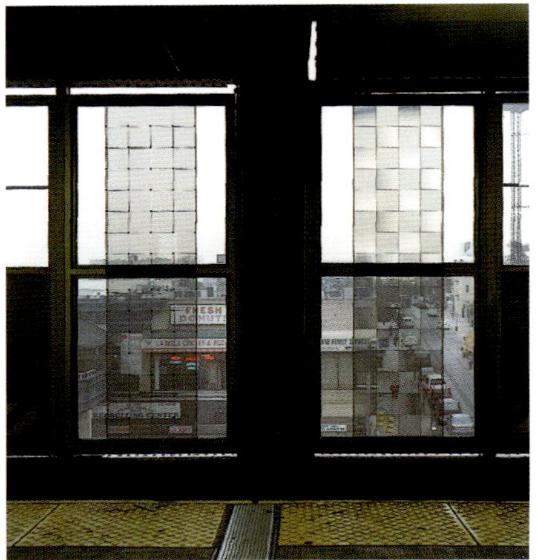

SIDNEY CASH

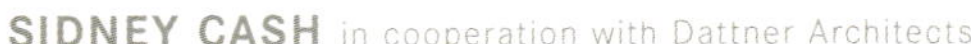

COLUMNS, 2000
Queensboro Plaza N W 7
Silkscreened glass panels
Fabricator: Viracon
Station Design: Dattner Architects
PHOTOGRAPHER: DAVID LUBARSKY

Sidney Cash describes his concept: "I envision installing interactive, optically kinetic, glass panels . . . that respond to the viewer's physical movement. As the viewer walks along the platform, he is able to watch the panels' imagery transform, as patterns appear and disappear in response to his movement . . . The patterns on the panels have been designed to relate to the style of embellishment of the Arts and Crafts architecture. As parts of the building are enhanced by diamond-shaped tiles, so are the patterns on the optical panels based upon the diamond shape. The vibrancy of movement and the patterns in the panels create a visual dialogue between the Arts and Crafts style, the motion of the trains, and the high-tech world of today . . . For the people who take the time to look, this installation becomes a moving exhibition."

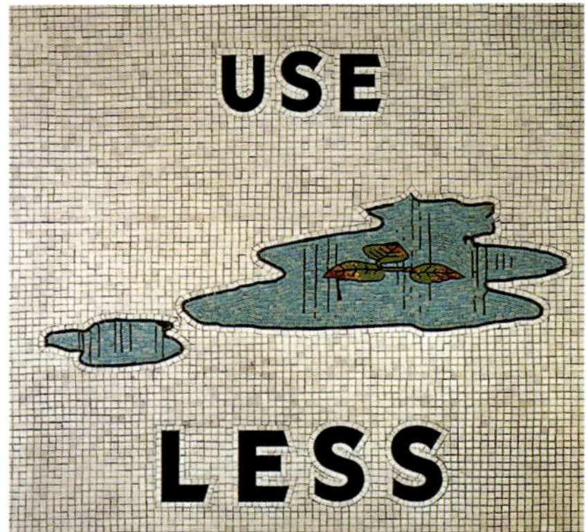

JACKIE CHANG

SIGNS OF LIFE, 2000
Metropolitan Avenue–Lorimer Street G L
Glass and ceramic mosaic and granite
Fabricator: Peter Columbo Artistic Mosaics
Station Design: MTA NYCT Architects/Engineers
PHOTOGRAPHER: DAVID LUBARSKY

Jackie Chang's *Signs of Life* murals are enigmatic. A rock is poised atop a pointed shape between two words, "faith" and "fate." Other words—"man," "kind," "it," "self"—seem to be endangered by a wave below them. Even the tenor of the implied messages is unclear. Are they optimistic or pessimistic? Are they speaking of the past or perhaps the future? This is entirely intentional. "I kept my titles brief," Chang says. "I wanted them to be challenging." In a sense, these snippets of what Chang calls "urban poetry" are an acknowledgment of some of the newest residents of the Greenpoint/Williamsburg neighborhood—young artists and writers—to whom enigma is a stock in trade.

JACKIE FERRARA

GRAND CENTRAL: ARCHES, TOWERS, PYRAMIDS, 2000
Grand Central–42nd Street S 4 5 6 7
Ceramic mosaic
Fabricator: Colorco
Station Design: Gruzen Samton
See page 36

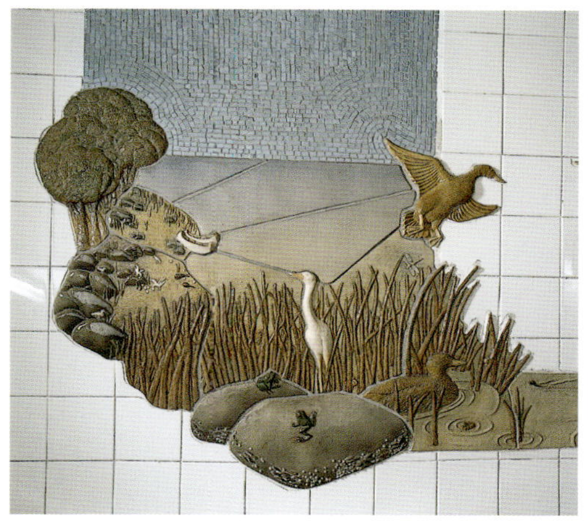

FRANK GIORGINI

PASSAGES, 2000

Whitehall Street R W

Handmade ceramic relief tiles, ceramic mosaic, cut granite floor tile, bronze, and forged steel

Fabricators: The artist; Leaping Beaver Forge; Peter Columbo Artistic Mosaics

Station Design: MTA NYCT Architects/Engineers

PHOTOGRAPHER: PATRICK J. CASHIN

Frank Giorgini designed a number of elements in ceramic, stone and metal, all of which blend with the historic elements of the Whitehall Street station. Beginning at the entrance of the station with a view of the city today, the images Giorgini created transport viewers backward through time. Scenes of the age of steamships are followed by a montage of New Amsterdam, the arrival of the first settlers, and finally the era before European settlement, with Native American canoes and a marshland of flora and fauna. In another area, groups of fish appear, in both two- and three-dimensional form, accompanying a mosaic of sea and sky. Nearby railings are in the form of cattails, topping off Giorgini's paean to a lower Manhattan of another era.

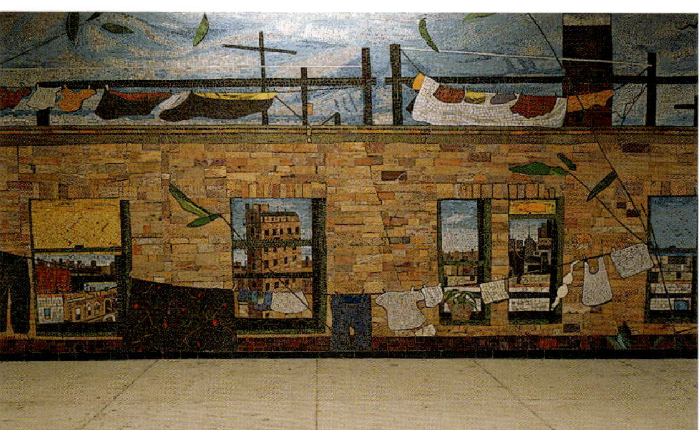

FRANK LESLIE HAMPTON

UPTOWN NEW YORK, 2000

Tremont Avenue B D

Glass mosaic

Fabricator: Franz Mayer of Munich

Station Design: MTA Architects/Engineers

PHOTOGRAPHER: PATRICK J. CASHIN

Uptown New York is a colorful, airy celebration of apartment life in the Bronx. Drawing from his childhood memory, Frank Hampton created a scene with a viewpoint from an actual rooftop location. The viewer, looking through a building, sees the neighbors' furniture, the continuing view of nearby rooftops, other apartment buildings, and further beyond to the scenery of skyscrapers in Manhattan. "I grew up in the Bronx gazing out of apartment windows that look out onto fire escapes, store signs, laundry, and buildings upon buildings," said Hampton. "These have always seemed like mosaics to me, colorful, interacting, and in constant motion. Windows played the role of a yard I didn't have."

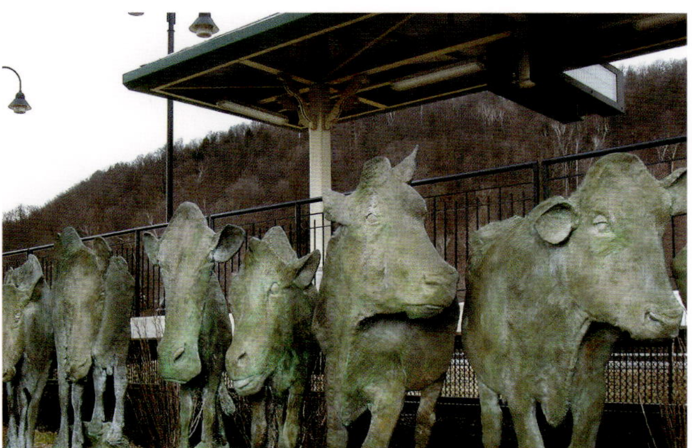

ANNE HUIBREGTSE

ARRIVAL, 2000

Wassaic Station, MTA Metro-North Railroad

Bronze

Fabricators: Argos Art Foundry; Jetstream

Station Design: MTA MNR Architects/Engineers; Clough Harbour & Associates; Jeff White

PHOTOGRAPHER: ROB WILSON

Arrival is a bronze bas-relief of life-size dairy cows that stand expectantly awaiting the next train. "I want the cows to remind both local residents and visitors of the region's rich farming past," says Anne Huibregtse. "The local agricultural economy may be shrinking, but it remains an important part of our community and rural landscape." The Wassaic area turned to dairy farming in the mid-nineteenth century; with the onset of the Civil War and the development of canned milk, the area was able to help fill a great demand created by Union soldiers. More recently, other regions have outpaced Wassaic in dairying, and farm after farm has turned to other uses.

FREDERICK DANA MARSH

MARINE GRILL MURALS, 2000
(created 1912 for the McAlpin Hotel)
Fulton Street–Broadway–Nassau A C J M Z 2 3 4 5
Glazed terra-cotta; painted cast and wrought iron
Donated by the New York City Landmarks Preservation Commission
Fabricator: Atlantic Terra Cotta Company
Conservators: Alan M. Farancz Painting Conservation Studio; Vel Riberto Consulting
Station Design: MTA NYCT Architects/Engineers
See page 104

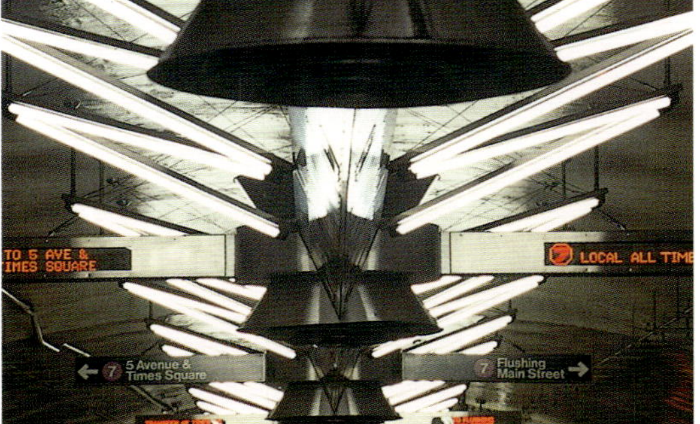

CHRISTOPHER SPROAT in collaboration with Gruzen Samton

V-BEAM, 2000
Grand Central–42nd Street S 4 5 6 7
Stainless steel, lighting, signage, LED, and fan system
Fabricator: Creative Light Source
Station Design: Gruzen Samton
PHOTOGRAPHER: MARY L. BACHMANN

V-Beam is both a functional structure and an aesthetic statement. In this piece, Christopher Sproat has combined standard utilitarian transportation hardware—signage, air circulation, and safety equipment—and his own artistic skill and imagination to integrate sculpture and the transit environment. The artwork takes the form of a large V, which Sproat judged to be the most practical shape in terms of access and stability, and is equipped with extruded aluminum panels and light-emitting diodes to carry out its functions.

2001

JACK BEAL

THE RETURN OF SPRING, 2001
THE ONSET OF WINTER, 2005
Times Square–42nd Street N Q R S W 1 2 3 7
Glass mosaic
Fabricator: Miotto Mosaic Art Studios
Station Design: William Nicholas Bodouva + Associates; Kohn Pedersen Fox
See page 28

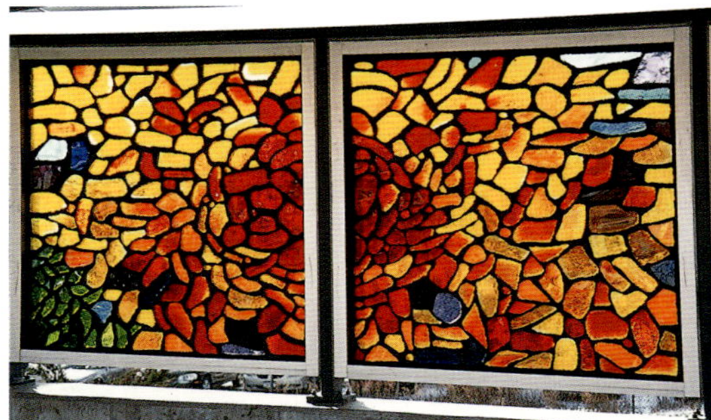

MARJORIE BLACKWELL

TRANQUILITY, 2001
Mount Vernon East Station, MTA Metro-North Railroad
Faceted glass
Fabricator: Gordon Stained Glass Studios
Station Design: MTA MNR Architects/Engineers; Sowinski Sullivan Architects
PHOTOGRAPHER: FRANK ENGLISH

Tranquility's twelve faceted-glass windscreen panels at Mount Vernon station create a shimmering impressionist effect in stained glass. Aptly named, it depicts a peaceful setting of trees, lake, and sky in calming shades of green, blue, and yellow. Marjorie Blackwell wanted the colors and dancing shapes to give commuters "something to play with, mediate with, and connect with at the station."

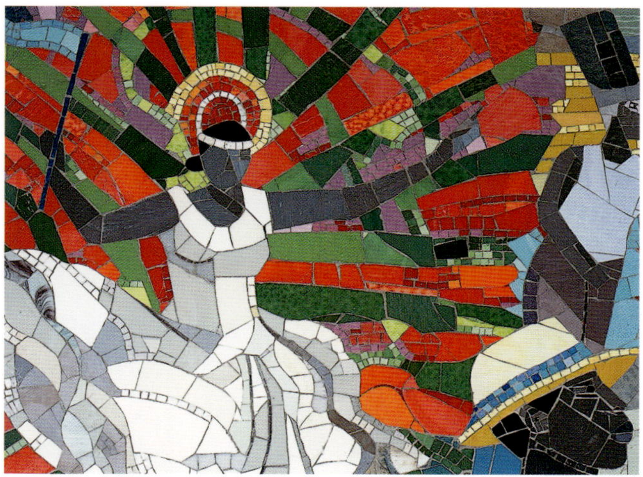

LOUIS DELSARTE

TRANSITIONS, 2001
Church Avenue 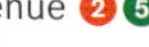
Glass mosaic
Fabricator: Franz Mayer of Munich
Station Design: Ellerbe Becket
PHOTOGRAPHER: PATRICK J. CASHIN

Brooklyn's Flatbush area has great ethnic diversity, including many recent immigrants who have contributed their own idiosyncratic flavor to the cultural life of the city. Among these relative newcomers are people from the Caribbean, who brought with them the idea for an event that has become one of the city's largest and most lively—the West Indian American Day Parade. In his murals at Church Avenue, Louis Delsarte evokes its color and energy. "This neighborhood has had many different groups moving in and out over the years. Now it's predominantly Caribbean, and I wanted to freeze a moment in its history," he says. In the part of the work called "Jump-Up," abstract shapes compete with more realistic figures to evoke a wild Carnival dance. "Avenue of Churches" is about Sunday morning reverence. In "The Neighborhood," children are shown happily jumping rope.

ERIC FISCHL

THE GARDEN OF CIRCUS DELIGHTS, 2001
34th Street–Penn Station A C E
Glass mosaic
Fabricators: Peter Columbo Artistic Mosaics; Franz Mayer of Munich
Station Design: MTA NYCT Architects/Engineers
See page 54

JACOB LAWRENCE

NEW YORK IN TRANSIT, 2001
Times Square–42nd Street N Q R S W 1 2 3 7
Glass mosaic
Fabricator: Miotto Mosaic Art Studios
Station Design: William Nicholas Bodouva + Associates; Kohn Pedersen Fox
See page 26

AL LOVING

BROOKLYN, NEW MORNING, 2001
Broadway Junction A C J L Z
Glass mosaic and faceted glass
Fabricator: Miotto Mosaic Art Studios
Station Design: Gruzen Samton
See page 130

WALTER MARTIN and PALOMA MUÑOZ

A GATHERING, 2001
Canal Street A C E
Bronze
Fabricator: Modern Art Foundry
Station Design: MTA NYCT Architects/Engineers
See page 92

ELIZABETH MURRAY

STREAM, 2001
23rd Street–Ely Avenue, Long Island City–Court Square E G V
Glass mosaic
Fabricator: Miotto Mosaic Art Studios
Station Design: MTA NYCT Architects/Engineers
See page 114

ROY NICHOLSON
MORNING TRANSIT, HEMPSTEAD PLAIN
EVENING TRANSIT, HEMPSTEAD PLAIN, 2001
Hicksville Station, MTA Long Island Rail Road
Glass mosaic
Fabricator: Miotto Mosaic Art Studios
Station Design: MTA LIRR Architects/Engineers
See page 152

TOM OTTERNESS in cooperation with Skidmore, Owings + Merrill
LIFE UNDERGROUND, 2001
14th Street–8th Avenue A C E L
Bronze
Fabricators: Tallix; Polich Art Works; Joel Meissner & Co.
Station Design: Skidmore, Owings & Merrill
See page 90

NANCY SPERO
ARTEMIS, ACROBATS, DIVAS, AND DANCERS, 2001
66th Street–Lincoln Center 1
Glass and ceramic mosaic
Fabricator: Peter Columbo Artistic Mosaics
Station Design: Lee Harris Pomeroy Architects
See page 88

2002

ACCONCI STUDIO in collaboration with di Domenico + Partners
WALL-SLIDE, 2002
161st Street–Yankee Stadium B D 4
Stone, tile, and fiberglass
Fabricators: M.A. Angeliades; Mozart Iron Craft; Miller Druck Specialty Contracting; Seal Reinforced Fiberglass
Station Design: di Domenico + Partners
See page 140

HELENE BRANDT in cooperation with Acconci Studio and di Domenico + Partners
ROOM OF TRANQUILITY, 2002
161st Street–Yankee Stadium B D 4
Glass, stone, and marble mosaic
Fabricator: Miotto Mosaic Art Studios
Station Design: di Domenico + Partners
See page 142

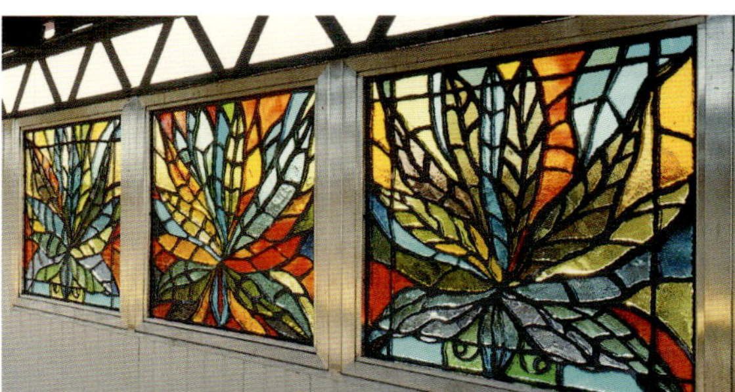

RON CALLOWAY
EUPHORBIAS, 2002
Kosciuszko Street J
Faceted glass
Fabricator: Willet Hauser Architectural Glass
Station Design: MTA NYCT Architects/Engineers
PHOTOGRAPHER: JEFFREY STURGES

In *Euphorbias*, Ron Calloway uses the imagery of plants as a metaphor for life and growth in the communities that surround the Kosciuszko Street elevated station. It seems as if energy is moving from the center of the striking, colorful images, radiating out to the tips of the forms. The colored plants, some suggesting the image of the sun and its rays, bloom in sixteen faceted-glass panels on the platform.

KANE CHANH DO / JANE GREENGOLD
ALMOST HOME, 2002
Pleasantville Station, MTA Metro-North Railroad
Bronze
Fabricator: Polich Art Works
Station Design: MTA MNR Architects/Engineers; Gruzen Samton
See page 146

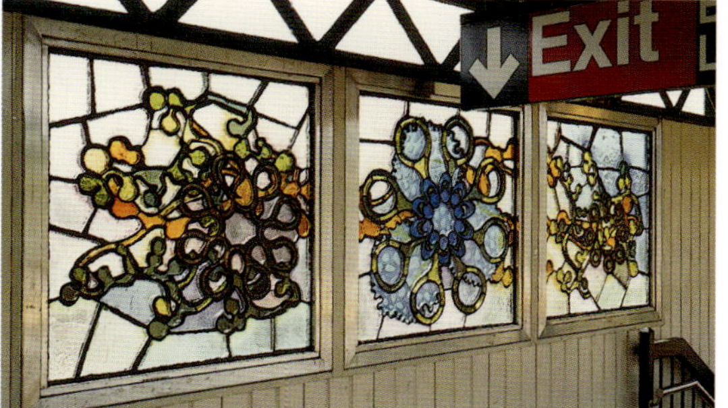

ANNETTE DAVIDEK
ROUNDLET SERIES, 2002
Lorimer Street J M
Faceted glass
Fabricator: Willet Hauser Architectural Glass
Station Design: MTA NYCT Architect/Engineers
PHOTOGRAPHER: JEFFREY STURGES

Annette Davidek's murals illustrate the fractured and fragmented language of nature's poetry. The abstract *Roundlet Series* invites free interpretation, at times recalling blossoming flowers, twisting branches, or meandering patterns that mimic genetic elements, and as the trains fly by, they create a kaleidoscopic effect. The faceted glass has a striking translucent quality, creating a dramatic contrast between the contours in the piece.

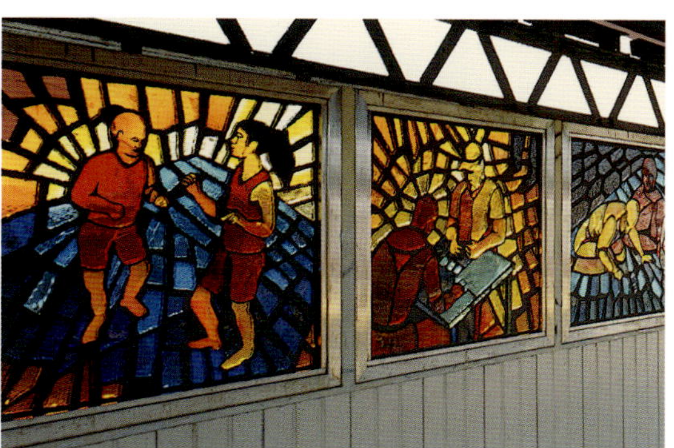

MARIA DOMINGUEZ
EL VIEWS, 2002
Chauncey Street J Z
Faceted glass
Fabricator: Willet Hauser Architectural Glass
Station Design: MTA NYCT Architects/Engineers
PHOTOGRAPHER: JEFFREY STURGES

In order to capture the area's spirit and energy, Maria Dominguez spoke with dozens of people and took numerous photographs of their neighborhood before creating the paintings that were the basis of *El Views*. Translated into sixteen panels of brilliantly colored faceted glass, her murals transform daily goings-on—people arriving home from school or work, buds in the trees on a warm spring day, and lights from the businesses surrounding the elevated structures—into powerful images. *El Views* is embedded with the sense of humanity created by the people and place that were its inspiration.

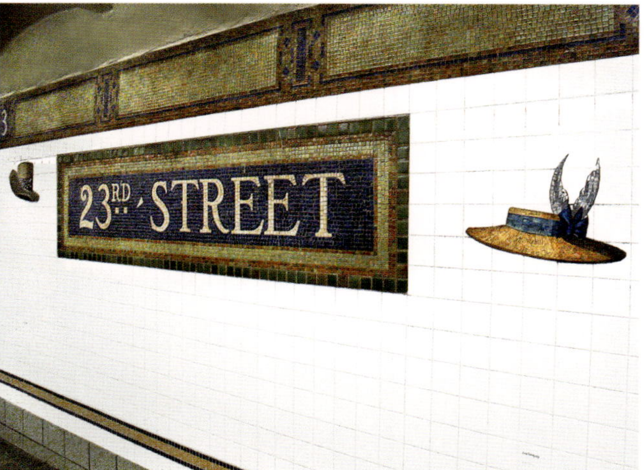

KEITH GODARD
MEMORIES OF 23RD STREET, 2002
23rd Street N R W
Glass mosaic
Fabricator: Miotto Mosaic Art Studios
Station Design: MTA NYCT Architects/Engineers
PHOTOGRAPHER: ROB WILSON

From the 1880s through the 1920s, 23rd Street was a major vaudeville, entertainment, and cultural section of the city. Ladies' Mile, the fashion and department store haven of that era, was nearby. In his *Memories of 23rd Street*, Keith Godard represents historic figures associated with Madison Square through the various hats they might have worn. Celebrities include Jim Brady, Oscar Wilde, Sarah Bernhardt, Mark Twain, Lillian Russell, and Stanford White. Godard says, "In addition to bringing back memories of the specific time period and people, and appealing to the viewers on a more common level as fascinating hats, this design can also serve as an interactive, playful, and witty landmark. As a diversion, passengers waiting for the subway train might try to picture people on the opposite platform 'wearing' the hats they are standing beneath!"

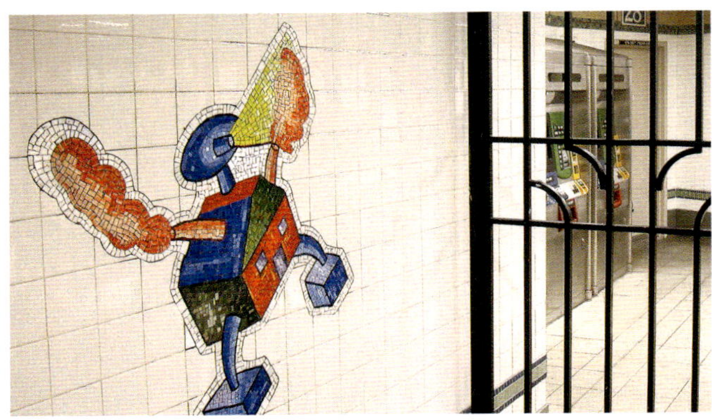

MARK HADJIPATERAS

CITY DWELLERS (FOR COSTAS AND MARO), 2002
28th Street N R W
Glass mosaic
Fabricator: Miotto Mosaic Art Studios
Station Design: MTA NYCT Architects/Engineers
PHOTOGRAPHER: ROB WILSON

The Toy Center and the Flatiron Building, both located near the station at 28th Street and Broadway, served as inspiration for Mark Hadjipateras who works in a funky cartoonlike style. His *City Dwellers* animates the platform walls with fanciful images of robotlike people. His creations may seem wacky, but the artist has used universal symbols and forms in the compositions to reference the neighborhood and its history involving technology, toys, and commerce. Hadjipateras's playful inventions invite riders to guess at their meanings; the images evoke a familiarity, yet the viewer is never quite sure exactly what they are.

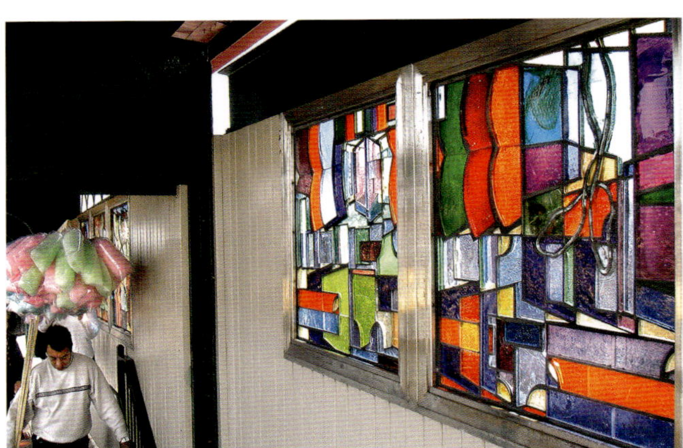

MARA HELD

EL IN 16 NOTES, 2002
Hewes Street J M
Faceted glass
Fabricator: Willet Hauser Architectural Glass
Station Design: MTA NYCT Architects/Engineers
PHOTOGRAPHER: ROB WILSON

In *El in 16 Notes*, abstract shapes couple with elegant lines to show patterns inventing themselves through a composite of layers and spatial relationships. The forms are derived from dress patterns, and the minimal, elegantly juxtaposed shapes are sometimes intercepted by playful and unexpected curves. Held paid particular attention to the density of colors and the way the colors animate the forms when illuminated. Riders see the neighborhood from a different perspective as the skyline emerges through the colored panes. The artist, daughter of artist Al Held, says, "In my work, vaguely reminiscent fragmented forms lock together to weave an image. Edges push against the forms to hold them in place."

ROBERT HICKMAN in cooperation with Dattner Architects

LACED CANOPY, 2002
72nd Street 1 2 3
Mosaic glass
Station Design: Gruzen Samton/Dattner Architects
See page 86

SAMM KUNCE

UNDER BRYANT PARK, 2002
42nd Street–Bryant Park B D F V 7
Glass mosaic and stone
Fabricator: Franz Mayer of Munich
Station Design: MTA NYCT Architects/Engineers
See page 34

ROY LICHTENSTEIN

TIMES SQUARE MURAL, 2002
Times Square–42nd Street N Q R S W 1 2 3 7
(Collage 1990, fabricated 1994)
Porcelain enamel
Fabricators: Windsor Fireform; Polich Art Works
Station Design: William Nicholas Bodouva + Associates; Kohn Pedersen Fox
See page 24

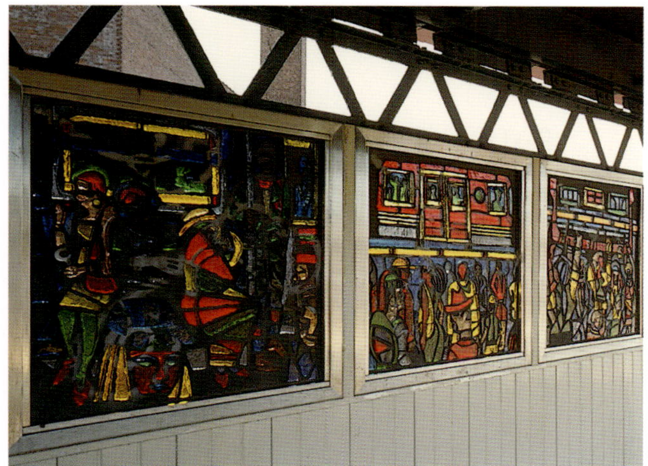

CHRIS WADE ROBINSON

DREAM TRAIN, 2002
Gates Avenue J Z
Faceted glass
Fabricator: Willet Hauser Art Glass Studios
Station Design: MTA NYCT Architects/Engineers
PHOTOGRAPHER: JEFFREY STURGES

In *Dream Train*, Chris Wade Robinson explores the spirit of the subway by intertwining organic and mechanical elements in a symphony of daily rhythm. Sixteen panels of faceted glass narrate moments of interaction between riders and the motions of trains. As Robinson observes, "A simple subway ride is a cultural exploration, a cross section of a city as it moves from past to present and on to tomorrow. All races, creeds, and colors interconnect on a common path to an endless variety of destinations. Each rider is enriched by daily discoveries of new faces, places, and things. Each individual work presented in this series is part of a larger whole, strung together, as it were, like the links in a chain or, more appropriately, the cars of a train. They are vignettes made of memory and experience; an ode to a lifetime spent riding in and dreaming on the train as it speeds through the darkness and into the light."

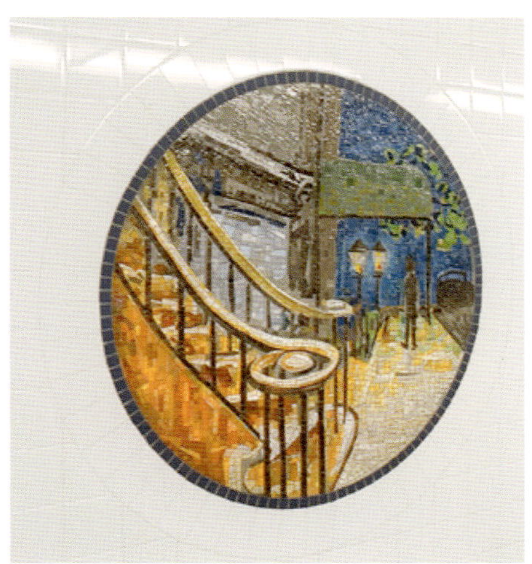

TIMOTHY SNELL

BROADWAY DIARY, 2002
8th Street-NYU N R W
Glass mosaic
Fabricator: Miotto Mosaic Art Studios
Station Design: MTA NYCT Architects/Engineers
PHOTOGRAPHER: ROB WILSON

Timothy Snell describes *Broadway Diary:* "The mosaic is composed of 40 'portholes' that depict scenes and historic sites of the neighborhood (Grace Church, Washington Arch, Cooper Union, Astor Place, the vista of Broadway) . . . The loose gestural rendering and free use of color with simplified imagery injects a light moment in the hectic schedule of the commuter passing through the station . . . Spreading the elements around the station in an architectural format . . . integrates the artwork with the space . . . This provides moments of diversion at various locations for people waiting and small surprises for repeat travelers in transit through this station. The repeat of elements . . . and loose use of line and color were devices to add motion and allow more abstract considerations to enter into the work with the hook of recognizable subject matter."

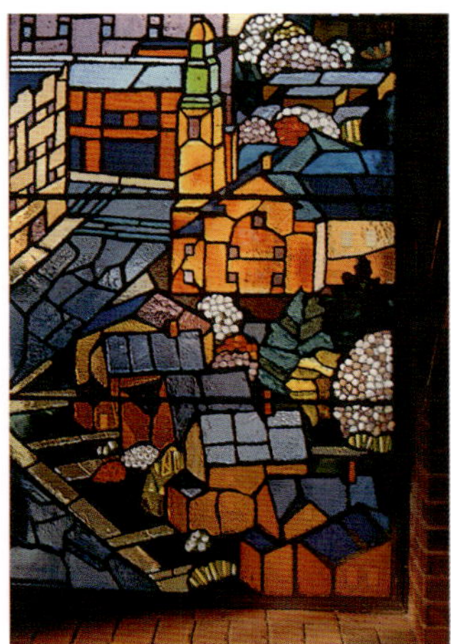

TOVA SNYDER

RAILROADS AND ROOFTOPS, 2002
Harrison Station, MTA Metro-North Railroad
Faceted glass
Fabricator: Helmut Schardt Master Craftsman
Station Design: MTA MNR Architects/Engineers; Sowinski Sullivan Architects
PHOTOGRAPHER: TOVA SNYDER

Railroads and Rooftops consists of twelve faceted-glass panels—four in the dormer windows of the station house and four in each of the two elevator towers. Tova Snyder focused on the streetscape of downtown Harrison for the panes in the dormer windows; for the windowed sections on the elevator towers, she created a series of images of commuters and trains. One tower shows contemporary scenes and the other depicts corresponding scenes in a historical context. While researching the history of Harrison, Snyder discovered how integral the railroad was to the development of the community. In Harrison, the railroad created the downtown and brought in the immigrant workers who eventually became part of the community, shaping its future—a relationship that Snyder attempts to capture.

2003

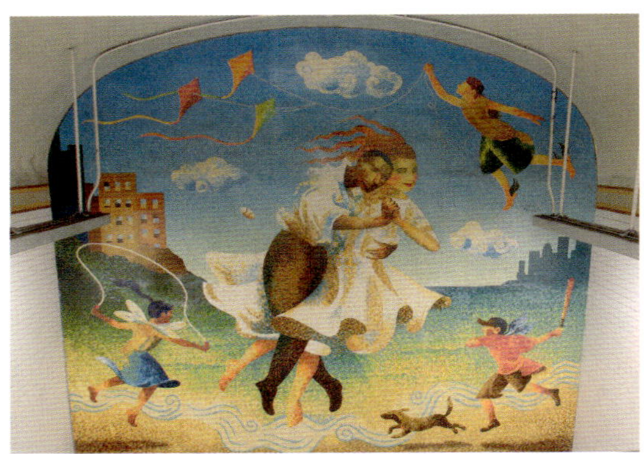

RAÚL COLÓN

PRIMAVERA, 2003
191st Street 1
Glass mosaic and faceted glass
Fabricators: Mosaïka Art & Design; Willet Hauser Architectural Glass
Station Design: MTA NYCT Architects/Engineers
PHOTOGRAPHER: PATRICK J. CASHIN

Raúl Colón recalls that when he was asked to submit a proposal, he paid a visit to Washington Heights in order to visualize a piece that its residents would notice and enjoy. He observed that it is a diverse neighborhood with a few parks nearby where children play, elements that he included in his work. However, Colón did not want to create a purely realist representation of the neighborhood, so he turned to early Renaissance paintings for inspiration. Colón adds, "The couple represented dancing is ethnically diverse, because it is a mixed neighborhood. It particularly represents the Hispanic and Latino culture."

LISA DINHOFER

LOSING MY MARBLES, 2003
42nd Street-Port Authority Bus Terminal A C E
Glass mosaic
Fabricator: Franz Mayer of Munich
Station Design: Dattner Architects
See page 32

VALERIE MAYNARD

POLYRHYTHMICS OF CONSCIOUSNESS AND LIGHT, 2003
125th Street 4 5 6
Glass mosaic
Fabricator: Miotto Mosaic Art Studios
Station Design: H2L2 Architects/Planners; B. Thayer Associates
See page 70

2004

ARTS FOR TRANSIT COLLABORATIVE

NEW YORK CITY ARCHITECTURAL ARTIFACTS FROM THE COLLECTION OF THE BROOKLYN MUSEUM, 2004
Eastern Parkway-Brooklyn Museum 2 3
Terra-cotta and glass mosaic
Fabricator: Miotto Mosaic Art Studios
Conservators: Alan M. Farancz Painting Conservation Studio; Vel Riberto Consulting
Station Design: MTA NYCT Architects/Engineers
See page 126

ELLSWORTH AUSBY

SPACE ODYSSEY, 2004
Marcy Avenue J M Z
Faceted glass
Fabricator: Willet Hauser Architectural Glass
Station Design: MTA NYCT Architects/Engineers
See page 132

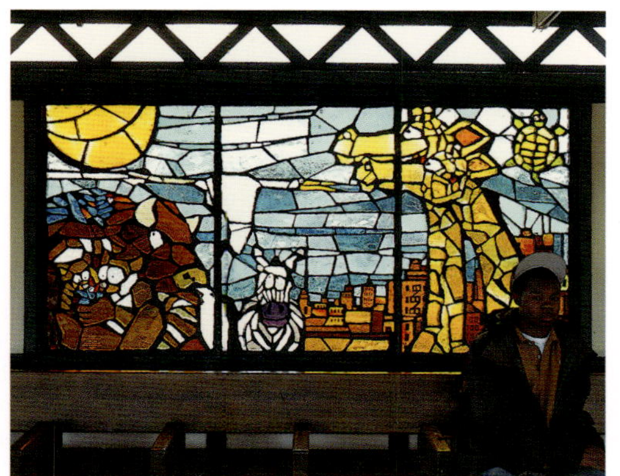

NAOMI CAMPBELL

ANIMAL TRACKS, 2004
West Farms Square–East Tremont Avenue 2 5
Faceted glass
Fabricator: Gordon Stained Glass Studios
Station Design: Urbahn Architects
PHOTOGRAPHER: JEFFREY STURGES

Naomi Campbell calls *Animal Tracks* "an oasis in the air." Campbell explains that she "plays on vision, using intense imagery to explore individual experiences" and uses "free play as a subtle language to communicate to the viewer. The viewer grapples with layers of space and the kinetics of movement and stillness to evoke a mood that is often uplifting and suggestive of powerful, poetic imagery." Locating her work at the West Farms Square–East Tremont Avenue station is not coincidental: *Animal Tracks* serves as an introduction to the nearby Bronx Zoo for visitors just arriving and a memento of the trip for those reboarding the train.

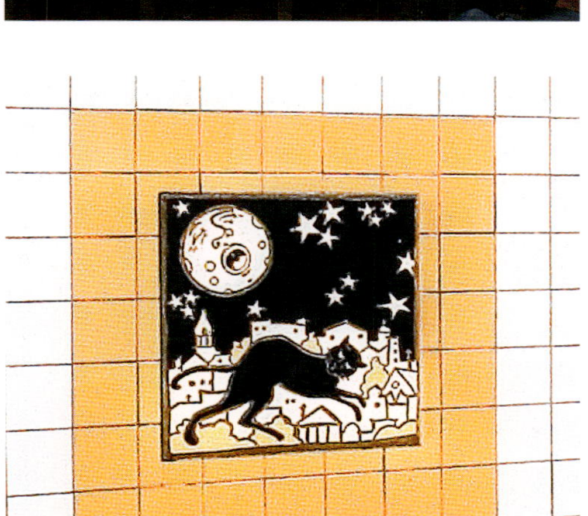

HUGO CONSUEGRA

GOOD MORNING AND GOOD NIGHT, 2004
Crown Heights–Utica Avenue 3 4
Ceramic tiles; bronze medallions
Fabricators: Frank Giorgini Handmade Tiles; Johnson Atelier
Station Design: Brennan Beer Gorman/Architects
PHOTOGRAPHER: ROB WILSON

Hugo Consuegra of Brennan Beer Gorman was already serving as the architect for the Crown Heights–Utica Avenue station when his responsibilities were expanded to creating artwork for it as well. *Good Morning and Good Night* mirror the flow of riders commuting in and out of their home neighborhoods day after day. *Good Morning* is on the inbound side of the station, which fills with commuters in the morning hours; *Good Night* welcomes travelers home as the evening arrives. Born in Cuba, Consuegra was a member of an influential abstract expressionist group, The Eleven, in the 1950s. The collective produced the largest portion of its work during the period of 1953 through 1955. In 1967, after participating in various exhibitions in Europe, Consuegra sought political asylum in Spain and eventually moved to New York City in 1970.

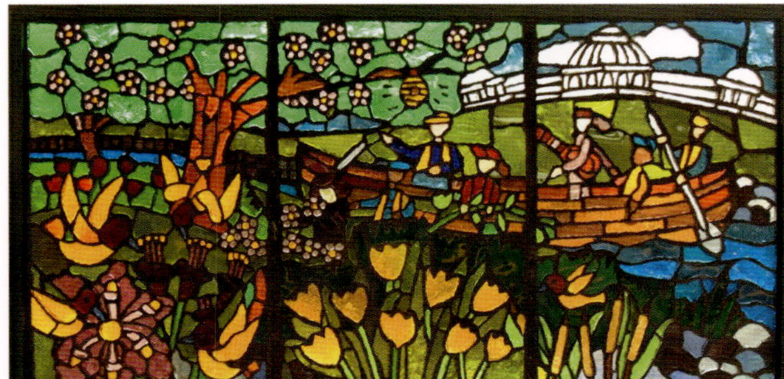

DANIEL DEL VALLE

A TRIP UP THE BRONX RIVER, 2004
174th Street 2 5
Faceted glass
Fabricator: Gordon Stained Glass Studios
Station Design: Urbahn Architects
PHOTOGRAPHER: PATRICK J. CASHIN

The ten faceted-glass panels of *A Trip up the Bronx River* show a group of people taking a canoe trip up the stream, visiting famous sites such as the Bronx Zoo and the Botanical Garden and passing by various neighborhoods. Daniel Del Valle also celebrates the local community, showing its members at a street festival, making masks, and planting trees. He adds, "Even though not everyone can take this magical trip up the river to view these sites, the 2 and 5 trains can provide easy access to these locations." Muralist Diego Rivera is an inspiration for Del Valle, who studied in Mexico and has a strong interest in Mexican art.

MING FAY

SHAD CROSSING, DELANCEY ORCHARD, 2004
Delancey Street–Essex Street F J M Z
Glass mosaic
Fabricator: Franz Mayer of Munich
Station Design: URS Group
See page 100

AL HELD in cooperation with Urbahn Architects
PASSING THROUGH, 2004
Lexington Avenue–53rd Street E V
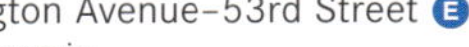
Glass mosaic
Fabricator: Miotto Mosaic Art Studios
Station Design: Urbahn Architects
See page 48

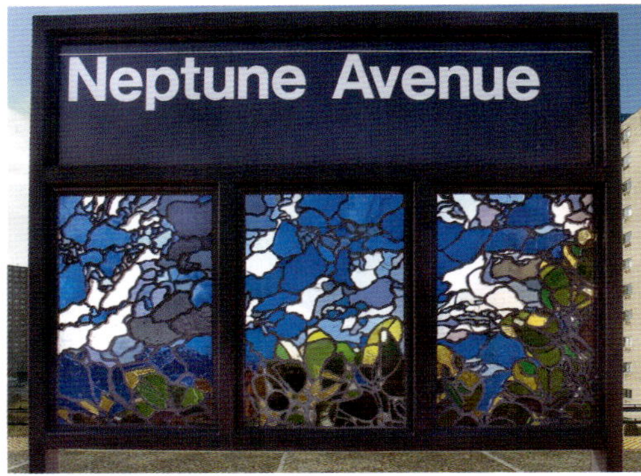

MICHAEL KRONDL
LOOKING UP, 2004
Neptune Avenue F
Faceted glass
Fabricator: Willet Hauser Architectural Glass
Station Design: Daniel Frankfurt
PHOTOGRAPHER: ROB WILSON

Michael Krondl describes *Looking Up* as "a series of photographically derived images that would act as an almost cinematic transition from the leafy terrestrial realm that exists in the immediate vicinity of the station to the airy fantastical world of Coney Island in the far distance. The imagery is highly site-specific and was chosen for its interplay of opacity and translucency." Pictorial elements derive from three sources—the nearby foliage, the sky (an element of the experience of riding the elevated train in Brooklyn), and Coney Island's famous Cyclone roller coaster.

ROBERT KUSHNER
4 SEASONS SEASONED, 2004
77th Street 6
Glass mosaic
Fabricator: Miotto Mosaic Art Studios
Station Design: David Elliot Leibowitz
See page 62

TOM PATTI
PASSAGE, 2004
74th Street–Broadway–Jackson Heights–Roosevelt Avenue E F G R V 7
Glass
Station Design: FXFOWLE Architects
See page 116

PETER SIS
HAPPY CITY, 2004
86th Street 4 5 6
Glass mosaic and etched stone
Fabricator: Franz Mayer of Munich
Station Design: David Elliot Leibowitz
See page 64

GEORGE TRAKAS in collaboration with di Domenico + Partners
HOOK (ARCHEAN REACH), LINE (SEA HOUSE), AND SINKER (MINED SWELL), 2004
Atlantic Avenue–Pacific Street B D M N Q R 2 3 4 5
Polished granite, brushed steel, limestone, and Rockville granite
Fabricators: Schiavone Construction; Santop Construction; Cold Spring Granite; New York Stone; Selco; Hatfield Metal Fab
Station Design: di Domenico + Partners
See page 124

ROBERT WILSON
MY CONEY ISLAND BABY, 2004
Coney Island–Stillwell Avenue D F N Q
Painted and laminated Vista glass brick
Fabricator: Franz Mayer of Munich
Station Design: MTA NYCT Architects/Engineers
See page 136

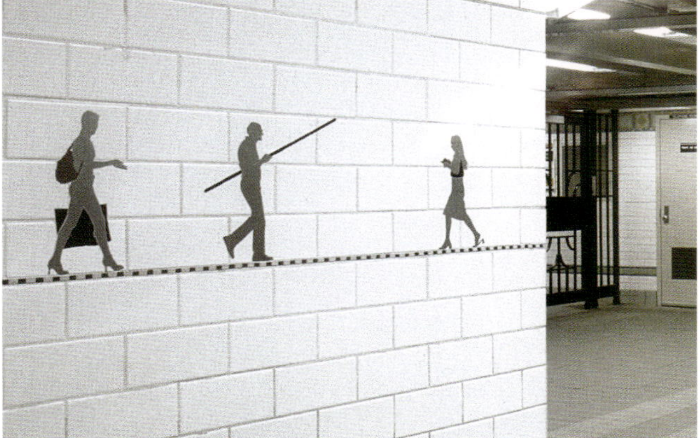

JANET ZWEIG and EDWARD DEL ROSARIO
CARRYING ON, 2004
Prince Street N R W
Steel, marble, and slate
Fabricators: Miotto Mosaic Art Studios; Surbeck Waterjet
Station Design: Brennan Beer Gorman/Architects
PHOTOGRAPHER: CATHY CARVER

Carrying On is composed of almost two hundred silhouettes of people and the many things they haul with them as they walk along the streets of the city. The artists worked from photographs depicting people moving around the city, in and out of the subway. The centerpiece is an enormous 1,200-foot storyboard on which combinations of images suggest scenarios, but viewers are invited to fill in the details. According to the artists, the title of *Carrying On* can be read in several ways: "People on the streets of New York are almost always carrying something, sometimes something huge and outlandish. After the 9/11 tragedy, New Yorkers felt that they must carry on with their lives. Finally, New Yorkers are notoriously opinionated and lively; they really do 'carry on.'"

2005

ACCONCI STUDIO in collaboration with Daniel Frankfurt
FACADE FOR WEST 8TH STREET SUBWAY STATION, 2005
West 8th Street–New York Aquarium F Q
Platform windscreens and seating
Fabricator: UAD Group
Station Design: Daniel Frankfurt
See page 134

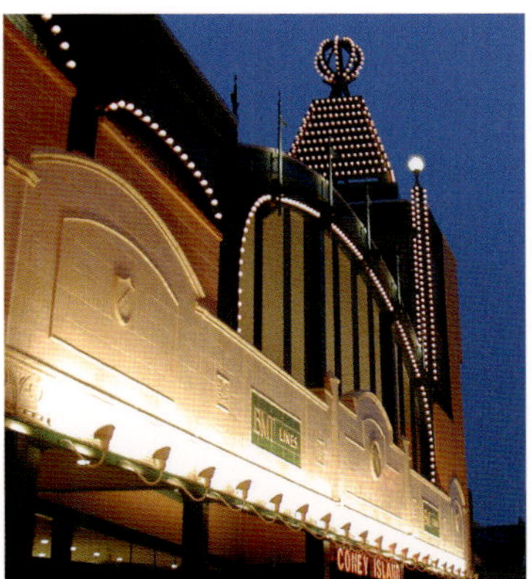

ATLANTIC TERRA COTTA COMPANY
BMT FACADE ON BUILDING ENTRANCE, 2005
Coney Island–Stillwell Avenue D F N Q
Building Design: di Domenico + Partners
Conservator: Alan M. Farancz Painting Conservation Studio
PHOTOGRAPHER: PATRICK PHILIPPEAUX

Architects di Domenico + Partners describe the new building at Stillwell Avenue as "a collage of elements that recall the 'Playland' character of Coney Island's past and strike the spark that will shape the area's future." The original facade from the BMT, complete with the green and red glazed tile logo, has been restored and incorporated into the building. A lighting scheme, created by Vel Riberto Consulting and Fisher Marantz Stone, recreates the feeling of the original Coney Island amusements, including Steeplechase Park, Dreamland, and Luna Park. The new building design, lighting, and historic terra-cotta evoke the old Coney Island and look forward to its future as a revitalized and re-energized residential community and recreation area.

RON BARON in cooperation with DMJM Harris
LOST AND FOUND: AN EXCAVATION PROJECT, 2005
Hempstead Station, MTA Long Island Rail Road
Bronze
Fabricator: Polich Art Works
Station Design: DMJM Harris
See page 150

ROBERT BLACKBURN assisted by Mei-Tei-Sing Smith
IN EVERYTHING THERE IS A SEASON, 2005
116th Street 6
Glass and ceramic mosaic
Fabricator: Franz Mayer of Munich
Station Design: MTA NYCT Architects/Engineers
See page 66

TOBY BUONAGURIO
TIMES SQUARE: 35 TIMES, 2005
Times Square–42nd Street N Q R S W 1 2 3 7
Ceramic plaques inset in glass-block wall
Station Design: William Nicholas Bodouva + Associates
See page 30

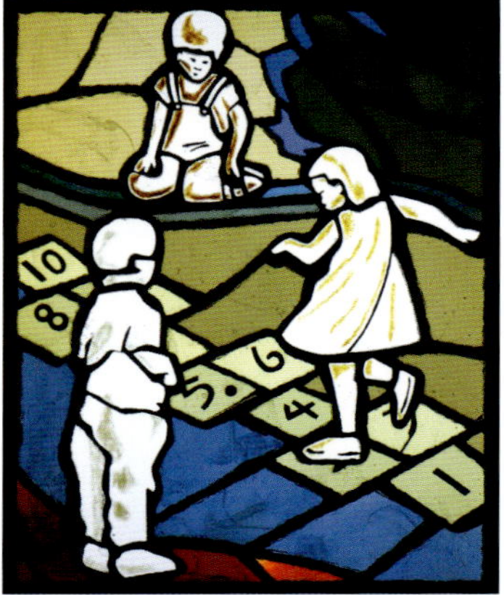

JOSIE GONZALES ALBRIGHT
CHILDREN AT PLAY, 2005
Woodlawn Avenue 4
Faceted glass
Fabricator: Willet Hauser Architectural Glass
Station Design: Urbahn Architects
PHOTOGRAPHER: ROB WILSON

Children at Play is a study of children moving through space—stopping to observe, spinning, crouching, sliding, and running. Josie Gonzales Albright says, "I arrived at a coloring for the children with jewel tones that would translate brightly to the stained glass. The scale of the children—to each other and the space that they're in—fills the frame with flowing colors that swirl around them. The effect is that they 'move through the colors' of their environment. Warm shadows are created by placing 'fritte' glass crystals fused over the glass, allowing for more flexibility and detail and adding a bubbly, raised texture. Lots of clear glass allows for light from adjacent colored glass pieces to spill over and create new color combinations throughout the day."

ELLEN HARVEY in cooperation with William Nicholas Bodouva + Associates
LOOK UP, NOT DOWN, 2005
Queens Plaza E G R V
Glass mosaic
Fabricator: Kolorines
Station Design: William Nicholas Bodouva + Associates
See page 112

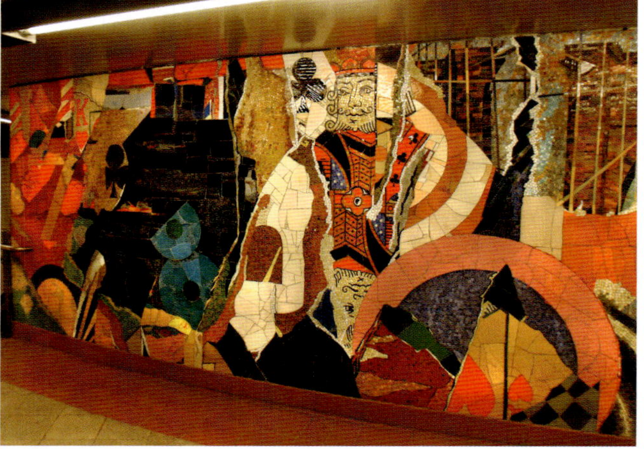

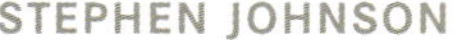

STEPHEN JOHNSON
DEKALB IMPROVISATION, 2005
DeKalb Avenue B M Q R
Glass mosaic
Fabricator: Franz Mayer of Munich
Station Design: Lee Harris Pomeroy Architects
PHOTOGRAPHER: ROB WILSON

Stephen Johnson intended these murals "to convey a sense of joy through an exuberant juxtaposition of colors, shapes, and familiar images . . . On the surface, the variety of colors and shapes makes the mosaics resemble collages and invites the traveler to consider the multiple layers of images found on city walls, particularly in the subway, where posters may tear, revealing previous images and forming exciting compositions. These wonderful juxtapositions of forms and thoughts are consonant with the dynamics of a vital, urban environment, which, like a collage, is a multi-layered community of individuals whose diversity brings into relief the character of a city . . . The glass is as diverse as the station's passengers, whose ethnic origins stem from Asia, Africa, and the Middle East . . . I wanted the abstract design to be balanced with realistic images that people can instantly get."

BARBARA SEGAL

MUHHEAKANTUCK (The River That Flows Two Ways), 2005
Yonkers Station, MTA Metro-North Railroad
Cast aluminum
Fabricator: Polich Art Works
Station Design: MTA MNR Architects/Engineers; Sowinski Sullivan Architects
See page 144

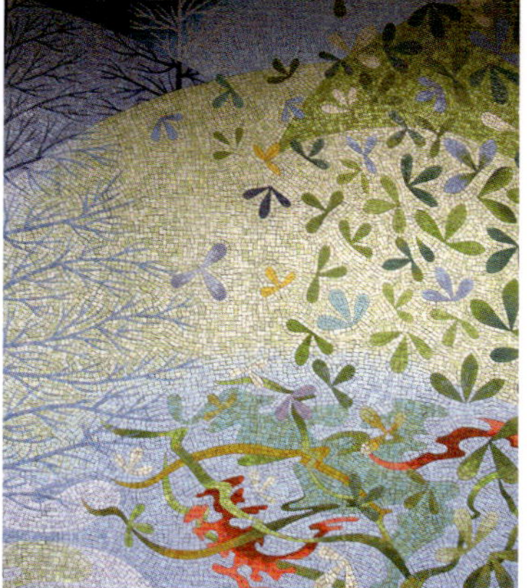

JOY TAYLOR

THE FOUR SEASONS, 2005
Larchmont Station, MTA Metro-North Railroad
Glass mosaic
Fabricator: Miotto Mosaic Art Studios
Station Design: MTA MNR Architects/Engineers; Sowinski Sullivan Architects
PHOTOGRAPHER: ANDY WAINWRIGHT

The Four Seasons shows the changes that the local plant life goes through during the year in suburban Larchmont. Joy Taylor explains, "Leaves are so commonplace in nature that we rarely consider them worthy of study. Yet when looked at closely they reveal themselves as marvels of efficiency and beauty. In a train station, time often means minutes to hurry, or to wait through. But this mural allows the traveler an opportunity for a different view. Like a time line, this mosaic reveals nature as a vehicle of change. Combining nature and time, I encourage the viewer to examine such changes and to appreciate the precious and fleeting quality of our world. The commuter may take a walk into April, or recall November, even as she hurries to an appointment or as he heads home from work."

ANITA THACHER

ILLUMINATED STATION, 2005
Greenport Station, MTA Long Island Rail Road
Lighting and projection
Sponsored by East End Seaport Museum and Marine Foundation
See page 158

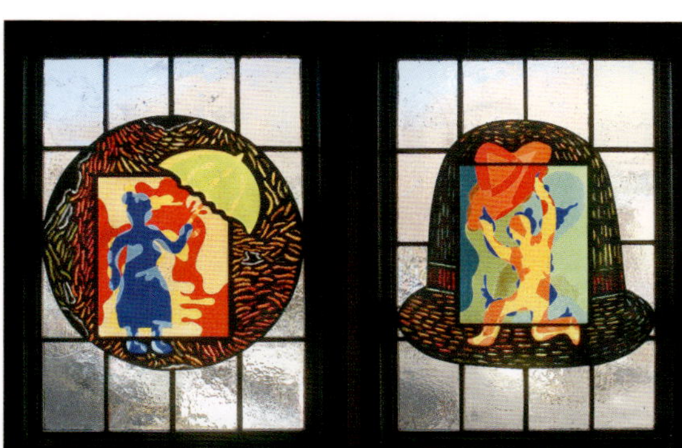

MOSES ROS

PATRIASANA WHOLESOMELAND, 2005
Fordham Road (4)
Faceted glass
Fabricator: Willet Hauser Architectural Glass
Station design: MTA NYCT Architects/Engineers
PHOTOGRAPHER: ROB WILSON

The brilliant colors and dancing figures in *Patriasana Wholesomeland* evoke the vibrant nature of the neighborhood. The bright human forms are offset by darker glass panels that surround them in shapes representing an umbrella, a hat, a coat, boots, pants, and gloves—objects that can be used to keep people warm and safe in foul weather. Clear glass outlines the darker shapes, creating further contrast, adding another layer to the design, and making the colors seem all the more lively. Moses Ros says, "Their energy is inspired by the brilliant colors, music, and dance of the Caribbean—the essence of life itself."

2006

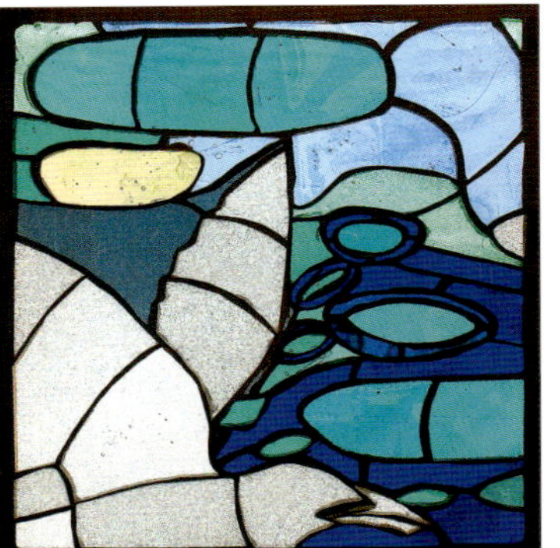

CANDIDA ALVAREZ

B IS FOR BIRDS IN THE BRONX, 2006
Bronx Park East 2 5
Faceted glass
Fabricator: Botti Studio of Architectural Arts, Inc.
Station Design: di Domenico + Partners
PHOTOGRAPHER: ROB WILSON

Candida Alvarez explains the presence of birds in her work: "I wanted to subvert them, and make them invisibly large and regal. By doing that, the birds in their emptiness, give attention to their transparency and how they hold a space for the trees, the bushes, the snow, the branches, the wind, the sky and the leaves to exist, like a still-life painting . . . where the space outside of the object really creates the form of the object . . . My birds are very still. They become templates of the possibility that wind and air filled them once and they have left a mark . . . like a footprint in the snow."

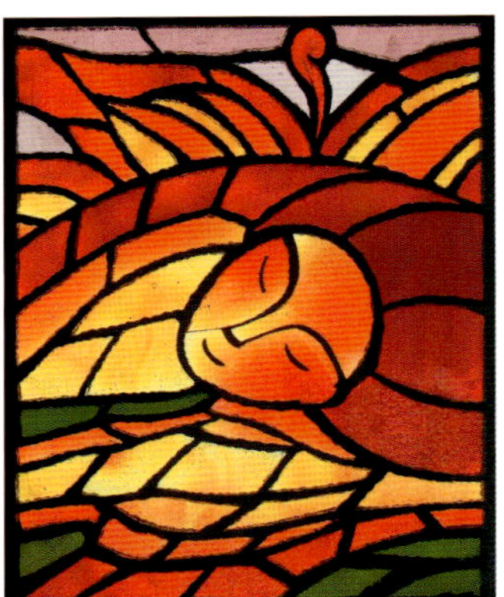

ANDREA ARROYO

MY SUN (MI SOL), MY PLANET (MI PLANETA), AND MY CITY (MI CIUDAD), 2006
Gun Hill Road 5
Faceted glass
Fabricator: Willet Hauser Architectural Glass
Station Design: di Domenico + Partners
PHOTOGRAPHER: ROB WILSON

Populated by colorful, lyrical figures, Andrea Arroyo's *My Sun (Mi Sol), My Planet (Mi Planeta), and My City (Mi Ciudad)* is composed of a series of faceted-glass windscreens that provide a focal point for the Gun Hill Road station. Inspired by life in the city, the artist strove to convey humanity, community, and harmony through the artwork. She explains, "In my work I celebrate nature and humanity, while examining the notions of gender, race and identity. My interest in the human form derives from my background in dance." Graced by vibrant figures in flight, the work conveys a sense of freedom and hope.

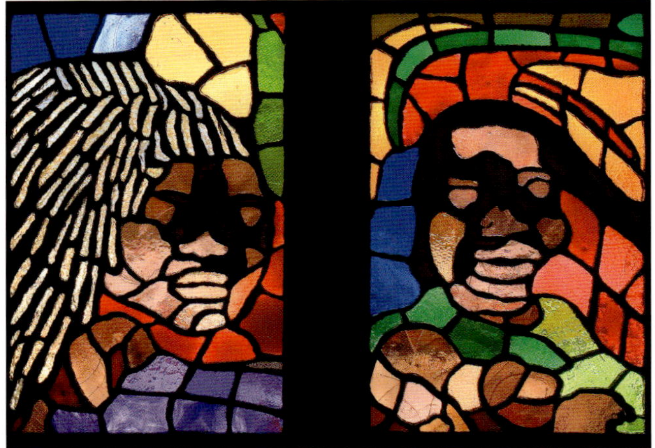

AMIR BEY

THE PROCESSION OF FOLK #3, 2006
Mount Eden Avenue 4
Faceted glass
Fabricator: Willet Hauser Architectural Glass
Station Design: MTA NYCT Architects/Engineers
PHOTOGRAPHER: ROB WILSON

Amir Bey describes *The Procession of Folk #3* as a vision of humanity's collective movements. The portraits are based on the faces of Bey's acquaintances, and in highlighting the unique qualities of each person, *The Procession* speaks to all riders in its celebration of individuality. Bey elaborates, "The identity of each face is specific, never to be repeated, even over thousands of generations, like the delicate changes of any flower's colors and shapes as it adapts to the sun's motion." Bey is fascinated with the complex nature of the human face: "The face can be a portrait or a stylized fantasy–even when I'm making a portrait of an individual. There is so much in the face, which is comprised of only a few components that can form complex expressions with endless variations, speaking a language that is universally understood."

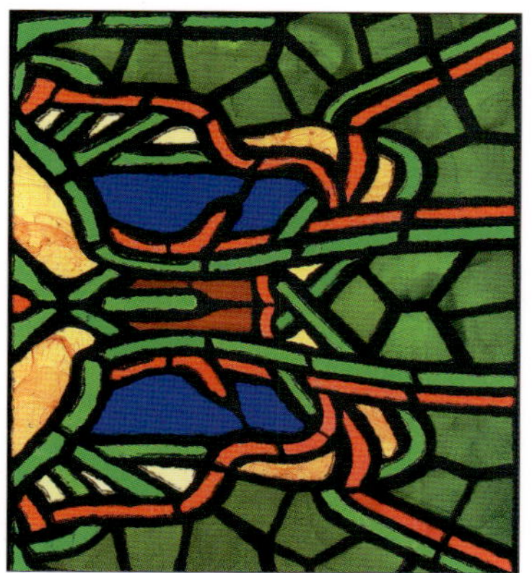

MICHELE BRODY

ALLERTON MANDALAS, 2006
Allerton Avenue 2 5
Faceted glass
Fabricator: Willet Hauser Architectural Glass
Station Design: di Domenico + Partners
PHOTOGRAPHER: ROB WILSON

Michele Brody based *Allerton Mandalas* on the 2 and 5 lines, which run from the Bronx through Manhattan to Brooklyn, as represented graphically on the MTA subway map. In the first stage of the work, she extracted the red and green lines and transformed them through a process of extrapolating, twisting, turning, and layering them. The final product, in faceted glass, captivates the viewer's attention with interlocking streams of colors. Fabricated into twenty panels and placed on the subway platform for the public to enjoy from inside as well as outside the station, the work is full of energy and excitement, almost mimicking the movement of a subway train.

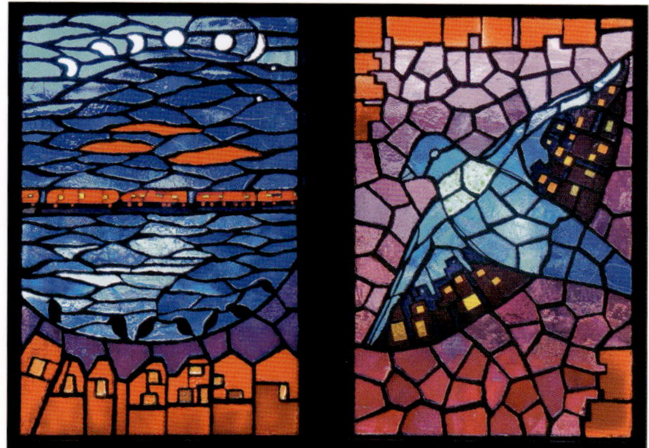

DINA BURSZTYN

VIEWS FROM ABOVE, 2006
170th Street 4
Faceted glass
Fabricator: Willet Hauser Architectural Glass
Station Design: MTA NYCT Architects/Engineers
PHOTOGRAPHER: ROB WILSON

As a daily rider of the trains in the area, Dina Bursztyn has become well acquainted with the "El" in the Bronx, which offers passengers a unique vantage point; she cites the extraordinary, even "magical," things that she has seen from the train as sources of inspiration. She has viewed tiny gardens of lushness and dreamed of the exotic animals living in the zoo nearby; the birds and the trees that she sees tell her stories. In the evening, sunsets fill the sky with a kaleidoscope of color and the train riders feel as if they might be rolling through the clouds. Bursztyn has been creating public art for more than twenty years and through it, she says, she seeks to create contemporary mythology and to present fresh possibilities, both literally and metaphorically.

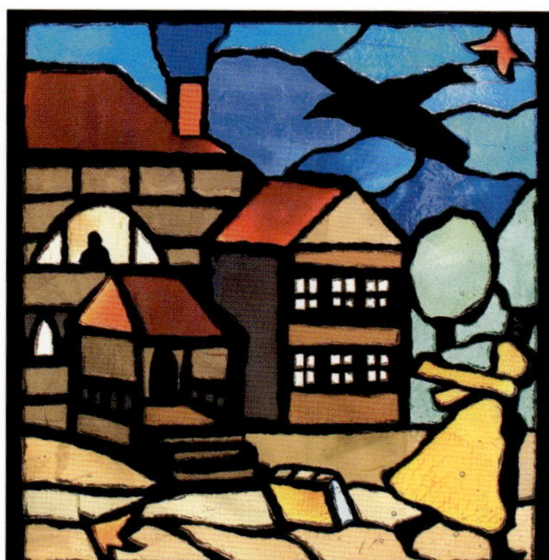

BÉATRICE CORON

BRONX LITERATURE, 2006
Burke Avenue 2 5
Faceted glass
Fabricator: Willet Hauser Architectural Glass
Station Design: di Domenico + Partners
PHOTOGRAPHER: ROB WILSON

In *Bronx Literature*, Béatrice Coron celebrates the rich literary heritage of the area, which has been the home and inspiration of writers as diverse as Edgar Allan Poe, Mark Twain, Sholem Aleichem, Allen Ginsberg, Chaim Potok, and Cynthia Ozick. The artist explains, "These authors tell the story of the borough from colonial times to suburban and contemporary community developments. Their works help us travel through time, into different social classes and communities making each of us an insider." In *Bronx Literature* Coron portrays four great writers' works, including Edgar Allan Poe's "Ulalume" and other poems, Sholem Aleichem's *Mottel, the Cantor's Son*, James Baldwin's *The Fire Next Time*, and Nicholasa Mohr's *El Bronx Remembered*.

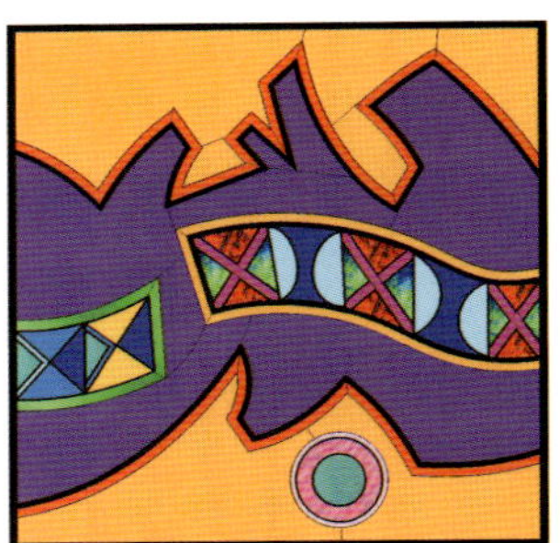

ROBIN HOLDER

MIGRATION, 2006

Flushing Avenue J M

Laminated glass

Fabricator: Däzzle Gläzz Studio

Station Design: MTA NYCT Architects/Engineers

PHOTOGRAPHER: ROBIN HOLDER

Robin Holder composed *Migration* with a series of brightly colored visual symbols that resemble the flags or signets of various countries. These banners appear to be undulating through a geographical space. The work evokes movement through city neighborhoods and the interaction of subway riders, traveling to work, home, and around the city.

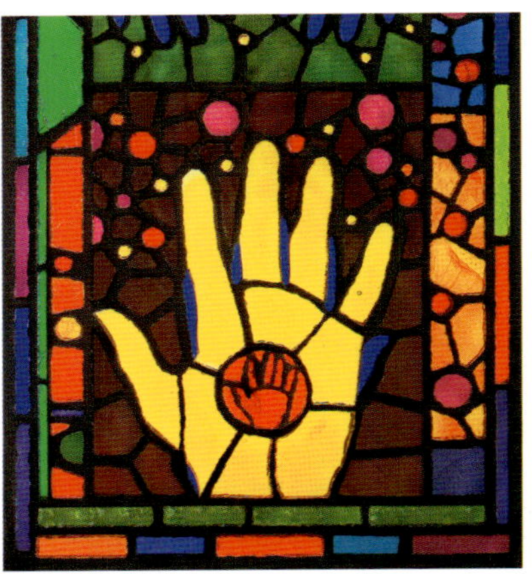

JUAN SÁNCHEZ

REACHING OUT FOR EACH OTHER, 2006

176th Street 4

Faceted glass

Fabricator: Willet Hauser Architectural Glass

Station Design: MTA NYCT Architects/Engineers

PHOTOGRAPHER: ROB WILSON

Reaching Out for Each Other allows warm streams of colored light to fill the 176th Street station. Human hands, the focus of the composition, transcend barriers to communicate meaning through a universal language. Using printed photographic images of hundreds of hands, Juan Sanchez cut and tore the paper, interspersing the pieces with bright colors and interesting shapes to produce a variety of seasonal collages. He explains, "The challenge was to create simple, direct, and consistent works for an urban train station. I wanted the artwork to be attractive and stimulating with much meaning and life. I wanted my art to visually convey people reaching and striving. I believe that art and life are inseparable. Art is life."

Pending Projects

These three projects are pending due to site and installation issues.

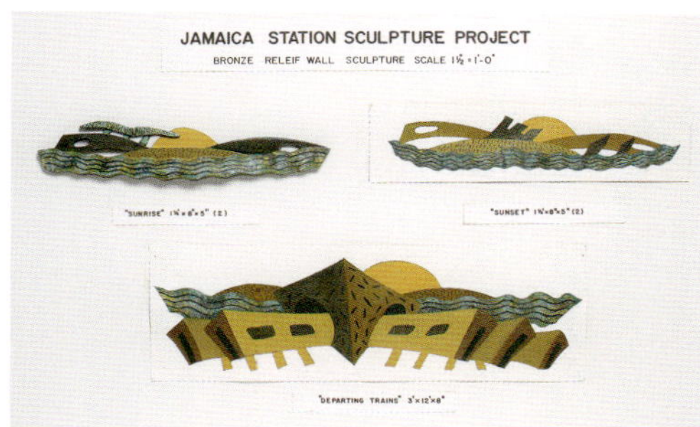

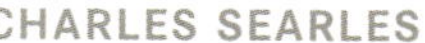

CHARLES SEARLES

SUNRISE, SUNSET, DEPARTING TRAINS
Bronze
Fabricator: Ryno Fab, Inc.
PHOTOGRAPHER: ANTHONY VERDE

Charles Searles designed a series of bronze reliefs with patinas in various greens, turquoise, and black for a wall of the Long Island Rail Road's Jamaica Station, rendering sun, water, rolling hills, flowers, and trees to create views that convey the sense of a train in motion. One portion shows trains in a setting that suggests the island of Jamaica, linking the art to the community of Jamaica, Queens. *Sunrise, Sunset, Departing Trains*, one of Searles's last works, is slated to be installed at a nearby subway station.

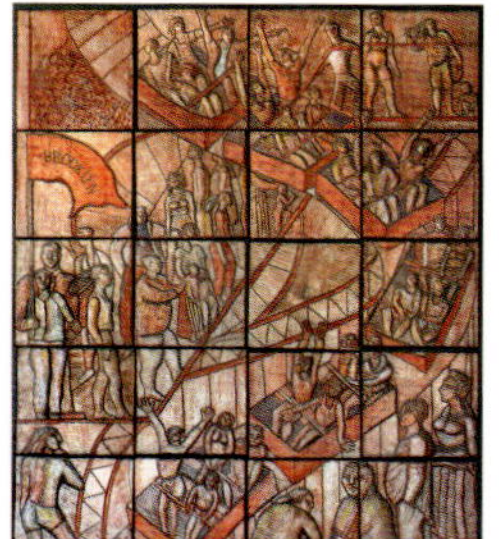

DEBORAH MASTERS

CONEY ISLAND RELIEFS
Concrete
PHOTOGRAPHER: ROB WILSON

Commissioned in 1991 for the station atop the Ocean Parkway Viaduct at Coney Island, *Coney Island Reliefs* responds to the architecture of the bridge beneath the station, which has niches akin to those created for ornamental tiles or sculpture. Influenced by Coney Island's annual Mermaid Parade, the artist designed striking concrete inserts of Mermaid and Neptune figures, which were to be surrounded by decorative tile borders that reflect the Coney Island seaside amusement park theme. Due to a drainage problem, the reliefs could not be installed safely.

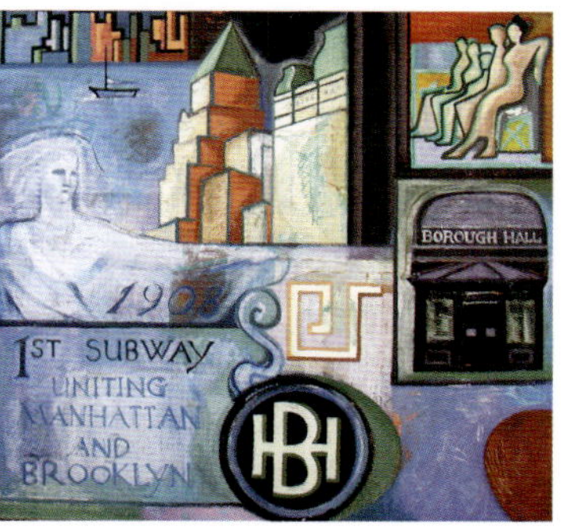

SUSAN MORRISON

BOROUGH HALL STATION: FIRST SUBWAY IN BROOKLYN
Mosaic
PHOTOGRAPHER: SUSAN MORRISON

Susan Morrison's proposed murals incorporate iconic subway elements, like tokens and tunnels, with views familiar to Brooklyn subway travelers, such as Manhattan from across the East River and Borough Hall's portico and tower. Morrison intended the murals to commemorate the station's opening in 1908, which connected Brooklyn and Manhattan by subway. She placed 1908 motifs alongside present-day images to evoke a timeless connection between past and present, while the color palette complements the station's existing ornamentation. Due to a change in the construction program, the murals could not go forward.

In Progress

Arts for Transit is currently working on fifty projects. Those listed below are in design or being fabricated as this book goes to press. Installation is expected within the next twelve to twenty-four months.

LISA AMOWITZ
URBAN RENEWAL
Simpson Street 2 5
Faceted glass

TOMIE ARAI
BACK TO THE GARDEN
Pelham Parkway 2
Faceted glass

LAURA BATTLE
HOW TO GET TO THE MOON...
Burnside Avenue 4
Laminated glass

NANCY BLUM
FLOATING AURICULAS
Dobbs Ferry MTA Metro-North Railroad
Glass mosaic

JAMES CARPENTER
James Carpenter Design Associates/Richard Kress, Principal Designer in collaboration with Nicholas Grimshaw + Partners
SOLAR REFLECTOR SHELL
Fulton Street Transit Center A C J M Z 2 3 4 5
Perforated aluminum panels and stainless-steel cable

ALFREDO CEIBAL
PERMANENT RESIDENTS AND VISITORS
Wakefield-241st Street 2
Faceted glass

AMY CHENG
LAS FLORES
Cleveland Street J Z
Faceted glass

NOEL COPELAND
LEAF OF LIFE
Nereid Avenue-238th Street 2 5
Faceted glass

GEORGE CRESPO
LATIN AMERICAN STORIES
Jackson Avenue 2 5
Faceted glass

JOSEPH D'ALESANDRO
HOMAGE
219th Street 2 5
Faceted glass

ANDREA DEZSO
COMMUNITY GARDEN
Bedford Park Boulevard-Lehman College 4
Mosaic

JANE DICKSON
THE REVELERS
Times Square-42nd Street N Q R S W 1 2 3 7
Glass mosaic

BARBARA ELLMANN
THE VIEW FROM HERE
Van Siclen Avenue J Z
Faceted glass

NICKY ENRIGHT
UNIVERSAL CITY
225th Street 2 5
Faceted glass

CADENCE GIERSBACH
FROM EARTH TO SKY
Myrtle-Wyckoff Avenues L M
Mosaic

CORINNE GRONDAHL
METROMORPHOSIS AND BIRTH OF A STATION
Mosholu Parkway 4
Laminated glass

SKOWMON HASTANAN
A SECRET GARDEN: THERE'S NO PLACE LIKE HOME
233rd Street 2 5
Faceted glass

DANIEL HAUBEN
THE EL
Freeman Street 2 5
Faceted glass

MICHAEL INGUI
UNTITLED
East 105th Street L
Faceted glass

JUNG HYANG KIM
WHEEL OF BLOOM-SOAK UP THE SUN
Crescent Street J Z
Faceted glass

MARGARET LANZETTA
CULTURE SWIRL
Norwood Avenue J Z
Faceted glass

SOL LEWITT
WHIRLS AND TWIRLS (MTA)
59th Street-Columbus Circle A B C D 1
Ceramic tile

MARIO MULLER
URBAN MOTIF
Kingsbridge Road (4)
Laminated glass

TAKAYO NODA
UNTITLED
Sutter Avenue (L)
Faceted glass

DENNIS OPPENHEIM
RISING AND SETTING, 2006
Riverdale Station, MTA Metro-North Railroad
Perforated painted steel

JOSE ORTIZ
MANY TRAILS
183rd Street (4)
Laminated glass

SCOTT REDDEN
UNTITLED
Alabama Avenue (J) (Z)
Faceted glass

SOL SAX
ANCESTRAL LETTERS IN SOL'SCRYPT
Halsey Street (L)
Faceted glass

DOUG and MIKE STARN
STARN STUDIO
UNTITLED
South Ferry Terminal (1)
Mosaic and glass, aluminum fence

CAROL SUN
A BRONX REFLECTION
167th Street (4)
Faceted glass

MARINA TSESARSKAYA
BRONX. FOUR SEASONS
Prospect Avenue (2) (5)
Faceted glass

EUGENIE TUNG
16 WINDOWS
New Lots Avenue (L)
Faceted glass

ALLAN and ELLEN WEXLER
OVERLOOK
Atlantic Avenue Terminal, MTA Long Island Rail Road
Granite and glass

PHILEMONA WILLIAMSON
SEASONS
Livonia Avenue (L)
Faceted glass

From its inception, the subway was considered a marvel of engineering, and it was the engineers who tackled the daunting logistical challenges posed by placing a transit system underground. Engineers continue to tackle similar challenges today. In addition to the engineering forces on board at the MTA agencies, each project requires numerous consulting engineers for its success. As much as the artists create the art, those behind the scenes–the engineers, architects, designers, planners, contractors–are the "artists" that create the opportunity for the art. While the architectural designer for each station is listed in the accompanying catalogue entry, this list is an attempt to include the balance of consulting engineers who have participated in the design of our revitalized stations.

Ammann & Whitney
B C Enterprises
BEM Systems, Inc.
Berger Lehman Associates
Bergman & Associates
Chu & Gassman
Cosentini Associates
Daniel Frankfurt
DMJM Harris
Duchscherer Oberst
EGIS
El Taller Collaborativo
Fay Spofford & Thorndike
Frederick R. Harris
Garg Associates
Goodkind & O'Dea
HAKS Engineers
Historical Perspectives
Joseph R. Martucci
Lebduska & Associates
Lewis Berger
The LiRo Group
Maitra Associates
Management Concepts Systems
Mariano Molina
Massand Engineering
Parsons Brinckerhoff
Parsons Transportation
Stone & Webster
STV
Sulton Campbell Britt Owens & Associates
Sverdrup & Parcel
TAMS Consultants
Tectonic Engineering
Thornton Tomasetti
Toporoff Engineers
URS
VJ & Associates
Vollmer Associates
Weidlinger Associates

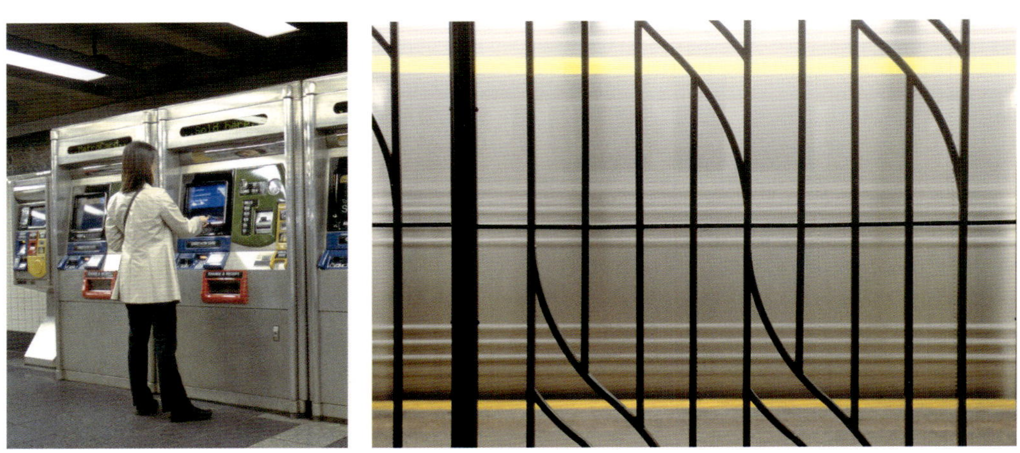

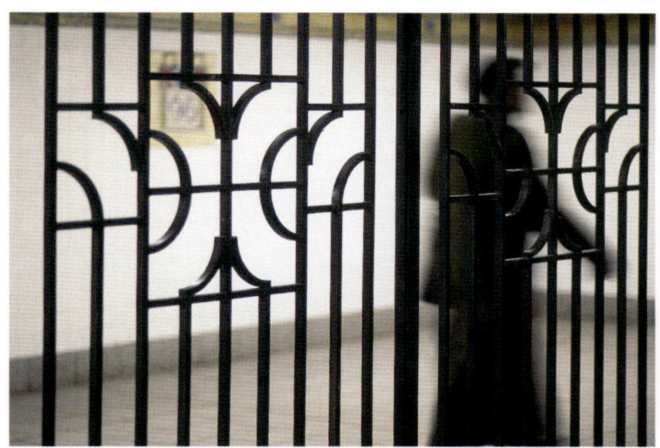

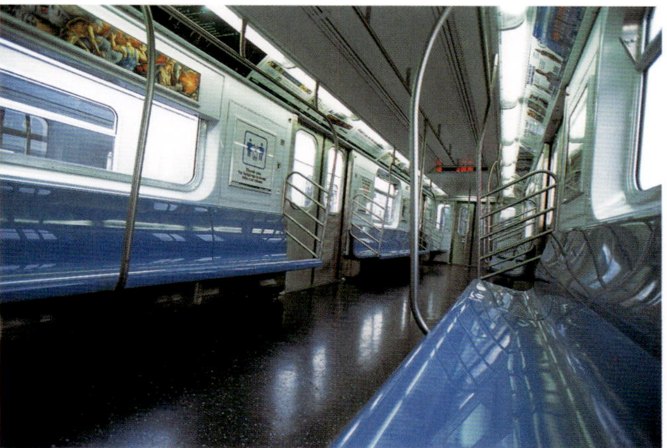

As the aesthetic eye of the MTA, Arts for Transit has been a driving force behind the design elements in the system, from vending machines to railings to new subway cars.

Opposite, Left: MetroCard Vending Machine
Masamichi Udagawa and Sigi Moeslinger, IDEO and Antenna Design
PHOTOGRAPHER: ANTENNA DESIGN

Opposite, Right: IND Railing: Wave
Laura Bradley
PHOTOGRAPHER: P. HAMBLIN

Above, Left: IRT Railing: Medallion
Laura Bradley
PHOTOGRAPHER: P. HAMBLIN

Right: R142 Subway Car
Masamichi Udagawa and Sigi Moeslinger, Antenna Design
PHOTOGRAPHER: PATRICK J CASHIN

Acknowledgments

Deep gratitude and thanks are owed to all those who contributed and shared their expertise to create this publication. The title "Along the Way" is taken from the 2005 exhibition of the same name shown in Manhattan at the UBS Gallery celebrating the twentieth anniversary of Arts for Transit.

In tandem with the authors, the Arts for Transit team became the core working group on this book. While there are photographs by many different photographers, more than half of those in the book were taken by Rob Wilson, long-time staff member at Arts for Transit, who has photographed MTA artwork beautifully for almost two decades. Yaling Chen headed the task force challenged with compiling images; Natalia de Campos handled publication permissions and copyright releases. Virginia Williams and Katherine Meehan provided invaluable assistance and editorial support, as did Lester Burg, who brought a keen eye to the review of the book. Amy Hausmann served as facilitator and sounding board. Lydia Bradshaw deserves special thanks: also a long-time member of the Arts for Transit team, she served as acting assistant director during much of this project and took on the challenging task of overseeing key operations while contributing insight, recollections, and hard facts to this publication. Also special thanks to Fred May, who became an ad hoc member of the team, providing advice and support throughout the project. Additionally, we are grateful to the photographers and others who waived fees for reproduction, making this publication possible.

It was a privilege to work with co-author William Ayres, chief curator at the Long Island Museum in Stony Brook, New York. Bill's contribution was made possible through a grant from the New York State Council on the Arts, Architecture, Planning, and Design Program and the New York Foundation for the Arts. Arts for Transit thanks The Monacelli Press for believing in the importance of the project; particular thanks are owed to Elizabeth White, managing editor, who believed in the significance of this book from the beginning and has brought a sharp organizational and editorial sense to its creation. Thanks also to John Clifford of Think Studio for his exceptional book design.

Producing public works in the nation's largest city for the nation's largest transit system is a monumental challenge. When the works involve the creative expression of artists, often unfamiliar with requirements of a large public agency, the challenges multiply. Add to the mix a system that moves millions of people on a daily basis and it becomes clear that it takes a multitude of supportive and cooperative individuals to achieve the beauty and lasting achievements seen on these pages. In my eighteen years with Arts for Transit, I have witnessed firsthand the unwavering cooperation of colleagues from other MTA departments and agencies. The publication of *Along the Way* is an example of this teamwork. The MTA legal, marketing, and procurement departments and the New York Transit Museum were steadfast partners in our efforts. And in the usual spirit of cooperation of our many partners, NYC Transit Capital Program Management, Marketing, and Stations departments provided the much needed support in compiling information and documenting the projects.

Finally, but most especially, we thank the artists whose work is celebrated in these pages for their talent and vision on behalf of the millions of riders who experience and enjoy this artwork every day.

SANDRA BLOODWORTH
DIRECTOR
ARTS FOR TRANSIT AND FACILITIES DESIGN

Credits

It is an impossible task to thank all of the hundreds of individuals who have played a role in the Arts for Transit program over the past twenty years. Each helped to build the great public art collection on which this publication is based. The program has grown from an initial handful of projects to one of the largest public art programs in the world. This was made possible because of the dedicated individuals that strove to create art that spoke to the people, especially the former staff: Wendy Feuer, director; Jodi Moise, assistant director, Erica Behrens, Mona Chen, Dorothy Desir-Davis, Kendal Henry, Kelly Pajek, Gabrielle Shubert, Cheryl Stewart, and Jackie Woods, managers; Maya Emsden and Nancy Reyner, program coordinators; Tania Duvergne and Theresa Tripoli, assistant managers; Andrea Abaquin, Monica Hudson, Dorel Reid and Bruce de Torres, support staff; and Brooke Anderson, Katie Corcoran, Lewis Feibelman, Elise Griffin, Heather Ho, Jackie Ivy, Jennifer Kronovet, Risa Loebenberg, Yvette Maddux, Pepi Marchetti Franchi, Nicole Murphy, Nell Ogorzaly, Yoon-Kyoung Seo, Rie Shintani, Elizabeth Slagus, and Elaine Szumanski, interns. During the formative years of the program numerous arts professionals and consultants lent their knowledge and experience, including Alexis Lalli, Joyce Pomeroy Schwartz, and Nancy Rosen; also, Nancy Kaufman and Suzanne Randolph, and, more recently, Vel Riberto and Ann Marie Baranowski, have focused on the management of artist/architect collaborations in upcoming downtown projects.

As early as 1982, there were efforts to include art in the subway, as the then New York City Transit Authority (NYCTA) began its massive rebuilding program. An art selection panel met at City Hall to select artists to create artwork for subway stations. Many of the meetings were coordinated by Patti Harris, the city's current first deputy mayor who was then an assistant to Mayor Edward Koch. Ronay Menschel, former deputy mayor and member of the MTA Board, with unparalleled vision and commitment, was a key figure in the pioneering artist selection process.

In 1985, Chairman Robert Kiley established a new office within the MTA, as part of its headquarters team, to administer an official art program, realizing that a permanent office with direct connections to management would have a greater chance of success than an ad-hoc task force or an outside consultant. He wanted the program to be broader than the visual percent-for-art program, including Music Under New York, the undertaking to present musicians in stations, and all other MTA arts programming.

From these early efforts emerged Arts for Transit. David Gunn, President of the NYCTA at that time, simultaneously emphasized the need to restore a sense of order to the system. This laid the groundwork for the office to play a leading role in the physical restoration in both the subway and commuter rail stations. Wendy Feuer became the founding director of the new office. Arts for Transit's purview grew and its influence was evident in all aspects of the transportation system, from artwork and decorative functional elements to participation in the design of subway cars, fare vending machines and the selection of architects for station designs. Ronay Menschel and Wendy Feuer, together with chief architect John Tarantino, lobbied to establish station design guidelines, in conjunction with NYC Transit's Office of Station Design. The guidelines provided a blueprint of criteria that formalized a process to preserve and protect historical elements while allowing for new art and architectural design. This goal was accomplished in 1990, carried out by Prentice & Chan, Olhausen. These efforts were instrumental in making the stations and the system an enticing place to be once again.

With the art and architecture now proceeding hand in hand, there was a need to build support for these efforts from within the arts community. Ronay Menschel chaired an arts advisory committee consisting of major arts figures to lend their prestige and expertise. The list is impressive: Bill Aguado, Kent Barwick, Barbara Bloemink, Robert Buck, Mary Schmidt Campbell, Luis Cancel, David Collens, Judy Collischan, Anita Contini, Houston Conwill, Paula Cooper, Barbara Fife, Leonard Fleischer, Susan Freedman, Henry Geldzahler, David Gibson, Agnes Gund, Patricia Harris, Alanna Heiss, David Hupert, Donald Kuspit, Harvey Lichtenstein, Maya Lin, Rolf Olhausen, Steve Polan, Harry Roseman, Harriet Senie, Isaiah Sheffer, Anne Van Ingen, David R. White, and William H. Whyte.

All told the interest, commitment, and dedication of so many firmly established the roots of an extraordinary program that will leave its mark for decades to come.

MTA leadership is proud of its collection and the importance of including art in the transportation environment. Chairman Peter S. Kalikow, Executive Director Katherine N. Lapp, and Deputy Executive Director Christopher P. Boylan, whose department Corporate and Community Affairs includes Arts for Transit, have each been steadfast in their support. Over the years, MTA Board Members have continually expressed their support for the Arts for Transit program. And none has been more enthusiastic than the current board: Joining Chairman Peter S. Kalikow are Vice Chairmen David S. Mack and Andrew M. Saul, and Board Members Andrew Albert, John H. Banks III, James F. Blair, Nancy Shevell Blakeman, Anthony J. Bottalico, Michael J. Canino, Donald Cecil, Barry Feinstein, James H. Harding Jr., Mark D. Lebow, James L. McGovern, Susan G. Metzger, Mark Page, Mitchell H. Pally, Francis H. Powers, James L. Sedore Jr., Ed Watt, and Carl V. Wortendyke. Former Board Member and current Director of the Permanent Citizens Advisory Committee Beverly Dolinsky has long been an energetic and consistent supporter of the program.

The program has been possible only with the ongoing support of MTA's constituent agencies, in particular their leadership: Lawrence G. Reuter, President, New York City Transit; Mysore L. Nagaraja, President, Captial Construction; James J. Dermody, President, Long Island Rail Road; Peter A. Cannito, President, Metro-North Railroad; Susan L. Kupferman, President, Bridges and Tunnels; Neil S. Yellin, President, Long Island Bus; and Thomas J. Savage, President, Bus Company.

The artists, architects, engineers, fabricators and various consultants whose contributions have been so vital are listed elsewhere in this book. Although it is not possible to name each administrator, planner, staff member, art and design professional, fabricator, and tradesperson who worked wonders to bring these projects to fruition, they are all deserving of praise, thanks and appreciation. Our gratitude to those whose names follow and apologies to anyone inadvertently omitted:

(In alphabetical order:) Stephanie Aaron, Mostafa Abolghasemi, Sharif Abou-Sabh, Lori Abraham, Tony Aceto, Roberto Aguirre, Camille Akeju, Emilio Albano, Marc Albrecht, Vincent Altrai, Tony Amato, Margie Anders, Albertine Anderson, Augustine Angba, Sheila Antman, John Anzalone, Robert Apfel, Mike Asher, Siraj Attia, Valery Baker, Gange Balagangeyan, Steven Balduzzi, Jean Banker, Dawn Banket, Don Bannon, Dave Barabas, Monica Barrow, Chris Bastian, Andrew Bata, Ken Bauer, Bobby Beard, Brian Bell, Roberta Bender, Bob Bergen, Joan Berkowitz, Marie Bernoth, Deborah Bershad, Art Bethel, Barry Bischoff, Don Bloomfield, Maureen Boll, Dan Borden, Dave Borges, Virginia Borkoski, Mary Kate Brangaccio, William Bratton, Susan Brophy, Russ Broshous, Alice Bruce, Louis Brusati, Dave Bumford, John Burke, Jim Burns, Joe Burzo, Michele Butchko, Colin Bynoe, Michelle Callabrass, Lachlin Cameron, Vivian Campbell, Gary Caplan, Jack Carter, Jackie Carter, Dan Caufield, Gricelda Cespedes, Sankar Chakraborty, Mike Charles, Carol Childers, Caron Christian, Margaret Coffey, Bernard Cohen, Mike Coleman, Clayton Conaway, Richard Coniglione, Maggie Connor, Michelle Constant, T. J. Costello, Paige Cowley, Izak Cozangi, Brad Craig, Connie Crawford, Jessie Crawford, Phil Cross, Fredericka Cuenca, Miriam Cukier, John Cunningham, Tom Czerniachowicz, Donna D'Ambrosio, Tony D'Amico, Cynthia Daniel, Diana David, Joan Davidson, Tito Davila, Michelle Davy, Gail Dawson, Larry Day, Jack Dean, John Dean, Richard Dean, Phillip DeCapua, Dorothy Dee, Jack Delaney, Joe Delaney, Gary Delaverson, Tom DeMaria, Neal DeNisco, Trevor Denny, Connie DePalma, Jimmy DePolo, Ron DeRubeis, Rajesh Desai, Bruce DeVito, Edward DeVito, Andrian Dias, Angel Diaz, Tony DiFiore, Jon DiLorenzo, Italo DiModica, Sheldon Dixon, Gean Dohman, Brian Dolan, Phil Dombkowski, Bill Donahue, Geoff Dopsch, Arethia Douglas, Mort Downey, Teena Doykos, Jim Dubbs, Ted Dunn, Uday Durg, Carol Durham, Wayne Ehmann, Mahmoud El-Attar, Fran El-Sawah, Russ Entin, Donna Evans, Joe Ewald, Tom Fackelman, Sophia Faivush, Anthony Fakas, Paul Fallon, Melissa Farley, Eddie Feizbakhsh, Michael Feinberg, Melissa Feldman, Martha Felix, Claretha Fennick, Joseph Ferrara, Victoria Fischer, Larry Fleischer, Linda Florio, David Foell, Nat Ford, Jerry Forman, Steve Frazzini, Lester Freundlich, John Frizziola, Frank Gaetano, John Gaito, John Gaul, Edmund Gbanite, Cheryl George, Mindy Gettler, Subrata Ghosh, Judy Giberstone, Arnold Gilbert, Pat Gilmartin, Jeanne Giordano, Michael Gleba, Michelle Goldstein, Hazel Gordon, Chuck Gordanier, Robert Gorvetzian, Arlene Grauer, Walter Green, Sharon Green-Lindsey, Stan Grill, Tony Guidice, George Guirguis, Craig Gustavson, Carlos Gutierrez-Solana, Suzanne Gyorgy, Wynton Haberstam, Ronnie Hakim, Doris Halle, Deborah Hall-Moore, Nuri Hamidi, Conrad Hardy, Suzanna Harrington, Fred Harris, Peter Harris, Mark Heavey, Ed Helenius, David Henley, Rob Hess, Wael Hibri, Joe Hofmann, Loriann Hoffman, Bob Holman, Keith Hom, Chuck Hoppe, Sarah Horowitz, Carmen Hung, Sheila Hutson, Drew Hyde, Donald Ianuzzi, Andy Igoe, Mike Iovino, Norman Jacklyn, Winston Jacobs, Mike Jaszcar, Debra Jean-Louis, Russ Jeck, William Jehle, David Jenkins, Dawn Jenkins, Michael Jew-Geralds, Nancy Jones, Marty Kaiser, Stan Karoly, Paul Kastner, Lori Katzman, Lamond Kearse, Tom Kelly, John Kennard, Alan Kiepper, Shawn Kildare, Sharon Killiebrew, Bill King, Ross Kapilian, Siu L. Ko, Stephen Klein, Linda Kleinbaum, Branko Kleva, Adrian Knight, Constantine Komandis, Alissa Kosowsky, Mel Krakowski, Larry Krasnoff, John Kriskiewicz, Roco Krsulic, Dick Kuczkowski, Greg Kullberg, Mike Kyriacou, Bob Laga, Anwar Lakhaney, Jan Lakin, Steve LaRocco, Howard Lau, Robert LaValva, Ellen Levanti, Ken Levy, Janet Lewis, Nancy Limeri, Jerry Litt, Talib Lokhandwala, Michael Lombardi, Robert Lombardi, Liz Lowe, Sharon Lubitz, Jackie Ludoff, Glen Lunden, Jack Lusk, Bill Madden, Dennis Maffettone, Mary Mahon, Miguel Maisonet, Dorothy Mancuso, Mark Mannix, Jeffrey Manthey, Gene Maounis, Alan Marder, Robert Marino, George Marinos, Joe Marra, Nancy Marshall, Alicia Martinez, Fernando Martinez, Bill Matheson, Paul Matthews, Jacques Mayard, Tom Mazzeo, Matt McElroy, Phil McGrade, Jesse McKinney, Bruce McIver, Ken McNutt, Mukesh Mehta, Carol Meltzer, Joe Mendola, Laura Messado, Mari Micelli, Jim Michaels, Betsy Miller, George Miller, Karl Miller, Richard Miras, Robert Moakler, Rhonda Moll, John Montemarano, Patricia Moore, Robert Moore, Steve Morris, Tom Mule, Shirley Moy, Abdul Muqtadir, Art Murphy, John Murphy, Robert Myers, Madan Naik, Richard Nazario, Ken Neal, Signe Neilsen, Tim O'Brien, Mike O'Connor, Danny O'Connell, John O'Grady, Tess O'Loughlin,

Michael O'Neill, Barbara Orlando, Bernie Ortiz, Richard Osborne, Mercedes Padilla, John Palamara, Bob Paley, Rosemary Paniagua, Thalia Panton, Anthony Paollilo, James Pappa, Anil Parikh, Patsy Park, Robin Parkinson, Jeremy Parness, Ashok Patel, Charlie Patterson, Debra Payne, Frank Peranio, Carlo Perciballi, Jorge Perez, Max Perez, Bob Petrides, Bob Petit, Jackie Phojanakong, Erol Pinnock, Steve Pirrelli, Julian Porta, Seymour Portes, Tom Prendergast, Pete Presvelis, Tracy Pruitt, Abe Puthota, Phyllis Rachmuth, Trish Raley, Valmiki Ramotar, Joe Raskin, Tom Reed, Joy Reid, John Reiter, Gabe Reves, Atefah Riaz, Randall Richardson, Catherine Rinaldi, Sarah Rios, Bob Riser, Henry Rissmeyer, Andy Ritchel, Tobey Ritz, Dan Ronan, Laura Rosen, Hal Rosenfeld, Terri Rouse, Charles Sachs, Janette Sadik-Kahn, Upasna Sagar, Porie Saikia-Eapen, Brenda Sanchez, Frank Sanchis, Gene Sansone, Ron Saporita, Bob Saraceni, Vijay Sawant, Erwin Schaeffer, Giuseppe Scalia, Steven Schecter, Joe Schick, Eric Schmidt, Suzanna Schroeder, Jennifer Schultz, Judith Schwartz, Lisa Schwartz, Morris Schwartz, Kathy Sekowski, Jim Sears, Butch Seay, Anthony Semancik, Joe Serrao, Walter Sewell, Brendan Sexton, Howard Schadt, Ashvin Shah, Ramdas Shanbhag, Chris Shieh, Suhas Sheth, Cliff Shockley, Gabrielle Shubert, Bill Shurbet, Joe Siano, Michael Sickenius, Brenda Sidberry, David Sierra, Jim Simpson, Mary Six Rupert, Darlene Slade, Lydia Sloan, Fred Smith, Kim Smith, Randy Solomon, Barbara Spencer, Kirke Stanfield, Emily Stedman, Fred Steers, Meyer Stender, Craig Stewart, Rick Stewart, Robin Stevens, Maggie Stevenson, Chantal St. Louis, David Stracquatanio, Franklin Streeter, Paul Streitz, Tony Suarez, Keith Summa, Doug Sussman, Melvin Sussman, Kathy Sweeney, John Tauranac, Adrienne Taub, Dexter Tee, Lois Tendler, Kenneth Teu, Albani Themo, Margie Thomas, Colin Thomson, Domenick Tinelli, Kyra Tirana, Fannie Todaro, Linda Tonn, Norma Toro, Steve Toth, Joe Trainor, Dick Trennery, Tom Triano, Joe Tripodi, Ed Valari, Carol Varnas, Vinny Verdisco, Vijay Verma, Richard Wackenheim, Chris Walsh, Peter Walsh, Karyn Ward, Gail Washington, Linda Watkins, Richard Webster, Hollie Wells, Bill Wheeler, Linda White, Reba White Williams, Dave Williams, Pierce Williams, Howard Wimmert, Dave Winfield, Leslie Wolf, Ray Wong, Hsin Wu, Marc Yanche, George Yee, Ron Yutko, Kurt Ziegler, and Franz Zwolensky.

Support for Arts for Transit has also come from many directions, friends, and allied agencies such as the Alliance for Downtown New York, Alliance for the Arts, American Craft Council, American Folk Art Museum, American Museum of Natural History, Art in General, Art Commission of the City of New York, Artists Space, The Battery Conservancy, Big Apple Greeters, Bronx Council on the Arts, Bronx Museum of the Arts, Bronx River Art Center, Brooklyn Academy of Music, Brooklyn Children's Museum, Brooklyn Museum, CITYarts, City Lore, Cityscape Institute, Cooper-Hewitt, Creative Art Workshops, Creative Time, Department of City Planning, Dia Art Foundation, Donnell Library Center of the New York Public Library, El Museo Del Barrio, Flushing Council on Culture & the Arts, Goddard Riverside Community Center, Grand Central Partnership, Henry Street Settlement, Hospital Audiences, Hudson River Museum Westchester, Huntington Township Art League, International Center of Photography, Islip Art Museum, Jazz at Lincoln Center, Landmarks Conservancy, Landmarks Preservation Commission, Lehman College Art Gallery, Lincoln Center Out of Doors, Lincoln Square BID, Long Island Museum, Longwood Arts Project, Lower Manhattan Cultural Council, Municipal Art Society, Museum of Arts and Design, Museum of the City of New York, Museum of Modern Art, The Museum of Television and Radio, National Conference of Arts, National Design Museum, National Museum of the American Indian, New York City Department of Cultural Affairs, New York City Department of Parks & Recreation, New York Public Library, New York Technical College, New York State Council on the Arts, North Westchester Center for Arts, NYC & Company, Partners for Livable Communities, Projects for Public Spaces, P.S.1 Contemporary Art Center, Public Art Fund, Queens Council on the Arts, Queens Museum of Art, Roy Lichtenstein Foundation, Snug Harbor Cultural Center, Staten Island Children's Museum, Studio in a School, Studio Museum in Harlem, Symphony Space, Times Square Alliance, Townscape Institute, Very Special Arts New York City, Wave Hill, Westchester Arts Council, Whitney Museum of American Art, and Women's Caucus for the Arts.

Selected Bibliography

Acconci, Vito, and Gloria Moure. *Vito Acconci: Writings, Works, Projects*. Ed. Gloria Moure. Barcelona: Ediciones Polígrafa, 2001.

Art En Route: MTA Arts For Transit. New York: Metropolitan Transportation Authority, 1994.

AskART, The American Artists Bluebook, <www.askart.com>.

Ayres, William, and Sandra Bloodworth. "Terra Cotta Incognita: Turn-of-the-Century Ceramic Art in the New York City Subway System." *19th Century* 11, nos. 3 and 4 (1992): 23–28.

Belle, John, and Maxinne R. Leighton. *Grand Central: Gateway to a Million Lives*. New York: W. W. Norton & Company, 2000.

Bender, Thomas. *New York Intellect: A History of Intellectual Life in New York City, from 1750 to the Beginnings of Our Own Time*. Baltimore, Md.: Johns Hopkins University Press, 1987.

Berman, Avis. "Lichtenstein's Mural Goes Back to Futures in Present N.Y." *Chicago Tribune*, September 21, 2002: 31.

Bischoff, Dan. "Subway Style." *Newark Star-Ledger*, June 26, 2005: Art sec.

Bonisteel, Sara. "Tracks of Change." *New York Resident*, June 20, 2005.

Bravo, Armando Alvarez. "Cuban Artist Hugo Consuegra Dies." *Miami Herald*, January 28, 2003.

Burns, Ric, James Sanders, and Lisa Ades. *New York: An Illustrated History*. New York: Knopf, 1999.

"Commuter Comfort." *The New Yorker*, June 10, 1991: Goings On About Town sec.

Coppola, Philip Ashforth. *Silver Connections*. Maplewood, N.J.: Four Oceans Press, 1994.

Cudahy, Brian J. *Under the Sidewalks of New York: The Story of the Greatest Subway System in the World*. Brattleboro, Vt.: Stephen Greene Press, 1979.

Diehl, Lorraine B. *Subways: The Tracks that Built New York City*. New York: Clarkson Potter, 2004.

Dunlap, David. "New Look for Bronx Civic Crossroads." *New York Times*, May 22, 2003, section 11.

Eccles, Tom, Dan Cameron, Katy Siegel, Jeffrey Kastner, and Anne Wehr. *Plop: Recent Projects of the Public Art Fund*. New York: Merrell, 2004.

Finkelpearl, Tom. *Dialogues in Public Art*. Cambridge, Mass.: MIT Press, 2000.

Fischler, Stan. *The Subway: A Trip Through Time on New York's Rapid Transit*. New York: H & M Productions II, 1997.

___. *Uptown, Downtown: A Trip Through Time on New York's Subways*. New York: Hawthorn / Dutton, 1976.

Fluegel, Jane, ed. *Art for the Public: The Collection of the Port Authority of New York and New Jersey*. New York: The Port Authority of New York and New Jersey, 1985.

Framberger, David J. "Architectural Design for New York's First Subway." *Historic American Engineering Record: Interborough Rapid Transit Subway*. New York: New York City Transit Authority, 1978.

Gargiulo, Joseph. "New Subway Terminal a Gateway to Coney Island's Future." *Community Gazette*, December 10, 2004, <www.gothamgazette.com/community/47/majorissues/172>.

Gayle, Margot, and Michele Cohen. *The Art Commission and the Municipal Art Society Guide to Manhattan's Outdoor Sculpture*. New York: Prentice Hall Press, 1988.

"Glass Artist to Present Raab Lecture." *Skidmore College Intercom* 1, no. 3 (January 2002).

Green, A. E. "Along the Way: MTA Arts for Transit Celebrating 20 Years of Public Art." *Brooklyn Spring Creek Sun*, June 10, 2005.

Guiney, Ann. "The Ultimate Ride." *The Architect's Newspaper*, March 23, 2004, <http://www.archpaper.com/feature_articles/the_ultimate_ride.html>.

Harrison, Helen A. "2 Artists View the World in Statements with 3,142 Images." *New York Times*, March 17, 1991: L.I. sec: 14.

Hayden, Dolores. *The Power of Place: Urban Landscapes as Public History*. Cambridge, Mass.: MIT Press, 1996.

Heartney, Eleanor. *City Art: New York's Percent for Art Program*. New York: Merrell Publishers in association with City of New York Department of Cultural Affairs, 2005.

Hershenson, Roberta. "To Grace Yonkers Station, Work That Mirrors River." *New York Times*, February 8, 2004: 14WC.

Hood, Clifton. *722 Miles: The Building of the Subways and How They Transformed New York*. Baltimore, Md.: John Hopkins University Press, 1995.

___. "Underground Pioneers." *City Journal* 4 no. 2 (Spring 1994): 82.

Jackson, Kenneth T. *The Encyclopedia of New York City*. New Haven, Conn.: Yale University Press, 1995.

Kay, Jane Holtz. "Architects Expand Use of Glass Art." *New York Times*, July 12, 1997: C1.

Kimmelman, Michael. "Stirring Up a Commotion on Canvas." *New York Times*, October 21, 2005: E2.31.

Kino, Carol. "A Visit with the Modern's First Grandmother." *New York Times*, October 1, 2005: 2.30.

Klitsch, Michael. "Subway Art." *The New Manhattan Review*, August 6, 1986: 20–23.

Lichtenstein, Roy. *Roy Lichtenstein*. Basel, Switzerland: Fondation Beyeler, 1998.

___. *Times Square Mural*. New York: Roy Lichtenstein Foundation and Mitchell-Innes & Nash, 2002.

Marshall, Bruce. *Building New York: The Rise and Rise of the Greatest City on Earth*. New York: Universe Publishing, 2005.

"Master Class," *Africana Heritage* 5, no. 3 (2005): 6–7.

Matus, Paul. "Brooklyn's New Coney Island Terminal." *The Third Rail Online*, May 1, 2003, <http://www.thethirdrail.net/0305/stillwell1.html>.

Melberg, Jerald L., and Milton J.Bloch, eds. *Romare Bearden: 1970–1980*. Charlotte, N.C.: Mint Museum, 1980.
Miro, Marsha. "Glass Transit." *The Urban Glass Art Quarterly* 97 (Winter 2005): 42–49.

"MTA Exhibit Celebrates 20 Years of Public Art." *Antique Review* 31, no. 7 (July 2005).

MTA Newsroom. "Aluminum Sculptures Adorn Yonkers Station." Metropolitan Transportation Authority, 2005, <http://mta.info/mta/news/newsroom/sculptures.htm>.

___. "Art Improves Public Transportation." Metropolitan Transportation Authority, 2005, <http://mta.info/mta/news/newsroom/west8.htm>.

"MTA Shows Off Two Decades of Subway Art at Midtown Gallery." NY 1 News, June 29, 2005: Transit.

Nasar, Jack L. *Design by Competition: Making Design Competition Work*. New York: Cambridge University Press, 1999.

Nesbett, Peter T., and Michelle DuBois, eds. *Over the Line: The Art and Life of Jacob Lawrence*. Seattle: University of Washington Press, 2001.

New York City Transit Authority. Historic American Engineering Record: Interborough Rapid Transit Subway. Compiled historical documentation.

The New York Subway: Interborough Rapid Transit. New York: Fordham University Press, 1991.

New York Transit Museum. *Subway Style: 100 Years of Architecture & Design in the New York City Subway*. New York: Stewart, Tabori & Chang, 2004.

New York Transit Museum and Vivian Heller. *The City Beneath Us: Building the New York Subways*. New York: W. W. Norton & Company, 2004.

O'Harrow, Robert. "Tunnel Vision." *Washington Post*, February 16, 2003: E1.

Oka Doner, Michelle. *Michelle Oka Doner: Natural Seduction*. Manchester, Vt.: Hudson Hills, 2003.

"One Hundred Years Later, Terra Cotta Tiles Return." Arts4All, <http://www.arts4all.com/newsletter/driftitem.asp?DID=341>.

Painting by Squire Vickers 1872–1947: Designing Architect of the New York Subway System. New York: Shepherd Gallery, Associates, Inc., 1992.

Raisman, A.I. "Evolution of the Subway System." *Civil Engineering* 2 no. 10 (October 1932): 606–609.

Raven, Arlene. "Saving Face." *Village Voice*, June 2, 1992.

___. "Train Soul." *Village Voice*, November 17, 1992.

___, ed. *Art in the Public Interest*. Ann Arbor, Mich.: UMI Research Press, 1989.

Sandler, Irving. *Al Held*. New York: Hudson Hills, 1984.

Sansone, Gene. *Evolution of New York City Subways: An Illustrated History of New York City's Transit Car 1867–1997*. New York: The New York Transit Museum Press, 1997.

Senie, Harriet F., and Sally Webster, eds. *Critical Issues in Public Art: Content, Context, and Controversy*. New York: HarperCollins Publishers, 1992.

Sheets, Hilarie M. "Underground Art, UBS Gallery Celebrates the MTA's Art Scene." *Time Out New York* 512 (July 21–27, 2005): 64.

"Shelia Levrant de Bretteville." *Yale University Newswire*, April 15, 1997.

Smith, Roberta. "The Rush-Hour Revelations of an Underground Museum." *New York Times*, January 2, 2002: Critic's Notebook sec.

Stern, Robert A.M., Gregory Gilmartin, and Thomas Mellins. *New York 1960: Architecture and Urbanism Between the Second World War and the Bicentennial*. New York: The Monacelli Press, 1995.

"Stillwell Avenue / Coney Island Complex." *Station Reporter*, May 2005, <http://www.station-reporter.net/coney.htm>.

Stookey, Lee. *Subway Ceramics: A History and Iconography*. 2nd ed. Vermont: Lee Stookey, 1994.

Tauranac, John. "Art and the I.R.T.: The First Subway Art." *Historic Preservation* XXV no. 4 (October–December, 1973): 26–31.

"The Ornamentation of the New Subway Stations in New York." *House and Garden* V no. 2 (February 1904): 287–292.

"Transit Agency Creates Art Havens in Subways." *New York Times*, November 6, 1989: B1.

Turner, Elisa. "Cuban Artists Reclaim Identity in Breaking Barriers." *Miami Herald*, October 26, 1997.

U.S. General Services Administration. *The Design Excellence Program Guide: Building a Legacy*. Washington: GSA, 2000.

Vickers, Squire J. "Architectural Treatment of Stations on the Dual System of Rapid Transit in New York City." *Architectural Record* 45, no.1 (January 1919): 15.

___. "Design of Subway and Elevated Stations." *Municipal Engineers Journal* 3 no. 9 (December 1917): paper 114.

___. "Designing Architect." *Public Service Record* III no. 1 (January 1916).

___. "Discussion." *Municipal Engineers Journal* 19, no. 1 (1993).

___. "The Design and Finish of the Subway Station." *Municipal Engineers Journal* 19, no. 1 (1993).

Vogel, Carol. "Inside Art." *New York Times*, March 2, 2001: E3.

___. "Inside Art." *New York Times*, May 2, 2003: E3.

Wei, Lilly. "Valerie Jaudon at Von Lintel." *Art in America* 93 no. 9 (October 2005): 179.

Whitman, Walt. *Leaves of Grass*. 1856. Facsimile edition, Ann Arbor: Microfilm International, 1980

Witzling, Lawrence, and Jeffrey Ollswang. *The Planning and Administration of Design Competitions*. Milwaukee, Wis.: Midwest Institute for Design Research, 1986.

Index of Artists

MTA Arts for Transit

Sandra Bloodworth, Director
Amy Hausmann, Assistant Director

Lydia Bradshaw, Manager
Lester Burg, Manager
Yaling Chen, Manager
Katherine Meehan, Manager
Rob Wilson, Conservator and Photographer
Virginia Williams, Assistant Manager
Gabriela Vazquez, Principal Executive Secretary

First published in the United States of America in 2006 by
The Monacelli Press, Inc.
611 Broadway, New York, New York 10012

Copyright © 2006 by The Monacelli Press, Inc. and Metropolitan Transportation Authority Arts for Transit
All works of art are commissioned by MTA Arts for Transit. Copyright to individual work is held by the artist or estate or MTA.

This publication is a sponsored project of the New York Foundation for the Arts with funding provided by the New York State Council on the Arts, Architecture, Planning, and Design Program.

All rights reserved under International and Pan-American Copyright Conventions.
No part of this book may be reproduced or utilized in any form or by any means, electronic or mechanical, including photocopying, recording, or by any information storage and retrieval system, without permission in writing from the publisher.
Inquiries should be sent to The Monacelli Press.

Library of Congress Cataloging-in-Publication Data

Bloodworth, Sandra.
Along the way : MTA arts for transit / Sandra Bloodworth and William Ayres ; foreword by Stanley Tucci.
p. cm.
Includes bibliographical references and index.
ISBN 1-58093-173-1
1. Public art–New York (State)–New York. 2. Subways–Decoration–New York (State)–New York. 3. Urban beautification–New York (State)–New York. 4. New York (State). Metropolitan Transportation Authority. I. Ayres, William II. Title. III. Title: MTA arts for transit.
N8845.N7B58 2006
709.747'1–dc22
2006014897

Design: Think Studio, New York

Printed and bound in China